This collection of essays adopts a unique interdisciplinary approach to a diverse group of texts produced in London during the Renaissance: eight literary scholars and eight historians from Britain and the United States have been paired to write companion essays on each text.

This collaborative method opens up rich insights into London's social, political and cultural life that would have eluded members of either discipline working in isolation. 'Theatrical' is used in a flexible sense, and is applied to the civic rituals and public spectacles of the capital (for example, the execution of King Charles I) as well as to the elite and the popular theatre. The eight texts therefore include historical accounts, political documents and polemical works as well as plays.

The volume originated in an interdisciplinary course at the University of Chicago, in which some of the contributors presented lectures. The result will be required reading for students and scholars of both English literature and history in the early modern period.

D1465602

The Theatrical City

The Theatrical City

Culture, Theatre and Politics in London, 1576–1649

Edited by
David L. Smith, Richard Strier and David Bevington

 CAMBRIDGE
UNIVERSITY PRESS

Published by the Press Syndicate of the University of Cambridge
The Pitt Building, Trumpington Street, Cambridge CB2 1RP
40 West 20th Street, New York, NY 10011–4211, USA
10 Stamford Road, Oakleigh, Melbourne 3166, Australia

First published 1995
Reprinted 1996

Printed in Great Britain at the University Press, Cambridge

A catalogue record for this book is available from the British Library

Library of Congress cataloguing in publication data
The theatrical city: culture, theatre, and politics in London, 1576–1649 / edited by
David L. Smith, Richard Strier, and David Bevington.
    p. cm.
    Includes index.
    ISBN 0 521 44126 9 (hc)
    1. English literature – Early modern, 1500–1700 – History and criticism. 2.
Politics and literature – England – London – History – 17th century. 3. Politics and
literature – England – London – History – 16th century. 4. English drama –
England – London – History and criticism. 5. Literature and anthropology –
England – London – History. 6. Theater – Political aspects – England – London –
History. 7. London (England) – Politics and government. 8. London (England) – In
literature. 9. London (England) – Civilization. I. Smith, David L. (David
Lawrence), 1963– . II. Strier, Richard. III. Bevington, David M.
PR421. T44 1995
942. 105'5–dc20 94–27825 CIP

ISBN 0 521 44126 9 hardback

WV

For John Morrill
and in memory of John M. Wallace

Contents

Plates

Notes on Contributors

Ian Archer is Fellow and Tutor in Modern History at Keble College, Oxford. His main publications are *The Pursuit of Stability: Social Relations in Elizabethan London* (1991), *The History of the Haberdashers' Company* (1991), and, with Caroline Barron and Vanessa Harding, *Hugh Alley's 'Caveat': The Markets of London in 1598* (1988). He is currently working on a book on rebellion and riot 1350–1650 for Macmillan.

David Bevington is Phyllis Fay Horton Professor in the Humanities at the University of Chicago. His books include *From 'Mankind' to Marlowe* (1962), *Tudor Drama and Politics* (1968), *Action is Eloquence: Shakespeare's Language of Gesture* (1984), and editions of the *Complete Works of Shakespeare* (Bantam, 1988, in individual paperbacks, and Harper Collins, 1992, in a one-volume format), and of *Medieval Drama* (1975) as well as of *The Macro Plays* (1972). He has also edited Lyly's *Endymion* for the Revels plays, and has co-edited an edition of *Doctor Faustus* for that same series, offering both the A and B texts complete.

Martin Butler is Senior Lecturer in English at the University of Leeds. He has written *Theatre and Crisis 1632–1642* (1984), Ben Jonson, *'Volpone', a Critical Study* (1987), and edited *The Selected Plays of Ben Jonson*, vol. 2 (1989). Currently he is working on a study of the Stuart masque, and an edition of *Cymbeline*.

Patrick Collinson is Regius Professor of Modern History at the University of Cambridge and a Fellow of Trinity College. He is the author of *The Elizabethan Puritan Movement* (1967), *Archbishop Grindal 1518–1583* (1979), *The Religion of Protestants 1559–1625* (1982) and *The Birthpangs of Protestant England* (1988). Some of his essays and articles are collected in *Godly People: Essays on English Protestantism and Puritanism* (1983) and *Elizabethan Essays* (1994). He has been working recently on the history of Canterbury Cathedral and of Emmanuel College, Cambridge, as well as on Elizabethan history.

Marshall Grossman is Associate Professor of English at the University of Maryland. His book *'Authors to Themselves': Milton and the Revelation of History* was published in 1987. He is now completing two books on the literary history of England: *Writing the Story of All Things: The Rhetoric of the Self in Renaissance Poetic Narrative*, and *Writing the Inside Out: Shakespeare, Milton, and the Supplement of Publication*, and editing a collection of essays on Aemilia Lanyer.

Derek Hirst is William Eliot Smith Professor of History at Washington University, St Louis. He has written extensively on the republican years 1649–60, and on interdisciplinary themes in literature and history. He is working on books in both fields, and has also published *Representative of the People?* (1975) and *Authority and Conflict: England, 1603–1658* (1986).

Keith Lindley is Senior Lecturer in History at the University of Ulster at Coleraine. He has published *Fenland Riots and the English Revolution* (1982) as well as numerous articles, mainly on seventeenth-century English history. He is currently completing a book on popular politics and religion in London during the English Civil War.

Lawrence Manley is Professor of English at Yale University. He is the editor of *London in the Age of Shakespeare: An Anthology* (1986), and author of *Convention, 1500–1750* (1980) and *Literature and Culture in Early Modern London* (1994).

Leah S. Marcus is Professor of English at the University of Texas, Austin. She is the author of *Childhood and Cultural Despair: A Theme and Variations in Seventeenth-Century Literature* (1978), *The Politics of Mirth: Jonson, Herrick, Milton, Marvell, and the Defense of Old Holiday Pastimes* (1986), and *Puzzling Shakespeare: Local Reading and its Discontents* (1988). More recently, she has wandered into the field of textual studies. Her next book project, *Unediting the Renaissance: Shakespeare, Marlowe, Milton*, is under contract with Routledge for publication in 1995.

Louis A. Montrose is Professor of English Literature, and Chairman of the Department of Literature, at the University of California, San Diego. He has published extensively on Elizabethan culture, and on theory and method in the historical analysis of literature. His essay in this volume is part of a more comprehensive study of *A Midsummer Night's Dream*, the Elizabethan theatre, and the Elizabethan state to be published by The University of Chicago Press.

Linda Levy Peck is Professor of History at the University of Rochester. She is the author of *Northampton: Patronage and Policy at the Court of James I* (1982), *Court Patronage and Corruption in Early Stuart England* (1990), and the editor of *The Mental World of the Jacobean Court* (1991). She is currently working on a study of political and material culture in the seventeenth century entitled *Britain in the Age of the Baroque*.

Paul S. Seaver is Professor of History and Director of the Program in Cultures, Ideas, and Values at Stanford University. His books are *The Puritan Lectureships, 1560–1662* (1970), *Seventeenth Century England*, ed. and intro. (1976), and *Wallington's World: A Puritan Artisan in Seventeenth-Century London* (1985). He is currently working on two papers: one on the work ethic and guild discipline in London 1560–1700, and a second on sorting out the middling sort in early modern London, an attempt to understand contemporary social categorisation.

David L. Smith is Fellow, Director of Studies in History, and Tutor for Admissions at Selwyn College, Cambridge. His publications include *Oliver Cromwell: Politics and Religion in the English Revolution, 1640–58* (1991), *Louis XIV* (1992), and *Constitutional Royalism and the Search for Settlement, c. 1640–1649* (1994). He is currently preparing a history of Britain, 1603–1707 for Blackwell.

Richard Strier is Professor of English and Humanities at the University of Chicago. He is the author of *Love Known: Theology and Experience in George Herbert's Poetry* (1983) and numerous articles on Renaissance poetry and modern criticism. He is the co-editor of *The Historical Renaissance: New Essays on Tudor and Stuart Literature and Culture* (1988). His new book is entitled *Resistant Structures: Particularity, Radicalism, and Renaissance Texts* (1995).

Frank Whigham is Professor of English at the University of Texas at Austin. He is the author of *Ambition and Privilege: The Social Tropes of Elizabethan Courtesy Theory* (1984), numerous articles on early modern English literature and culture, and of *Seizures of the Will in English Renaissance Drama*, forthcoming from Cambridge University Press.

Penry Williams taught history at the University of Manchester from 1951 to 1964 and then at New College, Oxford until his retirement in 1992. He has published *The Council in the Marches of Wales under Elizabeth I* (1958), *Life in Tudor England* (1963), and *The Tudor Regime* (1979); and edited, with John Buxton, *New College, Oxford, 1379–1979* (1979). He was an editor of the *English Historical Review* from 1982 until 1992. *Environed with War*, his volume on England 1547–1603 for the *New Oxford History of England*, is due to appear in 1995.

Preface

As our Introduction indicates, this book grew out of an interdisciplinary course at the University of Chicago concerned with the history and literature of London in the Renaissance. We wish to thank Professor John Boyer and others in the History Department who supported our endeavours from first to last. The students, both graduate and undergraduate, who took this class with us provided an intensity of interest and commitment without which the course could not have succeeded. We are of course very grateful to all those who have contributed essays to this volume for their collegiality and their willingness to explore the intellectual dimensions of this project as it grew well beyond its original boundaries in the classroom. We wish to thank our friends at the Cambridge University Press who have guided us throughout, especially William Davies. We owe thanks to the staffs of all the archives, libraries and museums listed in the Acknowledgements, and especially to Jean Miller and Barbara Mowat at the Folger Shakespeare Library.

Most of our editorial policies will be apparent to any reader of this book, but we might explain that we have modernised all primary sources in matters of spelling and punctuation to provide consistency and ease of reading; modern editions are sometimes presented in modern spelling and sometimes in original spelling, and the different handling of quotations in this book might well seem arbitrary without this kind of standardising. Also, in the footnotes the place of publication of books is to be understood as London unless otherwise stated.

Our dedication to John Morrill and John Wallace bespeaks our admiration and gratitude for the work of two scholars, one an historian and one (until his recent and much-lamented death) a literary scholar, one at Cambridge and one at Chicago, from whom we have received much sustaining friendship, encouragement and inspiration.

D.L.S.
R.S.
D.B.

Introduction

This book began in a pedagogical venture. Early in 1990, the director of an enterprise in the History Department at the University of Chicago called the Interdisciplinary Program for the Study of Europe (IPSE, for short) asked two of us, David Bevington and Richard Strier of the English Department, if we would be interested in participating in an interdisciplinary year-long course for 1990–1 to be called 'The City in Early Modern Europe'. The proposal was that a three-person team composed of the two of us and a historian of England (from England) be assigned to the spring quarter of that academic year (one of the aims of the Program was to bring over historians from Europe). The focus of our quarter was to be London. We readily agreed, and soon were able to enlist the collegial participation of David L. Smith, Fellow of Selwyn College, Cambridge.

The year-long course as a whole necessarily took a broad and somewhat schematic approach to urban culture in early modern Europe. The autumn quarter was to be devoted to the interrelations of history and art in Florence; the winter quarter chose Leipzig in order to study the connections between history and music; and the spring quarter adopted as its focus the relationship of history and literature, with a particular interest in the drama. Owing to staffing difficulties the scheme was not quite as interdisciplinary in the autumn and winter as had been hoped, though the subjects of investigation still remained Florence and Leipzig. In the spring, the original conception was fully borne out: a cross-disciplinary approach to London through a study of its drama and other literary genres in the context of the social, economic and political circumstances that gave rise to (or accompanied) the high Renaissance in England.

In working out our quarter, the three of us discovered that we were as interested in dramatic aspects of politics as we were in political and social aspects of theatrical productions and literary texts. For that reason, we entitled the course, 'London: The Theatrical City' – a version of the title of this present book. Our plan, then as now, was to employ the term 'theatrical' in a fairly plastic sense, covering popular as well as elite theatre and even 'dramatic' spectacles such as the execution of Charles I. We decided that texts did not have to be theatrical in any strict technical sense to be included in our deliberations. The theatricality of London itself, and of the court, gave us the backdrop we were looking for in our interdisciplinary dialogue. We decided that the course would cover the period from the building of the Theatre (1576) to the execution of the king (1649). This seemed like a convenient period, and these events announced the range of our concerns.

David Smith came to Chicago from Cambridge for the spring quarter of 1991. The living arrangement provided for him at the Bevingtons' house, and the close-knit character of the Hyde Park neighbourhood where the University of Chicago is located, made for frequent contact and intense, literally convivial cooperation. In the course, our usual procedure was to have David Smith lecture on historical subjects and to have Richard Strier and David Bevington take turns presenting texts. After David Smith had talked about the Elizabethan court, Richard Strier followed with a session on *A Midsummer Night's Dream*; David Smith's lecture on the political, social and economic anxieties at the end of Elizabeth's reign led into David Bevington's analysis of political, social and economic conflicts in Dekker's *The Shoemaker's Holiday*. And so it went, with numerous interventions during the lectures from the other instructors, the course assistants, and the students in the class, both graduate and undergraduate.

This experience was so rich and intellectually rewarding that we soon turned our minds to the possibility of a book-length project. The volume, we decided, would follow the shape of the course: it would retain its chronological scope, would construe theatricality broadly, and would take a liberal view of what would count as texts for analysis. We wanted to expand the interdisciplinary dialogue beyond the three of us, while still finding a way to capture in print the close collaboration and genuine dialogue that the course provided. The strategy we arrived at was to have each chapter of the volume consist of an essay by a historian on a particular text, set of texts, or event followed by an essay by a literary scholar on that same text, set of texts, or event. Some of the texts were chosen by us and had been used in the course; some were suggested by the participants themselves. It is worth noting that, despite major differences in approaches and interests, almost every historian or literary scholar we contacted was immediately enthusiastic about the project and readily agreed to participate in it. This readiness to participate not only gratified us but led us to think that our volume might speak to a real need, or at least a widespread desire.

The aim of the paired essay format was to establish true dialogue and true interdisciplinarity. We understand interdisciplinarity to require, logically and in practice, the existence of disciplinary difference. The existence, and productiveness, of disciplinary difference was part of the excitement of the course. We therefore asked each scholar to write within her or his discipline, whatever she or he took that to mean, and then to exchange drafts with the other half of the pair and see what effect such an exchange would have. The resulting volume gives us a picture not only of some aspects and productions of London in the English Renaissance but also of the current state, with regard to these matters, of the two

'disciplines' of literary and historical studies and of the relations between
them. Each essay in the volume is, we believe, worthwhile in itself. The
'pairs' speak to one another (and sometimes fail to do so) in ways that
we did not and could not mandate, but that we believe to be interesting
and significant in themselves.

We begin with a pair of essays on John Stow's *A Survey of London* (1598),
by way of introduction to the City itself. Ian Archer's approach to Stow
embraces at once our basic theme of the interrelatedness of social process
and the production of written texts. Archer sees Stow's work as an integral
product of the City's traditions, along with pageants, lord mayor's processions, stage plays, printed maps, epitaphs and much else; all are nourished by the City's physical reality, its wealth, its rapid development.
Archer is as concerned with Stow's worries about London as he is with
the laudatory handclapping; the Stow we meet in these pages is anxious
about undesirable change and the decline of social ideals. The result,
Archer argues, is a nostalgia for a medieval past of 'charity, hospitality
and plenty', and of ceremonials and pageants. Recognising Stow's nostalgia
enables Archer to provide insight into the reliability of Stow's observations,
for it shows us why Stow is so reluctant to see old customs fall away and
so ill equipped to comprehend London's resilience in coping with social
change and even with poverty. Stow is especially unable to measure the
worth of new forms of charity (by no means all of them institutionalised
and bureaucratic) that were taking the place of more traditional social
obligations. Archer shows Stow's ambivalence to be representative and
genuine, shared by no less an authority than Queen Elizabeth herself.

Lawrence Manley too connects Stow's *Survey* to ceremonial and theatrical
representation, and sees in Stow the paradox of a conservative response
to the erosion of late medieval traditions of hospitality coexisting with a
'progressive' celebration of new socio-economic mobility and metropolitan
growth. Part of what is new here is Manley's emphasis on the *Survey* as
a written document: on its influence as a model for the writing of urban
history; on its humanist and Aristotelian-Ramist assumptions that cities
could be analysed according to *res* and *homines*; on its organisational plan
of a district-by-district perambulation of London's wards, liberties and
suburbs. Manley reveals Stow's conception of London as a ceremonial
space, showing us what a wealth of information Stow provides on ceremonial routes, on the major feast days for such occasions, on guild
participation and the function of important buildings, and on the role of
jousting and sports. Stow's emphasis on pageantry in London, Manley
shows, provides the author ample opportunity for praise and dispraise:
praise for traditions like the disappearing Midsummer Marching Watch
and for those charitable Christians whose benefactions support the common
good, dispraise for those who seek private gain only and who suppress
older rituals without regard for civic sentiment. Stow deplores such things

as gospelling curates who pull down maypoles, public ostentation of wealth, the expansion of bureaucracy in Westminster, and the conversion of religious houses into gun factories. The new public theatres distress Stow with their heteroglot character and variegated audience, and he pays them scant attention. They do not suit his version of civic pride.

Shakespeare's *A Midsummer Night's Dream* (*c.* 1595) contains urban as well as courtly characters, and is therefore admirably suited to add awareness of the court to that of the City, and to suggest some aspects of their interaction. Penry Williams shows us that the festivals of Theseus's court are much like those of Elizabeth's. In both, ritual and display intersect with policy-making and patronage. Even if, as Williams argues, the marriages of *A Midsummer Night's Dream* need not point to a specific occasion in the 1590s, they do celebrate the political and social functions of marriage in the courtly world over which Elizabeth presided. In his analysis of this rich interplay of literature and history, Williams thus argues that Shakespeare's play embodies not only the mental world of the Elizabethan court but also the social world of Elizabethan London. It embodies division and conflict – between popular festivities and courtly entertainments, reason and passion, male and female – but also, and perhaps more importantly, it embodies, in Williams's view, a vision of the way in which social and political conflicts can be defused. Williams stresses the importance of this in the context of bad harvests and social unrest in the mid-1590s. He views Shakespeare's *A Midsummer Night's Dream* as helping us see how it could have been that the social fabric of London was not rent apart in that difficult moment. In the context of the volume, Williams leads us to see Shakespeare as having had an awareness of the 'resilience' of London that, in Archer's view, is overlooked by Stow.

Louis Montrose argues that the relationship of Queen Elizabeth to her subjects is at the heart of *A Midsummer Night's Dream*'s fascination with unstable hierarchies and categories of gender, rank and age. Bottom, for Montrose, is an exaggeratedly comic representation of those many males in Elizabeth's court who found themselves in a dependent, uncertain and partly eroticised relationship to a monarch who was capable of being (like Titania) benign and domineering, adoring and sinister, tender and imperious. As Montrose points out, Bottom is not simply a dependent child at Titania's sheltering bosom. He is also an artisan and a would-be actor. Although socially inferior to the nobles and gentlefolk who inhabit Theseus's court, he has a secure place in the civic and guild-oriented world that Shakespeare knew so well as his own heritage. The world of traditional guild theatre was one in which Elizabethan governmental policy was making itself severely felt. That policy was killing off or selectively appropriating an older theatre of Corpus Christi plays and folk ceremonials in favour of newer ceremonials designed to mythologise the Tudor state. We have seen, in our first pair of essays, how John Stow responded with alarm to the dismantling of Midsummer marches, maypole ceremonies and the like. Montrose's contribution to this discussion is to show how insistently *A Midsummer Night's Dream* alludes to the passing world of popular civic entertainment and to the celebration of royal authority that takes its place. Although Bottom and his colleagues are guild members, and although Bottom refers to the raging Herod of the cycles, the artisans' purpose in playing is no longer to observe the cycles of the agrarian and ecclesiastical calendar by recreating sacred history; it is to pay homage to a court wedding. Montrose shows that Shakespeare's presentation of such a transformation and of dependent relationships in a royal or ducal court is not without an element of critique. Bottom's allusion to 1 Corinthians in his comically jumbled evocation of 'a most rare vision' has the effect of inverting temporal and spiritual hierarchies. However absurd the vision in its manifestation of asses' ears and braying, its exponent in the play is the artisan-turned-actor. This droll representative of the Shakespearean theatre instinctively knows more about imaginative art (and spiritual mysteries?) than does his patron. Bottom thus unknowingly aligns himself with Puck as the spokesman for 'shadows'. By implication, Montrose argues, the social reality of dependence on Queen Elizabeth is transformed by the play's dreamwork into a fantasy of the artisan-poet-player-dramatist's control over the Faery Queen.

Thomas Dekker's *The Shoemaker's Holiday* is only three or four years later (1599/1600) than *A Midsummer Night's Dream*, and is similarly a play for a public company. Again, the worlds of artisans and of gentlefolk collide. Both plays are presided over by genial figures of royal or ducal power who reconcile differences and to whom homage is paid in the plays' closing moments. Both plays accept a significant degree of hierarchy while at the same time valourising the independence of various social groups and adopting the tolerant, whimsical pluralism that Renaissance English culture seems to have imagined as part of its national identity. Yet Dekker's play may also reflect the darker sense of anxiety and social tension that, as Penry Williams has hinted, was characteristic of Elizabeth's last years. Paul Seaver develops this view. He shows in some detail how conditions seemed to worsen towards the end of Elizabeth's reign: war with Continental Catholic powers dragged on; the Irish situation was exacerbated by the earl of Essex's ineffectual expedition; the economy stagnated amid rising inflation; and of course plague and the bad harvests alluded to in *A Midsummer Night's Dream* added to the misery. And over everything hung the uncertainty of the royal succession.

Seaver contends that Dekker's play is an enchanted rather than a reflecting glass with regard to contemporary social history. He shows that it deliberately distorts key aspects of London's social world in the direction of wish-fulfilment fantasy. Seaver points out that while a Simon Eyre did live in the fifteenth century and did indeed become lord mayor (and build

Leadenhall), he differs from his namesake in Dekker (and in Dekker's source, Deloney's *The Gentle Craft*) in one rather fundamental way: the historical Simon Eyre was not a shoemaker. He was an upholsterer and then draper. To the uninitiated this might seem like a trivial change, but to the social historian it is essential. What Seaver shows is that if Eyre had been a shoemaker, he could never have become lord mayor of London. No shoemaker ever did. Seaver shows that the guild that included shoemakers, the Cordwainers, cut a paltry figure in London's highly stratified world where Drapers, Goldsmiths and especially Grocers held a dominant position. The forbidding Sir Roger Oatley in Dekker's play is not a Grocer by accident. Dekker's vision of Simon Eyre is of a self-made, successful entrepreneur whose unhistorical rise to the top of London's social and economic world provided a dreamlike model of social mobility for the play's original audience at the Fortune Theatre – where the Admiral's men, headed by Edward Alleyn, offered stiff competition to Shakespeare's company, the Lord Chamberlain's men, and enjoyed a special affinity with London's bourgeoisie.[1] Seaver shows that Dekker's fantasy allowed this audience to explore tensions in London's social and economic structure while at the same time enjoying a holiday world of release in which all conflicts could finally be resolved. Scenes in Eyre's shop reveal struggles between the master and his 'covenanted' servants or workers; shoemakers are shown to be at odds not only with members of the other guilds but also with gentlemen in the City. The patronising manner and antagonisms in the encounters of all the rival social groups are greatly intensified when a noble like the Earl of Lincoln appears on the scene. The play's happy ending resolves all these tensions in a way that, as Seaver leads us to see, would have struck its original audience as a vision as 'rare' and fantastical as Bottom's.

David Bevington surveys this same scene of conflict and idealised resolution in terms of the play's literary genre. *The Shoemaker's Holiday* is a festive comedy, a splendid illustration of the viability of C. L. Barber's term.[2] Dekker's play celebrates holiday in a way that addresses the concerns of Stephen Greenblatt, Mikhail Bakhtin, Michael Bristol and others about containment and misrule.[3] Does this play endorse finally the co-optation by which political authority allows a degree of licence (including theatrical performance) merely in order to contain disorder and thereby return everything essentially to where things stood before, or is the play subversive in encouraging its audience to explore new possibilities about its social

---

[1] Andrew Gurr, *The Shakespearean Stage, 1574–1642* (Cambridge, 1970, 2nd edn, 1980).

[2] C. L. Barber, *Shakespeare's Festive Comedy* (Princeton, 1959).

[3] See, for example, Stephen Greenblatt, 'Murdering Peasants: Status, Genre, and the Representation of Rebellion', *Representations*, 1 (1983), 1–29; Mikhail M. Bakhtin, *Rabelais and his World* (Bloomington, Ind., 1984); and Michael D. Bristol, *Carnival and Theatre: Plebeian Culture and the Structure of Authority in Renaissance England* (1985).

and economic status? Bevington takes a mediating and synthesising position, arguing that the play's very genre encourages debate, exchange of views and presentation of multiple perspectives. For instance, in Bevington's view, when Sir Roger Oatley and the Earl of Lincoln meet in a flurry of mutual mistrust, the dramatist need not take sides; both are canny men, driven by self-interest, each willing to make use of the other in temporary alliance but finally contemptuous of what the other represents. Social aspiration and patrician snobbery cancel each other out in the audience's sympathies. Bevington shows that this balancing of apparent opposites pervades the play. The central figure, Eyre, is ebullient and shystering, generous and mistrustful, open and devious. All is jollity with him when it is not pure calculation. Eyre's wife, Margery, is fascinated by the accoutrements of social advancement even as she disclaims all such 'vanity' with pious moralisms. The romantic subplot trumpets its endorsement of virtuous poverty even as it invites sympathy for the rejected wealthy gentleman. The play's endorsement of the monarchy seems unalloyed with satire, and yet even here the comic exaggeration and the implicit advice to an English monarch to practise geniality bring the play to an Aristophanic close of hilarity and reconciliation. Bevington's essay thus complements the historical perspective of Seaver's by demonstrating the aptness of the play's literary genre to the kind of imaginative balancing act that Dekker undertook.

With our next play and pair of essays we move from texts that depict London and Elizabethan life as polyglot, and that imagine or survey multiple social realms, to a text that focuses exclusively on a single realm: the court. Yet even here, in John Marston's *Parasitaster, or The Fawn*, probably produced in 1604, only a year after the accession of King James, 'the court' is not a monolithic phenomenon. Instead, as Linda Peck demonstrates, the play presents us with two different courts, and two courts within a single court. Stressing the connection of the play to Queen Anne and her circle, Peck argues that *The Fawn*'s origin in this circle partly accounts for its presentation of noble women as at once political pawns and political powers. Still, the central focus of the play, as of the court, must be the ruler – with a clear allusion to King James, the British Solomon (as he liked to think of himself). Asserting the possibility of criticism even within the court, Peck argues that *The Fawn* at once flatters and criticises James. It presents a satirical portrait of a foolish would-be philosopher-duke who presides over the venal and trivial court of Urbino, a court that stands in ironic relation to the Urbino of Castiglione's *The Courtier*. At the same time the play presents an idealised picture of the Duke of Ferrara, who embodies much of the advice in King James's *Basilikon Doron* (1599), a book that was widely reprinted at his accession. The play is deeply aware of the power of that 'grateful poison, sleek mischief, flattery', and yet, by making the primary flatterer the good

Duke in disguise, the play suggests the possibility of the truly wise ruler seeing through flattery. Moreover, this ruler distinguishes himself not only by having full humanist awareness but also by supervising the marriage of his son in order to take care of the matter of the succession. Peck leaves open the question of whether the final effect of the play is satiric or laudatory. Perhaps the point is that it is both at once.

Frank Whigham's meditation on eroticism and flattery in *The Fawn* suggests that the play takes us very deeply into the hothouse world of the Jacobean court. He argues that this play and other disguised-ruler plays (including Shakespeare's *Measure for Measure*) are closely tied to the specific historical moment of the year or so following James's accession, when widespread plague prevented James from being visible to most of the nation in the ways that the moment seemed to demand. The ruler, in this situation, became an oddly private figure, but with all his abstract and actual powers intact. Whigham sees *The Fawn* as exploring the erotics of flattery from the point of view of an object of flattery who has come to experience it and to use it as a means of humiliation. The flatterer must tap into the desires of his (or her) object. Whigham sees in the potentially lustful monarch turned into revengeful flatterer the mutual obsession with sexuality that characterised the Elizabethan and Jacobean courts. The monarchies of these years were personal monarchies indeed. Marston's play resonates with the anecdotes Whigham cites about James crawling into bed with favourites who have just consummated their marriages (as opposed to the anecdotes about Elizabeth punishing consummation). The highly eroticised atmosphere of the court emerges into visibility in Marston's play and in Whigham's analysis of it. Finally, Whigham speculates on the importance of the comic mode of *The Fawn*, suggesting, as does Peck, that the play (and perhaps the culture at this moment) manages to keep its critical tendencies in balance with its more optimistic ones.

Issues of desire, repression and disguise are relevant not only to the Jacobean court but also to a figure, on the stage and in history, who played a major role in Stuart England but who has not yet become the focus of any of our essays: the 'hot Protestant' or 'Puritan'. Patrick Collinson shows that the greatest stage-Puritan of the period, Zeal-of-the-Land Busy in Ben Jonson's *Bartholomew Fair*, corresponded, in many of his activities and attitudes, including his alliance with a reforming magistrate, with actual Jacobean Puritans. Even the cry of 'Down with Dagon', with which Busy attacks the idolatrous and immoral puppet play in the Fair, was, as Collinson shows, unusual but not entirely unprecedented in the annals of actual Puritan activity in the period. Yet Collinson's is another essay in this volume that does not see the drama as merely 'reflecting' social realities. The startling claim that Collinson makes and suggestively documents is that the satiric figure of the stage-Puritan preceded rather than followed the historical existence of that figure, and indeed helped to make it a historical reality. Collinson argues that the satirical type of the Puritan – zealous, canting, hypocritical, 'Busy' – was, by a curious irony, created in response to a great series of anti-prelatical satirical works in the late 1580s, the 'Marprelate Tracts'. Richard Bancroft, the future archbishop, seems to deserve the credit (if that is the term) for seeing that satire would ultimately be more the enemy than the friend of the reforming movement. In the responses to the Martin Marprelate Tracts, Collinson proposes, the figure of the stage-Puritan was born. This figure, very different from that of 'Martin' himself, crystallised an element within the culture – not only for defenders but even for attackers of the establishment – that until then had only been nebulous, but that immediately became a major role on the public stage and in the public life of late Elizabethan and Stuart England.

Leah Marcus's essay helps us to think further about the culture's and Ben Jonson's ambivalence about both theatre and Puritanism. She suggests two readings of *Bartholomew Fair* (and, incidentally, of *The Alchemist*), readings which may be thought to correspond, as in Shakespeare's case, with the dual existence of these plays as both court and public entertainments and with the dual existence of these plays (in Jonson's case) as both plays and texts or 'works'. Marcus summarises her own compelling demonstration in an earlier study that, from the courtly or 'high culture' point of view, the play can be seen as a brief for the supervenience, in matters of 'sport' and entertainment, of tolerant royal authority over Puritanical local authorities (like those that Collinson documents in Busy's native town of Banbury). Yet Marcus now sees the play as demanding a more complex reading, especially in its existence on the public stage in 1614. She argues that Jonson is fascinated as well as repelled both by licence and by Puritanism. She sees Jonson as partaking of the full ambivalence of the location of the theatres in the 'liberties' of London, which were strongholds of religious nonconformity as well as of theatres, and she notes that some of the 'Puritans' were, like Jonson, economically dependent on the theatres that they professed to despise. She sees Jonson as intensely aware of both the sewage and the gardens of London (sewage reform, she points out, was one of the great achievements of the period). She speculates that the author and many of the spectators that took pleasure in the humiliation of Zeal-of-the-Land Busy were ambivalently exorcising a figure that they felt uncomfortably present in themselves. Marcus leaves us with a sense that both the Puritan and the theatre were highly cathected and ambivalent presences in the culture of the early Stuart world.

Our next pair of essays focuses on a play written and produced early in the reign of Charles I, Philip Massinger's *A New Way to Pay Old Debts* (published in 1633, probably written *c.* 1625). Keith Lindley sees this play as a meditation on a figure at least as troubling for the traditional culture of the period as the figure of the Puritan: the vastly wealthy London merchant. Lindley sees the play both as an idealised picture of traditional aristocratic values and as representing a response to powerful pressures that were exerted upon those values during the period. In his view, the play dramatises an assault on aristocratic values, an assault that – and here perhaps is the fantasy element in this play – is ultimately unsuccessful. The traditional aristocratic values, as Lindley explicates them, involve a combination of noble 'blood' (aristocratic lineage), proper condescension, 'honour' (with a military component), conscience, and the possession of a settled landed estate. This last item reveals the Achilles' heel of the system. Land can be bought. This was especially true in England in the Tudor–Stuart period. When a wealthy merchant buys land in the country, what happens to traditional status? Moreover, as Lindley points out, not only land but aristocratic titles, and even wives, were abundantly available for cash. All this social dislocation might have been less disturbing if the newcomers adopted, or at least paid lip service to, the traditional values. But what if they did not? This is the possibility that Lindley sees Massinger dramatising in Sir Giles Overreach. Overreach cares only for wealth and power. He has no regard for honour, reputation, conscience or condescension. He does not find wealth 'sordid'; his great value is 'industry'. Lindley shows how a figure like this is presented by Massinger as corrupting the whole fabric of elite social life in the countryside: the marriage market, the relations between neighbours, and the local system of justice (since at least some Justices of the Peace, in this play, are also for sale). Lindley notes the play's happy ending, but suggests that the figure of Overreach, and what he stands for, probably haunted the viewers and readers of the play in a way belied by the happy resolution.

Martin Butler's essay complicates our reading of *A New Way to Pay Old Debts*. He argues that what we see in the play is not a clash between aristocratic and other values but a dramatisation of tensions within the system of aristocratic values. He suggests that, despite Overreach's vaunted connections to the City (which may, Butler suggests, be a kind of smokescreen), Overreach is in fact nothing like the traditional City type who is set off against the 'gentlemen'. This difference immediately becomes clear when we compare Overreach with the equivalent figure in the play that is the 'source' for *A New Way to Pay Old Debts*, Middleton and Rowley's *A Trick to Catch the Old One* (c. 1605). Hoard is a typical usurer and miser; Overreach is not. Overreach is a spender rather than a hoarder. He maintains a first-rate cook and an extensive and expensive household. He is a conspicuous expender with nothing but scorn for the great 'bourgeois' virtue of thrift. He praises 'industry' for the spending power, not for the accumulation, that it produces. Overreach, then, shares and manifests a central – perhaps the central – value of 'traditional' aristocratic behaviour. He is himself a gentleman (a knight); he is not a hypocrite; and, almost as important as his gentlemanly 'port', he is not a coward, since he is quite ready to use his aristocratic sword. The play then becomes, for Butler, a competition between two different versions of aristocracy and patriarchy, a competition that is seen in political terms: Overreach is a model of tyranny, while the 'traditional' aristocrats are responsible, self-limiting rulers. Butler connects this antagonism to the conflict in the 1620s between court factions in which no less a person than Massinger's patron, the earl of Pembroke, was involved. Ultimately, Butler suggests, the object of criticism – indirectly, disguisedly, and from a great distance – may be the king. Still, there is nothing inherently revolutionary here. The ideal remains one of virtuous patriarchy. As both Butler and Lindley note, the servant who betrays Overreach, and thereby makes the happy ending possible, is roundly condemned for disobeying his master. Butler sees the play as deeply enmeshed in such tensions and potential contradictions.

Butler's essay, with its suggestion of tensions within the gentry class and of (disguised) criticism of the king, inevitably leads us to think ahead to the Civil War, even if this war was not itself 'inevitable'. The figure of the Puritan and the reformer, the possibility of a court insulated from reality (perhaps hinted at in *The Fawn*), the problem of whether disobedience could ever be justified – these would not disappear from the culture. The last two sections of our volume deal with the decade of the 1640s. The first pair of essays concerns two texts that illuminate the febrile mood of London on the eve of the Civil War, the 'Root-and-Branch' Petition and the 'Grand' Remonstrance. These differ from many of the texts in our volume in that they were generated in the turmoil of actual politics rather than composed as theatrical or literary works. Yet they are texts available to be carefully read. This present volume is profoundly uninterested in the difference between 'documents' and 'monuments'.[4] The two 'documents' now under discussion are not only evidence about the changing atmosphere of the capital between 1640 and 1642; they also embody and reveal ideas, feelings and visions. The context of this volume, moreover, leads us to the perception that these texts are intensely theatrical: the main 'actors' or participants behind them think of themselves as undertaking visible roles on a highly public stage.

David Smith's essay sets the texts within a specific historical context. Smith argues that when the Long Parliament met in November 1640 there was intense expectation in London and elsewhere that at last the opportunity had come to redress the political and religious grievances which had arisen under Charles I. The following month, Parliament received a petition, purporting to be signed by 15,000 Londoners, demanding that episcopacy 'with all its dependencies, roots and branches, may be aboli-

---

[4] For this distinction, see René Wellek, 'Literary Theory, Criticism, and History', in *Concepts of Criticism*, ed. Stephen G. Nichols, Jr (New Haven, 1963), p. 15.

shed'. Smith goes on to show how this demand sharply divided the political elite, and how the stance a figure adopted on this issue was often a predictor of allegiance in the Civil War: the majority of those who wished to preserve episcopacy rallied to the king, while those committed to its abolition generally became Parliamentarians. This division was most glaringly apparent in the acrimonious debates over the Remonstrance which Parliament presented to Charles I in November 1641. Against a volatile background of mass demonstrations in London and rebellion in Ireland, this comprehensive indictment of Charles I's rule passed the Commons by only eleven votes. Underpinning its 204 clauses was the belief that the king was in the clutches of a 'popish plot' to subvert 'the fundamental laws and principles of government'. Yet, to the king and a growing number of supporters, it seemed that the reforms advocated by Pym and his allies posed an even greater threat to established government and the rule of law. Hence, Smith argues, by the start of 1642, two symmetrical, opposed and self-sustaining conspiracy theories had emerged, both of which blamed England's troubles on a small minority of 'malignants'. Smith concludes by showing how this polarisation prompted Charles's decision to withdraw from London, a crucial error which, by physically separating the monarch from his Parliament, made civil war possible. Smith's essay is thus an exercise in the relationship between texts and contexts: it analyses how events and ideas shaped these two texts and were in turn influenced by them.

Richard Strier's essay complements this 'external' approach by presenting an 'internal' reading of the two texts. He stresses that the London petition actually uses the phrase 'roots and branches', never the singular form. He argues that this wording of the phrase underlines the vital point that the evil effects of episcopacy were thought to be widespread and pervasive, extending well beyond the rather narrow confines of Church government. The emphasis of the text, in Strier's terms, is not so much 'vertical' and causal as 'horizontal' and descriptive. The plurals, for Strier, are key. In his view, the real interest of the petition lies less in its critique of prelatical Church government as such than in its vision of the social and psychological effects of that government. Strier contrasts the petition's vision of pervasive social disruption with the analytic and programmatic stance of the Remonstrance. The Remonstrance identifies a single 'root' of those evils in a way that the petition never does. The great enemy is the 'malignant party'. Strier reveals the close link between this perception and Parliament's sense of its own identity. The first section of the Remonstrance, he argues, attacks Caroline policies not on the grounds of illegality (which was often difficult to establish) but because they undermined Parliament and justice. The remedy was to cast unconditional obedience aside. Strier draws out the extraordinary claims for Parliaments which especially pervade the second half of the Remonstrance. This vision of epochal parliamentary action leads to the 'Utopian' strain that Strier concludes by detecting in the document.

The essays by Smith and Strier both lead us into the mental world of John Pym and his allies, those who comprised the so-called 'Junto'. During the summer and autumn of 1642, as England moved into civil war, these were the figures who masterminded the creation of a parliamentarian army. Above all, these men were serious. One of the documents that reveals their outlook is the parliamentary 'order for stage-plays to cease', passed on 2 September 1642. This document laments that England is 'threatened with a cloud of blood by a civil war', and calls for 'all possible means to appease and avert the wrath of God'. It continues:

> Whereas public sports do not well agree with public calamities, nor public stage-plays with the seasons of humiliation, this being an exercise of sad and pious solemnity, and the other being spectacles of pleasure, too commonly expressing lascivious mirth and levity: it is therefore ... ordained ... that while these sad causes and set times of humiliation do continue, public stage-plays shall cease, and be forborn, instead of which are recommended to the people of this land the profitable and seasonable considerations of repentance, reconciliation, and peace with God, which probably may produce outward peace and prosperity.[5]

Here, in the stress on reconciliation with God through 'seasons of humiliation', we are able to sense some of the moral force and public concern of 'Puritanism'. Although some illicit plays continued to receive clandestine performances (even through 'public calamities'), the theatrical City was, for the indefinite future, closed to 'public stage-plays'.

Yet a central theme of our volume is the plasticity of the term 'theatrical'. We are concerned not solely with plays and theatres, but with spectacle and drama in the widest sense. Our contributors look beyond the world of the theatre and the court to the civic processions and public rituals of the capital. And of these rituals, none was more dramatic than the execution of Charles I in January 1649. This event marked the climacteric of the English Revolution. The piety that had earlier swept away public stage-plays as unseasonable now publicly tried and executed the tainted king as a 'man of blood'. These extraordinary events, unprecedented in history, are the topic of our final pair of essays.

Our text here is *Eikonoklastes*, John Milton's counterblast to the posthumous publication of 'the King's book', the *Eikon Basilike*. Derek Hirst argues that although a theatrical perspective on this polemical work may seem unpromising, in fact such a perspective illuminates both the text and its context. Taking as his theme the 'drama of justice' and its centrality to London's public life, Hirst shows how the regicide and its aftermath were widely seen in dramatic terms. Theatrical images recur throughout

---

[5] *Acts and Ordinances of the Interregnum, 1642–1660*, ed. C. H. Firth and R. S. Rait (3 vols., 1911), I, 26–7.

Eikonoklastes. Milton's attack on the image of the dead king was unusually vehement because, as Hirst argues, Milton's condemnation of Charles's spiritual and intellectual bankruptcy rested on a deep awareness of the relationship between national sin and political disintegration. The text returns to a profound sense of 'seasons of humiliation'. Only by recognising and atoning for the sins of the nation and of the king, in Milton's view, could God be propitiated and peace (and prosperity) be restored. Charles's self-serving image-making had to be laid bare. In entering the controversy which followed the king's execution and the virtually simultaneous publication of his *Eikon Basilike*, Milton saw himself (as did Parliament in Strier's account of the Grand Remonstrance) pleading at the bar of history. Here, once again, we return to the central theme of the drama of justice. Hirst concludes by emphasising the need to locate *Eikonoklastes* within the context of contemporary debate, arguing that this context provides the key to a historical reading of Milton's treatment of kingship and justice as well as to a new understanding of Milton's self-dramatisation as a pleader to posterity.

A similar wish to read *Eikonoklastes* not as an isolated work but as an integral part of contemporary exchanges following the regicide underpins Marshall Grossman's section of this chapter. Grossman locates *Eikonoklastes* as one of four pamphlets (the others were the *Eikon Alethine*, the *Eikon e pistes*, and the *Eikon Aklastos*) which, together with the original *Eikon Basilike*, make up the '*Eikon*' series. Grossman closely analyses how these pamphlets and their illustrations served to re-stage and counter-stage the king's death. Against this background, *Eikonoklastes* emerges not only as an assault on the king's image as propagated in royalist writings, but as an attack upon the connection between words and iconic representation. Alone among these works, *Eikonoklastes* moves directly from title to text, without the mediation of an image. Furthermore, Grossman argues, in using the king's own words to discredit both him and his image, Milton breaks the link between text and image. Grossman goes on to suggest that this desire to break the link between text and image transcends the specific polemical context of *Eikonoklastes* and can be found elsewhere in the Miltonic canon. An example of this anti-mimetic programme is the celebrated induction to hell in Book I of *Paradise Lost*. Here we see an intrusion of language between thought and image. Milton's language self-consciously resists visualisation in a way that fundamentally undercuts the strategies that produced the royalist 'eikon' of the king.

Although they focus on diverse texts and contexts from late Elizabethan to interregnum London, the essays in this volume are united by an attempt to suggest something of the variety of texts and practices that can usefully be characterised as 'theatrical' in this period. The sheer range of spectacles and experiences enacted in the English capital from the moment of the founding to the moment of the closing of the public theatres testifies to the existence of a theatrical culture of conscious dramatisation on all of the public stages. We have tried to show, through our paired explorations of texts, that a multiplicity and coordination of disciplinary perspectives is a fruitful way to gain insight into the productions and dynamics of this theatrical culture and its fiercely dynamic capital city.

1

John Stow's *Survey of London*

The Nostalgia of John Stow

Ian Archer

John Stow's *A Survey of London* was one manifestation of the celebration of the city's traditions, its physical fabric, its great benefactors, and the role of its citizens as supporters of the crown, which flourished at the turn of the sixteenth and seventeenth centuries.[1] One could hardly claim that such civic self-consciousness was a new development. Stow himself incorporated a description of London written in the twelfth century by William FitzStephen; the vogue of city chronicles in the fifteenth century testified to the growing self-importance of the capital and its rulers; the commonplace books of citizens with their lists of wards, parishes, monasteries and hospitals show an interest in the history and topography of the capital.[2] But the developments at the time Stow was writing are significant for the range of media involved and the sheer density of representations. As the morality tradition receded it became more common for the pageants accompanying the lord mayor's procession to include praise of the capital, 'rich and fortunate, / Famed through the world for peace and happiness'. On the London stage the stock figure of the city usurer was supplanted by more favourable representations of merchants as benefactors of the people and heroic defenders of the kingdom's rulers. The charitable activity of the city elite was also celebrated in epitaphs and monuments. The appearance of printed maps and panoramas, albeit initially produced largely by foreigners, helped Londoners to conceptualise their city as an integral body 'whole and entire of itself'. Stow's own work spawned derivatives like Anthony Munday's *A Brief Chronicle of the Success of Times* (1611) to which was appended 'A Brief Collection of the Original,

---

[1] J. Stow, *A Survey of London*, ed. C. L. Kingsford (2 vols., Oxford, 1908). For earlier treatments, see C. M. Clode, *The Early History of the Guild of Merchant Taylors* (2 vols., 1888), II, 298–305; R. Ashton, 'John Stow', *Transactions of the London and Middlesex Archaeological Society*, 29 (1978), 137–43; V. Pearl, 'John Stow', *Transactions of the London and Middlesex Archaeological Society*, 30 (1979), 190–4; H. R. Trevor-Roper, 'John Stow', in his *Renaissance Essays* (1985), pp. 94–102; L. Manley, 'From Matron to Monster: Tudor–Stuart London and the Languages of Urban Description', in *The Historical Renaissance*, ed. H. Dubrow and R. Strier (Chicago, 1988), pp. 347–74.

[2] Stow, *Survey*, II. 218–29; P. Clark, 'Visions of the Urban Community: Antiquarians and the English City Before 1800', in *The Pursuit of Urban History*, ed. D. Fraser and A. Sutcliffe (1983), pp. 105–24; C. M. Meale, 'The Compiler at Work: John Colyns and B. L. Harley MS 2252', in *Manuscripts and Readers in Fifteenth-Century England: The Literary Implications of Manuscript Study*, ed. D. Pearsall (Cambridge, 1983), pp. 97, 100.

Plate 1 Visscher's 'Long View of London', 1618

Antiquity, Increase, and Modern Estate of the Honourable City of London'.[3]

Quite why there should have been such an outpouring at this time is less clear. London's obviously enhanced role in the national economy, its physical expansion as a result of demographic growth, its contribution to royal finances at crucial times like the Armada scare of 1588, all fuelled a sense of civic pride. But to some extent the praise of London was a defensive reaction to the capital's critics. The 'Apology', probably by James Dalton, common pleader to the City, which Stow appended to his *Survey*, was directed against 'the opinion of some men, which think that the

[3] J. Knowles, 'The Spectacle of the Realm: Civic Consciousness, Rhetoric, and Ritual in Early Modern London', in *Theatre and Government*, ed. J. R. Mulryne (Cambridge, 1993), pp. 157–89; D. M. Bergeron, *English Civic Pageantry, 1558–1640* (1971), pp. 131–3; L. Manley, 'Proverbs, Epigrams, and Urbanity in Renaissance London', *English Literary Renaissance*, 15 (1985), 247–76; L. C. Stevenson, *Praise and Paradox: Merchants and Craftsmen in Elizabethan Popular Literature* (Cambridge, 1984); J. Howgego, *Printed Maps of London, c. 1553–1850*, (2nd edn, 1978), pp. 3–13; R. Hyde, *Gilded Scenes and Shining Prospects: Panoramic Views of British Towns, 1575–1900* (Yale, 1990), pp. 37, 40–3; A. Munday, *A Briefe Chronicle of the Successe of Times* (1611).

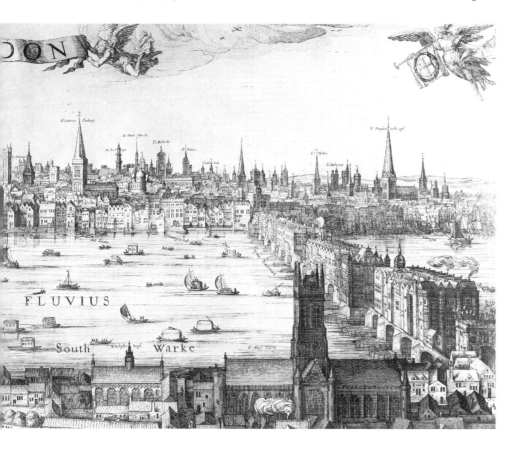

greatness of that City standeth not with the profit and security of this Realm'.[4] The growth of the City was not an unmixed blessing. The economies of provincial towns may have suffered as trade was sucked away to London, and the expansion of the capital placed strains on its own resources of housing and charity. Stow's work is notable because, for all his celebration of the City, he voices his anxieties about the changes he has witnessed within his lifetime, changes which offended against his social ideals.

Stow's social ideals owe much to the commonwealth tradition of the harmoniously functioning body politic of mutually interdependent social groups, all aware of their place in the hierarchy and their responsibilities towards others. In the past, says Stow, 'the inhabitants and repairers to this City of what estate soever, spiritual or temporal, having houses here, lived together in good amity with the citizens, every man observing the

---

[4] Stow, *Survey*, ii. 196–217; Ashton, 'Stow', p. 137.

customs and orders of the City, and chose to be contributory to charges
here'. But it was an ideal of which his contemporaries proved incapable.
His stress on the cooperation of social groups is at odds with the friction
between the citizens and the gentle and noble residents of the City. The
peace of the City streets was disturbed by repeated scuffles between
apprentices and gentlemen's servants; Londoners rioted against the Inns
of Court, the pretensions and immunities of whose denizens angered them;
and during the 1590s the aldermen repeatedly had occasion to complain
about the reluctance of gentlemen to contribute towards extraordinary
military rates.[5]

Other of Stow's ideals were at odds with developments in his lifetime.
His stress on the magnificent households, large retinues and lavish hospitality formerly maintained by the nobility stands at counterpoint to the
widespread conviction during the 1590s that the nobles and gentlemen
were neglecting their responsibilities at a time when the demands of the
poor were most pressing. Gentlemen were advised by the authors of
fashionable conduct books that the City life carried the advantage of
greater economy as the size of households could be cut and responsibilities
to entertain country yokels shirked. The crown fulminated against the drift
of the gentry to the capital and their neglect of their duties of hospitality.[6]
Stow's preoccupation with social boundaries, his sense that 'the sudden
rising of some men causeth them to forget themselves', is perhaps to be
explained by the fact that he was confronted with the reality of the dizzying
social mobility which brought men from relatively obscure provincial backgrounds to fabulous wealth and then sometimes dashed them down again.
Arrivistes like Sir John Spencer, the notoriously unpopular lord mayor in
the troubled year of 1595, ignored the paternalistic conventions: 'rich
Spencer', as he was known, failed to leave money for poor relief on his
death. Other aldermen like Sir Thomas Lodge and Thomas Starkey,
however, found themselves bankrupt through the misfortunes of trade.[7]
For anyone as concerned as Stow was about the public trust placed in
the magistrates – as shown by his hostility to the sale of offices in the
prisons and his sympathy for the petition against the farming of Leadenhall
in 1518 – the late Elizabethan and Jacobean decades offered the sorry

---

[5] W. R. D. Jones, *The Tudor Commonwealth* (1970); Pearl, 'Stow', p. 132; Stow, *Survey*, I. 85–91; I. W. Archer, *The Pursuit of Stability: Social Relations in Elizabethan London* (Cambridge, 1991), pp. 3–4; K. Lindley, 'Riot Prevention and Control in Early Stuart London', *Transactions of the Royal Historical Society*, 5th ser., 33 (1983), 113–14; *Acts of the Privy Council of England*, ed. J. R. Dasent (32 vols., 1890–1907), xx, 256–9, 269–71; xxi, 269–71; xxv, 295; xxvi, 228–9; xxvii, 287. Cf. Lawrence Manley, 'Of Sites and Rites', p. 49 below.

[6] Stow, *Survey*, I. 85–91; F. Heal, *Hospitality in Early Modern England* (Oxford, 1990), pp. 85–6, 102–11, 300–1; F. Heal, 'The Crown, the Gentry, and London: The Enforcement of Proclamation, 1596–1640', in *Law and Government Under the Tudors: Essays Presented to Sir Geoffrey Elton on his Retirement*, ed. C. Cross, D. Loades, and J. J. Scarisbrick (Cambridge, 1988), pp. 211–26.

[7] Stow, *Survey*, I. 133, 151–2, 179; L. Stone, 'The Peer and the Alderman's Daughter', *History Today*, 11 (1961), 48–55; C. J. Sisson, *Thomas Lodge and Other Elizabethans* (Harvard, 1933), pp. 7–53; T. S. Willan, *Studies in Elizabethan Foreign Trade* (Manchester, 1959), pp. 288–92.

spectacle of the privatisation of key areas of civic responsibility. This was the age of the projector, a time when courtiers with an eye for a ready profit devised schemes purporting the benefit of the commonweal but in fact designed to line their own pockets. It was a virus from which the City government was not immune; the enforcement of market regulations and the provision of work in Bridewell Hospital were farmed out to contractors in 1599 and 1602 respectively.[8]

Stow's *Survey* is thus suffused with nostalgia. He articulates the 'catholic' interpretation of the medieval past as a time of 'charity, hospitality and plenty'. Typical of his admiration for the charity of his medieval forbears is the passage in which he describes the support given to the bedridden people living in cottages by Houndsditch: 'devout people, as well men as women of this City, were accustomed oftentimes, especially on Fridays weekly, to walk that way purposely there to bestow their charitable alms, every poor man or woman lying in their bed within their window'. But by the time he was writing the farm at the Minories had been let out for garden plots, while the bedridden people of the cottages of Houndsditch had been replaced by 'brokers, sellers of old apparel, and such like'.[9] It was typical of what he saw as a collapse of community spirit to which he testifies most eloquently in the frequently cited passage about the Midsummer festivities:

There were usually made bonfires in the streets, every man bestowing wood or labour towards them; the wealthier sort also before their doors near to the said bonfires would set out tables on the vigils furnished with sweet bread and good drink, and on the festival days with meats and drinks plentifully, whereunto they would invite their neighbours and passengers also to sit and be merry with them in great familiarity, praising God for his benefits bestowed on them. These were called bonfires as well of good amity amongst neighbours that, being before at controversy, were there by the labour of others, reconciled and made, of bitter enemies, loving friends.

The fate of the Midsummer watches was shared by other recreations, such as buckler play, wrestling, May games and lords of misrule, which performed bonding functions, 'which open pastimes in my youth, being now suppressed, worser practices within doors are to be feared'.[10]

Stow also mourned the damage done to the physical fabric of the City over the course of his lifetime, the result of the twin pressures of population growth and the Reformation. The capital's growing population had been housed by a combination of the subdivision of existing properties and the

---

[8] Stow, *Survey*, I. 158–9, 351; J. Thirsk, *Economic Policy and Projects: The Development of a Consumer Society in Early Modern England* (Oxford, 1978), pp. 51–77; *Hugh Alley's 'Caveat': The Markets of London in 1598*, ed. I. W. Archer, C. M. Barron and V. Harding (London Topographical Society, 1988); A. L. Beier, *Masterless Men: The Vagrancy Problem in England, 1560–1640* (1985), p. 167.

[9] K. V. Thomas, *The Perception of the Past in Early Modern England* (Creighton Lecture, 1983), pp. 11–19; Stow, *Survey*, I. 126, 128.

[10] Stow, *Survey*, I. 95, 97–8, 101–4, 143–4.

proliferation of alleys. As the nobles moved away to the more fashionable west end the once grand mansions of nobles had been converted into petty tenements. Thus Suffolk House in Southwark had been sold to merchants who pulled it down, 'and in place thereof builded many small cottages of great rents to the increasing of beggars in that borough'. Worcester House and the Coldharbour underwent a similar fate.[11] Typical of the suburban housing developments was the street beyond Aldgate:

> Also without the bars, both the sides of the street be pestered with cottages, and alleys, even up to Whitechapel Church. . . . This common field . . . is so encroached upon by building of filthy cottages, and with other purprestures, enclosures and laystalls . . . that in some places it scarce remaineth a sufficient highway for the meeting of carriages and droves of cattle. Much less is there any fair, pleasant or wholesome way for people to walk on foot; which is no small blemish to so famous a city, to have so unsavoury and unseemly an entry or passage thereunto.

Images of dirt ('filthy') and disease ('pestered') recur in connection with the growth of the City.[12]

The pressure of a growing population was one force behind the disfigurement of the City; the Reformation was another. Many of the former monastic sites were themselves adapted to the demands of the expanding housing market. Holy Trinity Aldgate was converted into a town house for Lord Audley, and side chapels turned into tenements; St Katherine's was 'pestered with small tenements'; the Whitefriars became a fashionable gentry *quartier*. Others were adapted to industrial uses: the Minories became the centre of munitions production; the Crossed Friars (before it burned down in 1575) operated as a glass house.[13] These conversions were impious acts in Stow's eyes because of the iconoclasm with which they were attended. For example, he records an astonishing number of monuments in the former Greyfriars, many of them the tombs of City dignitaries (including four mayors), peers, even royalty: 'All these and five times so many more have been buried there, whose monuments are wholly defaced.' The attacks on images had also, in his opinion, disfigured the parish churches. To take a typical example, he notes of the church of St Mary Bothaw: 'Within this church, and the small cloister adjoining, divers noblemen and persons of worship have been buried, as appeareth by arms in the windows, the defaced tombs, and print of plates torn up and carried away.' It was a matter about which he felt so strongly that he omitted mention of many new monuments 'because those men have been the

---

[11] Stow, *Survey*, I. 237, 242, 247–8; II. 4, 15, 59–60. Cf. M. J. Power, 'The East and the West in Early Modern London', in *Wealth and Power in Tudor England: Essays Presented to S. T. Bindoff*, ed. E. W. Ives, R. J. Knecht, and J. J. Scarisbrick (1978), pp. 167–85; M. J. Power, 'John Stow and his London', *Journal of Historical Geography*, 11 (1985), 1–20.

[12] Stow, *Survey*, II. 72, 74–5. Cf. Manley, 'Of Sites and Rites', pp. 51–2 below.

[13] Stow, *Survey*, I. 124, 126, 139–41, 147; II. 47. Cf. J. Schofield, *The Building of London from the Conquest to the Great Fire* (1984), ch. 6.

defacers of the monuments of others, and so . . . worthy to be deprived of that memory whereof they have injuriously robbed others'.[14]

How reliable is Stow's presentation of the changes that had taken place over the course of his lifetime? This is an important question because of the frequency with which Stow is cited as a source for the texture of social relations in the capital.[15] But his laments for the loss of a sense of community and for the decay of hospitality have a timeless quality about them, and become arguably the less reliable when we consider the religiously conservative position from which Stow was writing.

Those historians who have turned to the archives to test Stow's observations have themselves come up with divergent conclusions. Some are impressed by the resilience of the sense of community in the capital: newcomers to the capital were integrated through the institution of apprenticeship; the persistence of small-scale production ensured that society did not become too sharply polarised and there were opportunities for advancement through the guild structure; although the Reformation destroyed some communal institutions like the fraternities, their functions devolved onto parishes and livery companies which remained foci for communal effort and loyalties. Others have argued that the 'optimists' have failed to take sufficient account of the stresses to which the City was subjected by the growth in its population and the consequent impoverishment: social polarisation was reflected in moves towards more limited participation in local government and guilds, in the fragmentation of sociability, and in an increasing preoccupation with the disciplining of the poor. The disagreements of historians reflect in part the different sources they have used: 'optimists' tend to draw upon institutional records of companies and parishes; 'pessimists' tend to make more use of the records of criminal justice which reveal more of the marginal population. But the disagreements are also a result of the ambiguity of much of the evidence. Take the issue of the fate of civic ritual.[16]

Stow is quite correct about the fate of the Midsummer Watch. Its decline was the result of the anxieties about public order which it focused; the discontent of the livery companies with the mounting costs of the pageants; and the ambitions of the crown for forms of mustering which were better suited to the provision of an effective defence force. The watch

---

[14] E. B. S. Shepherd, 'The Church of the Friars Minor in London', *Archaeological Journal*, 59 (1902), 266–87; Stow, *Survey*, I. 209, 210, 229, 272, 274, 319–22; II. 75; *Diary of John Manningham of the Middle Temple*, ed. J. Bruce (Camden Society, o.s., xcix, 1868), p. 103.

[15] C. Phythian-Adams, 'Ceremony and the Citizen: The Communal Year at Coventry 1450–1550', in *Crisis and Order in English Towns, 1500–1700: Essays in Urban History*, ed. P. Clark and P. Slack (1972), pp. 65–6; M. Berlin, 'Civic Ceremony in Early Modern London', *Urban History Yearbook* (1986), 18–19; S. Brigden, *London and the Reformation* (Oxford, 1989), p. 26; Archer, *Pursuit of Stability*, pp. 93–4.

[16] V. Pearl, 'Change and Stability in Seventeenth-Century London', *London Journal*, 5 (1979), 3–34; J. P. Boulton, *Neighbourhood and Society: A London Suburb in the Seventeenth Century* (Cambridge, 1987); S. Rappaport, *Worlds within Worlds: Structures of Life in Sixteenth-Century London* (Cambridge, 1989); Archer, *Pursuit of Stability*.

was cancelled at short notice in 1539 because of the costs the City had borne in the recent muster before the king; it suffered further disruptions through the mid-1540s in 'this busy time of wars'; and although an order for its permanent suppression in 1546 proved abortive, the revival of 1548 had more of the character of a muster, and the obsessive fears of insurrection under Edward VI and Mary prevented future revivals in their troubled reigns.[17] Under Elizabeth the main pressure for the revival of the watch came from the Armourers' Company: it was as a result of their lobbying that the shows were reinstated in the mid-1560s. But, as Stow himself remarks of the 1564 watch, it 'was to the commons of the city as chargeable as when in times past it had been more commendably done'. The communal and pageantic element was withering: bonfires were explicitly outlawed in the 1565 shows; the inclusion of pageants in the watch in 1567 was unusual; only in 1567 and 1568 were marching (as opposed to standing) watches held. The aldermen were unenthusiastic about the whole thing, only succumbing to even the limited standing watch with cressets in 1569 after the queen had expressed her displeasure at the lack of a suitable show. After 1570 the watches reverted to the late Edwardian pattern of double standing watches without illumination, music or bonfires, and the preoccupation with the maintenance of order manifested itself in instructions that all alehouses should be shut.[18]

Declining investment in the Midsummer watches was accompanied by the increasing elaboration of the lord mayor's procession on the occasion of his return from his oath-taking at Westminster. Stow's silence on the matter of the lord mayor's shows is striking, given his purpose in celebrating the traditions of the City, and given the way in which they so impressed foreign visitors and other English commentators.[19] Perhaps he felt that such recently invented traditions lacked an authentic quality, that they were a poor substitute for the incorporative rituals of the past. Certainly many historians would have agreed with him. Michael Berlin writes that the lord mayor's shows 'dwelt on the celebration of the office of the lord mayor as the apotheosis of the civic oligarchy ... and stressed the secular and privatized values of civic honour and pecuniary worth rather than

---

[17] *Calendar of State Papers Venetian*, ed. R. Brown, III, 136–7; *A Calendar of Dramatic Records in the Books of the Livery Companies of London*, ed. J. Robertson and D. J. Gordon (Malone Society Collections, II, 1954), pp. 1–26; *Wriothesley's Chronicle of England During the Reigns of the Tudors*, ed. W. P. Baildon (2 vols., Camden Society, n.s., XI and XX, 1875–7), I, 95–7, 100; II, 3; Corporation of London Records Office (CLRO), Jour. 14, fos. 142v, 147–8, 166–8; Rep. 10, fos. 85v–99v, 259, 329v, 331v; Rep. 11, fos. 77, 178, 192v, 445v; Rep. 12, fos. 238, 346.

[18] J. Stow, *The Annales of England from the First Inhabitation Untill 1601* (1601), pp. 1113, 1115, 1119; *Acts of the Privy Council*, VII, 107; CLRO, Rep. 15, fos. 347v, 436v, 437, 446; Rep. 16, fos. 49, 206, 362v, 475v; Rep. 17, fo. 160; Rep. 18, fos. 29, 230; Jour. 18, fos. 234v, 319, 319v, 332; Jour. 19, fos. 46v, 48v, 58v–60, 110v, 174, 243, 346v, 136v, 222v, 291, 412; British Library (BL), Lansdowne MS 11/21.

[19] Bergeron, *English Civic Pageantry*, p. 128; BL, Harleian MS 6363, fos. 6v–8; 'Journey Through England and Scotland Made by Lupold von Wedel in the Years 1584 and 1585', ed. G. von Bulow, *Transactions of the Royal Historical Society*, n.s., 9 (1895), 252–3.

the structural integration of contending social groups within communities'. This can only be part of the story, however, because the lord mayor's procession not only celebrated the power of the City elite but also emphasised its obligations to the poor. The procession attempted to present an idealised view of the social order, with the various levels of the mayor's company's hierarchy marching in due order distinctively dressed, the poor clothed in garments provided by subscription among the wealthier bachelors and bearing shields of the coats of arms of past mayors. Berlin is surely correct that the level of integration achieved was less than that of the Midsummer shows for the simple fact that the procession was provided by the lord mayor's own company alone; the liveries (generally the wealthier and older members) of other companies lined the streets, but there was no participation by the poorer members of the crafts.[20]

I have argued elsewhere that what the sixteenth century witnessed was not a collapse of community, but its articulation in different forms reflecting the working of social polarisation as society filled out at the bottom. Thus the dependence of the poor on the wealthier members of the community was constantly underscored although within a framework which also emphasised the obligations of the wealthy to relieve the poor. But this meant that rituals which had involved 'face-to-face' exchanges between rich and poor were undermined. Hence the assault on May Day, damaged by its associations with disorder particularly after the anti-alien riots of that day in 1517 and by the assaults of Protestant reformers. There are fewer signs of the involvement of the whole community in projects for the repair of the church in the Elizabethan period. Church ales and archery matches were rare in London after the early years of Elizabeth's reign; when the Jacobeans turned with apparent enthusiasm to the beautification of their churches it was by means of church rates. The disappearance of a whole gamut of religious processions at the Reformation probably worked to the same effect. Rogationtide processions, outlawed by Edward VI but allowed by Elizabeth with new and suitably Protestant prayers, continued to be celebrated in London parishes, evidently with increasing enthusiasm in the later decades of her reign; but they were poor and infrequent substitutes for the rich ritual life of processions on the days of patron saints, at Ascensiontide and Corpus Christi, which had preceded the Reformation.[21]

Arguments of this kind are vulnerable to the charges that the rise and decline of these rituals owed more to fashion than to changing patterns of social relations and that the vanished integrative rituals were soon replaced by new ones. It is true that the Protestant Church was developing

---

[20] Berlin, 'Civic Ceremony', pp. 17–21; Knowles, 'Spectacle of the Realm'; Archer, *Pursuit of Stability*, p. 54; Manley, 'Of Sites and Rites', pp. 47–8 below.

[21] Archer, *Pursuit of Stability*, pp. 92–9.

Plate 2 A detail of the lord mayor's procession, *c.*1614–15, from the album of Michael van Meer

its own ritual calendar as the celebration of Elizabeth's accession with bell ringing and sermons became widespread after 1570, a tradition on which the conservative Stow maintains a stony silence. But these were occasions orientated to the celebration of national rather than local loyalties, and in London they do not appear to have included the communal bonfires found elsewhere.[22] Likewise, the proliferation of dinners for vestrymen (the increasingly clearly defined parochial elite) was probably a poor substitute for the disappearance of the fraternities which had incorporated members of differing social status through commensality. And there are signs that although livery company feasting became more lavish, it also became more circumscribed in its capacity to incorporate the membership, if only because of the vast increases in the size of companies which meant that the assembly of all members in the hall was a physical impossibility.[23]

Nevertheless the corollary of this fragmentation of sociability was the increasing articulation of the social bond through the exercise of charity. This is an aspect of change in post-Reformation London on which Stow is most unreliable. The continual harping on the hospitality of yesteryear and the laments about the 'get-rich-quick mentality' of his own time convey the impression that charity had waxed cold. It is, of course, impossible to tell whether the informal charity by which Stow is so impressed really was declining in the later sixteenth century. Historians are now much less inclined to see a sharp break between the informal charity of the pre-Reformation era and the formalised and bureaucratised charity brought about by rating. Although hospitality may have been declining, there can be no doubting the huge surge in philanthropic giving in the sixteenth century. Data assembled by Susan Brigden and myself from the wills of Londoners has confirmed the massively increased participation in giving to the poor from the mid-Tudor decades. This investment meant that the yield of endowed charity leapt forward, outpacing the rate of inflation. This is a finding which could never have been inferred from Stow's *Survey*, the attitudes of which belong to the pre-Reformation era.[24]

Another aspect of his value system is the respect for the fabric of the parish churches of his native city. He is careful to record their embellishment and the donors responsible. Virtual rebuildings were undertaken at St Mary Hill (1490), St Peter Westcheap (1503), St Vedast (1510–20), St Mary Aldermary (after 1518), St Andrew Undershaft (1520–32), St Giles Cripplegate (1545), and St Anne and St Agnes (1548); new steeples

---

[22] D. Cressy, *Bonfires and Bells: National Memory and the Protestant Calendar in Elizabethan and Stuart England* (Berkeley, 1989), pp. 50, 55, 56.

[23] Archer, *Pursuit of Stability*, pp. 94–6, 116–20.

[24] W. K. Jordan, *The Charities of London, 1480–1660: The Aspirations and Achievements of the Urban Society* (1960); S. Brigden, 'Religion and Social Obligation in Early Sixteenth Century London', *Past & Present*, 103 (1984), 104–5; Archer, *Pursuit of Stability*, pp. 163–82.

adorned St Michael Crooked Lane (1501), St Katherine Cree (1504), St
Christopher le Stocks (1506), St Mary Bow (1512), and All Hallows
Lombard Street (1544); other churches, like St Bartholomew Exchange
and St Mary Woolnoth, acquired new aisles or chapels in the early
sixteenth century.[25] Stow's implication that the years after the Reformation
witnessed a collapse in Londoners' support for their churches is borne out
by the archival record. Investment in the church fabric in the later
sixteenth century was on a much smaller scale, and usually of a purely
functional nature, confined to the installation of pews and galleries and
the recasting of bells. Structural alterations were very rare and normally
only embarked upon when absolutely necessary, such as when the south
aisle roof of St Lawrence Jewry collapsed in 1578 during the excavation
of a vault for Sir John Langley's tomb. The low priority given to projects
for church repair is demonstrated by the exiguous numbers of Londoners
making bequests for these purposes: it seems that during the Elizabethan
decades only 3.2 per cent of wealthier testators and 0.36 per cent of poorer
testators left money for church repair (compared to 57 and 29 per cent
respectively for poor relief).[26]

Nevertheless, although parishioners were not investing heavily in the
fabric of their churches, there were other compensatory enterprises of
communal endeavour on which Stow is strangely silent. It is striking just
how many London parishes, using resources gained from the sale of church
goods under Edward VI or drawing on modest surpluses on the church
stock, sought to maximise resources for poor relief by constructing houses
to be rented to generate income for the poor. These were often built in
the churchyard or on sites adjacent to the church and, when mentioned
by Stow, it is in the context of complaints about the disfigurement of the
parish church: thus St Michael Cornhill was 'greatly blemished' by four
tenements built on the north side of the church. Thomas Bentley, author
of a parochial history of St Andrew Holborn, took a different line, lamenting
the way the church stock of his parish had been consumed in frequent
re-pavings of the lane and street about the church, and wishing that shops
were built about the walls to defray the costs of paving.[27] Unquestionably
the most significant of Stow's silences is his failure to discuss the involvement of Elizabethan Londoners in the promotion of God's word. There

---

[25] Stow, *Survey*, I. 142, 145, 181, 186, 202, 204, 208–9, 222, 252–3, 255–6, 299, 307, 313–14. Cf. *The British
Atlas of Historic Towns*, III: *The City of London*, ed. M. D. Lobel (Oxford, 1989), p. 48.

[26] Remarks based on survey of Elizabethan churchwardens' accounts; Guildhall Library (GL), MS 2590/1,
p. 56; *The Survey of London . . . Now Completely Finished by the Study of A. M., H. D. and Others this Present Yeere
1633* (1633), p. 826; Archer, *Pursuit of Stability*, pp. 170–3. Cf. J. Merritt, 'Religion, Government, and Society
in Early Modern Westminster, *c.* 1525–1625' (London Ph.D., 1992), ch. 5.

[27] Stow, *Survey*, I. 196; GL, MS 4249, fo. 233v; *The Accounts of the Churchwardens of the Parish of St Michael
Cornhill, 1456–1608*, ed. W. H. Overall (1883), pp. 69–70, 79, 84, 90, 91, 97. Cf. Public Record Office (PRO),
E117/4/11, 22, 67, 69, 87; GL, MSS 9235/1, fos. 18–22v, 24v, 25, 26; 1432/1, fos. 114v, 123; 4956/2, fo. 170;
7673/1, fos. 116v–18; 1568, p. 297.

could be no more eloquent testimony to his lack of sympathy for evangelical Protestantism than his failure to mention the endowment by leading London merchants of parochial lectureships and the support of others by means of subscription among parishioners: by the time of the publication of his *Survey* thirty-five parishes supported lectureships. The remarkable progress made in the creation of an effective preaching ministry went unpraised by Stow.[28]

Stow's contemporaries were sensitive to the implications of selective historical writing. On 2 December 1565 Stow's recently published *Summary* was denounced by Thomas Bickley, one of Archbishop Parker's chaplains, in a sermon at St Paul's Cross. Bickley accused Stow of seeking to conceal the embarrassing facts about Queen Mary's phantom pregnancy: 'It is known well enough how in Queen Mary's time there was talk of the queen's delivery, processions and bonfires for the same; but one John Stow in his chronicle, perceiving this to make against their vanity, hath left it clean out.'[29] Throughout the 1560s Stow's religious sympathies seem to have made him the subject of suspicion. In January 1569 he was interrogated in connection with his possession of the manifesto issued by the duke of Alva in response to the recently imposed English trade embargo with the territories of the king of Spain. The following month his study was raided by Bishop Grindal's chaplains who uncovered several 'old fantastical Popish books printed in the old time' together with 'books lately put forth in the realm of beyond the seas for defence of Papistry'.[30] Stow's manuscript jottings on events between 1561 and 1567 have a decidedly conservative cast. He expressed sympathy for the tribulations of mass priests; he was critical of those who wished to put the Marian bishops to death; he was bitterly sarcastic about the critics of the Elizabethan Settlement, 'the Puritans or unspotted lambs of the Lord', tarring them with the Anabaptist brush; and he struck out at the hypocritical pluralism of some of the capital's leading Puritan clergy, Robert Crowley and John Philpot.[31]

Nevertheless Stow was able to accommodate himself to the new regime in religion. Grindal's dour brand of Protestantism may not have been to his taste, but he enjoyed the patronage of Archbishop Parker, 'my especial benefactor'; and Archbishop Whitgift, the dedicatee of the *Annals* of 1592 he described as 'a man born for the benefit of his country and the good of the Church'.[32] Later editions of his historical works dropped references to support for the old religion under Mary, and Stow came to enjoy

---

[28] H. G. Owen, 'The London Parish Clergy in the Reign of Elizabeth I' (London Ph.D., 1957); P. Seaver, *The Puritan Lectureships: The Politics of Religious Dissent, 1560–1662* (Stanford, 1970), chs. 2, 5, 6.

[29] Bodleian Library, Tanner MS 50, fo. 30v; *Dictionary of National Biography* for Bickley.

[30] Clode, *Early History of Merchant Taylors*, II, 299–302; BL, Lansdowne MS 11/2–5; Stow, *Survey*, I. xvi–xvii.

[31] *Three Fifteenth-Century Chronicles with Historical Memoranda by John Stowe*, ed. J. Gairdner (Camden Society, n.s., XXVIII, 1880), pp. 121–2, 126, 135–6, 138, 139.

[32] Stow, *Survey*, I. xix–xxii, lxxix–lxxx.

patronage from City institutions dominated by Protestants of a hue with which the chronicler must still have felt uneasy. After 1579 he enjoyed a pension of £4 per annum from the Merchant Tailors' Company, raised to £6 per annum in 1600, and supplemented from 1593 by one of the new pensions established by the merchant tailor philanthropist, Robert Dowe. Among Stow's influential supporters within the Merchant Tailors' Company was the City's Recorder, William Fleetwood, a man of decidedly godly persuasions, but whose antiquarian interests gave him an intellectual affinity with Stow. Manningham records that a 'model' of Stow's portrait, later to form the frontispiece to the *Survey of London*, was found in the Recorder's study.[33] The court of aldermen recognised Stow's pains in advancing the honour of the City by granting him the reversion to the office of keeper of the Bay Hall and the profit of a freedom admission in 1583; the grant of another freedom followed in 1598.[34] Belated and perhaps grudging recognition of Stow's 'painful labours' came from the crown in the form of a licence 'to collect amongst our loving subjects their voluntary contribution and kind gratuities' in 1604.[35]

Whether the patronage of the City justified the aldermen's description of Stow as their 'fee'd Chronicler' in the 1590s is doubtful. Nevertheless his labours could undoubtedly be used in the City's service. Piers Cain has shown how the aldermen were coming to appreciate the importance of good record-keeping and a mastery of history in a climate where City liberties were under threat from predatory courtiers and where the City's defence of its claims depended on its ability to demonstrate that its position had the sanction of custom. Thus the aldermen drew upon Stow's expertise in their interminable dispute with the Lieutenant of the Tower and got him to set out the boundaries of the liberty of Cree church (formerly Holy Trinity Priory), purchased by the City from Lord Thomas Howard in 1592. Stow himself tells us with pride how his knowledge of boundaries was put to use by the inhabitants of Lime Street ward in withstanding a challenge from Aldgate ward; at a time when many taxes were levied on a local quota basis such disputes were hardly trifling matters.[36]

In the same way as Stow's researches could be of use to the City establishment, so too could they be of service to the ecclesiastical hierarchy. Archbishop Parker's patronage of Stow derived from his determination to set the Church of England on a firm historical base, demonstrating its early independence from Roman authority and showing how the Church of Rome had lost whatever purity it might once have possessed. Stow

---

[33] B. L. Beer, 'John Stow and the English Reformation', *Sixteenth Century Journal*, 16 (1985), 256–6; Clode, *Early History of Merchant Taylors*, II, 302–3; *Manningham's Diary*, p. 103.
[34] CLRO, Rep. 21, fo. 77; Rep. 24, fo. 303.
[35] Stow, *Survey*, I. lxvi–lxvii.
[36] Stow, *Survey*, I. xxiii, 161–2; P. Cain, 'Robert Smith and the Reform of the Archives of the City of London, 1580–1623', *London Journal*, 13.1 (1987–8), 143–62.

supplied Parker with the manuscripts of the *Flores Historiarum*, the chronicles of Matthew Paris, and Thomas Walsingham, which were published between 1567 and 1574. Stow's unpublished collection, the *Fundationes Ecclesiarum*, was much sought after by Elizabethan antiquarians. Medievalism could serve the interests of the new religion.[37]

Indeed, the intellectual world of Elizabethan England was not rigidly divided between the adherents of a Protestant view of a medieval dark age and a Catholic view of an idealised golden age. Protestants could appreciate the virtue that had existed in former times, and some of Stow's characteristic emphases surface in other more obviously godly writers. It is true that the reformers were keen to establish that their record of charitable provision put the Catholic Church to shame. In 1577 the controversialist William Fulke challenged his Roman adversary, William Allen: 'Show me, Mr Allen, if thou canst for thy guts, or name me any city in the world where Popery prevaileth, that hath made such provision for the fatherless children and widows and all other kind of poor, as in the noble city of London.' Andrew Willet set out in his monumental *Catalogue* of 1614 to prove that sixty years of the Gospel had brought forth more good works than twice as long of popery. And yet the stance taken by the godly depended on the audience they were addressing. In the teeth of Catholic polemicists they would assert the fruits of the Gospel; but confronted by congregations of businessmen intent on profits, they would lash out at the flinty-hearted Londoners. Willet himself had complained about the decay of charity in a St Paul's Cross sermon of 1592. Even so militant an antipapist as Laurence Chaderton was forced to admit in a sermon of 1578 that 'the papists always cast in our teeth the great and famous hospitals of their nobility and clergy, the building of abbeys, monasteries, and nunneries, cathedral churches, colleges, with many other outward works which indeed are such as do stop our mouths and put us Protestants to silence'.[38]

Stow's avowed purpose in recording the good works of preceding generations was the display of a 'godly example by the posterity to be embraced and imitated'. The value of memorialising benefactors as a spur to further charitable endeavour was widely appreciated in Elizabethan London. Good works were trumpeted in a variety of media. Tables of legacies in company halls were supplemented by statues, portraits and coats of arms of leading benefactors. The popular press churned out epitaphs mourning the passing of virtuous merchants and trumpeting their philanthropic works. In 1601

[37] F. J. Levy, *Tudor Historical Thought* (San Marino, 1967), pp. 114–22, 133–6; M. McKisack, *Medieval History in the Tudor Age* (Oxford, 1971), p. 41.

[38] Thomas, 'Perception of the Past', pp. 13–14; W. Fulke, *Two Treatises Written Against the Papists* (1577), II, 241; A. Willet, *Synopsis Papismi* (1614), p. 1219; A. Willet, *A Fruitfull and Godly Sermon Preached at Pauls Cross, 1592* (1592); L. Chaderton, *An Excellent and Godly Sermon . . . Preached at Paules Crosse the XXVI Daye of October An. 1578* (1580).

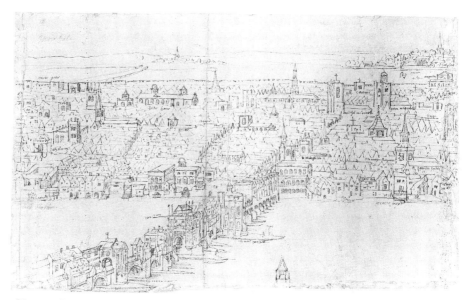

Plate 3   A section of the Wyngaerde panorama of London, *c.* 1550

William Jaggard, adopting a format reminiscent of Stow's section on the 'Honour of citizens, and worthiness of men in the same', provided *A View of all the Right Honourable Lord Mayors of this Honourable City of London*, with brief historical notes recording as appropriate their charities. Woe betide those of whom, like William Webb, lord mayor in 1591–2, he had to write, 'no monument, neither as yet any note of his bounty'! Philanthropy should always be accompanied by publicity, both for the sake of the donor's fame and for the encouragement to others. Stow's recovery of the tradition of charity in the City was therefore an important contribution to the surge in philanthropic endeavour characteristic of the turn of the century.[39]

Stow's concern about the wanton iconoclasm and spoliation of the churches was shared in quarters arguably more favourable to the cause of Protestantism. Elizabeth's own position on this was, of course, more conservative than that of most of her first generation of bishops. The ambiguity of the Elizabethan Settlement on the question of images marked a retreat from the high-water mark of iconoclasm under Edward VI, and the queen appears to have stepped in to protect certain categories of church possessions. Commemorative monuments were not to be attacked;

---

[39] Stow, *Survey*, I. 91, 104–17; I. W. Archer, *The History of the Haberdashers' Company* (Chichester, 1991), p. 74; Clothworkers' Company, Quarter Wardens' Accounts, 1566–7, fo. 7; 1573–4, fo. 7; 1594–5, fo. 26v; Mercers' Company, Acts of Court III, fos. 253v–4; *Ballads and Broadsides Chiefly of the Elizabethan Period*, ed. H. L. Collman (Oxford, 1912), pp. 18, 213, 227–9; A. Nixon, *London's Dove* (1612); N(icholas) B(our), *An Epitaph Upon . . . Lady Mary Ramsey* (1602?); *The Dramatic Works of Thomas Heywood*, ed. R. H. Shepherd (6 vols., 1874), I, 276–8; Stevenson, *Praise and Paradox*, pp. 108–10, 144–6; W. Jaggard, *A View of All the Right Honourable the Lord Mayors of London* (1601).

stained-glass windows were only to be destroyed with the permission of the bishop; and parishioners were subject to fine and imprisonment if they alienated their bells and lead.[40] Elizabeth's stand was supported by some of her subjects, even those of a Protestant hue. Thomas Bentley, the chronicler of St Andrew Holborn, leaves us in no doubt of his broadly Protestant sympathies, expressing hostility to the setting up of idolatry in the reign of Mary Tudor. But he was critical of the defacement of monuments under Elizabeth, suspicious of the iconoclasts' claims that these things had been done 'to the glory of God'. As for the sale of gravestones by the churchwardens in 1575, he doubts whether they were acting lawfully, and emphasises that their actions would discourage 'many well minded to bestow money that way when they see such abuse and defacing of monuments'. Bentley's purpose is similar to that of Stow albeit executed on a much smaller scale: his narrative is entitled 'Monuments of Antiquities worthy memory collected and gathered out of sundry old accounts . . .' Again, like Stow, he looks back nostalgically to the time when church repair was financed by means of plays, shooting matches, ales or drinkings, and is critical of churchwardens who seek to finance church repair by such dubious expedients as the sale of lead in 1579.[41]

Bentley's register provides a unique window into the reactions of an ordinary London parishioner to the changes he had witnessed in the fabric of parochial life. In some respects his outlook is similar to Stow's, but it is difficult to be sure how widely shared their attitudes were. There are some grounds for feeling that as the Elizabethan Church and the rituals of the Prayer Book became embedded in the consciousness of Londoners, regrets for the best of the Catholic past were strengthened. Certainly the transformation in attitudes to church repair at the turn of the century is striking. Within twenty years of the appearance of Stow's *Survey*, no less than thirty-two churches appear to have undergone programmes of repair and beautification. Aisle walls were rebuilt, windows enlarged and reglazed, steeples repaired and repointed, gravestones relaid, new galleries, pews and pulpits installed. In some cases the expense was enormous. The repair of St Botolph Bishopsgate in 1617 cost over £600, that of St Antholin in 1616 over £900; the enlargement of the increasingly fashionable church of St Anne Blackfriars in 1613 cost £1,546.[42]

The investment by Londoners in the fabric of their churches in the decades preceding the arrival of William Laud at the see of London in 1628 stands in stark contrast to the collapse of the Elizabethan decades.

---

[40] M. Aston, *England's Iconoclasts*, I: *Laws Against Images* (Oxford, 1988), pp. 294–342.

[41] GL, MS 4249, fos. 221, 222v, 233, 234. Bentley's register is printed in E. Griffith, *Cases of Supposed Exemption from the Poor Rates Claimed on Grounds of Extra-Parochiality, With a Preliminary Sketch of the Ancient History of the Parish of Saint Andrew Holborn* (1831), and discussed by C. M. Barron, *The Parish of St Andrew Holborn* (1979), ch. 4. For similar parochial reminiscences from a recusant standpoint, see *The Spoil of Melford Church: The Reformation in a Suffolk Parish*, ed. D. Dymond and C. Paine (2nd edn, Ipswich, 1992), pp. 1–9.

[42] *Survey of London . . . Now Completely Finished*, pp. 819–910.

It is a phenomenon very much in need of further investigation by historians. Should it be seen as a response to the new emphasis on 'prayer and praise' in Anglican apologetic, and a tapping of the conservative ceremonialist sentiments of the silent majority? Rather than seeing ceremonies as merely expedient, necessary for good order and obedience, Richard Hooker had treated them as a means of edification, good in themselves. In the words of Peter Lake this was 'little short of a reclamation of the whole realm of symbolic action and ritual practice from the status of popish superstition to that of a necessary, indeed essential, means of communication and edification'. Although Hooker may not have been widely read at the time, his ideas were shared by the avant-garde proto-Arminians some of whom, like Lancelot Andrewes, vicar of St Giles Cripplegate between 1589 and 1605, secured London livings at the turn of the century.[43] Alternatively, however, the greater investment in the church fabric may be read as a sign of the gradual implantation of a consensual Protestantism, an indication of the greater confidence of the Jacobeans in their Church. Not all the supporters of the beautification programme readily fit an Arminian mould, proto- or otherwise. Thus among the supporters of the Jacobean restoration of St Stephen Walbrook was Henry Andrewes, haberdasher, the donor of the window in the north chancel wall nearest the communion table showing the story of the stoning of St Stephen, the first martyr, and patron of the church. Henry Andrewes was no ritualist, for he also keenly supported the Puritan lecturer, John Downham. We have recently been reminded of the complexity of religious divisions in early seventeenth-century England: 'doctrinal preference did not necessarily coincide with liturgical taste'.[44] The sentiments expressed by Stow and Bentley, themselves writing from rather different religious standpoints, gained a sympathetic hearing in areas we do not readily associate with nostalgia for the Catholic past. In so far as a concern for the fabric of the church was hitched to a pride in the City, Stow's nostalgia may well have fed the explosion in the embellishment of London churches in the new century.

---

[43] P. Lake, *Anglicans and Puritans?: Presbyterian and English Conformist Thought from Whitgift to Hooker* (1988), pp. 164–9; BL, Add. MS 12222.
[44] GL, MS 593/2, acct. for 1613–14; PRO, PROB 11/Lee 127; P. White, 'The *Via Media* in the Early Stuart Church', in *The Early Stuart Church, 1603–42*, ed. K. Fincham (1993), pp. 211–30.

Of Sites and Rites

Lawrence Manley

The status of John Stow's *Survey of London* (1598) as both a record and an example of change in early modern London has been frequently celebrated. Reflecting the archaeological impulse of Renaissance humanism, stimulated by the work of the emerging Society of Antiquaries, based on painstaking archival research, and borrowing its method from the innovative chorographical techniques of William Lambarde's *Perambulation of Kent* (1576), Stow's *Survey* became a model for the writing of urban history. Its influence extends, through the continuations of Stow by Munday (1633) and Strype (1720) to such later avatars as the *Victoria County History*, the modern multi-volume *Survey of London*, and Derek Keene and Vanessa Harding's recent *Historical Gazeteer of London before the Great Fire* (1987–).

A feature of the *Survey* much admired and, in a way, imitated, among modern historians and literary scholars is Stow's concern, evident in his vivid descriptive style, with mundane detail, ordinary lives and routine social rhythms in the Tudor metropolis. For Stow, 'no facts', one historian writes, 'were trivial in themselves or because they were facts about obscure men'.[1] Less frequently noted, however, is the extent to which, for Stow, such facts are important because they are norms, exemplary instances of the ancient and continuing patterns of order the *Survey* is meant to celebrate. *The Survey of London* is as much a traditional testament of civic religion as it is an innovative work of historical anthropology. Part of its historical significance lies in the paradoxical relations between these two tendencies: between Stow's stress on the continuity of civic custom, tradition and ceremony, and his recognition of epochal change. On the one hand, Stow's still quasi-sacramental adherence, as a member of the traditional citizen class, to customary ceremonies and routines is a conservative response to the erosion of a late medieval commune by an alien world of change. On the other hand, Stow's civic religion is – in its very emphasis on ceremony and tradition – itself already implicated in the process of change; it is a dimension of the celebratory civic ideology, socio-economic mobility, and metropolitan growth that were transforming the life of London. In what

---

[1] F. Smith Fussner, 'John Stow and Local History', in *The Historical Revolution 1580–1640* (1962), p. 213.

it has to say about the transition from public ceremony to commercial theatre, Stow's *Survey* provides not only a picture of the changing metropolis but a striking example of the paradoxes of the citizen mentality, in which adherence to tradition reinforced a historic drift that transformed living civic norms into the facts of historical anthropology and Stow's civic religion into history.

The most original aspect of Stow's achievement is the central portion of the *Survey*, the district-by-district perambulation of the boundaries and monuments of the wards, liberties and suburbs of London. Yet this innovative topographical centre of the *Survey* is preceded and followed by sections more exclusively concerned with the traditional practices and values of the citizen class. Stow's account of civic traditions at the beginning of the *Survey* takes the form of a translation and extended commentary on passages from the *Descriptio nobilissimae civitatis Londoniae*, a twelfth-century account of the city forming part of a biography of Thomas à Becket by his secretary and fellow Londoner, William FitzStephen. In his commentary Stow follows Fitz-Stephen in a discussion of London's origins, walls, gates, conduits and bridges, together with a canvas of 'the orders and customs, sports and pastimes, watchings, and martial exercises, and . . . the honour and worthiness of the citizens'.[2] Stow returns to the question of civic honour and ritual at the conclusion of the *Survey* with an account of 'the policy and government, both ecclesiastical and civil, of London . . . maintained by the customs thereof, most laudably used before all the time of memory' (II. 124).

Built into the three-part structure of the *Survey*, then, is a distinction between physical fabric and populace, sites and rites, that was in line with current humanist theory – both with the Aristotelian-Ramist notion that cities could be analysed according to *res* and *homines*, and with the Aphthonian rhetorical scheme that, by appropriating to the praise of cities the topics for praising noble persons, dictated that while a city's physical features were like those of a person's body, worthy citizens were a city's equivalent to the worthy offspring of noble parents.[3] Furthermore, Stow's account of the 'honour of citizens, and worthiness of men' in London (I. 104–17) would have been supported by a wealth of ancient testimony, fashionable among humanists, to the effect that 'the men, not the walls . . . make the city'.[4] Yet the more likely source for Stow's distinction is his twelfth-century source, FitzStephen, whose declared aim in his *Descriptio* was to depict 'situm, et rem publicam Londoniae'.[5] Stow underlines Fitz-

[2] I quote throughout from the edition of the *Survey* by C. L. Kingsford (2 vols., 1908; rpt. Oxford, 1971), I, 117.

[3] Lawrence Manley, 'From Matron to Monster: Tudor–Stuart London and the Languages of Urban Description', in *The Historical Renaissance: New Essays on Tudor and Stuart Literature and Culture*, ed. Heather Dubrow and Richard Strier (Chicago, 1988), pp. 347–74.

[4] Thucydides, *History of the Peloponnesian War*, 7.77, tr. Thomas Hobbes (1629), *Hobbes's Thucydides*, ed. Richard Schlatter (New Brunswick, 1975), p. 501. Cf. Alcaeus, frag. 28; *Coriolanus*, 3.1.

[5] *Materials for the History of Thomas Becket*, ed. J. C. Robertson and J. B. Sheppard (7 vols., London, Rolls Series, 1875–85), III, 2.

Stephen's distinction by introducing the appended text of the *Descriptio* with a passage from John Bale's *Illustrium maioris Britanniae scriptorum summarium* (1548), stating that FitzStephen had written concerning 'the site and rites' (*de situ et ritibus*) of London.[6] Royally chartered as *caput regni* and *camera regis* (II. 202), London enjoyed special status as a ritual site, the only town in England 'found fit and able to entertain strangers honourably, and to receive the prince of the realm worthily', as James Dalton explains in the 'Apology of the City of London' that concludes Stow's *Survey* (II. 214). But for Stow, as for FitzStephen, whom Stow quotes approvingly, the deeper basis for London's ritual significance lies in the saturation of the traditional civic order by ritual and ceremonial observance: 'I do not think that there is any city wherein are better customs, in frequenting the churches, in serving God, in keeping holy days, in giving alms, in entertaining strangers, in solemnising marriages, in furnishing banquets, celebrating funerals and burying dead bodies' (I. 80).

In his expansive opening commentary on FitzStephen's account of the 'Orders and Customs' of London, Stow elaborates on the ceremonial patterns and ritual regulations – from market customs and military musters to mummings, triumphs and rites of almsgiving – that governed virtually all aspects of urban life. Alongside an elaborate round of seasonal recreations – springtime cockfights and football matches, summertime water-sports, martial games and dancing, wintertime ice-sports and venery – communal custom had prescribed a ritual calendar of religious and civic observances: the lords of misrule who presided at Christmas and throughout the festal season between All Hallows Eve and the Feast of the Purification, the Lenten ridings and Eastertide fetching in of greenery, the Corpus Christi processions and plays, the Midsummer Watch and shrieval elections, the summertime fairs on saints' feasts. Attended by nobility and clergy as well as citizens, the cycle of traditional events proves, Stow concludes, 'that in those days, the inhabitants and repairers to this City of what estate soever, spiritual or temporal, having houses there, lived together in good amity with the citizens, every man observing the customs and orders of the City' (I. 84–5). From this order of 'good amity' logically follows the roll of worthy citizen contributors to 'the common good of the City' (I. 164) with which Stow completes his commentary on FitzStephen and the first third of his book, all of it rounded off with Lydgate's assertion that London's 'faithful observance' and 'stableness aye kept in legiance' are among the reasons that 'The king's chamber of custom, men thee call' (I. 117).

The first Londoner named in Stow's list of worthies is none other than the martyred Becket of FitzStephen's *Descriptio*, whose effigy, Stow explains, adorned the City's official seal until the Cromwellian reforms of 1539 (I. 315). Stow would have encountered the *Descriptio* in another important

---

[6] *Illustrium maioris Britanniae scriptorum summarium* (1548), sig. Siiv.

source for the *Survey*, a fourteenth-century City custumal, the *Liber Custuma-rum*, where Andrew Horn, the City Chamberlain, had put FitzStephen's text at the head of the multitude of documents he assembled in connection with the City's defence of its franchises at the *iter* of 1321.[7] A major component of Stow's original research in such archives as the City letter-books, patent rolls, and the cartulary of Holy Trinity Aldgate was his study of the important custumals in which London's chief notaries had compiled the deeds, charters, trusts, regulations, precedents and rituals essential to the City's jealously guarded liberties and privileges. These custumals included the *Liber Albus* (1419) of John Carpenter, 'town clerk of London' (I. 109), the *Liber Dunthorne* (*c.* 1474) of William Dunthorne, town clerk, and the compilation of the London haberdasher Richard Arnold (*c.* 1502) who, Stow explains, 'being inflamed with the fervent love of good learning . . . and . . . matters worthy to be remembered of posterity . . . noted the charters, liberties, laws, constitutions and customs, of the city of London'.[8]

Most of these custumals were products of the fifteenth century, when, following a period of turbulence in the reign of Richard II, the City magistracy finally established its control over London's fractious guilds, and, led by the newly ascendant companies of international traders, arrived at the basic civic constitution that prevailed into Stow's time and beyond. Unlike their fourteenth- and fifteenth-century Italian counterparts, whose civic labours were creatively integrated with the dissemination of new classical learning, the members of the notarial class that helped to produce and perpetuate this civic order were relatively untouched by humanist scholarship,[9] which only emerged in England with the advent of printing and under the patronage of the Henrician state and the Elizabethan court. In both medium and outlook, London's citizen notaries belonged rather to the late medieval manuscript culture to which Stow, an early editor of Chaucer, alludes so frequently in the *Survey* – the culture of Gower, Lydgate and the 'moral and divine' author William Lichfield (I. 235), of the learned patron John Carpenter and the merchant manuscript dealer John Shirley (II. 23–4).[10] Stow alludes in the *Survey* only to Foxe and Camden among his great literary contemporaries. But he refers frequently to such citizen-chroniclers as Edward Hall, 'common sergeant of this City, and then

---

[7] *Liber Custumarum*, ed. H. T. Riley, in *Munimenta Gildhallae Londoniensis* (London, Rolls Series, 1860), II, 1–15. Kingsford notes that while Stow 'presumably . . . had access' to the *Descriptio* through the *Liber Custumarum*, he appears to have taken his text from an original closer to the versions in Lansdowne 398 and Marshall 75; see *Survey*, II. 387.

[8] *In this booke is conteyned the names of ye baylifs custos mairs and sherefs of london* (Antwerp, 1503), rpt. as *The Customs of London, Otherwise Called Arnold's Chronicle* (1811); Stow's comment on Arnold comes from the list of sources in his *Summarie of English Chronicles* (1565).

[9] Frank Freeman Foster, *The Politics of Stability: A Portrait of the Rulers in Elizabethan London* (1977), p. 5.

[10] See Derek Pearsall, *John Lydgate* (1970), p. 177; Thomas Brewer, *Memoir of the Life and Times of John Carpenter* (1856), pp. 62ff.

under sheriff' (I. 260) and 'Robert Fabyan alderman' (I. 197) as well as
to the contemporary manuscripts of such London notaries and legal special-
ists as the 'grave citizen' John Montgomery (I. 103), the 'learned gentleman,
and grave citizen' William Patten (I. 83) and the 'learned gentleman' and
'citizen born' James Dalton (I. 186).

Stow likely gained access to the London records through his association
in the Society of Antiquaries with William Fleetwood, the City Recorder,
who compiled the London custumal that bears his name. While his work
on London's past was shaped by the innovative techniques emerging in
the Society of Antiquaries, it was with something like a more traditional
notarial perspective that Stow, who had served on juries and wardmotes
and aided the City in property disputes, approached the historical labours
that he felt 'bound in love to bestow upon the politic body and members'
of London (I. xcviii). At the time of Stow's *Survey*, the Corporation was
involved in substantial efforts – including the recopying of the *Liber Albus*
and other custumals, the sequestering of records and the search for lost
volumes – to consolidate its archive. This effort, in which Stow was himself
recruited by the City,[11] was perhaps prompted by a number of political
exigencies,[12] but another important motive for the restoration of the archive
was the traditionalism of the civic mentality, a concern for the maintenance
of customary practices and ceremony. In 1571 the City created the new
position of Remembrancer, and in 1574–5 the first holder of the office,
Thomas Norton, compiled a manuscript calendar of civic rituals for the
lord mayor, noting that 'things . . . have their prescribed times, and so
be set under the titles of every several month'.[13] Printed calendars of the
civic year, meanwhile, had begun to be published periodically by 1568,
and in 1596 the Court of Aldermen required that

notes shall be set down in writing and hanged in the Guildhall what things appertain
either by charter, usage, Acts of Common Council or by custom to be yearly done
and performed by the Lord Mayor for the time being or by the Lord Mayor and
Court of Aldermen.[14]

It was important to observe civic rites because, as Fleetwood put it, 'it
hath ever been the use in . . . governing men's doings and policies always to
follow the ancient precedents and steps of the forefathers'.[15] The calendrical

---

[11] *Survey*, I. xxii, xxxiii.

[12] Piers Cain, 'Robert Smith and the Reform of the Archives of the City of London, 1580–1623', *London Journal*, 13.1 (1987–8), 3–16; Ian Archer, *The Pursuit of Stability: Social Relations in Elizabethan London* (Cambridge, 1991), pp. 35–7.

[13] *Instructions to the Lord Mayor of London, 1574–75*, in *Illustrations of Old English Literature*, ed. J. Payne Collier (3 vols., 1866), II, 14–15.

[14] *The ordre of my lorde mayor, the aldermen & the shiriffes, for their meetings throughout the yeare* (1568); *Generall matters to be remembred of the lord major throughout the whole yeare* (c. 1600); *The order of my Lord Major . . . throughout the yeere* (1621); CLRO, *Repertories*, 23, fo. 544v, cited in Cain, 'Robert Smith and the Reform of the Archives', p. 11.

[15] *The effect of the declaration made in the Guildhall by M. Recorder of London* (1571), sig. A2.

regularity of civic observance was especially important in maintaining the good order and stability of the City, which was, as James Dalton notes in the 'Apology' appended to Stow's *Survey*, governed 'by a pattern, as it were, and always the same, how oftensoever they change their magistrate' (II. 206). The regularity of London's government was enshrined not only in the custumals but also in the numerous City chronicles, most of them dating from the fifteenth century, that were so essential to Stow's research. Based on earlier lists of mayors and sheriffs, the numerous London chronicles commissioned or compiled by fifteenth-century City officials followed the annalistic practice of heading and identifying each year under the names of the City's newly elected leaders. The uninterrupted and secular rhythm of London's civic year remained a feature of Stow's own annalistic practice in both his *Summary of English Chronicles* (1565 ff) and his *Chronicles of England* (1580), and he took particular pride in the accuracy of his version of the mayoral and shrieval chronology, which he included in his account of 'temporal government' at the end of the *Survey*.[16]

Thomas Nashe mocked the citizen mentality of 'good Master Stow' and 'lay chronographers, that write of nothing but of mayors and sheriffs'.[17] But in so far as it was 'not to remain, but every year to be newly chosen',[18] the highly regular government of London was an essential counterbalance to the unpredictabilities of dynastic succession and changing royal policy. As the emerging Tudor state was becoming increasingly dependent on parliamentary financing, the regular customs, revenue and credit of London represented a dependable alternative to the summoning of unpredictable parliaments. The City's elaborate administrative machinery, furthermore, provided a means by which the nascent state, lacking mechanisms of its own, could carry out an 'ambitious programme of economic and social controls'.[19] The annual replacement of London's chief magistrate thus assured a perpetual stability: 'though the main authority of government [in him] may be said to die, yet it surviveth in other pelicans of the same brood'.[20]

An important corollary of the calendrical observance of a ritualised time in government was the transformation of the City into a sacred space, a physical embodiment of historic destiny and community spirit. The account of London's walls and gates, with which Stow begins the *Survey*, serves to delineate this theoretically inviolable space. Some vestige of the ancient

---

[16] See BL, Harleian MS 367, in *Survey*, I. lii.

[17] *Works*, ed. R. B. McKerrow (Oxford, 1958), I, 317, 194.

[18] *The Recorder of London's speech, on presenting the Lord Mayor, Sir John Spencer, to the Lord Chief Baron and his Brethren of the Exchequer* (1594), in *The Progresses and Public Processions of Queen Elizabeth*, ed. John Nichols (3 vols., 1823; rpt. New York, 1966), III, 256.

[19] Robert Ashton, *The City and Court, 1603–1643* (Cambridge, 1979), p. 17; G. D. Ramsey, *The City of London in International Politics and the Accession of Elizabeth Tudor* (Manchester, 1975), pp. 50–60.

[20] Anthony Munday, *Chrysanaleia: The Golden Fishing: or, Honour of Fishmongers*, in *Pageants and Entertainments of Anthony Munday*, ed. David M. Bergeron (New York, 1985), p. 107.

myth that a city's outline was laid out in the ritual acts of its founder remains in Stow's report, via Simeon of Durham, that London's walls were built by 'Helen the mother of Constantine the Great' and represent a people's capacity to 'look well to themselves' (I. 5–6). Within the civic space defined by these walls, Stow explains, the Lord Mayor ranks highest in the kingdom 'out of the king's presence' (II. 36). The fearsome giant effigies who, according to Stow, accompanied the mayor and sheriffs on the Midsummer Marching Watch (I. 103) also stood guard as *palladia* at London's gates – 'come custodi della città' – whenever monarchs made their ceremonial triumphs through the City.[21] In his survey of this sacral space, Stow includes mention both of the rebels – Wat Tyler, Jack Cade, the Bastard Fauconbridge, Sir Thomas Wyatt – who had violated it (I. 125) and of the many who had hallowed it – Becket and Erkenwald, whose cults had until recently been sustained by Londoners (III. 332), the martyred King Edmund, whose body wrought miraculous cures when it was brought into the City through Cripplegate (I. 33), Edward the Confessor, whose decision 'to make his sepulchre' on the former site of 'a Temple of Apollo' at Westminster lay at the root of London's status as a capital (II. 105).

In keeping with FitzStephen's claim that Londoners were ceremonially assiduous in 'burying dead bodies', and with Lewis Mumford's theory that the earliest form of the city was the burial ground, the physical space of Stow's London is furthermore hallowed by the dead, not simply by the 1,775 worthy persons whose monuments Stow, astonishingly, identifies by name (the Hebrew Bible, for comparison, contains 1,426 named personages), but also by the 'innumerable bodies of the dead' interred, in times of plague, in the mass graves of the suburbs – in East Smithfield, at the Charterhouse (containing 'above 100,000 bodies of Christian people'), and in the grounds of Bethlehem hospital, where in 1569 Mayor Thomas Roe buried his wife and countless other Londoners for 'the ease of such parishes . . . as wanted ground convenient' (I. 124, 165, II. 81–2). Indeed, Stow's archaeological impulse is inseparable from his spiritual membership in a community where the past was in a more or less continuous state of disinterral. Stow had seen what he believed were the remains of Romans, Britons and Saxons unearthed in the Spitalfield brickworks. He explains how the body of King Harold of the Danes, dug up and cast into the Thames by the vengeful Hardecanute, was returned by fishermen and buried in St Clement Danes (II. 96); how Alice Hackney came up 'uncorrupted more than one hundred years after she was buried'

---

[21] *La solenne et felice intrata delli Serenissimi Re Philippo, et Regina Maria d'inghilterra, nella Regal Città di Londra* (1554), cited in Sidney Anglo, *Spectacle, Pageantry, and Early Tudor Policy* (Oxford, 1969), p. 327. The City *palladia* made similar appearances at the triumphal entries for Henry V, Henry VI, the emperor Charles V, Mary and Elizabeth I.

in St Mary Hill (1. 209); and how Richard Whittington's grave was opened by a greedy Protestant parson who thought 'some great riches (as he said) to be buried with him' (1. 243). Though he is sceptical about the remains of giants found in London (1. 275, 389), Stow is in little doubt that the civic space is also a domain of spirits. He recalls having personally seen the claw-marks, 'three or four inches deep' (1. 196) and dating from his father's time, that were left by the devil on a midnight visit to St Michael in Cornhill.

Sacred space within the city was defined not only by shrines and sanctuaries but also by ritual observances, including the public processions and ceremonies that establish liturgically invariant routes and 'place(s) accustomed' for pageants and speeches.[22] As at Coventry, so in London, these civic rituals were organised as a 'ceremonial year', a complex cycle of annual events, divided into secular and religious semesters.[23] The shrieval election and confirmation of the chamberlain, clerk, chief sergeant and other officers coincided with the Midsummer Watch on the feasts of John the Baptist (24 June) and Saints Peter and Paul (29 June); it began the connected series of civic events that created a new City government – the swearing-in of the sheriffs on Michaelmas Eve, the Michaelmas mayoralty election, and the installation of the new lord mayor on the feast of Saints Simon and Jude (29 Oct.) and its morrow. These civic events left the new City government in place in time for the semester of religious feasts in which the mayor and aldermen played an important part – the series of fixed religious holidays that began on All Saints (1 Nov.) and ended with Candlemas (2 Feb.), and the moveable events of Easter week, Rogationtide, Whitsuntide and Corpus Christi, which could be dated as late as 24 June. In London as elsewhere in England, the guild-sponsored procession and plays that marked the closing of the Christological calendar on Corpus Christi also served to express, through the changing fortunes and prestige of the sponsors, 'diachronic changes within the social body', even while they also underlined the civic importance of 'status, hierarchy and the role of authority'. Stow mentions the Skinners' procession 'through the principal streets of the City' (1. 230) and the annual performance of 'some large history of Holy Scripture' by the parish clerks (1. 15) as things of the distant past. The relatively early disappearance of the Corpus Christi cycle at London and the absorption of its civic function into the more secular processions and pageants of the Midsummer Watch have been taken to indicate, with a shift in emphasis from the religious to the civic

---

[22] Stow, *The Annales, or Generall Chronicles of England, begun first by maister Iohn Stow, and after him continued . . . by Edmund Howes* (1615), fo. 517.

[23] Charles Phythian-Adams, 'Ceremony and the Citizen: The Communal Year at Coventry, 1450–1550', in *Crisis and Order in English Towns 1500–1700: Essays in Urban History*, ed. Paul Slack and Peter Clark (1972), pp. 57–85.

semester of the year, an unusually early consolidation of the London government and its merchant elite.[24]

In their processions and activities during this annual ceremonial cycle, the leaders of London literally followed in the 'steps of the forefathers', tracing out in a series of processions a highly ordered ritual space. The main civic event of the earlier sixteenth century, the Midsummer Marching Watch, had traditionally followed the longest east–west route in the City, processing, as Stow observes, 'from the little conduit by Paul's gate, through the West Cheap, by the stocks, through Cornhill, by Leadenhall to Aldgate' and then back to West Cheap (I. 102). Stow traces the watch to the reign of Henry III, and in the account that he takes from the *Liber Custumarum* of the rights of Robert Fitzwalter, one of the twelfth-century *barones* of the City, he unearths the ritual origins of the route. In time of war, Fitzwalter, the City bannerer, Stow explains, was to receive from the mayor and aldermen at the door of the cathedral the City's banner of St Paul. The leaders and commons of the City were then to assemble and 'go under the banner of Saint Paul, and the said Robert shall bear it himself unto Aldgate', where a council 'taken in the Priory of the Trinity near unto Aldgate' will complete the City's military plans (I. 63–4). Originating at St Paul's, London's traditional 'place of assembly to their folkmotes' where their 'common bell' was rung that 'all the inhabitants of the city might hear and come together' (I. 325), and terminating at the Holy Trinity, whose Prior, 'according to the customs of the City did sit in court and rode with the mayor and his brethren the alderman, as one of them ... until the year 1531' (I. 123), the route of the Midsummer Watch took in the route of the medieval bannerer and, not coincidentally, all of the principal pageant stations of coronation entries, which extended from the Tunne and conduit near St Peter and the Leadenhall in Cornhill to the Little Conduit at Paul's Gate.

A second civic processional route, followed on Whitsuntide, corresponded exactly with this main axis of the coronation route, as on Whitsun Monday the rectors, lord mayor and aldermen of London processed from St Peter's to St Paul's, where 'the hymn *Veni Creator* was chanted by the vicars to the music of the organ in alternate verses; an angel meanwhile censing from above'.[25] Stow is silent on the Whitsuntide processions, which had atrophied by the time of the *Survey* into a series of sermons attended by London officials,[26] but he is keenly aware of the ecclesiastical history that had made St Peter's and St Paul's (whose twin feasts coincided with the

---

[24] Mervyn James, 'Ritual, Drama, and Social Body in the Late Medieval English Town', in *Society, Politics and Culture: Studies in Early Modern England* (Cambridge, 1986), pp. 34, 38, 41.

[25] *Liber Albus*, ed. H. T. Riley (1862), p. 26; cf. *Calendar of Letter-Books of the City of London. Letter Book H*, ed. R. R. Sharpe (1907), p. 188; *Letter-Book I* (1909), p. 188.

[26] *The order of my Lord Mayor, the aldermen, and the sheriffs for their meetings* (1630), p. 24.

Midsummer Watch, and whose twin effigies were 'of old . . . rudely engraven' on the City's seal, I. 221) the two anchors of this processional route. As the church King Lucius founded as 'an archbishop's see, and metropolitan or chief church of his kingdom', St Peter's is for Stow a monument of the first Christianisation of Britain, when 'the temples of idols were converted into cathedral churches and bishops were placed where *Flammines* before had been' (II. 125). In the same way, St Paul's, believed in Stow's time to have been built on the site of 'a temple of Jupiter' (I. 333), commemorates in Stow's view the second Christianisation, when 'Ethelbert, King of Kent, builded in the city of London S. Paul's Church, wherein Melitus began to be bishop in the year 619' (II. 127). In John Speed's *Theatre of the Empire of Great Britaine* (1611), these twin hilltop churches, the one 'upon the East', the other 'in the west part', would form a diptych representing London's British and Saxon roots, respectively. For Stow, they define the City's central axis. At one end, St Peter's stands opposite the north-west corner of the Leadenhall, 'the highest ground of all the City' (I. 188); at the other end stand the precincts of St Paul's, 'the beauty of the city of London, the beauty of the whole realm',[27] whose walled churchyard, Stow notes, had 'crossed and stopped up' the thoroughfare of West Cheap, forming a sacred enclosure, with its cloisters and famous pulpit cross. Between them lies 'the high and most principal street of the City', which, passing the Stocks market 'in the midst of the City', forms both the City's main ceremonial route and the principal 'division of this City' that Stow follows in his perambulation of the wards from east to west (I. 117). In the architectural conceit that transforms London into a 'court royal' in Thomas Dekker's account of the coronation entry of James I, the series of pageant stations along this route defines a ceremonial crescendo, as the king passes from the 'great hall' of Cornhill to the 'presence chamber' of Cheapside to the 'closet or rather the privy chamber' framed by the passage from the Little Conduit into St Paul's Churchyard.

According to the writer who recorded the coronation passage of Elizabeth I through this space, 'a man . . . could not better term the city of London that time than a stage',[28] and indeed for Stow the theatrical significance of this setting – even and especially in its climactic segment – is as much a function of civic ritual as of royal charisma. Stow notes that the route is still frequently traversed by City officials during what he calls the 'days of attendance that the fellowships do give to the mayor at his going to Paul's' (II. 190). These 'days of attendance', according to the earlier

---

[27] 'Stowe's Memoranda', in *Three Fifteenth-Century Chronicles*, ed. James Gairdner (Camden Society, 77, 1880), p. 116.

[28] *The Quene's Majestie's passage through the citie of London* (1559), in *Elizabethan Backgrounds: Historical Documents of the Age of Elizabeth I*, ed. Arthur F. Kinney (Hamden Ct, 1975), p. 16.

custumals Stow consulted, originated in ritual processions, on fixed religious feasts between All Saints and Candlemas, along Cheapside to St Paul's from St Thomas de Acon in Cheap, the hospital and church raised to the memory of Thomas à Becket, who was still believed in Tudor times to have been born on the spot of the high altar on the feast of St Thomas the Apostle.[29] In its account of these ritual processions, the *Liber Albus* was adapting to a series of religious feasts a much older precept from the *Liber Ordinationum*, which declared that after his inaugural feast the mayor 'offered prayers at St Paul's for Bishop William [and then] led the aldermen in ritual chant at the Becket grave and in a torchlight procession through Cheap to the house of St Thomas'.[30] Aware that Bishop William had been venerated as a heroic defender of the City's medieval liberties, Stow explains the 'lord mayor's cause of repair to Paul's' in his *Annals*, observing that

through the great suit and labour of William the Norman, then Bishop of London, King William granted the charter and liberties to the same William Bishop, and Godfrey Portgreve and all the burghers of the City of London, in as large form as they enjoyed same, in the time of Saint Edward before the Conquest; in reward whereof, the citizens have fixed upon his grave, being in the midst of the west aisle of Saint Paul's, this epitaph following:

> These marble monuments to thee thy citizens assign,
> Rewards (O Father) far unfit to those deserts of thine,
> Thee unto them a faithful friend thy London people found,
> And to this town, of no small weight, a stay both sure and sound.
> Their liberty restored to them by means of thee have been,
> Their public weal by means of thee large gifts have felt and seen.
> Thy riches, stock and beauty brave, one hour hath them supprest,
> Yet these thy virtues and good deeds with valour ever rest.[31]

The civic importance to the two shrines of Bishop William and the sainted Becket explains not only the processions on religious feast days, continued in Stow's time, but the rituals that, until the sixteenth-century development of the inaugural shows, marked the inauguration of London's mayors. With the suppression of Becket's cult at the Reformation and the transfer of the property to the Mercers' Company,[32] the processions to St Paul's took on a more purely civic character by departing from the Guildhall, north of Cheapside at the head of Ironmonger Lane, rather than from St Thomas de Acon. Yet much of the old pattern remained,

---

[29] Henry Wriothesley, *A Chronicle of England During the Reigns of the Tudors*, ed. William Douglas Hamilton (2 vols., Camden Society, 1875), I. 87.

[30] *Liber Ordinationum*, fo. 174, cited in Gwyn A. Williams, *Medieval London: From Commune to Capital* (1963), pp. 30–1.

[31] *Annals*, fos. 108–9; cf. William Dugdale, *The History of St Paul's Cathedral*, ed. Henry Ellis (1818), p. 37.

[32] On the suppression of the cult of Becket, see Susan Brigden, *London and the Reformation* (Oxford, 1989), pp. 291–2; Eamon Duffy, *The Stripping of the Altars: Traditional Religion in England, c. 1400–c. 1580* (New Haven, 1992), p. 412.

including virtually all of the original route, from the foot of Ironmonger Lane at the Mercers' Chapel to St Paul's. The City's officials continued to process regularly to the cathedral on religious feasts, still doffing their gowns before entering, and circling the cathedral before donning them again. The days listed for such processions by Stow – All Saints, Christmas, St Stephen's Day, St John's Day, New Year's Day, Epiphany and Candlemas – are identical with the feasts listed in the early fifteenth-century *Liber Albus*, and are only slightly curtailed – lacking the feasts of Saints Stephen and John – in the published official calendars. The meaning of the route was kept alive, meanwhile, by the maintenance of the chapel at St Thomas by the Mercers (I. 269), and by the continued observance of the feast of St Thomas – when the *Liber Albus* had called for the hearing of mass and vespers at St Thomas de Acon – as the civic occasion when the lord mayor and every alderman was 'to sit in his ward in his violet gown and cloak furred', presiding over the Wardmote Inquest, the annual inquiry into the local order of each city ward, wherein 'theoretically, every householder could take part in civic government'.[33] Stow even notes in his memoranda for 1567 that the sergeants of London had concluded their annual feast by processing 'in their gowns, hoods and coifs to Saint Thomas of Ackars [Acon], and from thence to Saint Paul's'.[34]

Thus hallowed by civic routine, the portion of West Cheap between the Great Conduit and Paul's Gate forms, in Stow's view, the central core of the City's ceremonial space. It was here, Stow notes, that 'divers justings were made' in the reign of Edward III, and here too that the same monarch built 'the fair building of stone', still used in his own day, from which monarchs and ambassadors are accustomed 'to behold the shows of this City, passing through West Cheap' (I. 257, 268). Between this standing and the Mercer's chapel, from which Henry VIII beheld the Marching Watch of 1536, was the portion of the route that was double-railed during coronation entries, lined with the City companies, 'beginning with the mean and base occupations, and so ascending to the worshipful crafts; highest and lastly stood the mayor, with the aldermen' at the end of West Cheap.[35] It was here, by forming a buffer between the tumultuous London crowds behind them and the nobility and royalty processing before them, that the orderly ranks of London officials, in full regalia, served to underline the City's essential role in maintaining civil order. It was here, with the performance of the climactic pageants dramatising the *renovatio* or *initium seculi felicissimi* of the monarch's advent, that London officials delivered the gifts and harangues embodying the element of popular *acclam-*

---

[33] *The order of my Lord Maior* (1621), p. 20; Foster, *The Politics of Stability*, p. 37.
[34] 'Stowe's Memoranda', p. 142.
[35] Edward Hall, *The Union of the two noble and illustrate famelies of Lancastre and Yorke* (1548), sig. AAaiiv.

atio essential to the making of English kings.[36] It was here that the status of London's mayoralty was affirmed when the Lord Mayor received from entering monarchs the sword or mace with which he then led the remaining phase of the procession.[37] And it was here, finally, that the Lord Mayor's inaugural show, a novel development in Stow's lifetime, reached its culminating phase, as 'the whole fabric of the Triumph'[38] was finally assembled in processional order.

It is surprising that Stow has so little to say about the mayoral inauguration, the concluding event of the civic semester that, with the sixteenth-century suppression of the Midsummer Watch, had come to replace the beginning of the civic semester in ceremonial importance. It is true that Stow mentions the lord mayor's inaugural feast (I. 273), and his chronology of mayors takes account of many of the developments that had gone into the making of the inauguration – the freedom of electing mayors (II. 151), the presentation of the new mayor before the Barons of the Exchequer in Westminster (II. 156), the journey to Westminster by barge (II. 175), the routine courtesy of bestowing knighthood on the mayor (II. 181). Furthermore, in keeping with the principle that early modern processions 'displayed the *dignités, qualités, corps*, and *états* of which the social order was thought to be composed',[39] Stow's list of the principal city and mayoral officials – the sheriffs, chamberlain, common sergeant, sword-bearer, common cryer or mace-bearer (I. 187–8) – follows quite closely the sequence of protocols in a contemporary description of the inaugural procession by the herald William Smith.[40] Had Stow not believed that James Dalton was going to publish a work on the 'public government' of London, he might have included a fuller account of the inaugural ceremonies in his 'unperfected' notes (II. 186–7).

Insofar as Stow concerns himself with 'what London hath been of ancient time' and not with 'what it is now' (I. xcviii), it may be the relative novelty of the inaugural show, and its implications for the changing tenor of London ceremonials and society, that led to its omission from the pages of the *Survey*. The spotty documentation suggests that the inaugural show was not yet a

---

[36] Janet L. Nelson, 'Symbols in Context: Inauguration Rituals in Byzantium and the West in the Early Middle Ages', *Studies in Church History*, 13 (1976), 97–119; Ernst Kantorowicz, *Laudes Regiae* (Berkeley, 1946), pp. 79–80; Gordon Kipling, 'Richard II's "Sumptuous Pageants" and the Idea of the Civic Triumph', in *Pageantry in the Shakespearian Theater*, ed. David M. Bergeron (Athens, Ga., 1985), p. 85.

[37] On this point, as on the 'buffer' of the city liveries, see R. Malcolm Smuts, 'Public Ceremony and Royal Charisma: The English Royal Entry in London, 1485–1642', in *The First Modern Society: Essays in History in Honour of Lawrence Stone*, ed. A.L. Beier, David Cannadine and James P. Rosenheim (Cambridge, 1989), pp. 72–3.

[38] Thomas Middleton, *The Triumphs of Health and Prosperity* (1626), in *Works*, ed. A. H. Bullen (8 vols., rpt. New York, 1964), VII, 409.

[39] Robert Darnton, *The Great Cat Massacre and Other Episodes in French Cultural History* (1984; rpt. New York, 1985), p. 116.

[40] 'A breffe description of the Royall Citie of London', BL, Harleian MS 6363, printed in Nathan Drake, *Shakespeare and His Times* (1838; rpt. New York, 1969), p. 424.

fully established ceremony at the time the *Survey* was published.[41] The only sixteenth-century examples of the sort of printed pageant-texts that began to appear with regularity in the Jacobean period date from 1585, 1590 and 1591. This, together with Stow's allusions to intermittent attempts to revive the Midsummer Marching Watch, suggests that ceremonially, as in the many other respects detailed in the *Survey*, London was still in a process of transformation, as the inaugural show was beginning to absorb some of the functions of the Midsummer Watch, which had in turn replaced the feast of Corpus Christi as the principal event of the civic year.

By replacing communal celebration with cultic exaltation of the Lord Mayor and his company, the new inaugural shows of the late Elizabethan and Jacobean age adopted a new ideological slant. In their overt myth-making, they reflected the forces that were undermining the traditional community – a heightened emphasis on acquisition, mobility, wealth and status, and a deepening symbiosis between London and the centralised, bureaucratic state. William Nelson's 1590 inaugural pageant for the Fishmongers, for example, was an early contribution to the wave of civic myth-making contemporary with the emergence of the inaugural show. Focusing on the former fishmonger William Walworth, Nelson alleged that Walworth's slaying of the rebel Jack Straw was the occasion both for the inclusion of a sword in the City's official arms and for the custom of knighting lord mayors:

> First knight was I of London, you may read,
> And since each ·mayor gains knighthood by my deed.[42]

Together with a play on *The Life and Death of Jack Straw* (1593), which may originally have been connected with the same fishmonger mayoralty of 1590,[43] Nelson's pageant was an early instance of what became a corpus of works, in both pageant and theatre, devoted to the magnanimity, virtue and chivalric élan of worthy Londoners. This new mythology sought to ameliorate the socially disruptive effects of the developing urban order, accommodating the newly ambitious citizen mentality and behaviour to a state apparatus cloaked in the values of traditional English society, even while masking the mobility and aspirations of the state's entrepreneurial servants as manifestations of true nobility.[44]

---

[41] There are references to pageants in 1535 and 1540 and in Machyn's diary for 1553-7, and pageant texts or text commissions survive from 1561, 1566 and 1568. See *A Calendar of Dramatic Records in the Books of the Livery Companies of London*, ed. Jean Robertson and D. J. Gordon, *Malone Society Collections* (1954), II, 37, 40, 42-4, 46, 48-50; *The Diary of Henry Machyn*, ed. J. G. Nichols (Camden Society, 1848), pp. 48, 73, 96, 118, 155.

[42] *The Device of the Pageant, set forth by the Worshipful Companie of Fishmongers, for the right honorable Iohn Allot: established Lord Maior of London* (1593), sigs. A3v-A4.

[43] See Robert Withington, 'The Lord Mayor's Show for 1590', *Publications of the Modern Language Association*, 30 (1915), 110-15; and David M. Bergeron, 'Jack Straw in Drama and Pageant', *The Guildhall Miscellany*, 2.1 (1968), 459-63.

[44] L. C. Knights, *Drama and Society in the Age of Jonson* (1937; rpt. New York, 1968), ch 8; Louis B. Wright, *Middle-Class Culture in Elizabethan England* (Chapel Hill, 1935), ch. 2; Laura Caroline Stevenson, *Paradox and Praise: Merchants and Craftsmen in Elizabethan Popular Literature* (Cambridge, 1984), pp. 108-29.

Stow certainly includes service and loyalty to monarchs among the civic virtues of Londoners, and he is not loath to praise the readiness with which they defended their liberties. But the deeds most frequently celebrated in the *Survey* are those of local Christian benefactors who show less regard for 'their own private gain, than the common good of the City' (1. 164). In a sharp rebuke almost certainly referring to the Fishmongers' pageant and play of 1590, Stow assails the Fishmongers as 'men ignorant of their antiquities' on a variety of counts, including both the person of Jack Straw, who had actually been 'adjudged by the said mayor' according to due process, and the meaning of the City arms, which depicted 'the cross and sword of Saint Paul, and not the dagger of William Walworth'. Stow explains that Walworth had indeed in self-defence wounded another rebel, Wat Tyler, who was then killed by 'an esquire of the king's house'. But for Stow, just as important as this achievement of Walworth – 'a man wise, learned, and of incomparable manhood' – was his endowment of the college of priests in St Michael's Crooked Lane (1. 215, 219–20).

Just as Stow's Walworth humbly demurs at the prospect of knighthood, maintaining that 'he was neither worthy nor able to take such estate upon him, for he was but a merchant, and had to live by his merchandise only', so his Richard Whittington is not the plucky entrepreneur emerging in contemporary legend[45] but a pious benefactor to the religious, charitable and civic endowments of London. While Stow is proud enough to report that 'noble men of this realm, of old time, as also of later years, have dealt in merchandises' (1. 203), or that the property of the great Lord Neville in Leadenhall had passed into the hands of the prosperous alderman Hugh Offley (1. 203, 151), he is troubled by the pride of Londoners whose ostentation exceeds their traditional estate. He makes it a point that Alderman John Champneys was blinded for building a 'high tower of brick' to overlook his neighbours (1. 133); that Richard Wethell, Merchant Taylor, was too lamed with gout to 'take the pleasure of the height' of a similar tower (1. 151); that Sir John Crosby, sheriff and alderman, died too soon to enjoy 'his large and sumptuous building . . . the highest at that time in London' (1. 172); and that one 'Buckle, a grocer', while 'greedily labouring to pull down the old tower' given by Edward III to the College of St Stephen Westminster, was 'so sore bruised . . . that his life was thereby shortened' (1. 260).

Opposed to such *campanilismo* and devoted to civic virtue, Stow's traditional mentality is what leads him to appeal to 'modern' historical accuracy as a means of resisting the newer and more grandiose modes of theatricality emerging in the metropolis. Commissioned by the new class of professional entertainers associated with the developing commercial theatres, the pageant texts of the new inaugural show overlaid the collective

---

[45] Caroline M. Barron, 'Richard Whittington: The Man Behind the Myth', in *Studies in London History*, ed. A. E. J. Hollender and William Kellaway (1969), pp. 197–250.

rites of civic religion with those 'private-distinctive' features – idiosyncracy, novelty, variety and commerciality – that in Victor Turner's terms characterise the sort of 'liminoid' culture that begins to make free with the social heritage.[46] Commercial necessity was often the mother of invention in the pageants, whose function, as the pageant-writers put it, was to 'descend . . . to the modern use' of 'ancient and honourable things', to 'view / Old customs kept, and (in them) things anew'.[47] Economic and artistic rivalry among the pageant authors, as between the companies themselves, made it necessary not to 'run in the same course of antique honour: but rather to jump with time, which evermore affecteth novelty, in a new form'.[48] It is perhaps this 'contingent and instrumental use of allegorical symbols' in the newer types of grandiose pageants that, by frustrating 'the desire to protect the valued symbols from both inadvertant and wilful misinterpretation',[49] provoked Stow's outburst against the 'fabulous book' of the Fishmongers' inaugural show. Anthony Munday would soon enough be apologising to the Drapers for having appropriated their 'worthy', Henry Fitz-Alwin, for the Goldsmiths' pageant of 1611, 'to the disgrace of the forenamed company and mine own deep discredit'.[50]

Stow's silence on the new inaugural shows may be linked to his relative silence on London's new commercial theatres, whose leading writers were also being commissioned by the City for the scripts of the mayoral pageants. Although he includes several comments on drama in medieval London, Stow merely mentions in passing that 'of late time . . . certain public places have been erected' for modern performances; he even omits from the 1603 edition of the *Survey* the names of The Theatre and The Curtain, which he included in 1598. In Stow's silence may be read an endorsement of the anti-theatrical bias of the London government, whose persistent attempts to restrict playing stemmed from many of the same concerns sounded in the pages of the *Survey* – including a sense of weakening control over the suburbs, with their illicit mingling of a shadowy variety of unenfranchised strangers, aliens and nonconformists.[51] Disturbingly heteroglot in nature, as Stow and the London officials saw them, the theatres were frequented by a newly variegated and mobile population – of fashionable gentry, provincial strangers, foreigners and underworld denizens – that was drawn by the growth of the capital but did 'not contribute to such charges' of the City as 'other citizens do'. Protected by courtiers,

---

[46] 'Liminal to Liminoid in Play, Flow, and Ritual: An Essay in Comparative Symbology', in *From Ritual to Theatre: The Human Seriousness of Play* (New York, 1982), pp. 20–60.

[47] Middleton, *The Triumphs of Integrity, Works*, VII, 385; Heywood, *Londini Emporia* (1633), sig. B.

[48] Munday, *Metropolis Coronata* (1615), in *Pageants and Entertainments*, p. 87.

[49] Michael Bristol, *Carnival and Theater: Plebeian Culture and the Structure of Authority in Renaissance England* (New York, 1985), pp. 82–4.

[50] *Himateia-Poleos* (1614), in *Pageants and Entertainments*, p. 73.

[51] See esp. Steven Mullaney, 'Toward a Rhetoric of Space in Elizabethan London', in *The Place of the Stage* (Chicago, 1988), pp. 1–25.

who were making their own inroads into traditional London franchises, the players fostered the sort of sceptical and individualistic outlook that would lead to condescending 'girds at citizens' in the theatres.[52]

In his preference for an explicitly integrated urban order, where the articulations of custom, hierarchy, order and degree were visibly and ritually affirmed as a matter of routine – an order where 'The inhabitants and repairers to this City of what state soever . . . lived together in good amity, every man observing the customs and orders of the City' – Stow registers his distaste for a theatricalisation of public life that he associates with the coming of the Reformation, acquisitive individualism and the secular bureaucratic state. According to Stow, the gospelling curate who incited a London mob to destroy the great maypole of St Andrew Undershaft struck a blow against the whole ceremonial order of things, maintaining that 'the names of the days of the week might be changed, the fish days to be kept any days . . . and the Lent any time, save only betwixt Shrovetide and Easter' (I. 144). The corollary to such assaults on the fixed temporal order and its collective, ritual observances is for Stow the transformation of familiar public symbolism into a manipulative theatricality marked by hypocrisy, ostentation and divisive individualism. The 'open pastimes in my youth, being now suppressed' in the post-Reformation climate of religious surveillance and state control, Stow sourly speculates that 'worser practices within doors are to be feared' (I. 95). The pattern of introversion is reinforced by 'purpresture' – the feverish encroachment of formerly common space, which encouraged the replacement of outdoor, public recreation with indoor, commercialised leisure. 'By the mean of closing in the common grounds', Stow notes, 'our archers, for want of room to shoot abroad, creep into bowling alleys and ordinary dicing houses nearer home, where they have room enough to hazard money at unlawful games' (I. 104). Once restricted to the precincts of Northumberland House, London's 'ancient and only patron of misrule', such dubious establishments now honeycomb the city, 'in all places . . . increased and too much frequented' (II. 79); 'common to all comers for their money' (I. 149), their commercial nature erodes traditional distinctions while creating new ones between wealth and poverty, fashionable expense and prudent thrift.

The new distinctions are nowhere more apparent than in the public ostentation that Stow associates with the individualised withdrawal from community. Commenting on congestion caused by the newly fashionable coach, Stow observes that 'the riding in whirlicotes and chariots' was formerly 'forsaken, except at coronations and such like spectacles', but 'now of late years . . . there is neither distinction of time nor difference

---

[52] Francis Beaumont, *The Knight of the Burning Pestle*, Induction, l. 8. On the paradoxes involved in the City's commissioning of playwrights for the inaugural shows, see Theodore B. Leinwand, 'London Triumphing: The Jacobean Lord Mayor's Show', *Clio*, 11 (1982), 137–53.

of persons observed; for the world runs on wheels with many, whose parents were glad to go on foot' (i. 84). In the spectacle of the public making a spectacle of itself, Stow sees a ceremonial and civic heritage transformed. The common grounds north of the city, once fiercely defended against the saying that 'no Londoner ought to go out of the City but in the high ways', are now lost to public use

by means of inclosure for gardens, wherein are builded many fair summer houses and other such places of the suburbs, some of them like midsummer pageants, with towers, turrets and chimney tops, not so much for use or profit, as for show and pleasure, bewraying the vanity of men's minds, much unlike the citizens who delighted in the building of hospitals and alms houses for the poor, and therein both employed their wits and spent their wealths in preferment of the common commodity of this our city.

In noting this reappropriation of the pageantry of the Midsummer Watch, the ceremonial occasion of 'good amity amongst neighbours' on which he has lavished his greatest attention, Stow adds a bitter marginal pun on the decline of ceremony, equating 'banqueting' with 'banqueroutes bearing great show and little worth' (ii. 78).

It is primarily in the topographical centre of the *Survey*, the perambulation of the wards, that Stow canvasses the many developments that, in transforming the city's sites, had also transformed its rites and social fabric – the conversion of religious houses into biscuit bakeries, gun foundries, glass manufactories and storehouses; the subdivision into mazes of tenements of the houses of the old nobility, whose successors were abandoning the City to take up residence, sometimes in former bishops' properties, in the burgeoning west end; the pestering of the suburbs and liberties with a swollen population of strangers; the expansion of the state bureaucracy in Westminster; the pillage of monuments and charitable bequests by 'bold and greedy men of spoil' (i. 208). In the sharp disjunctures, sudden expansions and disruptive realignments of the contemporary urban space – the subject of the middle third of the *Survey* – Stow confronts a register of change at odds with the temporal continuities stressed at the beginning of the *Survey* in his account of the ceremonial practices of the citizen class, and at the end of the *Survey* in his chronology of leaders and procession-like lists of the City's holidays, officers and companies. The variegated terrain he perambulates lays bare in irrefutably physical form the types of historical and social discontinuity that work against the ritual habits of following 'the ancient precedents and footsteps of the forefathers'. If Stow's opening and closing accounts of ritual help to establish, in the manner of a map, a symbolic terrain that inscribes the civic order and its past upon the urban landscape, his personal survey of that contemporary landscape reveals, as do the endlessly varied routes actually walked by a city's population, a mobility and heterogeneity on which no symbolic or ritual system could hope to impose a complete or stable order.[53]

But if, in its approach to the disarticulation between sites and rites, Stow's *Survey* less than wholeheartedly celebrates the contemporary capital – it was after all still a daringly conservative act to have begun and ended the *Survey* with a portion of the biography of the outlawed saint Becket, a London Thomas martyred by a royal Henry[54] – Stow's apparently conservative allegiance to the civic religion is itself a symptom of the very changes he laments. Stow could not, of course, express in print any allegiance to the doctrines and beliefs of Catholicism; but it would seem that his greatest devotion is reserved for the old religion's social and communitarian dimensions.[55] Presumably Stow is not simply being ironic when he quotes the ballad-writer William Elderton to the effect that once-venerated statues, now so few in London, can still be seen in the personified civic virtues gracing the porch to the Guildhall (I. 272). For Stow, much of the piety that might once have been reserved for religious veneration has now become invested in a civic religion based on veneration for the past. Indeed, even the most innovative aspect of the *Survey*, the topography of the wards, beginning in each case with an outline of the ward boundaries and ending with a tally of its rates and Wardmote panel, involves Stow's creative adaptation of an ancient religious rite, the Rogationtide circumambulation of parish boundaries 'for the better knowing and retaining of the circuit of your parish, and for the obtaining of God's blessings upon the fruits of the ground',[56] to the civic entity of the ward. The last visit in the *Survey* is to a stained-glass window – not the famous one at St Thomas de Acon, but one

in the Guildhall above the stairs, the mayor is there pictured, sitting in habit, parti-coloured, and a hood on his head, his sword-bearer before him with an hat or cap of maintenance; the common clerk and other officers bareheaded, their hoods on their shoulders (II. 194).

As a record of London's sites and rites, upholding in the guise of a traditional order what was in many respects an innovative civic religion, Stow's *Survey* was first pressed into service – ironically but not surprisingly – by the very ceremonial innovators he neglected (or despised too much) to

---

[53] See Michel de Certeau, 'Walking in the City', in *The Practice of Everyday Life*, tr. Steven F. Rendall (Berkeley, 1984), pp. 91–110. On the uses of spatial disjunction to figure temporal discontinuity, see Michel Foucault, 'Questions on Geography', in *Power/Knowledge*, ed. Colin Gordon (New York, 1980), pp. 69–70.

[54] In 1571, the year that he became London's first Remembrancer, Thomas Norton delivered a well-received attack in Parliament on the 'Reball Bp Beckett', assailing him for clerical meddling in state affairs; see M. A. R. Graves, 'Thomas Norton the Parliament Man: An Elizabethan M.P., 1559–1581', *The Historical Journal*, 23: 1 (1980), p. 21.

[55] Fussner, 'John Stow', pp. 218–20.

[56] Bishop Bickley of Chichester, 1586, quoted in David Cressy, *Bonfires and Bells: National Memory and the Protestant Calendar in Elizabethan and Stuart England* (Berkeley, 1989), p. 23.

mention, the literary professionals who created the new inaugural show. His accounts of various City companies and their famous worthies were taken over wholesale – by Munday for the Goldsmiths in 1611, for example, and by John Webster for the Merchant Tailors in 1624. While Stow's work as the 'fee'd chronicler' of the City had merely been a free-lance consultation on City real estate, the example of Stow's *Survey* and its potential contribution to a still-evolving civic religion led to the creation of the office of 'City chronologer' in 1620, within a few years of his death.[57] In the inaugural shows of Thomas Middleton, the first holder of the post, as in the work of Munday and Heywood, Stow's contribution to civic religion continued to have normative force, but in a new form that put less stress on commensality than on hierarchy and deference, less stress on the stability of ritual tradition than on individual mobility and commercial achievement. Yet in many respects the latter emphases were the historical corollaries and consequences of the former. Embedded in this very continuity was the basis for the changes Stow depicts and for those which, as citizen and historian, he embodies in his account of civic religion.

---

[57] W. H. Overall, ed., *Analytical Index to the Remembrancia* (1876), p. 305; R. R. Sharpe, *London and the Kingdom* (3 vols., 1894), II, 439; R. C. Bald, 'Middleton's Civic Employments', *Modern Philology*, 31 (1933), p. 67.

2

Shakespeare's *A Midsummer Night's Dream*

Social Tensions Contained

Penry Williams

Seeking for the context of *A Midsummer Night's Dream*, many commentators have begun by locating it in the occasion of the play's first performance. For Paul Olson and for several others this probably took place during the celebrations following a court wedding, perhaps with the queen herself present.[1] The most favoured candidate is the marriage of Elizabeth Carey, granddaughter of Lord Hunsdon, to Thomas, son of Lord Berkeley, in February 1596. The evidence adduced for asserting that the play was first performed for a particular court wedding is largely internal: the concern of the play with marriage; its ending in actual marriages; the availability of boys from the noble household to play the part of fairies; and a reference to Queen Elizabeth, suggesting that she was actually present.[2] However, the only direct evidence about the Carey/Berkeley wedding, Smyth's *Lives of the Berkeleys*, has nothing to say about the festivities, which suggests that they were nothing out of the ordinary; and the play itself would seem rather long to be part of an evening's entertainment after a wedding – a masque was more usual on such an occasion. Moreover, there is no evidence that Shakespeare ever composed a play for a specific court occasion.

The reference to the queen seems at first sight more intriguing and, because it is specific, more plausible. It is made in Oberon's speech to Puck, instructing him to fetch the flower called love-in-idleness (a contemporary name for the pansy). Oberon tells Puck how, seated on a promontary, he saw

> Cupid all armed: a certain aim he took
> At a fair vestal, throned by the west,

Quotations from the play are taken from the Arden edition, edited by Harold F. Brooks (1979), and abbreviated as *MND*.

[1] Paul A. Olson, 'A Midsummer Night's Dream and the Meaning of Court Marriage', *English Literary History*, 24 (1957), 95–119.

[2] For the arguments in favour of *MND* having been a play in celebration of a court wedding, see Harold F. Brooks, Introduction to the Arden edition (London, 1979), pp. liii–lvii; for arguments against, Stanley Wells, Introduction to New Penguin edition (Harmondsworth, 1967), pp. 12–14, and 'A Midsummer Night's Dream Revisited', *Critical Survey*, 3.1 (1991), 14–29; and Marion Colthorpe, 'Queen Elizabeth I and A Midsummer Night's Dream', *Notes and Queries*, 232, n.s., 34. 1 (1987), 205–7.

> And loosed his love-shaft smartly from his bow
> As it should pierce a hundred thousand hearts.
> But I might see young Cupid's fiery shaft
> Quenched in the chaste beams of the watery moon;
> And the imperial votaress passed on,
> In maiden meditation, fancy-free.
>
> (2.1.157–64)

While there can be no doubt at all that the fair vestal or imperial votaress stood for Elizabeth, this hardly constitutes evidence that she saw the first presentation of the play. If the Carey/Berkeley wedding was indeed the occasion of this performance, it is unlikely that she attended, since she was then at Richmond and the event took place in February, a poor time for travelling. She may well, of course, have attended another performance of the play at court, but we cannot be at all sure about this and no inferences can be drawn from this supposition. While we can still leave open the possibility that the first performance took place at court, even that it may have been connected with an actual wedding, it would be unwise to draw any conclusions from this about the play. The most we can say is that it was almost certainly intended for performance both at court and on the public stage.

This is not to deny that the occasion of a first performance can be important in discussions of early modern drama. For instance, Greg Walker has shown how Henrician plays like *Hick Scorner* and *Magnyfycence* can be illuminated by studying the role of patronage in their creation and the circumstances of their production.[3] At a later date, the Jacobean and Caroline masques of Jonson and others can only be penetrated with knowledge of the immediate circumstances at hand. But the plays of Shakespeare and his fellow dramatists are in a different category from these, since they were intended to be performed on the public stage as well as at court. They had not only to please the queen, but also to make their way by attracting paying customers.

To be fair, the interpretation of *A Midsummer Night's Dream* presented by Olson does not depend upon its having first been performed at a court wedding. The text has enough about the preparations and celebrations for weddings to make marriage an important theme. Yet it was not the only theme; and there is some danger that, by starting from the circumstances of performance, we bring the marriages so far into the foreground that other themes are obscured.

If we cannot rely on the occasion of the first performance to guide our analysis of its courtly significance, are we simply to enjoy *A Midsummer Night's Dream* as a poetic fantasy of lovers, fairies and rude mechanicals? It is, of course, that, and very enjoyably so; yet it also enables us to enter

---

[3] Greg Walker, *Plays of Persuasion: Drama and Politics at the Court of Henry VIII* (Cambridge, 1991), esp. ch. 3.

the social world of the late Elizabethan court, of which it was both a part
and a forming activity. To do that we need to examine context rather
than occasion.

A Midsummer Night's Dream works by contrasts. Court is set against
country; Athens against the wood; reason against nature and passion; day
against night; waking against dreaming; everyday against carnival; nobles
against artisans. Such concepts are not alternatives but polarities, for each
element requires its opposite: dreaming means nothing without waking,
night cannot exist without day, nobles and artisans depend upon each
other. The action moves between these interdependent and contrasting
worlds, with two royal courts governing events, the Athenian court of
Theseus and the fairy court of Oberon. Between them they display some
of the many faces of the royal court of Elizabeth, with its theatre of ritual,
magic and display, and its arena of policy-making and patronage. While
neither court stands exclusively for one type of world, for there is ritual
and display in the court of Theseus as well as in the court of Oberon,
by and large Theseus stands for city, reason, daylight and wakefulness,
Oberon for the wood, nature and magic, poetic imagination, night, and
dreams.

Both the courts in *A Midsummer Night's Dream* contain and exploit
festivity, though the festivals are of many kinds.[4] In its title and its text
the play calls up popular rites and carnivals, Theseus remarking of the
lovers in Act 4 that

> No doubt they rose up early, to observe
> The rite of May . . .
>
> (4.1.131–2)

They had not of course done any such thing, Lysander and Hermia having
attempted elopement, with Helena and Demetrius following after them;
and his reference to the rite of May when the title of the play refers to
midsummer is confusing. However, the two festivals were in many ways
similar. May Day remained very popular throughout the reign of Elizabeth,
to the disgust of Puritans like Philip Stubbes:

Against May . . . all the young men and maids, old men and wives run gadding over
night to the woods, groves, hills, and mountains, where they spend all the night in
pleasant pastimes; and in the morning they return, bringing with them birch and
branches of trees, to deck their assemblies withall, and no marvel, for there is a great
Lord present amongst them, as superintendent and Lord over their pastimes and
sports, namely Satan, prince of Hell . . .[5]

---

[4] On festivity see C. L. Barber, *Shakespeare's Festive Comedy: A Study of Dramatic Form in Relation to Social Custom* (Princeton, 1959), ch. 6; François Laroque, *Shakespeare's Festive World: Elizabethan Seasonal Entertainment and the Professional Stage*, trans. Janet Lloyd (Cambridge, 1991), passim; Annabel Patterson, *Shakespeare and the Popular Voice* (Oxford and Cambridge, Mass., 1989), pp. 57–70; David Underdown, *Revel, Riot and Rebellion: Popular Politics and Culture in England, 1603–1660* (Oxford, 1985), chs. 2–5.

[5] Philip Stubbes, *Anatomie of Abuses*, p. 149, quoted in Laroque, *Shakespeare's Festive World*, p. 112.

Running into the woods, sexual licence, crowning of the May Queen, dancing round the maypole, and morris dancing were the marks of the May festival, and the midsummer festival was similarly associated with confusion and revelry. The transformations and wanderings of the play could easily be associated with either occasion, as the popular festivals of May Day and midsummer are called up in *A Midsummer Night's Dream* by the artisans' play and by the disruption and confusion that reign in the wood.

Popular festivals were under pressure in the late sixteenth and early seventeenth centuries. As Louis Montrose shows, Elizabeth's government had suppressed the civic religious drama of pre-Reformation England by the middle years of her reign; and secular occasions had often been taken over, especially in the towns, by governmental and urban authorities.[6] William Kethe, rector of Childe Okeford, Dorset, complained about the profanation of the sabbath: 'Where God calleth it his holy sabbath, the multitude call it their revelling day, which day is spent in bull-baitings, bear-baitings, bowlings, dicing, carding, dancings, drunkenness and whoredom'. William Harrison, writing in 1576, was more optimistic: while he condemned the 'superfluous numbers of idle wakes', he claimed that they had been 'well diminished' in recent years.[7] The attacks on rural festivals seem to have been launched mostly by regional elites – Puritan preachers, town magistrates and county notables – fearing moral corruption and social disorder. By contrast, the crown defended the professional London theatre against the City fathers and, under James I, protected popular sports. In spite of the attacks, much popular festivity survived into the seventeenth century. Plymouth had its morris dancers until 1605; there were florists' feasts in Norwich as late as the 1630s; the hobby-horse dance at Abbots Bromley, Staffordshire, survived into the Interregnum; and at All Cannings, Wiltshire, there was an annual assembly of 'the youth of the parish at the parsonage house' on the Sunday after Twelfth Night, 'and after supper many then and there present went to dance'.[8]

The festivals of Theseus's court are more staid and controlled than these occasions, and in some ways they resemble the rituals of the Elizabethan court. One marriage feast of Elizabeth's reign, that of Anne Russell and Henry Somerset, Lord Herbert, in 1600, has been well recorded, both in contemporary letters and in a remarkable picture. Elizabeth, borne in a litter and accompanied by her courtiers, went in procession from Blackfriars to the church, then to dinner at Lady Russell's house, and finally to Lord Cobham's, where eight ladies performed a masque, in which the queen

[6] Louis Montrose, 'A Kingdom of Shadows', pp. 70–3, below.
[7] Underdown, *Revel, Riot and Rebellion*, pp. 47, 49.
[8] *Ibid.*, p. 46.

Plate 4   Eliza Triumphans, or *Queen Elizabeth going in Procession to Blackfriars in 1600*, attributed to Robert Peake

herself danced.[9] The Athenian ceremonies are, of course, different, entertainment being provided by Bottom and his friends; but the role of Philostrate echoes that of the Master of the Revels in Elizabeth's court; and Theseus expects masques and dances to while away the hours between supper and bedtime, although he chooses *Pyramus and Thisbe*. Other Elizabethan occasions are called to mind by *A Midsummer Night's Dream*, especially those alfresco entertainments which greeted the queen on progress, like that at Elvetham in 1591, when a fairy queen appeared and claimed to be wife to Oberon. An earlier festivity, at Kenilworth, residence of the earl of Leicester, in 1575 contained even more of the elements of *A Midsummer Night's Dream*. Elizabeth was greeted on her arrival by a Savage Man – a favourite figure on these occasions and significantly a denizen of the woods; next morning the 'lusty lads and bold bachelors' of the parish presented a burlesque marriage before the queen, and in the afternoon the citizens of Coventry performed their Hock Tuesday play commemorating the victory of the English over the Danes in 1002. On the third day of her visit Elizabeth was treated to a more formal masque, held on the banks outside the castle walls, during which Triton appeared, swimming

---

[9] Roy Strong, *The Cult of Elizabeth* (1977), ch. 1. The picture, fully described by Strong, is *Queen Elizabeth going in Procession to Blackfriars, 1600*, attributed to Robert Peake.

on a mermaid to petition the queen to save the lady of the lake from a cruel knight.[10] Obviously, there are many differences between these performances and *A Midsummer Night's Dream*, and there is no reason, beyond Kenilworth's nearness to Stratford, for supposing that Shakespeare witnessed these events. What they show is the same combination of popular festivities, citizen drama and formal masques that he later used in his play, a combination that was common form at the court.

The May games and the riot of carnival were often directed to the theme of marriage, while *A Midsummer Night's Dream* revolves around the preparations for a wedding, ending with the celebration of that wedding and of two others. Love is an important theme of the play as it was in the court of Elizabeth. Sir John Harington, writing after the queen's death, described the climate of her reign:

> Her mind was often like the gentle air that cometh from the westerly point in a summer's morn; 'twas sweet and refreshing to all round her. Her speech did win all affections, and her subjects did try to show all love to her commands; for she would say, 'her state did require her to command what she knew her people would willingly do from their own love to her'.[11]

Love was a major topic in discussions of courtly virtues and conduct, where the contest between reason and passion had a central place. The potentially tragic conflict between reason and passion was described by Philip Sidney in the *Arcadia* and by Shakespeare himself in *Romeo and Juliet*. The dangers and distortions arising from love are laid out in *A Midsummer Night's Dream* in the antics of the lovers, the burlesque of *Pyramus and Thisbe*, and the enchantments laid by Oberon and Puck upon Titania and the lovers. Good sport is had, but underlying it all is serious matter about the nature of love and its dangers. Helena forewarns us of these perils early on, lamenting Demetrius's sudden infatuation with Hermia:

> Things base and vile, holding no quantity,
> Love can transpose to form and dignity:
> Love looks not with the eyes, but with the mind,
> And therefore is winged Cupid painted blind;
> Nor hath Love's mind of any judgement taste:
> Wings and no eyes, figure unheedy haste.
>
> (1.1.232–7)

As Helena interprets events, the 'mind', or imagination, has become infected by passion and so has overcome reason and distorted vision. This happens to Demetrius before the opening of the play when he abandons Helena for Hermia; to Lysander when, under the magic spell of Puck, he

---

[10] Described by Robert Laneham in F. J. Furnivall, ed., *Captain Cox, his Ballads and Books: or Robert Laneham's Letter* (Ballad Soc., 1871), passim.

[11] Quoted in Stephen Greenblatt, *Renaissance Self-Fashioning* (Chicago, 1980), p. 168, from N. E. McClure, ed., *The Letters of Sir John Harington* (Philadelphia, 1930), p. 122.

deserts Hermia for Helena, and again when Puck releases him from the spell; and finally to Titania when she becomes infatuated with the transfigured Bottom – certainly something base and vile.[12] Lysander tells Helena that reason has prompted him to love her:

> The will of man is by his reason swayed,
> And reason says you are the worthier maid.
>
> (2.2.113–15)

Helena thinks he is mocking her, but the audience knows better than both, having seen Lysander bewitched by Oberon and Puck. And Bottom hammers home the point when Titania tells him of her love:

Methinks, mistress, you should have little reason for that. And yet, to say the truth, reason and love keep little company together nowadays. (3.1.137–9)

Finally, Theseus compares lovers with madmen:

> Lovers and madmen have such seething brains,
> Such shaping fantasies, that apprehend
> More than cool reason ever comprehends.
> The lunatic, the lover, and the poet
> Are of imagination all compact.
>
> (5.1.4–8)

Love cannot be directed by reason, for it is blind; but it can and must be controlled by reason so that distortion of the imagination and of judgement is avoided or at least diminished. Yet it is not exactly reason that restores balance and order in the disordered world of *A Midsummer Night's Dream*. Oberon tames Titania by sexually humiliating her, while Theseus controls Hippolyta, first through violence, and then by marrying her:

> Hippolyta, I wooed thee with my sword,
> And won thy love doing thee injuries . . .
>
> (1.1.16–17)

Hippolyta may once have been

> . . . the bouncing Amazon
> Your buskined mistress, and your warrior love . . .
>
> (2.1.70–1)

but by the end of Act 4, scene 1 she has been tamed. Men are firmly on top, as of course they were not, however much they may have wanted to be, in the court of Elizabeth.[13]

---

[12] On imagination, see R. W. Dent, 'Imagination in *A Midsummer Night's Dream*', *Shakespeare Quarterly*, 15 (1964), 115–29; and Olson, 'The Meaning of Court Marriage', pp. 95–119.

[13] This aspect of the play has been convincingly explored by Louis Montrose, in '"Shaping Fantasies": Figurations of Gender and Power in Elizabethan Culture', *Representations*, 2 (1983), 61–94.

In the final act, Theseus and his court are at last confronted by Bottom and his company, their actions having thus far run parallel without ever quite intersecting: the nobles encounter the plebs; the high culture of the Duke and the lovers meets the popular culture of the artisans. These meetings occur at a time of famine and dislocation, described by Titania in her rebuke to Oberon in 2.1, when she accuses him of disturbing the sport of herself and her followers and thus causing the winds to suck up

> Contagious fogs; which, falling in the land
> Hath every pelting river made so proud
> That they have overborne their continents.
>
> (2.1.90–2)

The result has been rotting of the corn, diseases of flocks and of men, alteration of the seasons. During the last decade of the century, when *A Midsummer Night's Dream* was first performed, England suffered from a run of four successive bad harvests – 1594, 1595, 1596 and 1597 – with that of 1596 perhaps the worst in the century.[14] Wheat prices, which had averaged 19.9 shillings in 1590–2, rose to 50.07 in 1596–7. At harvest-time in 1596, a correspondent told Lord Burghley that 'I greatly fear that this year will be the hardest year for the poor people that hath happened in any man's memory'; and, sadly, he was right.[15] It was reported from Newcastle-on-Tyne that there were 'sundry starving and dying in our streets and in the fields for lack of bread'.[16] London was the scene of mounting disorder from 1590, the worst disturbances coming in 1595, when apprentices rioted against fishwives, butter-sellers and alien merchants, culminating in assaults on corporation officials upon Tower Hill. In November of the following year came the so-called Oxfordshire Rising, a protest against enclosures and the high price of corn. Three ringleaders tried to raise men to pull down enclosures, seize the weapons of the gentry and march on London to join the discontented apprentices. In the event, only four men turned up at the rendezvous and the 'rising' never took place. Even so, the Privy Council was profoundly disturbed: suspects were interrogated and tortured, the offence was treated as treason.

England, by contrast with many countries across the Channel, escaped serious social upheaval: rural risings petered out and urban authorities maintained their control. Yet the coercive power of the government was weak and much depended upon the manipulation of rhetoric and the preservation of social cohesion. John Stow wrote that 'the estate of London for government is so agreeable a symphony with the rest, that there is no fear of popular discord to ensue thereby'.[17] While his picture of the City

---

[14] Patterson, *Shakespeare and the Popular Voice*, ch. 3.
[15] John Walter, 'A "Rising of the People"? The Oxford Rising of 1596', *Past & Present*, 107 (1985), 91 and passim.
[16] A. B. Appleby, 'Disease or famine?', *Economic History Review*, 26 (1973), 419.
[17] John Stow, *A Survey of London*, ed. C. L. Kingsford (2 vols., Oxford, 1908), II. 207; Ian Archer, *The Pursuit of Stability: Social Relations in Elizabethan London* (Cambridge, 1991), passim.

was too bland, for there certainly was a real fear of the populace, the social order was preserved by a careful attention on the part of the lord mayor and aldermen to the condition of the propertyless. The poor were succoured by the establishment of hospitals and the careful administration of relief; attention was paid to the provision of food; and the authorities listened and responded to grievances. They were supported by the Privy Council, which issued directives for maintaining the supply of grain to London and blamed hoarders of corn, 'liker to wolves or cormorants than to natural men', for the shortage of food.

These consensual attitudes are mirrored in *A Midsummer Night's Dream*, where, in spite of aristocratic disdain for Bottom and his company, the artisans are presented affectionately by the author and treated with laughter rather than hostility by the courtiers. When Theseus chooses to hear *Pyramus and Thisbe* rather than the alternatives offered him by Philostrate, his Master of the Revels, the latter tries to avoid subjecting the mechanicals' play to the scorn he feels it deserves:[18]

> No, my noble lord,
> It is not for you: I have heard it over,
> And it is nothing, nothing in the world;
> Unless you can find sport in their intents,
> Extremely stretched and conned with cruel pain
> To do you service.
>
> (5.1.77–81)

However, Theseus insists that such efforts by lowly men have their place in the courtly scheme of things:

> For never anything can be amiss
> When simpleness and duty tender it.
>
> (5.1.83–4)

And when Hippolyta then tries to reinforce the doubts of Philostrate, not wanting the players to be mocked, Theseus defines the spirit in which the play is to be watched:

> Our sport shall be to take what they mistake:
> And what poor duty cannot do, noble respect
> Takes it in might, not merit.
>
> (5.1.90–2)

In other words, his reception of the play will give it the value that its performers intend but cannot provide; and he calls to mind 'great clerks', who came to give him welcome and dried up in the middle of their speeches.

---

[18] In the Folio edition of 1623, almost all Philostrate's lines are given to Egeus; and in the *Oxford Shakespeare*, ed. Stanley Wells and Gary Taylor, Egeus takes the lot and Philostrate is eliminated from the cast. While the Folio seems better dramatically, for the sake of consistency I have remained with the Quarto and Arden.

This is reminiscent of Elizabeth herself, who treated her lowly subjects with famous consideration. Very early in her reign, during her procession through London in January 1559, it was reported that 'a branch of rosemary given to her Grace with a supplication by a poor woman about Fleet Bridge, was seen in her chariot till her Grace came to Westminster'. Later, in 1578, when she visited Norwich, she found the local schoolmaster, Stephen Limbert, waiting nervously to deliver an oration in her honour. She went up to him and, 'thinking him fearful, said graciously unto him: "Be not afraid"'. When his speech was over she spoke to him again, praising his speech: '"it is the best that ever I heard; you shall have my hand"; and [she] pulled off her glove and gave him her hand to kiss'.[19]

Theseus comments on his own, very similar response:

> Out of this silence yet I picked a welcome,
> And in the modesty of fearful duty
> I read as much as from the rattling tongue
> Of saucy and audacious eloquence.
> Love, therefore, and tongue-tied simplicity
> In least speak most, to my capacity.
>
> (5.1.100–5)

When, a little later, in the course of *Pyramus and Thisbe*, Hippolyta bursts out with a frustration familiar to any of us who have dutifully watched inept amateur performances, with the words 'This is the silliest stuff that ever I heard', she is calmly rebuked by Theseus:

> THESEUS: The best in this kind are but shadows; and the worst are no worse,
>   if imagination amend them.
> HIPPOLYTA: It must be your imagination then, not theirs.
> THESEUS: If we imagine no worse of them than they of themselves, they may
>   pass for excellent men.
>
> (5.1.207–12)

In passing, we may note some ambivalence here, for although Theseus is defending the performers, he does so by suggesting that the professionals are not really much better. Courtiers may scoff at amateurs, but the rational sovereign – and Theseus is nothing if not that – will be indulgent to all: the words may be Shakespeare's, but the sentiments are unlikely to be those of a professional actor and playwright.

Annabel Patterson has expounded the social content of the play, emphasising its promotion of 'common society and loving friendship'; and she has even seen it as 'part of a conscious analytic project', as a 'social play that could cross class boundaries without obscuring them'.[20] While much

---

[19] John Nichols, *The Progresses and Public Processions of Queen Elizabeth* (3 vols., 1823), I, 19; II, 155, 159.

[20] Patterson, *Shakespeare and the Popular Voice*, pp. 65, 69. Although I have registered some disagreement with Patterson, I wish to acknowledge the help that her work has given me and my accord with the main lines of her interpretation.

of her account is original and convincing, this presentation of Shakespeare as a deliberate social analyst with a specific message for his audience seems too easily to ascribe intention without much evidence; and class boundaries are hardly crossed in the play, for the separation of courtiers and artisans remains fixed. But the play does mirror the beliefs of the Privy Council and the civic authorities that artisans are to be treated with kindness, though not with respect; and it is worth observing, with Patterson, that in *A Midsummer Night's Dream* the mechanicals arouse mockery rather than fear, the play having none of the social confrontations presented in *Coriolanus*, a play written at the time of the Midlands Rising of 1607.

On one reading of *A Midsummer Night's Dream* the rationality of Theseus seems to be dominant; yet his great speech on imagination at the start of Act 5 is undermined by Hippolyta. For Theseus the events of the night are 'more strange than true', the products of disordered and uncontrolled imagination (5.1.2–22):

> And as imagination bodies forth
> The forms of things unknown, the poet's pen
> Turns them to shapes, and gives to airy nothing
> A local habitation and a name.
>
> (5.1.14–17)

But we know, and Hippolyta knows, that there is more to it than that, for as she says:

> . . . all the story of the night told over
> And all their minds transfigured so together,
> More witnesseth than fancy's images,
> And grows to something of great constancy;
> But howsoever, strange and admirable.
>
> (5.1.23–7)

This world of magic is associated with a symbol that dominates the play from first to last: the moon. Theseus tells us in his opening lines that 'four days bring in / another moon' (1.1.2–3), when his marriage to Hippolyta will be celebrated; and at the end Puck alludes to the fairies

> . . . that do run
> By the triple Hecate's team
> From the presence of the sun,
> Following darkness like a dream . . .
>
> (5.1.369–72),

Hecate being an alternative name for Diana, the moon-goddess. However, if the moon gives a unity of imagery to the play, it helps to foster the sense of inconstancy, illusion and uncertainty. To begin with, there is uncertainty about the phase of the moon during the play. Theseus tells us that it is waning and that the wedding will be at the time of the new

moon; but Quince, worried about lighting problems for his play, looks at
the calendar and finds that the moon will shine that night, which it would
hardly do if it were new (3.1.45–54). In most senses we are in the dark.

The moon provides some of the element of menace in the play when
Titania tells us that, as a result of Oberon's quarrel with her,

> Therefore the moon, the governess of floods,
> Pale in her anger, washes all the air,
> That rheumatic diseases do abound.
> And thorough this distemperature we see
> The seasons alter . . .
>
> (2.1.103–7)

Matters become even more confused when we know that Titania was
another name for Diana, and that Diana was frequently a symbol for
Elizabeth. Diana had in classical and Renaissance mythology three aspects.
Known as Luna or Cynthia in the heavens, she was a goddess of chastity,
and hence a favourite identity for Elizabeth; on earth she was Diana,
goddess of woods and of the chase; under the earth she was Hecate or
Proserpina, a more sinister presence. Thus, confusingly, the moon stood
for chastity – 'the chaste beams of the watery moon' (2.1.162) – but also
in the person of Titania for something more earthy, both in her devotion
to her Indian votaress and in her infatuation with Bottom; and the moon
is also the cause of disease and alteration of the seasons. If all this is
confusing, making it difficult to match up the characters with their symbols,
and casting contradictory beams upon Elizabeth-Titania-Diana-Cynthia-
Hecate, then one can only say that this is fully in the spirit of the play;
and if an identification of Elizabeth with Titania seems far-fetched, then
one must reply that the commonest names for the queen in the 1590s
were Diana and Cynthia, both associated with the moon.

A Midsummer Night's Dream thus leads us into a world of uncertainty
and transformations, a complex place and time of ambivalences and multiple values. This is the imaginative world of the Elizabethan court, where
popular festivities competed with courtly masques, reason with passion,
male dominance with the reality of a female monarch. The multiplicity
of names for Elizabeth – Diana and Cynthia as well as Belphoebe, Gloriana
and Astraea – is paralleled by the metamorphoses of the play; and while
its conclusion provides harmony and reconciliation, it does not eliminate
competing forces.

To readers who are unpersuaded by this search for meaning in the
play, I would say that I began by being sceptical and ended by being
convinced that much more is going on here than the romantic comings
and goings of lovers, dreamy evocations of fairy-land and the comic antics
of the mechanicals. A great deal of the play is unintelligible unless it is
comprehended in the light of contemporary ideas. That is not to say that
all members of Shakespeare's audience understood these matters; but some
of them would have done and the play can be enjoyed at many levels.

Within the image, the inscription reads:

ViVat. ViñCat. Regnet,
ELISABETHA,
AngLiæ, FranCIæ ac HiberniÆ
Regina,
FIDei DefenfatriX
HenrICI 8ti RegIs F:
Anno regnIs ViXXXVII.

Plate 5   Elizabeth I with a Crescent-Moon Jewel in her Hair, by an unknown artist, 1594–5

A Kingdom of Shadows

Louis A. Montrose

I

In *A Midsummer Night's Dream*, the interplay among characters is structured
by an interplay among categories – namely, the unstable Elizabethan
hierarchies of gender, rank and age. For example, Titania treats Bottom
as if he were both her child and her lover – which seems entirely appropriate, since he is a substitute for the changeling boy, who is, in turn,
Oberon's rival for Titania's attentions. Titania herself is ambivalently
benign and sinister, imperious and enthralled. She dotes upon Bottom,
and indulges in him all those desires to be fed, scratched and coddled
that render Bottom's dream recognisable to us as a parodic fantasy of
infantile narcissism and dependency. But it is also, at the same time, a
parodic fantasy of upward social mobility. Bottom's mistress mingles her
enticements with threats:

> Out of this wood do not desire to go:
> Thou shalt remain here, whether thou wilt or no.
> I am a spirit of no common rate;
> The summer still doth tend upon my state;
> And I do love thee: therefore go with me.
> I'll give thee fairies to attend on thee;
> And they shall fetch thee jewels from the deep,
> And sing, while thou on pressed flowers dost sleep:
> And I will purge thy mortal grossness so,
> That thou shalt like an airy spirit go.
>
> (3.1.145–6)[1]

The sublimation of matter into spirit is identified with the social elevation
of the base artisan into the gentry: Titania orders her attendants to 'be
kind and courteous to this gentleman' (3.1.157), to 'do him courtesies'
(167), and to 'wait upon him' (190); she concludes the scene, however,
with an order to enforce her minion's passivity, thus reducing him to the
demeanour prescribed for women, children and servants: 'Tie up my love's
tongue, bring him silently' (104).

---

[1] Quotations follow *The Arden Shakespeare* edition of *A Midsummer Night's Dream*, ed. Harold F. Brooks (1979),
abbreviated to *MND* and cited by act, scene and line.

Titania vows that she will purge Bottom's mortal grossness and will make him her 'gentle joy' (4.1.4); Bottom's own company hope that the Duke will grant him a pension of sixpence a day for his performance as Pyramus. It is surely more than dramatic economy that motivated Shakespeare to make the artisan who is the queen's complacent paramour also an enthusiastic amateur actor who performs before the Duke. Bottom is a comically exorbitant figure for the common masculine subject of Queen Elizabeth. His interactions with the Queen of Faeries and with the Duke of Athens represent distinct modes of relationship to his sovereign: in the former, that relationship is figured as erotic intimacy; in the latter, it is figured as collective homage. Within Elizabethan society, relationships of authority and dependency, of desire and fear, were characteristic of both the public and the domestic domains. Domestic relations between husbands and wives, parents and children, masters and servants, were habitually politicised: the household was a microcosm of the state; at the same time, socio-economic and political relationships of patronage and clientage were habitually eroticised: the devoted suitor sought some loving return from his master-mistress. The collective and individual impact of Elizabethan symbolic forms frequently depended upon interchanges or conflations between these domains.

Like their companion Bottom in his liaison with Titania, the mechanicals are collectively presented in a childlike relationship to their social superiors. They characterise themselves, upon two occasions, as 'every mother's son' (1.2.73; 3.1.69); however, they hope to be 'made men' (4.2.18) by the patronage of their lord, Duke Theseus. Differences *within* the mortal and faery courts of *A Midsummer Night's Dream* are structured principally in terms of gender and generation. However, by the end of the fourth act, the multiple marriages arranged within the Athenian aristocracy and the marital reconciliation arranged between the King and Queen of Faeries have achieved domestic harmony and reestablished hierarchical norms. When Bottom and his company are introduced into the newly concordant courtly milieu in the final scene, social rank and social calling displace gender and generation as the play's most conspicuous markers of difference. The dramatic emphasis is now upon a contrast between the socially and stylistically refined mixed-sex communities of court and forest, and the 'crew of patches, rude mechanicals' (3.2.9), who 'have toiled their unbreathed memories' (5.1.72) in order to honour and entertain their betters. In the coming together of common artisan-actors and the leisured elite for whom they perform, socio-political realities and theatrical realities converge. Implicated in this particular dramatic dénouement are several larger historical developments: the policies and attitudes abetting Elizabethan state formation; the enormous growth of London as an administrative, economic and cultural centre; and the institutionalisation of a professional, secular and commercial theatre with a complex relationship to the dynastic state and the royal court on the one hand, and to the urban oligarchy and the public market on the other. In the present essay, I seek to articulate some of these implications.

II

The immediate reason for the presence of Bottom and his companions in *A Midsummer Night's Dream* is to rehearse and perform an 'interlude before the Duke and the Duchess, on his wedding-day at night' (1.2.5–7). However, their project simultaneously evokes what, only a generation before the production of Shakespeare's play, had been a central aspect of civic and artisanal culture in England – namely, the feast of Corpus Christi, with its ceremonial procession and its often elaborate dramatic performances. The civic and artisanal status of the amateur players is insisted upon with characteristic Shakespearean condescension: Puck describes them to his master, Oberon, as 'rude mechanicals, / That work for bread upon Athenian stalls' (3.2.9–10); and Philostrate describes them to his master, Theseus, as 'Hard-handed men that work in Athens here, / Which never laboured in their minds till now' (5.1.72–3). In the most material way, Bottom's name relates him to the practice of his craft – the 'bottom' was 'the core on which the weaver's skein of yarn was wound' (Arden *MND*, p. 3, n. 11); and it also relates him to his lowly position in the temporal order, to his social baseness. Furthermore, among artisans, weavers in particular were associated with Elizabethan food riots and other forms of social protest that were prevalent during the mid-1590s, the period during which *A Midsummer Night's Dream* was presumably written and first performed.[2] Thus, we may construe Bottom as the spokesman for the commons in the play – but with the proviso that this *vox populi* is not merely that of a generalised *folk*. Bottom is primarily the comic representative of a specific socio-economic group with its own highly articulated culture. He is not the voice of the dispossessed or the indigent but of the middling sort, in whose artisanal, civic and guild-centred ethos Shakespeare had his own roots.[3] During his childhood in Stratford, Shakespeare would have had the opportunity and the occasion to experience the famed Corpus Christi play that was performed annually in nearby Coventry. Bottom

---

[2] On the connection between weavers and social protest, see Theodore B. Leinwand, "'I believe we must leave the killing out": Deference and Accommodation in *A Midsummer Night's Dream*', *Renaissance Papers* (1986), 11–30, esp. pp. 14–21; also Annabel Patterson, *Shakespeare and the Popular Voice* (Oxford and Cambridge, Mass., 1989), pp. 56–7. On Elizabethan food riots, see John Walter and Keith Wrightson, 'Dearth and the Social Order in Early Modern England', *Past & Present*, 71 (1976), 22–42; Buchanan Sharp, *In Contempt of All Authority: Rural Artisans and Riot in the West of England, 1586–1660* (Berkeley, 1980); John Walter, 'A "Rising of the People"? The Oxford Rising of 1596', *Past & Present*, 107 (1985), 90–143.

[3] On the playwright's social origins and his father's position in Stratford, see S. Schoenbaum, *William Shakespeare: A Compact Documentary Life* (Oxford, 1977), pp. 14–44.

himself, the most enthusiastic of amateur thespians, makes oblique allusion to the figures and acting traditions of the multi-pageant mystery plays.[4] Thus, Bully Bottom, the weaver, is an overdetermined signifier, encompassing not only a generalised common voice but also the particular socio-economic and cultural origins of William Shakespeare, the professional player-playwright – and, too, the collective socio-cultural origins of his craft. *A Midsummer Night's Dream* simultaneously acknowledges those origins and frames them at an ironic distance; it educes connections only in order to assert distinctions.

Recent studies in sixteenth-century English social history have emphasised that a major transformation in cultural life took place during the early decades of Elizabeth's reign, and that this cultural revolution manifested a complex interaction among religious, socio-economic and political processes. Mervyn James concludes that

the abandonment of the observance of Corpus Christi, of the mythology associated with the feast, and of the cycle plays . . . arose from the Protestant critique of Corpus Christi, in due course implemented by the Protestant Church, with the support of the Protestant state. . . .

The decline and impoverishment of gild organizations, the pauperization of town populations, the changing character and role of town societies, increasing government support of urban oligarchies, were all factors tending toward urban authoritarianism. As a result, urban ritual and urban drama no longer served a useful purpose; and were indeed increasingly seen as potentially disruptive to the kind of civil order which the magistracy existed to impose.[5]

In a study of the world the Elizabethans had lost, Charles Phythian-Adams emphasises that

for urban communities in particular, the middle and later years of the sixteenth century represented a more abrupt break with the past than any period since the era of the Black Death or before the age of industrialization. Not only were specific customs and institutions brusquely changed or abolished, but a whole, vigorous and variegated popular culture, the matrix of everyday life, was eroded and began to perish. . . .

If the opportunity for popular participation in public rituals was consequently largely removed, that especial meaning which sacred ceremonies and popular rites had periodically conferred on the citizens' tangible environment also fell victim to the new 'secular' order.[6]

The brilliant scholarship of these studies appears to proceed from a position that sees in the advent of the early modern Protestant state the fragmen-

---

[4] See Clifford Davidson, '"What hempen home-spuns have we swagg'ring here?" Amateur Actors in *A Midsummer Night's Dream* and the Coventry Civic Plays and Pageants', *Shakespeare Studies*, 19 (1987), 87–99.

[5] 'Ritual, Drama and Social Body in the Late Medieval English Town' (1983), rpt. in Mervyn James, *Society, Politics and Culture: Studies in Early Modern England* (Cambridge, 1986), pp. 16–47; quotation from pp. 38, 44. James emphasises the centrality of the feast of Corpus Christi to late medieval urban culture in England, and the dialectical relationship between procession and play.

[6] Charles Phythian-Adams, 'Ceremony and the Citizen: The Communal Year at Coventry 1450–1550', in *Crisis and Order in English Towns, 1500–1700: Essays in Urban History*, ed. Peter Clark and Paul Slack (1972), pp.

tation and loss of a pre-existing organic community. This tendency has been challenged recently in the work of Miri Rubin. Of Corpus Christi, she observes bluntly that 'a procession which excluded most working people, women, children, visitors and servants, was not a picture of the community. . . . By laying hierarchy bare it could incite the conflict of difference ever more powerfully sensed in a concentrated symbolic moment.'[7] Taking her point, I wish to emphasise a shift not from sacramental civic *communitas* to disciplinary state hierarchy but rather from a culture focused upon social dynamics within the local community to one that incorporates the local within and subordinates it to the centre.

Throughout most of the sixteenth century, the Tudor regime had been engaged in a complex process of consolidating temporal and spiritual power in the hereditary ruler of a sovereign nation-state. Consistent with this project, the Elizabethan government was actively engaged in efforts to suppress traditional, amateur forms of popular entertainment, including the civic religious drama. The Elizabethan state perceived this culture to be tainted by the superstitions and idolatrous practices of the old faith; because its traditional loyalties were local, regional or papal, it was regarded as a seedbed for dissent and sedition. Popular and liturgical practices, ceremonial and dramatic forms, were not wholly suppressed by the royal government but were instead selectively appropriated. In court, town and countryside, they were transformed by various temporal authorities into elaborate and effusive celebrations of the monarchy and of civic oligarchies; they became part of the ideological apparatus of the state. Such ceremonies of power and authority are epitomised by the queen's occasional progresses to aristocratic estates and regional urban centres; by her annual Accession Day festivities, celebrated at Westminster with pageants and jousts, and in towns throughout England with fanfares and bonfires; and by the annual procession and pageant for the lord mayor and aldermen of London, and analogous ceremonies maintained by other local, urban elites.[8]

The suppression of religious and polemical drama and the curtailment of popular festivities were policy goals vigorously pursued by the Elizabethan regime from its very inception. The custom of celebrating the queen's Accession Day began to flourish following the suppression of the northern rebellion and the York Corpus Christi play in 1569, and the promulgation of the Papal Bull excommunicating Queen Elizabeth on

57–85; quotations from pp. 57, 80. Also see his monograph, *Desolation of a City: Coventry and the Urban Crisis of the Late Middle Ages* (Cambridge, 1979).

  [7] Miri Rubin, *Corpus Christi: The Eucharist in Late Medieval Culture* (Cambridge, 1991), p. 266.

  [8] On the process by which cultural practices were appropriated and invented in order to aggrandise the Tudor state, see Roy Strong, *The Cult of Elizabeth* (1977); Penry Williams, *The Tudor Regime* (Oxford, 1979), pp. 293–310, 351–405; Philip Corrigan and Derek Sayer, *The Great Arch: English State Formation as Cultural Revolution* (Oxford, 1985), pp. 43–71; David Cressy, *Bonfires and Bells: National Memory and the Protestant Calendar in Elizabethan and Stuart England* (Berkeley, 1989), pp. 1–129.

Corpus Christi Day 1570. The process of suppressing the mystery plays was virtually complete by 1580. As Mervyn James puts it, 'under Protestantism, the Corpus Christi becomes the Body of the Realm'.[9] At the same time, the queen's Privy Council and the court nourished the professional theatre – if only to the limited extent that it could be construed as serving their own interests. Commencing scarcely two decades before the writing of *A Midsummer Night's Dream*, resident professional acting companies, under the patronage of the monarch and her leading courtiers, were established in the vicinity of the City of London and the royal court at Westminster. Thus, the beginning of the fully professional, secular and commercial theatre of Elizabethan London coincides with the effective end of the religious drama and the relative decline of local amateur acting traditions in the rest of England.[10] As a means of entertaining the court and the people, the professional theatre seems to have been perceived by the crown as potentially if indirectly useful, both as an instrument for the aggrandisement of the dynastic nation state and for the supervision and diversion of its subjects.

The decay of Coventry's traditional civic culture during the mid- and late sixteenth century paralleled the city's economic decline. Such cultural changes were abetted, however, by the Tudor state's active suppression or cooptation of popular ceremonies and recreations. Some specific instances of this general process can provide a context for construing Shakespeare's comic representation of civic, artisanal culture and its relationship to the state. Queen Elizabeth visited Coventry on progress in 1566. In his speech of welcome, the City Recorder alluded to the role of Coventry in the overthrow of the Danes, 'a memorial whereof is kept unto this day by certain open shows in this City yearly'; the reference is to the elaborate and rowdy annual Hock Tuesday play, in which the role of women

---

[9] See Mervyn James, *Society, Politics and Culture*, p. 41; Harold C. Gardiner, S. J., *Mysteries' End* (New Haven, 1946); R. W. Ingram, 'Fifteen-seventy-nine and the Decline of Civic Religious Drama in Coventry', in *The Elizabethan Theatre VIII*, ed. G. R. Hibbard (Port Credit, Ontario), pp. 114–28.

[10] Rubin points out that 'in those towns where political power and wealth were exercised through craft gilds, like York, Coventry, Beverley, Norwich, dramatic cycles were supported and presented by the crafts, expressing both the processional-communal and the sectional elements in town life.' (*Corpus Christi*, p. 275).

In some significant respects, the dramatic traditions of late medieval London differed from those of such towns. Mervyn James maintains that in London, even in the late middle ages, 'the celebration of Corpus Christi never acquired a public and civic status, and play cycles of the Corpus Christi type never developed. London had its great cycle plays; but the London cycle was performed by professional actors, and had no connection either with Corpus Christi or the city gilds.' (*Society, Politics and Culture*, pp. 41–2). Rubin appears to dispute this assertion, and presents a more complex picture of processional and dramatic elements in the capital's Corpus Christi festivities. She starts from the position that 'once we discard a view which imputes a necessary development of the Corpus Christi drama into full-cycle form we are better able to appreciate the variety of dramatic forms which evolved for Corpus Christi, and the ubiquity of dramatic creation.' (*Corpus Christi*, p. 275). She maintains that, although 'London never developed a town-wide celebration for the feast, a project which is almost unthinkable in so large and varied a city', it nevertheless sustained 'a series of processions related to parish churches, fraternities, crafts'. The most comprehensive of these was the 'great play' organised by the Skinners' Company, presented over several days 'in the form of *tableaux vivants*' (pp. 275–6).

combatants was prominent. Upon her actual entrance into the city, the queen viewed the pageants of the Tanners, Drapers, Smiths and Weavers that formed parts of the Corpus Christi play.[11] Two years later, under the pressure of reformist preachers, the civic celebrations of the Hocktide shows were banned. Despite this, the queen had a subsequent opportunity to witness them at first hand. According to a putative eyewitness account, this was in 1575, during her celebrated visit to the earl of Leicester's estate at Kenilworth. Led by a mason who styled himself Captain Cox, the 'good-hearted men of Coventry' daringly presented their quaint show among the spectacular entertainments and displays with which the earl courted and counselled his royal mistress. The Coventrymen intended to make 'their humble petition unto Her Highness, that they might have their plays up again'.[12] Nevertheless, it appears that, after 1579, the citizens of Coventry ceased to entertain themselves with either their Hocktide show or their Corpus Christi play. At about the same time, in the city records for 1578, there occurs the first of a number of extant entries for payments in connection with celebrations 'on the quee[n']s holiday' (*Records of Early English Drama: Coventry*, p. 286). In these fragmentary records, we glimpse instances of the complex ideological process by which traditional ceremonial forms and events that were focused upon the articulation and celebration of the civic community itself either became occasions for the city's celebration of a royal visit, or were displaced outright by a newly instituted calendar of holidays that promoted the cult of the queen by honouring her birthday and her Accession Day.

A Midsummer Night's Dream incorporates allusions to this changed and diminished world of popular civic play forms. In its very title and in passing allusions – to the festivals of Midsummer Eve and St John's Day, to the rites of May and to St Valentine's Day – the play gestures towards a larger context of popular holiday occasions and customs that mixed together pagan and Christian traditions. In this context, it is significant that Corpus Christi, though a moveable feast, was nevertheless a summer festival, occurring between 21 May and 24 June – a circumstance that made possible its extensive open-air ceremonies and entertainments.[13]

---

[11] See the documents printed in *Records of Early English Drama: Coventry*, ed. R. W. Ingram (Toronto, 1981), pp. 233–4. Also see Ingram, 'Fifteen-seventy-nine'.

[12] See Robert Langham, *A Letter*, with Introduction, Notes and Commentary by R. J. P. Kuin (Leiden, 1983), pp. 52–5. The performance of the Hocktide show was preceded by a rustic brideale, complete with such village pastimes as morris dancing and running at quintain (pp. 49–52). Significantly, neither of these common and amateur entertainments is mentioned in George Gascoigne's self-promoting courtly account, *The Princely Pleasures at the Court at Kenilworth* (1576).

[13] On allusions to the rites of May in *MND*, see 1.1.167, 4.1.132; on St Valentine's Day, 4.1.138. On the inseparability of St John's Day and Midsummer Night 'in the religious and folk consciousness of the sixteenth century', see Anca Vlasopolos, 'The Ritual of Midsummer: A Pattern for *A Midsummer Night's Dream*', *Renaissance Quarterly*, 31 (1978), 21–9; esp. pp. 23–6. On rites and games of May Day and Midsummer Eve and Day, also see C. L. Barber, *Shakespeare's Festive Comedy: A Study of Dramatic Form in Relation to Social Custom* (Princeton, 1959), pp. 119–24; François Laroque, *Shakespeare's Festive World: Elizabethan Seasonal Entertainment and the Professional*

Furthermore, the institutional basis of civic ritual drama in the craft guilds survives in Shakespeare's *A Midsummer Night's Dream* in the names of the mechanicals, as enumerated by Peter Quince: 'Nick Bottom, the weaver', 'Francis Flute, the bellows-mender', 'Robin Starveling, the tailor', 'Tom Snout, the tinker', 'Snug the joiner'. The identification of the mechanicals in terms of both their particular crafts or 'mysteries' and their collective dramatic endeavour strengthens the evocation of the Corpus Christi tradition. Nevertheless, despite the conspicuous title of Shakespeare's play, and despite the oblique allusions to the guild structure of the civic community, the occasion for the artisans' play-within-the-play is not the marking of the traditional agrarian calendar, nor the articulation of the collective urban social body through the celebration of customary holidays. Neither is it the observance of the ecclesiastical calendar, the annual cycle of holy days, nor the dramatisation of the paradigmatic events of sacred history from the Creation to the Final Doom. Instead, the rude mechanicals pool their talents and strain their wits in order to dramatise an episode from classical mythology that will celebrate the wedding of Duke Theseus – an event that focuses the collective interests of the Commonwealth upon the person of the ruler.

III

As has long been recognised, *A Midsummer Night's Dream* has affinities with Elizabethan royal iconography and courtly entertainments. The most obvious features are Shakespeare's incorporation of a play performed in celebration of an aristocratic wedding, and Oberon's allusion to 'a fair vestal, throned by the west. . . . the imperial votaress' (2.1.158, 163) – the latter being invoked in a scenario reminiscent of the pageantry presented to the queen on her progresses.[14] From early in the reign, Elizabeth had been directly addressed and engaged by such performances at aristocratic estates and in urban centres. In these pageants, masques and plays, distinctions were effaced between the spatio-temporal locus of the royal spectator/actress and that of the characters being enacted before her. Debates were referred to the queen's arbitration; the magic of her presence civilised savage men, restored the blind to sight, released errant knights from enchantment, and rescued virgins from defilement. Such social dramas of celebration and coercion played out the delicately balanced relationship

---

Stage, trans. Janet Lloyd (Cambridge, 1991), passim. On Corpus Christi as a summer festival, see Rubin, *Corpus Christi*, pp. 208–9, 213, 243, 271, 273.

[14] In his Introduction to the Arden edition of *MND*, Brooks comments that 'Oberon's description of the mermaid and the shooting stars . . . reflects Shakespeare's acquaintance with the kind of elaborate courtly entertainment which combined a mythological water-pageant with fireworks, rather like those presented to Elizabeth by Leicester at Kenilworth [1575] and the earl of Hertford at Elvetham [1591]' (p. xxxix).

between the monarch and the nobility, gentry and urban elites who constituted the political nation. These events must also have evoked reverence and awe in the local common folk who assisted in and witnessed them. And because texts and descriptions of most of these processions, pageants and shows were in print within a year – sometimes within just a few weeks – of their performance, they may have had a cultural impact far more extensive and enduring than their occasional and ephemeral character might at first suggest. Such royal pageantry appropriated materials from popular late medieval romances, from Ovid, Petrarch and other literary sources; and when late Elizabethan poetry and drama such as Spenser's *Faerie Queene* or Shakespeare's *A Midsummer Night's Dream* reappropriated those sources, they were now inscribed by the allegorical discourse of Elizabethan royal courtship, panegyric and political negotiation. Thus, the deployment of Ovidian, Petrarchan and allegorical romance modes by late Elizabethan writers must be read in terms of an intertextuality that includes both the discourse of European literary history and the discourse of Elizabethan state power.

There is an obvious dramaturgical contrast between *A Midsummer Night's Dream* and the progress pageants, or panegyrical court plays such as George Peele's *Arraignment of Paris*. In such courtly performance genres, the resolution of the action, the completion of the form, is dependent upon the actual presence of the monarch as privileged auditor/spectator. Her judgement may be actively solicited, or, *in propria persona*, she may become the focus of the characters' collective celebration and veneration; frequently, as in Peele's play, the two strategies are combined.[15] However, there are also Elizabethan plays that do not require the queen's active participation in the action but instead refer the dramatic resolution to an onstage character who is an allegorical personage readily if not wholly identifiable with the queen. Such is the authoritative figure of Cynthia, the queen/goddess who presides over the action in both John Lyly's *Endymion* and Ben Jonson's *Cynthia's Revels*. These formal strategies are presumably motivated in part by the practical concern to make the play playable in more than one venue, and for more than one audience. The professional players had more people to please than the monarch alone. In any case, the queen was frequently unavailable to play her part; and – as Ben Jonson discovered, having written her into *Every Man Out of His Humour* (1599) – for someone else to have explicitly personated the monarch would have been a grave offence.[16] The formal and dramaturgical responses to such manifestly practical concerns may have had larger implications. Such plays

---

[15] See Louis A. Montrose, 'Gifts and Reasons: The Contexts of Peele's *Araygnement of Paris*', *ELH, A Journal of English Literary History*, 47 (1980), 433–61.

[16] See Helen M. Ostovich, '"So Sudden and Strange a Cure": A Rudimentary Masque in *Every Man Out of His Humour*', *English Literary Renaissance*, 22 (1992), 315–32; Richard Dutton, *Mastering the Revels: The Regulation and Censorship of English Renaissance Drama* (Iowa City, 1991), pp. 136–7.

preserve the theatrical illusion of a self-contained play world. In doing so, they necessarily produce a more mediated – and, thus, a potentially more ambiguous – mode of royal reference and encomium than do those plays which open the frame of the fiction to acknowledge the physically present sovereign and defer to her mastery of acting and action. Thus, plays performed in the playhouses had a relatively greater degree of both formal and ideological autonomy than did exclusively courtly entertainments.

In royal pageantry, the queen was always the cynosure; her virginity was the source of magical potency. And in courtly plays such as Lyly's *Endymion*, such representation of the charismatic royal virgin continued to enact such a role – although the limitations and resources of dramatic representation opened up new and perhaps unintended possibilities for equivocation and ambiguity in the apparent affirmation of royal wisdom, power and virtue. Like Lyly's *Endymion, A Midsummer Night's Dream* is permeated by images and devices that suggest characteristic forms of Elizabethan court culture. However, Shakespeare's ostensibly courtly wedding play is neither focused upon the queen nor structurally dependent upon her actual presence or her intervention in the action.[17] Nor does it include among its onstage and speaking characters a transparent allegorical representation of the queen – a character who enjoys a central and determining authority over the action. It has often been suggested that the original occasion of *A Midsummer Night's Dream* was an aristocratic wedding at which Queen Elizabeth herself was present.[18] Whatever the truth of this attractive but unproven hypothesis, what we know for certain is that the title page of the first quarto, printed in 1600, claims to present the play 'As it hath been sundry times publicly acted, by the right honourable the Lord Chamberlain his servants'. Despite the legal fiction that public performances served to keep the privileged players of the Chamberlain's Men in readiness for performance at court, and despite whatever adaptations may have been made in repertory plays to suit them to the conditions of particular court performances, the dramaturgical and ideological matrix of Shakespearean drama was located not in the royal court but in the professional playhouse.

Although perhaps sometimes receiving their first and/or most lucrative performances at court or in aristocratic households, all of Shakespeare's plays seem to have been written with the possibility in mind of theatrical as well as courtly performance. Certainly, this practice provides evidence for the shared tastes of queen and commoner. And, needless to say, the

---

[17] Compare G. K. Hunter, *John Lyly: The Humanist as Courtier* (London, 1962), pp. 329–30.

[18] The leading contenders for the aristocratic wedding at which the play was supposedly first performed are that of William Stanley, earl of Derby, with Lady Elizabeth Vere, daughter of the earl of Oxford and granddaughter of Lord Burghley (26 January 1594/5), and that of Thomas, son of Lord Berkeley, with Elizabeth, daughter of Sir George Carey and granddaughter of Lord Hunsdon, the lord chamberlain and patron of Shakespeare's company (19 February 1595/6). For a summary of the arguments, see *MND*, liii–lvii.

advertisement that a play had been performed at court or before the queen was intended to enhance the interest of Elizabeth's theatre-going or play-reading subjects, who might thereby vicariously share the source of Her Majesty's entertainment. Nevertheless, despite the broad social appeal of Shakespearean and other plays, we should resist any impulse to homogenise Elizabethan culture and society into an organic unity. The courtly and popular audiences for Shakespeare's plays constituted frequently overlapping but nevertheless distinct and potentially divergent sources of socio-economic support and ideological constraint. The writing of plays that would be playable in both the commercial playhouses and in the royal court points towards the conditions of emergence of the professional theatre at a historically transitional moment. This theatre was sustained by a frequently advantageous but inherently unstable conjunction of two theoretically distinct modes of cultural production: one, based upon relations of patronage; the other, upon market relations.

IV

In *A Midsummer Night's Dream*, the playwright's imagination 'bodies forth' the ruler and patron in the personage of Theseus. Shakespeare's antique Duke holds clear opinions as to the purpose of playing; and these opinions take two forms. One is that the drama should serve as a pleasant pastime for the sovereign, as an innocuous respite from princely care:

> Come now; what masques, what dances shall we have,
> To wear away this long age of three hours
> Between our after-supper and bed-time?
> Where is our usual manager of mirth?
> What revels are in hand? Is there no play
> To ease the anguish of a torturing hour?
> Call Philostrate. . . .
> Say, what abridgement have you for this evening,
> What masque, what music? How shall we beguile
> The lazy time, if not with some delight?
>
> (5.1.32–41)

The Office of the Revels had been established in the reign of Queen Elizabeth's father, and its purpose had been 'to select, organise, and supervise all entertainment of the sovereign, wherever the court might be'.[19] The expansion of the role of this court office to include the licensing

---

[19] Gerald Eades Bentley, *The Profession of Dramatist in Shakespeare's Time 1590–1642* (1971; rpt. Princeton, 1986), p. 147. On the Revels Office, also see E. K. Chambers, *The Elizabethan Stage* (4 vols., Oxford, 1923), I, 71–105; Janet Clare, *'Art made tongue-tied by authority': Elizabethan and Jacobean Dramatic Censorship* (Manchester, 1990); and Dutton, *Mastering the Revels*.

of public dramatic performances as well as the provision of courtly ones indicates that the Elizabethan regime was attempting to subject the symbolic and interpretive activities of its subjects to increasing scrutiny and regulation – at the same time that it was inventing new sources of revenue for itself and its clients. In the personage of Philostrate, Shakespeare's play incorporates the courtly office of Master of the Revels, but limits it to its original charge, which was to provide entertainments for the monarch. Like the ambivalent term *licence*, Philostrate's alliterative title as Theseus's 'manager of mirth' suggests an official concern simultaneously to allow and to control the expression of potentially subversive festive, comic and erotic energies.

Of the four proffered entertainments, the first two – 'The battle with the Centaurs, to be sung / By an Athenian eunuch to the harp' and 'the riot of the tipsy Bacchanals, / Tearing the Thracian singer in their rage' (5.1.44–5; 48–9) – are dismissed by Theseus, ostensibly because their devices are overly familiar. (As I have suggested elsewhere, both allude to the play's classical mythological subtext of sexual and familial violence – a subtext over which the play's patriarchal comedy keeps a precarious control.)[20] The third prospect is excluded because it smacks of social protest:

> 'The thrice three Muses mourning for the death
> Of learning, late deceased in beggary'?
> That is some satire, keen and critical,
> Not sorting with a nuptial ceremony.
>
> (5.1.52–5)

This conspicuous irrelevance has two operative points: the first, that its subject is the familiar complaint of Elizabethan cultural producers that they lack generous and enlightened patronage from the great; the second, that Duke Theseus does not want to hear about it. His taste is for something that

> is nothing, nothing in the world;
> Unless you can find sport in their intents,
> Extremely stretched and conned with cruel pain
> To do you service.

This is the play that Theseus will hear, 'For never anything can be amiss / When simpleness and duty tender it' (5.1.78–83). Thus, the other form taken by Theseus's opinions concerning the drama is that it should serve as a gratifying homage to princely power, simultaneously providing a politic opportunity for the exercise of royal magnanimity:

---

[20] See Louis Adrian Montrose, '"Shaping Fantasies": Figurations of Gender and Power in Elizabethan Culture', *Representations*, 2 (1983), 61–94; rpt. in *Representing the English Renaissance*, ed. Stephen Greenblatt (Berkeley, 1988), pp. 31–64. I have incorporated some passages from this earlier study into the present one;

Our sport shall be to take what they mistake:
And what poor duty cannot do, noble respect
Takes it in might, not merit.
Where I have come, great clerks have purposed
To greet me with premeditated welcomes;
Where I have seen them shiver and look pale,
Make periods in the midst of sentences,
Throttle their practised accent in their fears,
And, in conclusion, dumbly have broke off,
Not paying me a welcome. Trust me, sweet,
Out of this silence yet I picked a welcome,
And in the modesty of fearful duty
I read as much as from the rattling tongue
Of saucy and audacious eloquence.
Love, therefore, and tongue-tied simplicity
In least speak most, to my capacity.

(5.1.90–105)

The opinions of Shakespeare's Athenian duke bear a strong likeness to those of his own sovereign, as these were represented in her policies and in her own public performances. Thus, in the metatheatrical context of the play's long final scene, Duke Theseus is not so much Queen Elizabeth's masculine antithesis as he is her princely surrogate.

Theseus's attitude towards his subjects' offerings has analogues in the two printed texts that describe the queen's visit to the city of Norwich during her progress of 1578. In a curiously metadramatic speech directly addressed to Elizabeth, the figure of Mercury describes the process of creating and enacting entertainments for the queen – such as the one in which he is presently speaking:

And that so soon as out of door she goes
(If time do serve, and weather waxeth fair)
Some odd device shall meet Her Highness straight,
To make her smile, and ease her burdened breast,
And take away the cares and things of weight
That princes feel, that findeth greatest rest.[21]

On another occasion, as the queen returned toward her lodgings,

within Bishops Gate at the Hospital door, Master Stephen Limbert, master of the grammar school in Norwich, stood ready to render her an oration. Her Majesty drew near unto him, and thinking him fearful, said graciously unto him: 'Be not afraid.' He answered her again in English: 'I thank Your Majesty for your good encouragement'; and then with good courage entered into this oration.

---

in revised form, both will be incorporated into a more comprehensive study of *MND*, the Elizabethan theatre, and the Elizabethan state.

[21] Thomas Churchyard, *A Discourse of The Queen's Majesty's Entertainment in Suffolk and Norfolk* (1578), rpt. in *Records of Early English Drama: Norwich, 1540–1642*, ed. David Galloway (Toronto, 1984), p. 302.

After printing the oration in the original Latin and in English translation, the account continues by describing the queen as

very attentive, even until the end thereof. And the oration ended, after she had given great thanks thereof to Master Limbert, she said to him: 'It is the best that ever I heard.'[22]

The tone in which Theseus responds to the mechanicals' 'palpable gross play' catches the element of hyperbole in the queen's reported speech, and turns its gracious condescension towards mockery. For example, as Theseus says to Bottom: 'Marry, if he that writ it had played Pyramus, and hanged himself in Thisbe's garter, it would have been a fine tragedy – and so it is, truly, and very notably discharged' (5.1.343–7). I have suggested analogues from royal pageantry performed by children and amateurs because such performances most clearly equate to the mechanicals' performance of *Pyramus and Thisbe* within Shakespeare's play. However, the queen's attitude towards the uses of the adult, professional and commercial theatre seems to have differed little from what it was towards the uses of other forms of royal entertainment. As early as 1574, a company of professional players under the patronage of the earl of Leicester were licensed by the queen to perform in public so that they would be in readiness to play at court, 'as well for the recreation of our loving subjects as for our solace and pleasure when we shall think good to see them'.[23]

Despite the apparently indifferent attitude of the sovereign – or, perhaps, precisely because of it – in *A Midsummer Night's Dream* Shakespeare calls attention to the artistic distance between the professional players and their putatively crude predecessors; and he does so by incorporating a comic representation of such players into his play. This professional self-consciousness is the very hallmark of the play's celebrated metatheatricality – its calling of attention to its own artifice, to its own artistry. Such metatheatricality prescribes the interpretive schema of much modern scholarship in literary and theatre history, which envisions Shakespearean drama as the culmination of a long process of artistic evolution. *A Midsummer Night's Dream* parodies antecedent dramatic forms and performance styles: the amateur acting traditions that had been largely suppressed along with the civic drama by the end of the 1570s, and the work of the professional companies active during the 1570s and earlier 1580s; and it juxtaposes to them the representational powers of the Lord Chamberlain's Men and their playwright.[24] This contrast was made manifest by Shakespeare's

---

[22] B[ernard] G[arter], *The Joyful Receiving of the Queen's Most Excellent Majesty into Her Highness' City of Norwich* (1578), rpt. in *Records of Early English Drama: Norwich*, pp. 266–7, 271.

[23] Patent of 10 May 1574, rpt. in Chambers, *Elizabethan Stage*, II, 87–8.

[24] Davidson convincingly suggests that the mechanicals' rehearsal and performance of *Pyramus and Thisbe* is designed to burlesque 'the older dramatic styles (including . . . the theatrical styles of the public theatre fashionable before *c.* 1585) with their tendency toward bombastic language and clumsy use of mythological subjects'; and to conjoin this burlesque with one directed toward the acting capacities of the amateurs who

company in the very process of performing *A Midsummer Night's Dream*. In particular, it was demonstrated in what we may presume was their consummately professional comic enactment of the mechanicals' vexed rehearsals and inept performance of *Pyramus and Thisbe*. The dramaturgical problems with which the mechanicals struggle show them to be incapable of comprehending the relationship between the actor and his part. They have no skill in the art of personation; they lack an adequate conception of playing. The contrast between amateur and professional modes of playing is incarnated in the performance of Bottom – by which I mean the Elizabethan player's performance of Bottom's performance of Pyramus. The amateur actor who wants to be cast in all the parts, the only character to be literally metamorphosed, is also the one who, despite his translations into an ass-headed monster and a fabled lover, remains immutably – fundamentally – Bottom. The fully professional collaboration between the imaginative playwright and the protean player of the Lord Chamberlain's Men creates the illusion of Bottom's character precisely by creating the illusion of his incapacity to translate himself into other parts.

The play-within-the-play device calls attention to the theatrical transaction between the players and their audience. In the process of foregrounding the imaginative and dramaturgical dynamics of this transaction, *A Midsummer Night's Dream* also calls attention to its socio-political dynamics. Shakespeare's Duke Theseus formulates policy when he proclaims that 'The lunatic, the lover, and the poet / Are of imagination all compact'; that 'Lovers and madmen have such seething brains, / Such shaping fantasies, that apprehend / More than cool reason ever comprehends' (5.1.7–8, 4–6). The social order of Theseus's Athens depends upon his authority to name the forms of mental disorder and his power to control its subjects. Theseus's analogising of the hyperactive imaginations of lunatics, lovers and poets accords with the orthodox perspective of Elizabethan medical and moral discourses. The latter insisted that the unregulated passions and disordered fantasies of the ruler's subjects – from Bedlam beggars to melancholy courtiers – were an inherent danger to themselves, to their fellows, and to the state.[25] For Theseus, no less than for the Elizabethan Privy Council, the ruler's task is to *comprehend* – to understand and to contain – the energies and motives, the diverse, unstable and potentially seditious apprehensions of the ruled. But the Duke – so self-assured and benignly condescending in his comprehension – might also

---

performed in the civic religious drama, which had been largely suppressed by the early 1580s ("'What hempen home-spuns have we swagg'ring here?'", p. 88).

[25] Among modern critical and historical studies, see Lawrence Babb, *The Elizabethan Malady: A Study of Melancholia in English Literature from 1580 to 1642* (East Lansing, Mich., 1951); Michael MacDonald, *Mystical Bedlam: Madness, Anxiety, and Healing in Seventeenth-century England* (Cambridge, 1981); Lacey Baldwin Smith, *Treason in Tudor England: Politics and Paranoia* (Princeton, 1986); Karin Coddon, '"Suche Strange Desygns": Madness, Subjectivity, and Treason in *Hamlet* and Elizabethan Culture', *Renaissance Drama*, n. s., 20 (1989), 51–75.

have some cause for *apprehension*, for he himself and the fictional society over which he rules have been shaped by the fantasy of a poet.

Theseus's deprecation of lunatics, lovers and poets is his unwitting exposition of the scope and limits of his own wisdom. The wonderful musings of the newly awakened Bottom provide a serio-comic prelude to the Duke's set piece. Fitfully remembering his nocturnal adventure, Bottom apprehends something strange and admirable in his metamorphosis and his liaison with Titania:

I have had a most rare vision. I have had a dream, past the wit of man to say what dream it was. Man is but an ass if he go about to expound this dream. . . . The eye of man hath not heard, the ear of man hath not seen, man's hand is not able to taste, his tongue to conceive, nor his heart to report, what my dream was. I will get Peter Quince to write a ballad of this dream: it shall be called 'Bottom's Dream', because it hath no bottom; and I will sing it in the latter end of a play, before the Duke.

(4.1.203–16)

Bottom's (non-)exposition of his dream is a garbled allusion to a passage in St Paul's First Epistle to the Corinthians:

And we speak wisdom among them that are perfect: not the wisdom of this world, neither of the princes of this world, which come to nought.

But we speak the wisdom of God in a mystery, even the hid wisdom, which God had determined before the world, unto our glory.

Which none of the princes of this world hath known; for had they known it, they would not have crucified the Lord of glory.

But as it is written, The things which eye hath not seen, neither ear hath heard, neither came into man's heart, are, which God hath prepared for them that love him.

But God hath revealed them unto us by his Spirit; for the Spirit searcheth all things, yea, the deep things of God.

(1 Corinthians 2: 6–10; *Geneva Bible*, 1560 ed.)

This allusion has often been remarked. Insufficiently remarked, however, is the political resonance that the passage may have had for Elizabethan playgoers and readers; and the possibility that, in selecting it for parody, the playwright may have had a point to make, however oblique its expression.[26] The New Testament passage is built upon an opposition between the misconceived and misdirected profane knowledge possessed

---

[26] The 'context of profound spiritual levelling' implied by Shakespeare's biblical parody is noted in Patterson, *Shakespeare and the Popular Voice*, p. 68. Patterson pursues the 'genial thesis' that *MND* imagines 'an idea of social play that could cross class boundaries without obscuring them, and by those crossings imagine the social body whole again' (p. 69); accordingly, she focuses upon the integrative 'Christian communitas' suggested in 1 Corinthians 12: 14–15, rather than upon the obvious and immediate oppositional context of 1 Corinthians 2: 6–10. For another recent study of the relationship between late Elizabethan social conflict and the tensions of rank within *MND*, see Leinwand, '"I believe we must leave the killing out"'. Less sanguine than Patterson, Leinwand concludes that 'Shakespeare criticises the relations of power in his culture, but does so with remarkable sensitivity to the nuances of threat and accommodation which animate these relations' (p. 30).

by 'the princes of this world' and the spiritual wisdom accessible only to those who humble themselves before a transcendent source of power and love. The biblical text does more than construct a generalised opposition between the profane and the sacred: it gives that abstract moral opposition a political edge by proposing an inverse relationship between the temporal hierarchy of wealth and power and the spiritual hierarchy of wisdom and virtue.

The attitude displayed by the professional playwright towards Bottom, and towards the artisanal culture that he personifies, is a complex mixture of affection, indulgence, condescension and ridicule; and the complexity of that mixture is nowhere more conspicuous than in the speech about Bottom's dream. The comical garbling of the allusion and its farcical dramatic context function to mediate the sacred text, allowing Shakespeare to appropriate it for his own dramatic ends. An opposition between sacred and profane knowledge is displaced into an opposition between Bottom's capacity to apprehend the story of the night and Theseus's incapacity to comprehend it. Shakespeare's professional theatre implicitly repudiates Theseus's attitude towards the entertainer's art precisely by incorporating and ironically circumscribing it. I am suggesting, then, that Shakespeare evokes the scriptural context in order to provide a numinous resonance for the play's temporal, metatheatrical concerns; and that these concerns are rooted in the distinction and relationship between the instrumental authority of the state, as personified in Queen Elizabeth, and the imaginative authority of the public and professional theatre, as personified in the common player-playwright. At the same time, Bottom's dream mediates the relationship of the socio-economically ascendant artist-entrepreneur to his modest roots. It is fitting that the play's chosen instrument for its scriptural message of socio-spiritual inversion is a common artisan and amateur player named Bottom – one who, earlier in the play, has alluded to the raging tyrant of the Nativity pageants in the mystery cycles (1.2.19, 36). By casting Bottom to play in 'an interlude before the Duke and the Duchess, on his wedding-day at night' (1.2.5–7), Shakespeare's play firmly records the redirection of the popular dramatic impulse toward the celebration of 'the princes of this world'. Nevertheless, Bottom's rehearsal of his wondrous strange dream is an oblique marker, an incongruous evocation, of an ethos that *A Midsummer Night's Dream* and its playwright have ostensibly left behind – a trace of social, spiritual and (perhaps) autobiographical filiation.

V

When Puck addresses the audience in the epilogue to *A Midsummer Night's Dream*, his reference to 'we shadows' (5.1.409) implies not only the personified spirits in the play but also the players of Shakespeare's company who have performed the play. Theseus registers this meaning when he says of the mechanicals' acting in *Pyramus and Thisbe*, that 'The best in this kind are but shadows; and the worst are no worse, if imagination amend them' (5.1.208–9). The statement itself, however, is belied on two counts: on the one hand, the rehearsal and performance of the play-within-the-play invite the audience to make qualitative distinctions between the best and the worst of shadows; and, on the other hand, the onstage audience at the Athenian court refuses to amend imaginatively the theatrical limitations of the mechanicals. When Puck addresses his master as 'King of shadows' (3.2.347), the appellation recognises Oberon as the principal player in the action, whose powers of awareness and manipulation also mark him as the play's internal dramatist.[27] Although Titania has a limited power to manipulate Bottom, an artisan and an amateur actor, she herself is manipulated by this 'King of shadows', who is also her husband and her lord. Thus, in the triangulated relationship of Titania, Oberon and Bottom, a fantasy of masculine dependency upon woman is expressed and contained within a fantasy of masculine control over woman. And, more specifically, the social reality of the Elizabethan players' dependency upon Queen Elizabeth is inscribed within the imaginative reality of a player-dramatist's control over the Faery Queen.

The relationship of Shakespeare's play and its production to traditions of amateur and occasional dramatic entertainments is at once internalised and distanced in the mechanicals' ridiculous rehearsal and performance of *Pyramus and Thisbe*. And by the way in which it frames the attitudes of Theseus and the play-within-the-play's courtly audience, *A Midsummer Night's Dream* internalises and distances the relationship of the public and professional theatre to the pressures and constraints of noble and royal patronage. Its resonances of popular pastimes and amateur civic drama on the one hand, and of royal pageantry and courtly entertainments on the other, serve to locate *A Midsummer Night's Dream* in relationship to its cultural antecedents and its socio-economic context. Through the play of affinity and difference, these resonances serve to distinguish Shakespeare's comedy from both amateur and courtly modes, and to define it as a production of the professional and commercial theatre. The much noted metatheatricality of *A Midsummer Night's Dream* is nowhere more apparent and striking than in this process by which the play assimilates its own cultural determinants and produces them anew as its own dramatic effects. When I suggest that the play simultaneously subsumes and projects the conditions of its own possibility, I am not making a claim for its timelessness and universality. On the contrary, I am attempting to locate it

---

[27] For 'shadow' as 'applied rhetorically . . . to an actor or a play in contrast to the reality represented', see *OED*, s.v. 'Shadow', sense 1.6.b. The earliest usages cited by *OED* are in Lyly, *Euphues*, and Shakespeare, *A Midsummer Night's Dream* and *The Two Gentlemen of Verona*.

more precisely in the ideological matrix of its original production. The foregrounding of theatricality as a mode of human cognition and human agency is a striking feature of Shakespearean drama. Such theatricality becomes possible at a particular historical moment. By this means, the professional practitioners of an immensely popular and bitterly contested emergent cultural practice articulate their collective consciousness of their place in the social and cultural order – the paradoxical location of the theatre and of theatricality at once on the margins and at the centre of the Elizabethan world.

3

Thomas Dekker's *The Shoemaker's Holiday*

The Artisanal World

Paul S. Seaver

Dekker's *The Shoemaker's Holiday*, staged for the first time on 1 January 1599/1600 in the midst of the festive twelve days of Christmas, must have been experienced as an antidote to a grim season in a grim time: a holiday indeed. At first glance, the play seems little more than a piece of commercial escapism, a release from the frightening social and political tensions of the time, a droll tale in which love conquers all, a happy denouement engineered by a madcap lord mayor aided by his clever and patriotic shoemakers and presided over by a benign and amused king in which Court and City are at least temporarily reconciled in a happy feast. And yet would not a London audience have seen a much more problematic drama scarcely disguised beneath the surface innocence of the play? The actual experience of those playgoers almost four centuries ago is beyond our reach, but what follows is an attempt to sketch some of the knowledge and perceptions that a London audience might have brought to that initial performance in the dark season following the winter solstice.

By the end of the 1590s both Court and City were in need of a holiday. The war with Spain had dragged on for a dozen years with no end in sight. The Protestant wind which had dispersed the Spanish Armada in 1588 had humbled Philip II but had not changed his purposes, and early in 1598 the English government learned that a Spanish fleet ferrying 7,500 troops had set sail for England, only to turn back in the face of autumn storms.[1] English troops were engaged in France and the Low Countries and since 1595 against Tyrone and the Ulster rebels in Ireland as well.[2] The mustering of Ralph Damport, Simon Eyre's journeyman, was an event repeatedly seen on the streets of London during these years. In the spring of 1598 the earl of Essex had sailed for Ireland with an army of 12,000,

---

[1] *Calendar of State Papers, Domestic Series, Elizabeth, 1598–1601* (henceforth, *CSPD*), pp. 27–9. In February, 1598, Lord Admiral Nottingham wrote to the Privy Council of his defensive measures at Chatham and elsewhere on the lower Thames to prevent a hostile fleet from reaching London; *ibid.*, p. 32.

[2] For England's foreign engagements during the 1590s, see Wallace T. MacCaffrey, *Elizabeth I. War and Politics 1588–1603* (Princeton, 1992), passim.

but within months the Council was contemplating the dispatch of another 4,000. At the end of August London was ordered to muster 400 reinforcements for the troop of 2,100 to be dispatched to Ireland, and in late December London was ordered to supply another 600.[3] War on such a scale far outran the resources of the English government. In August 1598 the Privy Council wrote to Sir Richard Saltonstall, lord mayor, to the aldermen 'his brethren' and to the Common Council, requesting a loan of £20,000 from the livery companies; in December John Chamberlain reported that, despite the granting of parliamentary subsidies and the levying of forced loans, the queen was contemplating borrowing £150,000 from the City, which, Chamberlain suspected, was an amount 'hardly to be had, the City being so impoverished through decay of trade'.[4]

The festive, celebratory mood of *The Shoemaker's Holiday* is all the more remarkable for coming at the end of a decade in which the Four Horsemen of the Apocalypse seemed loosed on the land. In 1593 the pestilence returned, and, although not as devastating a visitation as that of 1603, more than 10,000 Londoners perished of the plague in that summer and autumn.[5] Later in the decade bad harvests led to sky-rocketing prices: the cost in London of meat and flour rose 30 per cent, beer 48 per cent, and although wages also responded to inflationary pressures, those of skilled workmen like Ralph, Hodge and Firk rose a mere 10 per cent.[6] Vagrants and the unemployed flocked to London, competing for work and poor relief with the discharged and 'maimed' soldiers, and in 1598 Parliament gave statutory authority to the great Elizabethan Poor Law, a measure which doubled the poor rates in some London parishes.[7]

Rather than a golden Elizabethan sunset, the last years of the century seemed to usher in an age of iron, a decline symbolised by Sir Philip Sidney's wasted death and by the refusal of the aging queen to commit herself to a vigorous Protestant war. As well she might, for as war swallowed increasing resources in the midst of a stagnant economy, the progressive corruption of her court and government became an open scandal (it 'glowed like rotten wood' in Raleigh's phrase), as her capacity to reward her henchmen declined and the unseemly scramble for place and profit reached scandalous proportions.[8] The increasingly poisonous

---

[3] *CSPD*, pp. 43, 51; *Acts of the Privy Council* (henceforth, *APC*), *1598–9*, pp. 97, 391. In October the government learned that some 200 of the London troops had mutinied at Towcester, before reaching the port of embarkation at Chester: *APC, 1598–9*, pp. 214–15.

[4] *APC, 1598–9*, pp. 40, 62; *CSPD*, pp. 129–30.

[5] Paul Slack, *The Impact of Plague in Tudor and Stuart England* (1985), p. 151.

[6] Steve Rappaport, *Worlds within Worlds: Structures of Life in Sixteenth-Century London* (Cambridge, 1989), pp. 140–1, 147.

[7] See, for example, Edwin Freshfield, ed., *The Account Books of the Parish of St Bartholomew Exchange. Church Wardens Accounts of St Bartholomew Exchange 1596–1698* (1890). For collections for maimed soldiers, see, e.g., *APC, 1597–8*, pp. 173, 205, 341.

[8] Lawrence Stone, 'The Inflation of Honours: 1558–1641', *Past & Present*, 14 (1958), 45–70; L. Stone, *The Crisis of the Aristocracy, 1558–1641* (Oxford, 1965); Wallace T. MacCaffrey, 'Place and Patronage in Elizabethan

politics at court polarised in a struggle between Sir Robert Cecil (his father, Lord Burghley, had died in August 1598) and the earl of Essex, leader of the swordsmen since the death of the earl of Leicester in 1588, and that struggle had come to a climax in the months immediately before *The Shoemaker's Holiday* appeared on the stage. Essex had returned from Ireland precipitously and contrary to orders, and the furious queen had dismissed him from court. In late December 1599 it was known that the queen was 'not well pleased' with either the bishop of London or the archbishop of Canterbury, whom she blamed for the fact that a number of the London clergy, including several preachers at Paul's Cross, had openly prayed for the earl.[9] Did she fear that the popular earl might lead a sympathetic City into armed rebellion (as in fact Essex attempted but a few weeks later)?

And does that tense and dangerous political atmosphere explain in part Dekker's placing of his drama in an ambiguous historical time, at once contemporary in its preoccupations and yet firmly set a century and a half in the past? For Simon Eyre is not entirely a fiction; a quite historical Simon Eyre had been elected sheriff in 1434, alderman for the ward of Walbrook a decade later, and lord mayor in 1445. Eyre had indeed built Leadenhall, although originally its intended use had been as a City granary.[10] Further, the king, never named in the play, would theoretically have to be the ill-fated Henry VI, the last Lancastrian monarch, although the fictional monarch of Dekker's play is really a reflection of Tudor ideals – appreciative of his commons, always willing to do justice, a combination warrior and gift-giver – precisely those qualities that Elizabeth lacked but hardly characteristic of the hapless Henry VI. In the 1440s the war with the resurgent French monarchy would shortly resume, following the breach of the Truce of Tours by English arms, and the deaths in 1447 of the royal dukes of Gloucester and Bedford, the king's uncles, would open the way for Richard duke of York's bid for supremacy at court, a threat greater than that posed by Elizabeth's Essex, for York was, for a brief period, the heir apparent. In short, for Londoners who knew their English chronicles the setting of the play must have resonated like a sly wink in the smiling countenance of the drama.

The temporal setting of the play itself must have carried its own freight of meanings, for the play moves towards its climax on Shrove Tuesday, pancake day, the last day of feasting before Lenten fasting. Shrovetide and May Day were the two spring holidays belonging peculiarly to youth, but whereas May Day was a holiday particularly for young lovers, when

Politics', in *Elizabethan Government and Society*, ed. S. T. Bindoff *et al.* (1961), pp. 95–126; Linda Levy Peck, *Court Patronage and Corruption in Early Stuart England* (Boston and London, 1990).

[9] *CSPD*, pp. 365–6.

[10] Alfred B. Beaven, *The Aldermen of the City of London* (2 vols., 1908), II, 9, 164; John Stow, *A Survey of London* (1603), ed. C. L. Kingsford (2 vols., Oxford, 1908), I, 153–4.

Plate 6 A drawing of Simon Eyre by Roger Leigh, Clarenceux King of Arms, *c.* 1446–7

couples were supposed to flock to the suburbs to gather green branches, Shrovetide had become a season of youthful licence, of ritualised rioting by the City apprentices. Certainly neither the Privy Council nor the City magistrates underestimated their potential for dangerous breaches of the peace. By the 1590s it has been estimated that there were in London at least 15,000 apprentices and another 12,000 journeymen, many, like Firk, unmarried and as ready as the apprentices to take to the streets.[11] Under pressure from the Privy Council, the lord mayor regularly ordered the aldermen of every ward to 'give notice to every householder ... not to suffer their apprentices and servants to wander abroad in the streets ... upon Sunday, Monday and Tuesday' of Shrovetide – to little effect, despite the fact that it became customary to order double watches of armed citizens into the streets at that season.[12]

It would be a mistake, too, to see such responses as merely the reaction of old and crabbed authority to youthful high spirits. Although the first surviving evidence for attacks on bawdy houses comes from a few years later, the new playhouses had been objects of riot as early as 1580, and in 1595 the lord mayor complained to the Privy Council that plays contained 'nothing but profane fables, lascivious matters, cozening devices, and other unseemly and scurrilous behaviours, which are so set forth as that they move wholly to imitation and not to the avoiding of those vices' and were in fact to blame for the 'late stir and mutinous attempt of those few apprentices and other servants who we doubt not drew their infection from these and like places'.[13] Not that apprentices seemed to need the example of the theatre or indeed much excuse of any kind to indulge in unruly behaviour. In July 1599, less than six months before Dekker's play was staged, the lord mayor complained that divers 'riotous and unruly' apprentices in 'troops to the number of two or three hundred', armed with 'long staves and other weapons', had gathered in the summer evenings 'under colour of going to a place called the Old Ford to bathe themselves', in the course of which they had gone about 'setting men's corn growing in the fields on fire, breaking down glass windows and signs hanging at men's doors, thrusting down of bricks with their staves from the tops of brick walls, pulling up of gates and stiles, breaking into orchards and stealing of fruits, beating of Her Majesty's watches, and divers other rebellious parts'.[14] Old Ford in suburban Hackney was of course the locale of Mayor Sir Roger Oatley's rural retreat in Dekker's play, which trans-

---

[11] Rappaport, *Worlds within Worlds*, p. 11.

[12] See the mayoral precept of 16 Feb. 1587/8, Corporation of London Records Office (henceforth, CLRO), Jour. 22, fo. 156v; a precept of 18 Feb. 1598/9 repeated the order to keep apprentices within doors in order to prevent 'sundry outrages' during Shrovetide, and by the late 1590s it had become customary to call out double watches whenever such outrages were feared: Jour. 25, fos. 22r, 28v, 72v, 87r.

[13] Ian Archer, *The Pursuit of Stability: Social Relations in Elizabethan London* (Cambridge, 1991), p. 3; CLRO, Remembrancia, I, nos. 9, 662; II, no. 103.

[14] CLRO, Jour. 25, fo. 72v.

forms this locus of youthful rioting to the scene of romantic pastoral, just as Dekker's Simon Eyre, for all his anarchic verbiage, feasts the apprentice cordwainers on Shrove Tuesday rather than unleashing them to their customarily riotous celebrations.

In keeping with the holiday mood of the drama is the social fantasy of Simon Eyre's precipitous rise to the mayoralty. As Dekker's London audience well knew, no cordwainer ever rose to be lord mayor, for London had long been a highly stratified society, dominated by a mercantile elite, and its lord mayors all belonged to the liveries of one of the twelve great livery companies – Mercers, Grocers, Drapers, Haberdashers, Merchant Taylors, Clothworkers, Goldsmiths, Skinners, Ironmongers, Salters, Fishmongers and Vintners. Simon Eyre, the historic figure, had begun his career as a freeman in the Upholsterers' Company but had secured his translation to the more prestigious Drapers some fifteen years before his election as sheriff.[15] All London guilds or companies had both a livery and a yeomanry; the company's governors, the master, wardens and assistants, were drawn from among the livery, the wealthier members of the company who were entitled to wear the company livery and to march in the lord mayor's inaugural procession on 29 October.[16] A handful of spectacularly successful members of minor companies were elected aldermen in Elizabeth's reign, but all of these slated for election to the mayoralty were translated beforehand to one of the more prestigious twelve, typically the Grocers or Drapers.[17]

The Cordwainers were an old company, and their royal charter and a company hall dated from the 1440s.[18] However, unlike Dick Whittington, whose rise from rags to riches and the mayoralty had become a popular myth by the end of Elizabeth's reign, no mere shoemaker was likely to follow in his footsteps, for Whittington had been apprenticed to a merchant, and the mythic element in his story had to do with his success without any capital (except for a cat). The Cordwainers in contrast were engaged in the production of necessary, but cheap, commodities – shoes primarily, but also leather pantaloons, jerkins and gloves. The manufacture of leather belonged to another company, the Tanners, and the trade in leather to the Leathersellers. In short, the opportunities for a mere shoemaker to expand his trade were severely limited. Production took place in household shops, and a yeoman cordwainer as old as Simon Eyre would have been entitled to take on as many as four apprentices, so long as he also employed a journeyman for each two apprentices.[19] Obviously in an urban metropolis fast approaching a quarter of a million inhabitants there were necessarily

[15] Beaven, *Aldermen of London*, II, 164.
[16] William F. Kahl, *The Development of London Livery Companies* (Boston, 1960), passim.
[17] Beaven, *Aldermen of London*, II, 329–31.
[18] Jennifer Lang, *The Worshipful Company of Cordwainers 1439–1979* (1980), pp. 43–4.
[19] Guildhall Library MS (henceforth, GLMS) 8033, Cordwainers' Charters and Ordinances, Exemplification out of the Court of Exchequer, 28 November, 13 Elizabeth, p. 16.

a great many shoemakers (in 1604, 39 paid dues at the quarter court as liveried members of the company, 138 paid as yeomen, and another 88 as cobblers, qualified to repair but not manufacture shoes; in that year masters in the company indentured 152 apprentices).[20] On the other hand, although large, the company was neither prestigious nor wealthy. When the order of precedence was fixed in 1515, the Cordwainers were assigned the twenty-seventh place, despite the fact that they were among the twelve oldest companies in the City, and when in 1627 the crown demanded £60,000 from the livery companies as their share of the forced loan of that year, the Cordwainers were assessed £360, a sum that seems derisory compared to the Merchant Taylors' £6,300 or the Drapers' £6,000.[21]

As a consequence, Dekker's Simon Eyre rises not through the diligent pursuit of his vocation, but rather by a *deus ex machina* supplied by a Dutch captain who, as an alien merchant, could not sell his shipload of goods directly on the London market but needed a citizen broker, and by Lacy, disguised as Hans, who supplies the capital and engineers the bargain. However unlikely, there was nothing illegal about Simon's sudden launching as a merchant. One of the peculiarities of the freedom of London, which would have been known to Dekker's audience, was the right of any freeman of the City, regardless of his company affiliation, to engage in any trade: thus there were Grocers who ground lenses for eyeglasses and Fishmongers who engaged in the cloth trade. Dekker's Simon, then, had the right to set up as a merchant, and the real difficulty, recognised in the play by both Eyre and Hans, was not the legalities of the situation but the difficulty that a mere shoemaker had in acquiring the necessary capital, a problem solved ingeniously by a combination of the captain's necessity, Hans's purse, and Eyre's appearing to negotiate the transaction dressed in aldermanic robes. Such events do not happen in real life. A shoemaker's credit would enable him to purchase leather from a tanner and to run up a bill at the alehouse, but the purchase of a shipload of high-value goods – and this is not presented as a cargo of coal from Newcastle or of pine timber from Norway, but of sugar, civet, almonds and cambric, luxury goods of small weight and great price – required not only fast talking and deception, but on the part of the audience a certain suspension of disbelief, accomplished in part by Eyre's constant creation of a kind of holiday high spirits that prevents one from asking whether indeed any of this could happen in a workaday world.[22]

Firk's offhand remark that the ship's lading was worth 'two or three hundred thousand pounds' must have been a further clue that the audience was being presented with a happy piece of wish fulfilment rather than

[20] GLMS 7351/1, Cordwainers Audit, Apprentice and Freedoms Book, 1595–1636, no fo.

[21] Lang, *Worshipful Company of Cordwainers*, p. 34; CLRO, Jour. 34, fo. 196r.

[22] For the credit economy of the small artisanal shopkeeper, see, e.g., Paul S. Seaver, *Wallington's World: A Puritan Artisan in Seventeenth-Century London* (Stanford, 1985), pp. 122–4; Peter Earle, *The Making of the English Middle Class: Business, Society and Family Life in London 1660–1730* (Berkeley and Los Angeles, 1989), pp. 112–30.

any kind of mercantile reality, for Firk's wildly exaggerated sum was closer to the size of the crown debt than to the value of any conceivable shipload of commodities. For example, London imports of sugar for the year beginning on Michaelmas 1595 totalled in weight about 832,000 pounds at a time when the retail value of a pound of refined sugar was close to 20 pence. In other words, the total value of the sugar imported to London in the mid-1590s, representing the cargo of many ships, when refined and sold on the retail market carried a value of no more than £70,000.[23] A century later in 1697 the merchant partnership of Perry and Lane, the largest London importer of tobacco by that year, recorded shipments of 4.8 million pounds of that popular colonial commodity worth an estimated £137,800; however, in the fashion typical of London merchants, the firm of Perry and Lane did not own or even charter their own fleet but rather bought shares – a sixteenth or thirty-second – in ships owned by others, in 1719 employing a total of some fifty ships altogether.[24]

Dekker's exaggerations are not gratuitous. Whereas the historic Simon Eyre traded successfully for more than a decade before being elected sheriff and for a quarter of a century before his mayoralty, the fictitious Simon Eyre's rise is necessarily more rapid, and for that to be even dramatically plausible, Simon had to achieve instant wealth. Dramatic compression requires Dekker's hero to pass from a mere shoemaker to sheriff and then lord mayor in time to succeed Sir Roger Oatley at the end of the latter's year as the head of London's government. But while the speed of the rise is dramatic licence, the progress from wealth to office was virtually inevitable. London lacked a hereditary patriciate, and given the extraordinarily high rate of urban mortality, neither the London elite nor the urban population as a whole was able to reproduce itself biologically – not for want of trying, for most Londoners had large families, and Dekker's Eyre, still childless though eager for children at the advanced age of fifty-six, is clearly exceptional. Nevertheless, fewer than half the children born in the poorer parishes of London survived to the age of fifteen, and the expectation of life at birth was only about thirty-five. Because apprentices were not permitted to marry, and freedom in a company and citizenship could not be achieved before the age of twenty-four, Londoners married late, women on average in their twenty-fourth year, men in their twenty-eighth. The consequence of late marriages and high infant and child mortality was that Londoners did not reproduce themselves, and the City grew – in

---

[23] These calculations are based on figures from T. S. Willan, *Studies in Elizabethan Foreign Trade* (Manchester, 1959), p. 315.

[24] Jacob M. Price, *Perry of London: A Family and Firm on the Seaborne Frontier, 1615–1753* (Cambridge, 1992), pp. 21, 41–2. For the value of imports and exports to and from London in the later seventeenth century, see W. E. Minchinton, *The Growth of English Overseas Trade in the 17th and 18th Centuries* (1969), pp. 96–7; for a summary of the imports and exports of the firm of Marescoe and David between 1664 and 1678, see Henry Roseveare, *Markets and Merchants of the Late Seventeenth Century: The Marescoe-David Letters, 1668–1680* (Oxford, 1987), pp. 577–8.

Dekker's lifetime from perhaps 70,000 to 250,000 – as a result of constant and massive immigration: for example, more than 80 per cent of the young men apprenticed in the period came from further away than the Home Counties.[25] Given such a demographic regime, London's rulers were an oligarchy of wealth, not birth. Unhappy Hammon is the one character in the play who is presented to us as a second generation Londoner, the inheritor of an independent income, and Hammon, despite his wealth, does not succeed in marrying either Mayor Oatley's daughter or Ralph's supposed widow, and he exits vowing not to marry at all.

Great wealth did not automatically lead to high office, but London's ruling elite was drawn from among the wealthiest of the mercantile inhabitants. The City's *cursus honorum* normally led from nomination by a ward to the bench of aldermen to election to the shrievalty, but serving as sheriff first, as Simon Eyre does in Dekker's play, was not unheard of and occurred when all the eligible aldermen had already served in that office.[26] Once elected for one of the twenty-six wards, a London alderman who lived long enough could predict when his election to the mayoralty would take place, for that office normally went to the senior alderman who had not yet served. Eyre's accelerated election as lord mayor is explained by Lacy (4.3.15–16; 15.15–16)[27] as the consequence of the 'death of certain aldermen', presumably those junior aldermen who stood in seniority between Eyre and Mayor Oatley. Great wealth was seen as a prerequisite, for service as a sheriff, alderman or mayor was a source of expense, not profit, a fact that Mayor Oatley acknowledges (3.1.71–2; 9.71–2), when he remarks that Eyre, newly made sheriff, 'shall spend some of his thousands now'. It was possible to escape the highest office, but escape too had its price. When Alderman Masham asked for his discharge from the aldermanry in 1594 on the purported grounds (he lived another six years) that he was 'grievously tormented with gout, colic and stone, unwieldiness and disability of body', his request was granted but at the cost of a stiff fine of £600.[28] Dekker's madcap shoemaker is no Masham, for Eyre not only accepts high office but uses it in exemplary fashion, feasting the apprentice shoemakers and then the king, suing for a royal pardon for Lacy, and endowing Leadenhall as a legacy to his city.

Yet for all the rollicking good humour of the play, its happy ending and benign view of City life, *The Shoemaker's Holiday* does little to hide or deny the tensions of urban life. Indeed it dramatises these tensions.

---

[25] For the basis of these demographic generalisations, see Roger Finlay, *Population and Metropolis: The Demography of London 1580–1650* (Cambridge, 1981), passim.

[26] Frank Freeman Foster, *The Politics of Stability: A Portrait of the Rulers in Elizabethan London* (1977), p. 61.

[27] Textual references in this essay are to Fredson Bowers, ed., *The Dramatic Works of Thomas Dekker*, vol. I (Cambridge, 1953), giving act, scene and line numbers; and to R. L. Smallwood and Stanley Wells, eds., *The Shoemaker's Holiday* (Manchester, 1979), giving scene and line numbers.

[28] CLRO, Rep. 23, fo. 146, as quoted in Foster, *The Politics of Stability*, p. 65.

Entrance into the civic society of London was through membership in a
craft, trade or mystery, and freedom in one of the guilds or livery companies
had long been a prerequisite for citizenship. The vast majority of working
males entered urban life and came to their freedom as a consequence of
apprenticeship, and symbolic of the connection between company and city
was the fact that an apprentice's indentures were enrolled both by the
company clerk and by the City chamberlain. It was possible to achieve
one's freedom by patrimony (i.e., inheritance) or purchase, but only a
small percentage came to their freedom and citizenship in this fashion.
For example, on 15 July 1575, the Carpenters' Company admitted ten
new freemen, nine by apprenticeship, and one by purchase or redemption;
for the year following 14 September 1601, the company admitted thirty-five
to the freedom, thirty-one by apprenticeship, three by patrimony, and one
by purchase.[29] Ben Jonson was free of the Tylers' and Bricklayers' Company by patrimony and briefly exercised his freedom before becoming a
soldier.[30] Redemption or purchase permitted foreign or stranger merchants
and tradesmen to buy and sell in London freely, and it was precisely the
lack of that freedom that forced the Dutch captain in Dekker's play to
seek a citizen broker in order to sell his cargo. However, while a company's
freedom was a necessary prerequisite to participation in the City's economic
and political life, all freemen citizens were not equal.

The Shoemaker's Holiday shows us two kinds of inequality. Hodge, Firk
and Ralph are all freemen cordwainers and citizens of London, but they
are also journeymen who call Simon Eyre master. In the terminology of
the times they are 'covenanted servants', which implied that they had
entered into a contract with their master, normally for a year at a time,
to serve their master for a specified wage to be paid at the conclusion of
their service. Firk's prickly belligerency, his insistence on his rights and
his willingness to walk off the job, when Eyre hesitates to hire Lacy
disguised as the shoemaker Hans (1.4.44–61; 4.50–71), is a function at
least in part of his anomalous position – at once a freeman and citizen
but at the same time a servant living in his master's household. Hodge,
on inheriting Eyre's shop at the end of the play, achieves the real-life
ambition of all London artisans: to cease to be a servant and to become
the master of one's own shop, capable of taking on apprentices, and, if
successful, of moving up from the yeomanry to the livery of one's company.

    The second inequality is the stuff of one of the two major social dramas
of the play, the clash between the shoemakers' world and that of Hammon
and Mayor Oatley. Dekker dramatises the gulf between their two worlds by
introducing Eyre and his journeymen at work in Eyre's shop in the City,

---

[29] GLMS 4329/2, Worshipful Company of Carpenters: Wardens' Account Book 1573–1594, no fo., entry
dated 15 July 1575; GLMS 4329/3, Worshipful Company of Carpenters: Court Book 1600–1618, entries from
14 Sept., 1601, to 6 Sept., 1602.
[30] GLMS 3051/1, Tylers' and Bricklayers' Company, Quarterage Book 1588–1616, entry for St Mark's Day,
1599.

while Hammon is introduced, not in the world of work, but rather in the world of the hunt. To be sure, the audience sees Hammon and his companions hunting not in their own deer park – they are City gentlemen, not true country gentry – but in suburban London at Old Ford, where Mayor Oatley has his summer mansion. In actuality these suburban retreats were not so much a place at which the successful merchants of London could play at being gentry, as they were a means to escape the polluted air of the City which in the hot, humid summers was thought to carry disease. Nevertheless, in the play Old Ford serves to contrast the urban world of the journeymen shoemakers with the leisured world of pastoral romance played out in suburban Hackney. The contrast is heightened by the fact that we first see the shoemakers suddenly made serious by the conscription of Ralph for the French wars, a scene in which the social responsibility of the citizens is contrasted with the helplessness of Lacy and the King's captains, who cannot release a pressed journeyman, even though he is newly wed. Just how different is the social world of the City gentlemen is shown not only by Hammon's appearance as a hunter, pursuing the sport of the gentry and aristocracy, but even more by the rhetorical skill displayed by both Rose and Hammon in their exchange of rhymed lines in which the hunting of the hart becomes the hunting of Rose's heart. Rose's maid Sybil, who is equivalent to Firk in the lord mayor's household, mocks the couple's romantic sentiments with plebeian realism, their elevated pretensions having been deflated for the audience by the fact that Sybil and the other servants have already dispatched the hunted deer with a very plebeian flail and pitchfork, butchered the beast for the mayor's table, and, surely significantly, 'unhorned him' (2.2.2–9; 6.2–11).

One cannot help wondering how Dekker's audience reacted to this scene which presented such a direct assault on aristocratic sensibilities. Some years earlier Lord Burghley had complained to the lord mayor that the queen and the nobility had been offended by the 'excessive spending of venison and other victuals' at company feasts, a reprimand to which the lord mayor bowed, leading the Common Council to forbid the consumption of venison in company halls. Nevertheless, courtiers, who were regularly invited to the great company feasts, and the City folk knew that this interdict was flouted with some regularity. Just six months after Dekker's play was first staged, the Fishmongers' Company, by no means the wealthiest or proudest of the livery companies, recorded the arrangements for their election day feast, and included baked venison in the menu for the first mess between the roast goose and the boiled pike.[31]

Hammon, for all his graces, belongs to the world of the City, and not to the wider world of the landed aristocracy represented by the Earl of Lincoln and his nephew Lacy, and it is this that makes him such an

---

[31] J. H. Hexter, *Reappraisals in History* (2nd ed., Chicago and London, 1979), p. 98; GLMS 5570/1, Fishmongers' Company Court Minutes, 9 June 1600, p. 243; see also p. 313.

acceptable potential son-in-law to Mayor Oatley. In contrast to Lacy, who is gentle by birth and lineage, but whom Oatley views as hopelessly profligate, Hammon is 'a proper gentleman', by which Oatley means that he is 'a citizen by birth, fairly allied' (2.2.58–9; 6.60–3). It is a prejudice endorsed and shared by Simon Eyre, who, while not urging Hammon's suit, nevertheless advises marriage within one's class: 'A courtier? – wash, go by! Stand not upon pishery-pashery. . . . No, my fine mouse, marry me with a Gentleman Grocer like my Lord Mayor your father. A grocer is a sweet trade, plums, plums!' And Eyre completes this disquisition on proper marriage partnerships by insisting that 'had I a son or daughter should marry out of the generation and blood of the shoemakers, he should pack' (3.3.40–6; 11.42–9).

Hammon himself shares these urban prejudices, for, disappointed by Rose's rejection of his suit, he does not turn to an alternative among the daughters of the country gentry but rather to another City marriage, one with the supposedly widowed Jane, whom he discovers keeping shop in Ralph's absence. For, unlike the country gentry and aristocracy, who were constrained in their choice of marriage partners by their need for powerful alliances and an heir to perpetuate a lineage and inherit a landed estate, the citizen was little constrained by the considerations of family and lineage, and the bulk of his property, even when inherited rather than earned (as in Hammon's case), tended to be personal rather than real. Hence, Hammon is free to reject 'enforced love', when Oatley offers to force Rose into an unwanted marriage, and, since, as he says, 'it is not wealth I seek; / I have enough', he is free to seek a love match with Jane (3.1.50–5; 9.50–5). The stark contrast between the mercenary world of the real aristocracy, where marriages were frequently arranged for dynastic reasons of wealth and power, and the plebeian marriages of the City, where marriages were based on choice and affection, is drawn more sharply in the play than in real life, but it was a contrast that Dekker's audience would have recognised as approximating social reality.[32]

Jane, pictured in these later scenes as an independent entrepreneur, free to accept or reject Hammon's suit, would not have struck Dekker's audience as anomalous. Unlike spinsters, who could not open a shop except in partnership with a citizen father or brother, wives and widows of freemen were not so limited. Jane's resort to shopkeeping is in fact anticipated in the first scene. When Ralph is marched off in Lacy's regiment, Jane, in despair, asks what she is to do, and Firk promptly replies, 'be not idle', to which Eyre adds that Jane 'must spin, must card, must work', naming in the process those parts of textile manufacturing largely in the hands of

---

[32] Lawrence Stone, *Family, Sex and Marriage in England 1500–1800* (New York and London, 1977), pp. 178–94; Ralph A. Houlbrooke, *The English Family 1450–1700* (London and New York, 1984), pp. 63–95; John R. Gillis, *For Better, For Worse: British Marriages, 1600 to the Present* (Oxford, 1985), pp. 21–3, 85–9.

women (1.1.207–9; 1.215–16). Widows of citizens in particular were privileged, and although most young widows soon remarried, widows had the right to keep a shop, to buy and sell, and to hire journeymen and indenture apprentices.[33]

Nevertheless, although a wealthy citizen might choose to woo a widowed shopkeeper, preferring love to social and economic advantage, there was a clear gulf between the world of artisan shoemakers and that of the wealthy merchant members of the Grocers' Company. Oatley patronises Eyre and his journeymen at Old Ford, and they in turn are properly deferential to 'his lordship', just as they are on familiar terms with the maid, Sybil. However, all freemen, whether Cordwainers or Grocers, were citizens, and City politesse wears thin late in the play where the journeymen shoemakers confront Hammon on his way to an anticipated marriage with Jane. When accosted by Hodge, Hammon replies, 'unmannerly rude slave, what's that to thee?', the familiar form of address being doubly and deliberately insulting, and yet although the shoemakers bridle at being called 'villains', Hodge recognises the social distinction by addressing Hammon's party as 'my masters and gentlemen' (5.2.23–30; 18.26–35). As the quarrel progresses, such acknowledgement of social difference is submerged in the general equality of all freemen; 'Master Hammon' becomes 'Sirrah Hammon', and Firk, always the most outspoken of the shoemakers, addresses Hammon as an equal, deserving no title: 'Look not, Hammon; leer not. I'll firk you!'

Shortly after, the shoemakers confront Oatley and the Earl of Lincoln; here the social gulf is too great to be bridged by any rude familiarity. This time there is no direct challenge to visible authority, no 'cry clubs for prentices'. Even so, when Lincoln addresses Firk as 'villain', Firk punctiliously denies the implication of unfreedom in the appellation (villain, villein, or serf) and slyly replies, 'Punish the journeyman villain, but not the journeyman shoemaker' (5.2.145–7; 18.159–61). Nevertheless, if a citizen might stand on his freedom, the difference in social power between the mere citizen and a member of the titled aristocracy was immense, and the confrontation between the thwarted Lincoln and the now Lord Mayor Eyre, who champions the marriage of Lacy and Rose, could not be resolved by a contest of power – the inequality was too great – but only by the mediation of the King himself. And the King does not so much deny Lincoln's charge that Rose's 'blood is too too base', as find an exception to the accepted concept of hierarchy in the notion that 'love respects no blood, / Cares not for difference of birth or state' (5.5.102–4; 21.104–6).

---

[33] Vivien Brodsky, 'Widows in Late Elizabethan London: Remarriage, Economic Opportunity and Family Orientations', in *The World We Have Gained*, ed. Lloyd Bonfield, Richard Smith and Keith Wrightson (Oxford, 1986), pp. 122–54.

Nevertheless, despite the play's happy ending in which these social clashes are resolved, and despite its surface geniality, it seems profoundly hostile to the landed aristocracy. For all the animus between the shoe-makers and Oatley and Hammon, artisans and merchants are at one in their hostility to the nobility. In Oatley's eyes courtiers 'will in silks and gay apparel spend / More in one year than I am worth by far' (1.1.13–14; 1.13–14), a sentiment echoed in a later scene where Eyre remarks that 'courtiers' are 'silken fellows', whose 'inner linings are torn' (3.3.41–2; 11.43–5). Oatley's and Eyre's contempt is that of the producers of wealth for a class of social parasites. Like Thomas Deloney's *Jack of Newbury*, Dekker's play creates a world in which the traditional aristocracy has lost its social function as a warrior class. In fact, it seems a class that has lost its attractiveness even to its privileged members. Lacy avoids the field of battle to pursue his plebeian love, and it is Ralph, the journeyman shoemaker, who must leave the comforts of a new marriage to defend England's honour on the fields of France. Lacy in turn redeems himself not by an act of martial valour but by engaging in the trade of cordwainer, the 'gentle craft'. As a consequence, in the final scene, Simon Eyre, now lord mayor, can defend Lacy – not as the traitorous nephew of a peer, a traitor to both his class and his king, as Lincoln views him, but rather, as Eyre sees him, as 'my fine journeyman here, Roland Lacy' (5.5.121–2; 21. 123–4), a man made acceptable again, at least in City terms, by honest labour. And what is the audience to make of Eyre's repeated reference to 'the gentle craft', the 'gentle trade', and 'gentlemen shoe-makers', if it is not an assertion of a new gentility to be gained not by birth but by honest labour? Is there not a suggestion in the final scene that the King and the City are now the dominant forces in the land, and is this not implied in the last lines where the King pauses to 'revel it at home' with the shoemakers before returning to his war in France?

Theatre as Holiday

David Bevington

If we measure Dekker's *The Shoemaker's Holiday* in terms of the social and economic issues it explores, the play begins to sound like a dramatised social 'survey of London'. Social conflict between the nobility and the London bourgeoisie, romantic notions of marriage across social boundaries, solidarity among artisans and apprentices in the London guilds, resentment of foreign labour from the Lowlands, labour-management relations between shopkeepers and their restive employees, struggles for mastery in the selection of lord mayor among the more powerful guilds, profiteering and other economic sharp practices, patriotism and resistance towards war with Catholic states on the Continent, problems of domestic and economic readjustment for returning war veterans, sexual rivalries between gentlemen and London citizens, Protestant moral attitudes about chastity in marriage and the 'vanity' of sartorial extravagance, appeals to an idealised notion of monarchy as a buffer against social conflict – the wonder is that Dekker managed to include so much in a lucid, cheery, fast-moving, five-act entertainment.

Such inclusiveness raises a number of critical issues about the play. How are its various themes related to one another in the structure of the drama, and how does Dekker go about controlling tone in his adjudication of social conflict? How, that is, does he balance social and economic antagonisms, appealing to his London audience while at the same time exploring contrastive points of view? Is the play, in Stephen Greenblatt's terms, one of containment in which the potentially destructive energies of social conflict are allowed their moment of 'holiday' only to subside thereafter into business as usual,[1] or is a more revisionary and even rebellious process of change at work? Such questions lend complexity to the very notion of 'holiday' celebrated in the play's title.

I will argue that, among other things, Dekker's play is about drama itself as holiday, about the ways in which drama engages with social conflict

---

[1] Stephen Greenblatt, 'Invisible Bullets', in *Shakespearean Negotiations* (Berkeley, 1988), pp. 21–65. David Scott Kastan, 'Workshop and as Playhouse: Comedy and Commerce in *The Shoemaker's Holiday*', *Studies in Philology*, 84 (1987), 324–37, argues that 'social dislocations are rationalized and contained in a reassuring vision of coherence and community' (p. 325). I have been considerably influenced by Kastan's essay.

in such a way as to contain and simultaneously liberate. Containment and social change are not as incompatible as the terms might suggest; both can go on in the holiday world of drama. By literally acting out and resolving social conflict in the theatre, *The Shoemaker's Holiday* gives substance to 'play' in its many forms – as make-believe, reenactment, and enabling mirror of social reality. The word 'contain' is similarly ambivalent, suggesting as it does that Dekker's play can act as an escape valve in Greenblatt's sense and yet also embody a social process. In other words, containment need not be as 'containing' as Greenblatt would have us believe. This play encourages audience members to feel reconciled to the circumstances of their daily lives, but only by providing them with a partly fantastic vision of how to make the most of their opportunities, to prosper with the changing times. The medium is the message in Dekker's 'festive' comedy; his strategy of having it both ways with satire and romantic idealism is a perfect emblem for his age of how drama can 'negotiate' its complex interaction with the society on which it must depend but which it can nonetheless also criticise.[2]

The play begins, appropriately, neither with shoemakers in their shops nor with romantic lovers, but with two wary old men staking out their respective claims. The lord mayor, Sir Roger Oatley, is plainly introduced as an anticipatory foil to the play's once and future mayor, Simon Eyre. We see in Oatley the kind of mayor one might realistically expect to find in late medieval and sixteenth-century London: calculating, outwardly polite in a frosty way but chary of commitment, proud of his station, possessive of his daughter and coolly contemptuous of those courtiers who might aspire to steal his daughter's heart to repair the ravages of their own extravagance. 'Poor citizens must not with courtiers wed, / Who will in silks and gay apparel spend / More in one year than I am worth by far' (1.1.12–14; 1.12–14),[3] he protests to the Earl of Lincoln. Oatley's characterisation of himself as a 'poor citizen' is a bit of wry and hypocritical self-deprecation used in addressing a great lord; in fact, Oatley is rich and proud of it. He is, we learn later, a 'Gentleman Grocer' (3.3.43; 11.46), meaning that he belongs to one of London's most powerful guilds. Firk's contemptuous reference to him as 'Sir Roger Oatmeal' (4.1.30; 13.34) bespeaks the envy and resentment that shoemakers must have felt towards this pillar of the London bourgeois establishment; the shoemakers,

---

[2] See Greenblatt, 'The Circulation of Social Energy', in *Shakespearean Negotiations*, pp. 1–20.

[3] For the convenience of readers wishing to consult a play that is sometimes edited in five acts and sometimes in sequentially numbered scenes only, textual references to the play in this essay are double: by act, scene, and line, Fredson Bowers, ed., *The Dramatic Works of Thomas Dekker* (Cambridge, 1953), vol. 1; and, by scene and line, R. L. Smallwood and Stanley Wells, eds., *The Shoemaker's Holiday*, Revels Plays (Manchester, 1979). The idea of 'festive' comedy as containment is lucidly set forth in C. L. Barber, *Shakespeare's Festive Comedy: A Study of Dramatic Form in Relation to Social Custom* (Princeton, 1959). See also Mikhail M. Bakhtin, *Rabelais and His World*, trans. H. Iswolsky (Cambridge, Mass., 1968) and Michael D. Bristol, *Carnival and Theatre: Plebeian Culture and the Structure of Authority in Renaissance England* (1985).

as Paul Seaver shows in the companion to this present essay, never in fact succeeded in promoting one of their own to the office of mayor.

Oatley's opponent in the play's opening contest of wills is Sir Hugh Lacy, Earl of Lincoln, caricature of the haughty nobleman, who views the prospect of a marriage between his spendthrift nephew Rowland Lacy and the daughter of a London bourgeois with about as much enthusiasm as he has bestowed on young Lacy's improvident whim of apprenticing himself to the shoemakers' trade. 'Then seek, my lord, some honest citizen / To wed your daughter to' (1.1.36–7; 1.36–7) is his condescending advice to Oatley.

Neither uncle nor father, then, favours the love match between young Lacy and Oatley's daughter Rose. The two old men concur in a plan to ship young Lacy off to France in command of soldiers destined for the king's wars on the Continent. So much for patriotic idealism, it would seem, and so much for romantic idealism as well. This cynical pact between landed nobleman and London bourgeois, aimed at sustaining their traditional enmity rather than overcoming it, establishes a structural bond between two central elements of the play, for Lincoln and Oatley are hereby set up as blocking characters in both a romantic and socially realistic sense. They are visibly recognisable as the parental figures of Plautine and neo-classical comedy whose function it is to oppose young love on fiscal and dynastic grounds in the name of patriarchal family interests. Thus their opposition sets in motion, and anticipates the eventual resolution of, a plot of young lovers who must devise a 'trick to catch the old ones' and thus finally confirm the romantic (and socially subversive) proposition that 'love respects no blood, / Cares not for difference of birth or state' (5.5.103–4; 21.105–6). At the same time, because Lincoln and Oatley are particularised as landed nobleman and London merchant, their simmering duel establishes the play's fascination with social conflict and contests of power. Their aim is to keep apart the social groups they represent. They resist the play's festive idealism, which celebrates romantic love as a potentially upsetting force in a hierarchical social world.

In the spirit of productively ambivalent aims, Dekker's manipulation of point of view in the opening action is nicely balanced. Lincoln and Oatley are the blocking characters of the play who must eventually be foiled, and accordingly are shown to be wily and hypocritical. 'Well, fox, I understand your subtlety' (1.1.38; 1.38), comments the lord mayor aside on the gambits of his patrician opponent. Oatley's readiness to suspect hypocrisy in his opponent springs in part from his own skill at telling bland lies, as when he later protests to Lincoln that he has the earl's best interests at heart: 'Not that I scorn your nephew, but in love / I bear your honour, lest your noble blood / Should by my mean worth be dishonoréd.' This gambit deserves the acid aside it receives from Lincoln: 'How far the churl's tongue wanders from his heart!' (4.4.19–22; 16.19–22). For his part, Lincoln is equitably calm in his direct dealings with Oatley, only to comment to his nephew, after the mayor's departure, 'I know this churl even in the height of scorn / Doth hate the mixture of his blood with thine. / I pray thee, do thou so' (1.1.78–80; 1.78–80). The advice is cynical in its worldly practicality. At the same time, Dekker invites his audience to consider whether there is not something in what these two old gentlemen have to say. Young Lacy has indeed squandered all his money abroad; 'A verier unthrift lives not in the world' (l. 17), as the disappearance of over a thousand pounds in one half year (ll. 32–3) plainly attests. Shoemaking as an expedient is certainly what we would call reverse social mobility, however it may lend lustre to the trade by suggesting that there are worse ways for nobles to spend their time.

Similarly, Lacy's attitude towards military service is not perhaps wholly consistent and admirable. He protests that 'Where honour beckons, shame attends delay' (l. 97), but is ready enough to dodge the draft when romance or other opportunities beckon. This mix of attitudes is not unlike that of Hodge, Firk and the rest of the shoemakers, either; Hodge is wholly resistant at first to the idea of Rafe's going into service ('Rafe, thou'rt a gull, by this hand, an thou goest', 1.1.171; 1.179), but collapses only moments later into patriotic stereotypes when the departure seems inevitable ('Thou'rt a gull, by my stirrup, if thou dost not go', 1.1.181; 1.189).[4] Simon Eyre is ready enough to buy his apprentices out of being called up (1.1.131–3; 1.134–7), since trained men are expensive to replace, but he beats the drum in his public utterances when his efforts at polite bribery fail.

> Well, let him go. He's a proper shot. Let him vanish. Peace, Jane. Dry up thy tears; they'll make his powder dankish. Take him, brave men. Hector of Troy was an hackney to him; Hercules and Termagant, scoundrels; Prince Arthur's Round Table – by the Lord of Ludgate – ne'er fed such a tall, such a dapper swordsman.
>
> (1.1.162–7; 1.169–74)

War invokes a comically inconsistent response, and thus establishes at the start of this play a tone of mixed amusement and admiration that applies in varying degrees to all social groups.

A common denominator in social representation, then, is that rich and poor alike have their foibles, their hypocrisies, their self interest. Drama provides this common ground by creating dialogue *in utramque partem*.[5] Even while *The Shoemaker's Holiday* invites traditional sympathy for the young and relatively dispossessed, it crosses that sympathy with a perception that Dekker's protagonists are not very dispossessed after all (Hans

---

[4] Some editors, including Bowers and the Revels editors, emend Rafe's first remonstrance to Ralph by adding a crucial 'not': 'an thou goest not'. The editors thus miss, in my view, all the fun of Hodge's inconsistency of attitude toward patriotic duty, an inconsistency that parallels Eyre's own. The word 'not' first appears in Q4, a quarto that does appear to have some manuscript authority, so that the reading is defensible.

[5] The term is definitively studied in Joel Altman, *The Tudor Play of Mind: Rhetorical Inquiry and the Development of Elizabethan Drama* (Berkeley, 1978).

LXIII.

Sutor.

The Shoo-maker.

Plate 7 A depiction of a shoemaker, from Johann Amos Comenius, *Orbis sensualium pictus*, 1672

is the nephew of an earl, Simon Eyre is already a prospering merchant) and that they are not as different from autocratic authority figures as a romantic view might suppose.

Simon Eyre is the major success story of *The Shoemaker's Holiday*. His rise to glory designedly appeals to the dreams of London's mercantile population. Eyre owns a thriving business, and is admired and liked by his workmen, who see his success as the pathway to their own advancement. Quick promotion to the rank of master sheriff and then alderman gives Eyre the opportunity to savour the advantages of political influence and sartorial splendour that attend upon his new office. 'Here's a seal ring, and I have sent for a guarded [i.e., embroidered] gown and a damask cassock,' he tells his men. 'See where it comes.' Indeed, just at this point the Boy enters *'with a velvet coat and an alderman's gown'*. His men avidly applaud: 'Ha, ha! My master will be as proud as a dog in a doublet, all in beaten damask and velvet,' crows Firk, while Hodge puts more stress on the sheer power of title: 'I warrant you, there's few in the City but will give you the wall, and come upon you with the "Right Worshipful"' (2.3.93–106; 7.107–20). In short order, Eyre is elected to the 'worshipful vocation of Master Sheriff' (3.2.4–5; 10.5), and soon enters as such onstage, *'wearing a gold chain'* (3.2.127.1; 10.145.1).

His men share his dream and revel vicariously in his success, as presumably their counterparts in a London audience would also do. 'To it, pell-mell', says Hodge, 'that we may live to be lord mayors, or aldermen at least' (4.1.3–4; 13.3–4). The dream comes true, at least for Eyre, with all the sumptuous splendour that should attend such an elevation. 'By the Lord, my Lord Mayor is a most brave man,' exclaims Hodge. 'Let's feed and be fat with my lord's bounty.' All 'good fellows' are to 'dine at my Lord Mayor's cost today' (5.2.183–7; 18.201–6). Stage directions and dialogue are unusually pointed in their specific references to gowns, coats, gold chains, rings and the like, along with the various delicacies (venison pasties, fritters, pancakes, beef, hens and oranges, collops and eggs, and still more) that are to be consumed at the Lord Mayor's feast. Even the King is impressed: 'Is our Lord Mayor of London such a gallant?' (5.3.1; 19.1). Simon Eyre and his fellows have all lived 'as merry as an emperor' (5.5.143; 21.145). The proud implication is that though king and emperor may enjoy more wealth and power, no one lives as well as Eyre, the quintessential London craftsman.

What is more, all this success has come to one who gives the appearance of shunning ambition – the ambition, at any rate, of turning his back on his mercantile origins and on those brethren of his trade who have accompanied him to the top. He is as loyal and expansive towards his crew of shoemakers as Tamburlaine is towards Theridamas, Techelles and Usumcasane. 'Prince am I none, yet am I princely born' is his perennial cry, and he often explains what that means in terms of social and economic origins: 'as being the sole son of a shoemaker' (2.3.42–3; 7.49–50). He is, in his followers' eyes, the 'brave lord of incomprehensible good-fellowship', an 'eternal credit to us of the Gentle Craft' (5.2.200–9; 18.219–29).

Eyre seems to deserve his good fortune because he is so ebullient, jolly, irrepressible. 'Care and cold lodging brings white hairs', he admonishes the King with the kind of sententious lecturing that London's royal entries and other street pageants sometimes used in offering advice to the monarchy. 'My sweet Majesty, let care vanish. Cast it upon thy nobles. It will make thee look always young, like Apollo, and cry "Hump!"' Then, again, the refrain: 'Prince am I none, yet am I princely born' (5.5.30–4; 21.32–6). The saying has a particular resonance when spoken to a king, for it suggests the kind of defensive mercantile pride that London manifested towards the court even while it acknowledged the king's authority.

Eyre is, moreover, the presiding genius of the 'holiday' evoked in the play's title. The play of which he is the dominating personality is *The Shoemaker's Holiday* or *The Shoemakers' Holiday*, either and both; no modern spelling rendition can capture the perfect ambivalence of the original *The Shoemakers Holiday*.[6] He is in himself a kind of metonymy for the Gentle Craft and for the city in which it flourishes. And since Eyre embodies not

---

[6] As David Scott Kastan points out, in his 'Workshop and/as Playhouse', pp. 324–37, editors are divided on the placement of the apostrophe in the title: Fredson Bowers's edition argues for *Shoemakers'*, while Smallwood and Wells, in their Revels edition, argue for *Shoemaker's*.

only London but its merriment and spirit of holiday, he might seem to have a special kind of authorial claim in this play as spokesman for what drama can best do: celebrate saturnalian release and its purging of social discontent through Eyre's attainment of his own dream. Certainly in Dekker's source, Deloney's *The Gentle Craft*, Eyre is an unabashed hero in the author's eyes, and Dekker acknowledges his *hommage* to Deloney by his refrain-like references to 'the Gentle Craft'. What's more, paying members of Dekker's audience presumably read their Deloney with a straight face, much as they flocked to Thomas Heywood's quaintly revisionist plays (*If You Know Not Me You Know Nobody*, etc.) that presented the building of the Royal Exchange, the rising of the prentices and similarly bourgeois events as the milestones of a new view of British history.

Yet Dekker is not content to idolise Simon Eyre. From a scene in which Lacy, Firk and Hodge encounter the skipper of a Dutch vessel laden with a valuable cargo from the eastern Mediterranean (2.3.1–22; 7.1–27), we learn how this mayor-to-be has garnered some of his wealth.[7] The ship's contents are luxury goods, the very opposite of the shoemakers' normal stock in trade – sugar, civet, almonds, cambric and the like. For reasons left unexplained (perhaps, as Paul Seaver suggests, his not enjoying the 'freedom' of one of the guilds or livery companies that would enable him to sell his cargo), the 'merchant owner of the ship dares not show his head'. Eyre is ready to act as middleman on terms very favourable to himself: by arranging a 'reasonable day of payment' some time in the future, Eyre will be able to 'sell the wares by that time, and be an huge gainer himself'. Hans acts as go-between because of his conversancy in Dutch and as provider of the 'earnest' money. Eyre evidently incurs no risk at all other than the unspoken hazard of dealing with a foreign merchant shipper and an ambiguously irregular purchase. Eyre is diversifying his portfolio, it seems, in the spirit of many a multinational corporation. Firk and Hodge are morally neutral in their comments: they are ready to help, glad to see the prospect of money, but still circumspect rather than defiantly gleeful. The dominant impression is not of villainy but of business-as-usual. Eyre is doing something legal and familiar, though on the shady side from the point of view of moralists who inveighed against this kind of profiteering in their pamphleteering and on stage (as in Thomas Lupton's *All for Money*, *c.* 1577). The deal is potentially huge in its profitability, and is a big step for Eyre. Paul Seaver in his essay makes clear how common was the practice but how totally fantastic the numbers are in this case: these goods are 'worth the lading of two or three hundred thousand pounds', much more than a single ship cargo could be worth and more than a shoemaker could guarantee.

---

[7] Discussed in Kastan, 'Workshop and/as Playhouse'.

Eyre is often free with money, but in ways that can be construed as calculating. Faced one day with a small insurrection in his shop, he expansively sends the Boy off to the Boar's Head to 'fill me a dozen cans of beer for my journeymen', only to add, in a cautionary aside intended to be heard by this same Boy, 'An the knave fills any more than two, he pays for them.' Then, once more, aloud, 'A dozen cans of beer for my journeymen!' (2.3.67–71; 7.77–82). The celebratory feast he bestows on his followers when he is chosen mayor employs somewhat the same pragmatic largesse. The feast is gargantuan, by all accounts, but Dekker's dramatic emphasis is less on the sheer sybaritic delight than on how the feast celebrates Eyre's greatness as the lord of misrule on 'Saint Hugh's Holiday' (5.2.206; 18.226). Eyre's banquet is a potlatch destined to show that he is more munificent than anybody except perhaps the King. Modern anthropologists have taught us to see a calculating dimension in most gift-giving, at least on an epic scale.[8] The point here is that Dekker seems consciously and amusedly aware of the art of gift-giving in Elizabethan London. However droll and beneficent Eyre may seem, he knows exactly what he is doing with his gestures of largesse.

The Shoemaker's Holiday is studiously circumspect as to the means by which Eyre becomes lord mayor. Outwardly he appears to do so by financial success and charisma. But how, one wonders, does he replace Oatley, that powerful gentleman grocer? Oatley is still very much in evidence after Eyre's elevation to the mayoralty, and still in cahoots with Lincoln, though now demoted in style of address to plain 'Sir Roger Oatley' (5.2.161; 18.175). Oatley's animus against Eyre is partly occasioned by Eyre's daring to stand in defence of Hans's marriage to Rose ''Gainst any that shall seek to cross the match' (5.2.154; 18.168), but one surmises that political rivalry may be a motive as well. Oatley's resentment of Eyre's rising fortunes is of long standing. Ironically, Oatley is responsible for Eyre's having been named master sheriff, in the hope that the financial burden of being sent for 'to the Guildhall' will force Eyre to 'spend some of his thousands now' (3.1.71–2; 9.71–2). The financial cost of being alderman or sheriff is real enough: in the real London world of the 1590s, merchants elected to these posts were willing to accept fines of £500 to £600 to escape the financial burdens of office, which might run as high as £1,200 to £1,500.[9] Yet in Dekker's play world, Eyre survives this

---

[8] On potlatch rituals, see Marcel Mauss, *The Gift: The Form and Reason for Exchange in Archaic Societies*, trans. W. D. Halls (New York, 1990); Claude Lévi-Strauss, *The Elementary Structures of Kinship* (rev. edn, 1969); Helen Codere, *Fighting with Property: A Study of Kwakiutl Potlatching and Warfare 1792–1930* (Seattle, 1950); Abraham Rosman and Paula G. Rubel, *Feasting with Mine Enemy: Rank and Exchange among Northwest Coast Societies* (New York, 1971); Philip Drucker and Robert F. Heizer, *To Make My Name Good: A Reexamination of the Southern Kwakiutl Potlatch* (Berkeley, 1967); and Forrest E. LaViolette, *The Struggle for Survival: Indian Cultures and the Protestant Ethic in British Columbia* (Toronto, 1961).

[9] Frank Freeman Foster, *The Politics of Stability: A Portrait of the Rulers in Elizabethan London* (1977), pp. 61–2, 65 and 147–8.

economic challenge and goes on to use his offices as a power base for further advancement, so that Oatley is eventually hoist on his own petard.

The rivalry intensifies as Eyre moves up the aldermanic ladder. When Rafe learns from Hodge that 'seven of the aldermen be dead, or very sick', Rafe sees the likely outcome: 'then my Master Eyre will come quickly to be Lord Mayor' (4.1.34–8; 13.39–43). Eyre is by this time one of the aldermen himself. How would new vacancies insure his own rise to the mayoralty, given the continued presence on the council of Oatley? Dekker here seems to be relying on the City politics of his own time, as one might expect. One of the two sheriffs was almost invariably the oldest junior alderman who had not yet served in that office, and so the process of 'election' to this office could be predicted with considerable certainty. Custom dictated, moreover, that the lord mayor, at the end of his term, was to be replaced by the senior alderman who had not yet served as mayor. The vote taken by the Congregation (Common Hall) was pro forma; hence the logic of Rafe's deduction that Eyre's election is a sure thing when so many aldermen have died or become ill. Oatley, however much he may despise Eyre, is in no position to stop the process; Oatley is presented as too conservative to contemplate changing London custom.

At the same time, Dekker treats his London audience to a heady dose of fantasy about this political struggle. In the actual London of his day, the Merchant Adventurers were still the dominant mercantile interest in the City, and most of the aldermen were Merchant Adventurers regardless of the livery company to which they belonged; they were not yet seriously challenged by the rising Levant and East India merchants. No doubt the Merchant Adventurers' ascendancy helps explain why shrieval and mayoral elections came to be automatic and uncontested. Yet Dekker imagines a world in which gentlemen shoemakers are now in the ascendant and the once-powerful gentlemen grocers in the eclipse. All this is muted in Dekker's drama in order to allow his whimsical jollity to have its play, and to suggest that success is the inevitable and just reward of a conscientious shoemaker, but the more matter-of-fact political explanation is there as well. Eyre's fantasied triumph over the grocers is designed to appeal to shoemakers and other disenfranchised guild members in Dekker's London; every Londoner would know that the cordwainers were never in the ascendant, the grocers never in decline.[10]

We are invited to view with amiable scepticism Eyre's disingenuous claim that 'I am a handicraftsman, yet my heart is without craft' (5.5.9–10; 21.10–11). Indeed, so ironic is that pronouncement, and so self-aware is the wordplay, that the very epithet of Eyre's calling, 'the gentle craft',

---

[10] See Paul Seaver, 'The Artisanal World', above. I am further indebted to Seaver for a number of detailed observations and factual observations given to me in our exchange of correspondence. Our two essays have been revised and brought together through extensive collaboration.

begins to resonate with multiple meanings. 'Gentle' can mean mild, kind, tender; noble, generous, courteous; and, in its earliest etymological senses, well-born, well-bred, honourable, spirited. What kind of social claim is 'the gentle craft' attempting to make for itself? 'Craft' moves easily as a word from occupation and calling to strength, might, force, skill and on to artifice, deceit, guile and fraud. Firk elaborates this figure when, in reply to Oatley's charge that he is a 'base, crafty varlet', Firk insists that he is not 'crafty neither, but of the Gentle Craft' (5.2.139–41; 18.152–5). Whatever his station, Firk does not accept that he is of low moral character.

Firk also extends this verbal duelling to a familiar wordplay on 'mean' and 'base': he and his fellows may be 'but mean', he concedes, but they are not 'base'. Firk's distinction allows him to occupy the middle ground as in the musical analogy of tenor and bass voices, thus divesting 'mean' of its implications of inferiority, abjectness and ignoble small-mindedness. His attitude towards lowness of social station is usefully ambivalent: he seems to accept the shoemakers' place in the traditional social order ('I am but mean'), only to take refuge in other semantic meanings that give to 'mean' the qualities of moderation and freedom from the arrogance that afflicts his social superiors.

'The honour of the Gentle Craft' is, in this play, both a lofty ideal and a congeries of conflicting attitudes about authority, economic competition and ethnicity. However unwilling Eyre's men may be to serve in the military, once conscripted they resolve to 'fight for the honour of the Gentle Craft, for the Gentlemen Shoemakers, the courageous cordwainers, the flower of Saint Martin's, the mad knaves of Bedlam, Fleet Street, Tower Street, and Whitechapel' (1.1.211–15; 1.221–5). Because they view themselves as belonging to an international brotherhood, they are eager to hire on the spot an 'uplandish' workman – by which they probably mean 'outlandish' – who enters their shop singing his Dutch songs, and are ready to walk off the job if Eyre does not accede to their demands (1.4.36–62; 4.42–72). Solidarity against the employer is an article of faith among the shoemakers, much as they adulate Eyre and propose to follow him right on up to the mayoralty. This solidarity is both spirited and comically absurd, for virtually anything will do as an excuse for a job action. The men are touchy about any interference with Monday as their 'holiday' (2.3.25; 7.31), and are ready to walk off the job at an imagined slight from the boss's wife, Margery; indeed, they provoke her into making one flippant remark and then proceed to make an issue of it, obliging the harried shopowner to placate them by calling his wife every name in the book. Eyre's role as employer is similarly comic: he resists his workers' demands as long as he can until, faced with labour unrest beyond his control, he does his best to take credit for having a progressive attitude.

The shoemakers' insistence on hiring a seeming immigrant Dutchman is more than a stratagem to hamper Eyre with strident demands from his employees; it is also a chance for these English workers to give safe expression to their gleeful scorn of foreign artisans. From the start, Firk's motive in urging that Hans be employed is satiric. 'Hire him, good master, that I may learn some gibble-gabble; 'twill make us work the faster' (1.4.44–5; 4.50–2). Firk finds hilarity in repeating and parodying every phrase of the supposed Hans. The play's amiable satire is partly directed at Firk's good-natured bigotry, so characteristic of his social origins. Yet Dekker manages to have it both ways with his audience about xenophobic stereotypes: they can laugh at Firk and yet condescend to Hans's beer-drinking German drollery. Hans's language revels in stereotyped stage dialect (ambivalently German or Dutch) called for in the ethnic spellings and no doubt exaggerated onstage by the Lord Admiral's players in 1599. *Henry V* and *The Merry Wives of Windsor*, written about the same time, suggest how great was the appetite of London audiences for caricatures of French, Welsh, Irish and so on in the plays they flocked to see.

Firk is allowed a fair amount of verbal ethnic violence, and yet is presented as an amiable man who would do much to preserve Hans's right to earn a living in Eyre's shop and to marry Sir Roger Oatley's daughter. Moreover, Firk's xenophobic humour is balanced by the ethnically neutral attitude of Hodge, who wants to hire Hans because he appears to be well qualified: ''Fore God, a proper man and, I warrant, a fine workman' (1.4.54; 4.63–4). Dekker's presentation of attitudes towards foreigners is delicately ambivalent, at once friendly and satirical.

This evenhandedness is remarkable in view of the strength of feeling in London about cheap immigrant labour. That feeling had been exacerbated by a disastrous overexpansion and then collapse of the wool industry in 1551, leading to widespread unemployment, followed by a wave of Protestant refugees from the Low Countries after 1567 and especially after the Spanish sacking of Antwerp in 1574. Flemish rogues who speak a thick Germanic stage dialect are common in plays like *Wealth and Health* (c. 1554–5), *Trial of Treasure* (1567), *Like Will to Like* (1562–8), and *The Tide Tarrieth No Man* (1576). These hated foreigners carouse drunkenly and huddle together in crowded tenements, encouraging grasping landlords to evict honest Englishmen from their rented dwellings. The Lowlanders work for such minimal wages that native Londoners are driven out of the labour market. Exhortations to 'buy English' and to restrict fiscal abuses encouraged by cheap immigrant labour were sounded again and again in tracts like *A Discourse of the Common Weal* (1549), Edward Hakke's *A Touchstone for the Time Present* (1574), and Philip Stubbes's *The Anatomy of Abuses* (1583).[11] Dekker plays off these feelings and does not repudiate what his characters say, choosing instead to dramatise multiple and discordant voices in a comic dialogue about the viability of the English Commonwealth.

---

[11] See David Bevington, *Tudor Drama and Politics: A Critical Approach to Topical Meaning* (Cambridge, Mass., 1968), pp. 133–5.

Eyre's wife, Margery, is the focus of a different but related set of contradictory attitudes: about the role of women in London's social and economic life, about attitudes towards 'vanity' in dress and in other worldly aspirations. From the first, she is treated with humorous and sexist condescension by her husband and his workers. 'This wench with the mealy mouth that will never tire is my wife,' Eyre introduces her (1.1.127–8; 1.130–1). The men view her as a 'scold' (2.3.23; 7.29) and use her tongue as their flimsy excuse for a work stoppage. Shrewishness is of course one of the classic defamations in stereotyping women. Margery's social origins are unpromising, as her husband never tires of reminding her: 'Have not I taken you from selling tripes in Eastcheap, and set you in my shop, and made you hail-fellow with Simon Eyre, the shoemaker?' (2.3.60–2; 7.69–71). His insulting epithets for her – Cisly Bumtrinket, Dame Clapperdudgeon, Lady Madgy, midriff, wench, kitchen stuff, brown bread Tannikin, powder-beef quean, chitterling and the like – poke fun at her anatomy, her menial status, her appetites, her sexuality and her tongue; 'Clapperdudgeon' suggests that her tongue rattles like a beggar's clapdish. Her unintentional sexual double entendres (see, for example, 1.1.152–6; 1.158–62) brand her as a humorous type. In reality, however, Margery is devotedly loyal to her husband and tractably silent much of the time. Is Dekker endorsing the sexism of his male speakers or criticising them on Margery's behalf? The presentation is so ambivalent that we cannot be sure whom Dekker privileges in the war of the sexes; the genre of festive comedy allows him to have it both ways. The conflict itself is his chief delight.

Dekker is similarly ambivalent in portraying Margery's delight in finery. She is humanly vain about the sartorial splendour that becomes her due as an alderman's and then lord mayor's wife. 'Art thou acquainted with never a farthingale-maker, nor a French-hood-maker?' she inquires of Hodge. 'I must enlarge my bum' (3.2.32–3; 10.36–8). Her desire for social prominence is almost erotic, as she unconsciously acknowledges: 'I do feel honour creep upon me, and, which is more, a certain rising in my flesh; but let that pass' (2.3.133–5; 7.151–3). Yet the humour lies not in any inappropriate hauteur, but rather in the comic contrast between her innocent joy in dressing up and her constant reminders to herself that such pleasures are but vanity. 'Indeed, all flesh is grass,' she announces as her scriptural text, even in the act of asking Hodge where she can acquire 'a false hair for my periwig' (3.2.37–41; 10.42–6). 'Fie upon it, how costly this world's calling is!' she exclaims. 'Perdie, but that it is one of the wonderful works of God, I would not deal with it' (3.2.46–8; 10.51–3).

This simultaneous embracing and denial of worldly pleasure, and the transparent rationalisation that accompanies such a hard reconciliation, are sometimes labelled as marks of Puritan sensibility, as in Ben Jonson's savage portrayal of Zeal-of-the-Land Busy and Tribulation Wholesome, and in Dekker's own later *If This Be Not a Good Play, The Devil Is In It* (1611–12). Here, on the other hand, we sense that Dekker is still reaching out to his London auditors in an accommodating spirit. Margery's mannerisms of speech, including such mild asseverations as 'fie', 'yea', 'nay', 'by my troth', 'indeed', 'truly' and 'but let that pass', recall those 'pepper-gingerbread' oaths that Hotspur ridicules as suited only for 'Velvet-guards and Sunday citizens' (*1 Henry IV*, 3.2.252–4). They characterise a bourgeois temperament: pious, mild, respectable. They are labelled not as Puritan mannerisms but as humorous foibles, expressive of the festive, contradictory character of the very Londoners who are invited to watch this play.

The bourgeois view of sex and marriage that Dekker uses to characterise the fondly combative marriage of Eyre and his wife is essential also to the plot of Rafe, his wife Jane and Master Hammon. Moreover, in this plot sexual and social rivalries coincide. Hammon, first an unsuccessful wooer of Rose and then the rival to Rafe for Jane's love, is 'a proper gentleman, / A citizen by birth, fairly allied' (2.2.58–9; 6.60–1), while Jane is a 'wench' who 'keeps shop in the Old Change' during her husband's absence on military service abroad (3.1.51; 9.51). This situation is one that will be exploited in the next decade or two by city comedy: a citizen, his wife and a gentlemanly wooer.[12] Yet whereas city comedy in the private theatres will portray this triangle satirically at the expense of the gullible citizen and his randy wife, Dekker chooses to idealise London's adherence to orthodox sexual mores. Despite the apparent news of her husband's death in battle and the attendant pressures on her to succumb to Hammon's proposal of marriage, Jane is resolute. She scorns to use the 'witchcraft' of 'sunshine smiles and wanton looks' or to be 'coy, as many women be' (3.4.65–7; 12.65–7). If Rafe lives still, she will choose to live in poverty, 'And rather be his wife than a king's whore' (ll. 78–9). If Rafe is dead, 'My love to him shall not be buried' (l. 106). Her only concession to Hammon is to allow that 'If ever I wed man, it shall be you' (l. 122).

Confronted at last with a choice between the importunate Hammon and her husband, who has returned safely after all, albeit with a symbolically suggestive wound in the left leg (''Twas a fair gift of God the infirmity took not hold a little higher,' observes Margery, 3.2.64–5; 10.73–4), Jane finds her choice a simple one. 'Whom should I choose? Whom should my thoughts affect / But him whom heaven hath made to be my love?' (5.2.53–4; 18.62–3). Humbly virtuous poverty triumphs over Hammon's corrupting gold. 'Sirrah Hammon, Hammon', Rafe taunts him, 'dost thou think a

---

[12] See Lawrence Venuti, 'Transformation of City Comedy: A Symptomatic Reading', *Assays*, 3 (1985), 99–134. Paul Seaver, in his accompanying essay in this volume, discusses Hammon as a city gentleman making urban choices in his wooing and free to do so because much of his property is presumably personal rather than 'real'.

shoemaker is so base to be a bawd to his own wife for commodity?' Significantly, Rafe answers in the name of his trade, not just as an offended husband; his fellows are present and ready to back him up. 'Sell not thy wife, Rafe', urges Hodge; 'make her not a whore' (5.2.78–82; 18.88–94). As Hodge has insisted moments earlier, 'shoemakers are steel to the back, men every inch of them, all spirit' (5.2.31–2; 18.36–7).

Yet for all the melodrama inherent in such a triumph of virtue, the issues for Dekker are nuanced. Hammon is oddly ill-suited to the role of villain. When, earlier, he is repulsed by Rose, despite her father's liking for a prospective son-in-law so 'fairly allied' (2.2.59; 6.61), Hammon urges the father to respect his daughter's preference for a single life: 'If she can live an happy virgin's life, / 'Tis far more blessed than to be a wife' (3.1.34–5; 9.34–5). Even if this is a recognisably Roman Catholic position, it also bestows implicit praise on Queen Elizabeth's choice to remain single, much in the vein of Theseus's admiration for those 'thrice-blessed' souls who 'master so their blood / To undergo such maiden pilgrimage' (*A Midsummer Night's Dream*, 1.1.74–5). Moreover, Hammon does not wish to be the unwelcome intruder: 'Enforcèd love is worse than hate to me' (3.1.50; 9.50). If this virtuous posture is at variance with his importunacy towards Jane, we must nevertheless allow that Hammon never offers her anything less respectable than marriage. 'I love you as a husband loves a wife,' he tells her. 'That, and no other love, my love requires' (3.4.51–2; 12.51–2). Whether the letter he produces as proof of Rafe's death in France is a forgery, as Jane suspects (l. 95), is never clear.

In any case, Hammon's final resolution to remain single and chaste after Jane's refusal of him ('no woman else shall be my wife', 5.2.92; 18.102) is in keeping with the fine moral elevation of those shopkeepers he would have bought out if he could. The gentle craft has shown its moral superiority to a gentleman, and indeed can edify and even reform a gentleman like Hammon who is at last capable of honour. Ambivalence is to be found on both sides: Jane does offer Hammon an option when she agrees to marry no one other than him, and the erotic potential of a seduction is never far away. Rafe is given ample cause to be jealous when he is asked to make a pair of shoes for his wife's wedding; he determines to be at St Faith's church on the morrow to see if his wife prove true or not (4.2.3–68; 14.4–75). Social conflict is thus mediated through a love plot that celebrates the triumph of London bourgeois morality while allowing that gentlemen need not be so bad after all.

This plot of virtue triumphant is deftly juxtaposed with the nominally central love plot of *The Shoemaker's Holiday*, in which moral considerations are subordinated to the timeless and ultimately Plautine 'trick to catch the old one'. Oatley is the blocking parental figure, Lacy and Rose the resourceful young lovers, and Firk the clever servant. His identity as such allows him to cross freely between this love plot and the comedy of social conflict. The dramatic conventions through which we are invited to react to this plot are mildly satirical: Oatley gets what his graspingness deserves, whereas the young are vindicated by their cleverness. Disguise is at once the mechanism of the plotting against authority and the means by which this comedy attains its seemingly effortless closure. Love's difficulties are an illusion. At the same time, Dekker takes care not to offend the norms of London morality. Rose is without blemish; she seeks marriage rather than an affair, unlike her counterpart in Ariosto's *I Suppositi* and other eroticised neo-classical comedies from the Continent.

Moreover, the familiar contours of this demure sex comedy are aligned with the plot of social conflict. The triumph of Lacy and Rose is a means to defeat the aspirations of the play's most opprobrious characters: a grasping lord mayor who has lost touch with many honest and hard-working Londoners, and a formidable hereditary peer who cannot even be true to his temporary political allies. When we add to this the discomfiture of a gentleman in the Hammon–Jane–Rafe plot, we arrive at a veritable hit list of enemies for that part of London's bourgeois population that Dekker is particularly addressing. The fact that these enemies are not very opprobrious in *The Shoemaker's Holiday* is evidence of Dekker's genial strategy in dealing with social conflict. Such a strategy is itself not untypical of the bourgeois class that Dekker both represents and gently mocks.

Dekker's ultimate stratagem in *The Shoemaker's Holiday* is to embrace the monarchy, or at least a sentimentalised version of it, as endorser of his happy ending. As Michael Manheim has pointed out, the king we are shown is more like Henry V, the monarch with the common touch, than the hapless Henry VI, who in fact reigned at the time of Eyre's mayoralty.[13] The unnamed king of this play is suitably impressed with Eyre's irrepressible rise to power, and willingly bestows his blessing on a wedding 'knit by God's majesty' (5.5.63; 21.65). God's majesty and the King are of one regal mind; neither will allow anyone to 'offend Love's laws' (5.5.75; 21.77). Romantically and with no semblance of social realism, this king denies to a powerful London ex-mayor and to a baleful nobleman the right to block the marriage of Rose and Lacy. The King aligns himself with the spirit of festively romantic comedy itself, thus reinforcing our impression that Dekker's play is self-consciously aware of its own role in the idealised resolution of social conflict. Dekker's strategy credits himself and his audience with being loyal subjects of the king; they are the true monarchists, whereas Oatley and Lincoln are the stumbling blocks to social harmony as well as to the marriage now in hand.

---

[13] Michael Manheim, 'The King in Dekker's *The Shoemakers' Holiday*', *Notes and Queries*, n.s., 4 (1957), 432. See also W. K. Chandler, 'The Source of the Characters in *The Shoemaker's Holiday*', *Modern Philology*, 27 (1929), 175–82.

Eyre, as final spokesman for the idea of holiday that is the very *raison d'être* of festive comedy, urges the King to embrace a madcap spirit with him and all the shoemakers, for they can teach enlightened authority what holiday is all about. 'My sweet majesty', he admonishes, 'let care vanish. Cast it upon thy nobles' (5.5.31–2; 21.33–4). The nobles are appropriately the scapegoats of this comedy. Their discomfiture leaves in its wake an alignment between an idealised monarchy and a London bourgeois culture that knows the value of worldly prosperity even while it knows also how to place that prosperity in a suitably Christian perspective. Social discontent is purged in the play's closure by the fact that Eyre and his shoemakers get what they want, yet without undue abrasiveness. The victory is confined to the realm of festive comedy, and does not promise a comparable victory in the real world; indeed, the absurdities of the dream, and the unstableness of a comic vision, are no more absent from the finale than they are in Aristophanes. Comedy of this sort is utopian. What it does achieve, nonetheless, is a victory for festive comedy itself as the suitable arena for such a bloodless battle to be fought out and reduced finally to forgiving laughter.

4

John Marston's *The Fawn*

Ambivalence and Jacobean Courts

Linda Levy Peck

John Marston's *The Fawn* tickles its audience with a story of a duke who preens himself on his wisdom, courtiers who personify different vices, and strategies for access and preferment at court based only on extravagant flattery.[1] Written in 1604 or 1605, a year or two after James VI of Scotland ascended the English throne as James I, Marston's satire titillates because it apparently mirrors aspects of Jacobean court life.[2] James claimed the mantle of King Solomon, a trope faithfully repeated in contemporary English literature and art culminating in Rubens's Banqueting Hall ceiling; later scandals surrounding the king's favourite, Robert Carr, earl of Somerset, including the Essex divorce and Overbury murder trial, aroused prurient interest throughout the country; Jacobean courtiers carried flattering language to flowery heights; and the portrait of the court as drunken and lecherous continued to resonate through propaganda written in the Civil War period and Commonwealth.[3] Philip Finkelpearl, developing the earlier suggestion of Alexander W. Upton, suggests that *The Fawn* may provide the 'only full-length portrait of the ruling sovereign in Elizabethan drama'.[4]

Finkelpearl, who has convincingly situated Marston's work in the legal culture of early seventeenth-century London, identifies James I with the character of Duke Gonzago of Urbino. Further, he argues that Marston's aim in *The Fawn* is 'to display Duke Gonzago at length', revealing him

---

I am grateful to the editors of this volume and to A. R. Braunmuller and Michael Neill for their comments on earlier drafts of this essay.

[1] On the dating of the play see David A. Blostein, ed., *Parasitaster or The Fawn* (Manchester and Baltimore, 1978), pp. 32–6 and Kenneth Tucker, *John Marston: A Reference Guide* (Boston, 1985). I quote hereafter from the former.

[2] For the traditional view of the Jacobean court see, for instance, D. H. Willson, *King James VI and I* (1956).

[3] Anthony Weldon, 'The Court and Character of King James', in *Historical and Biographical Tracts*, ed. George Smeeton (2 vols., Westminster, 1820), first published in 1650; Arthur Wilson, *The History of Great Britain Being the Life and Reign of King James I* (1653); Francis Osborne, *Traditional Memoirs of the Reign of King James I* (1658). William Sanderson, *Aulicus Coliquinariae* (1650); several of these tracts were reprinted in Sir Walter Scott, *Secret History of the Court of James the First* (2 vols., Edinburgh, 1811).

[4] Philip Finkelpearl, *John Marston of the Middle Temple* (Cambridge, Mass., 1969), p. 223; Alexander W. Upton, 'Allusions to James I and his Court in *The Fawne*', *Publications of the Modern Language Association*, 44 (1929), 1048–65.

to be 'an utterly witless credulous fool'.[5] Other commentators, such as David Blostein, have been less sure of the play's satiric target, noting that Duke Gonzago is neither the focus of the play nor its leading character.[6] In fact, *The Fawn* is at least as much a study of the disguised Duke of Ferrara, who cleverly triumphs over court vice, achieves a secure succession and the union of Ferrara and Urbino, as it is the foolishness of the Duke of Urbino who thinks he is wise.[7] While Queen Elizabeth had failed to provide for a successor, King James, with a wife and three children, immediately provided his subjects with a secure succession to the English throne and offered as well the possibility of the Union of England and Scotland. Even as Marston wrote, James, unlike Elizabeth, pursued a deliberate policy of fostering marriage among former rival families at court such as Essex, Cecil and Howard. Does *The Fawn* then celebrate the court's uxoriousness, the king as father of his country and husband of Britain, or his foolishness? Or does Marston tease his audience by embedding his text with multiple readings? And what are the political implications of his treatment of noble women? As historians have revised their views of early seventeenth-century court life we can bring a somewhat differently inflected political reading to *The Fawn*.[8]

The Fawn is a deliberately multivalent reading of the Jacobean court rather than a realistic portrait of King James. The Jacobean court was not monolithic; it was composed as well of the court of Queen Anne and, later, of Prince Henry. Their households were havens for political and religious views that differed from the king's and offered a space for satire.[9]

Marston, the Middle Temple man, Elizabethan satirist and Jacobean court critic, had court connections as did other contemporary writers. *The Fawn* was performed by the Children of the Queen's Majesty's Revels who secured the queen's patronage in 1604. One of Marston's central sources

---

[5] Finkelpearl, *John Marston of the Middle Temple*, pp. 229, 223.

[6] Blostein, ed., *Parasitaster or The Fawn*, p. 32.

[7] MacDonald P. Jackson and Michael Neill, eds., *The Selected Plays of John Marston* (Cambridge, 1986), xv.

[8] For more recent views see Jenny Wormald, 'James VI and I: Two Kings or One?', *History*, 68 (1983), 79–101. Linda Levy Peck, ed., *The Mental World of the Jacobean Court* (Cambridge, 1991); idem, *Northampton: Patronage and Policy at the Court of James I* (1982). The view that Gonzago was a thoroughgoing portrait of James founders as well on the problem of age: Gonzago is an old fool with a daughter of marriageable age; James is 38 with three children, the eldest of whom is 10.

[9] On Queen Anne see Leeds Barroll, 'The Court of the First Stuart Queen', in *The Mental World of the Jacobean Court*, ed. Peck, pp. 191–208; Linda Levy Peck, *Court Patronage and Corruption in Early Stuart England* (1990), pp. 68–74. On Prince Henry see Roy Strong, *Henry, Prince of Wales, and England's Lost Renaissance* (New York, 1986). Gerald Smith in the introduction to his edition of *The Fawn* (1964) notes the several plays that attracted official censure including *Philotas, Eastward Ho!, The Dutch Courtesan*. 'Oddly enough, these were the plays produced by the company that was patronised by the Queen.' See Anthony Caputi, *John Marston, Satirist* (Ithaca, 1961), p. 204. E. K. Chambers, *The Elizabethan Stage* (Oxford, 1923), I, 325. Hercules describes Donna Philocalia 'whose ample report hath struck wonder into remotest strangers, and yet her worth above that wonder' to which Nymphadoro replies 'There were a lady for Ferrara's Duke: one of great blood, firm age, undoubted honour, above her sex, most modestly artful, though naturally modest; too excellent to be left unmatched, though few worthy to match with her' (3. 153–70). Could this be a compliment to Queen Anne?

Plate 8   Queen Anne at Oatlands, by Paul van Somer, 1617

for *The Fawn* was John Florio's translation of Montaigne's *Essays*.[10] Florio, the Italian humanist, became a member of Queen Anne's Household in 1604 and dedicated *The Essays* to several powerful women at the Jacobean court: Lucy, countess of Bedford, and Lady Anne Harrington, her mother;

---

[10] See for instance Blostein, ed., *Parasitaster or The Fawn*, pp. 32–42.

Elizabeth, countess of Rutland, daughter and heir to Sir Philip Sidney, Lady Penelope Rich, sister of the earl of Essex, Lady Elizabeth Grey, daughter to the earl of Shrewsbury, and Lady Marie Neville, daughter to Lord Treasurer Buckhurst and wife of Sir Henry Neville.[11] These members of the Sidney–Essex circle were restored to prominence under the Stuarts. The countess of Bedford, a leading court patron, was a member of the queen's Household.[12] Florio's interest in Montaigne was shared at the court itself. King James owned a copy of Florio's Montaigne as did Ben Jonson.[13] Jonson, patronised by the same circle of aristocratic women, inscribed a copy of *Volpone* to Florio, calling him 'loving Father and aide of his Muses'. Samuel Daniel, the poet-historian, who was also a member of Queen Anne's Household, was a close friend as well of both Florio and Marston.[14] Marston married Mary Wilkes, daughter of William Wilkes, James's chaplain, with whom they lived before 1605, and in 1610 took holy orders.

Marston's career and connections thus reveal how through the linkages of court, city and stage, a nascent public sphere existed in late sixteenth- and seventeenth-century London in which satire and sycophancy could coexist.[15] 'The nimble form of Comedy', Marston wrote in his prologue to *The Fawn*, was 'mere spectacle of life and public manners'.[16] *The Fawn* celebrates and castigates at one and the same time the Good King and the Bad King, the practices of courtiers whose language of benefits is Senecan but whose behaviour is shaped by greed and delineates the power of noble women within the court where they assert political power beyond their assigned roles.

Yet if Marston shared the intellectual tastes of King James and Queen Anne, his plays like those of others at the moment of transition often challenged the boundaries of censorship. He was imprisoned in 1605 along with Ben Jonson and George Chapman for *Eastward Ho!* even though within months he also wrote Latin verses for the reception of Christian IV of Denmark in 1606. He wrote an entertainment for Ashby on the occasion of the betrothal of Anne Stanley, daughter of Alice, countess of Derby and Grey Brydges, fifth Lord Chandos in 1607, and yet in 1608 may have had a hand in a play, now lost, in which he attacked the Scots and 'represented the king himself as a drunken, bad-tempered sot'.[17] In

---

[11] See Frances Yates, *John Florio* (1934).

[12] Peck, *Court Patronage and Corruption* (1990), pp. 47–8, 68–74.

[13] Yates, *John Florio*, p. 248.

[14] Jonson's dedication of *Volpone* to his 'worthy friend' is in the British Library copy, *STC* 14783. I am grateful to A. R. Braunmuller for these points.

[15] On the importance of such a public sphere see Jurgen Habermas, 'The Public Sphere', in *Jurgen Habermas on Society and Politics* (Boston, 1989), pp. 231–6. See also Susan Wells, 'Jacobean City Comedy and the Ideology of the City', *ELH, A Journal of English Literary History*, 48 (1981), 37–60.

[16] Blostein, ed., *Parasitaster or The Fawn*, Prologus, pp. 19–20.

[17] Jackson and Neill, eds., *Selected Plays of John Marston*, xv.

reprisal all the theatres were shut, and Marston was summoned before the Privy Council and imprisoned. Still, Marston's *The Dutch Courtesan*, despite its anti-Scots satire, was performed in 1613 during festivities for the marriage of Princess Elizabeth to the Elector Palatine.[18] But, after taking holy orders in December 1609, Marston retired to a country parish and cut himself off from that public sphere of debate and criticism that was characteristic of the early years of James's reign. When his collected works were published in 1633 he tried to have his name removed from the volume.[19]

The Fawn then should first be placed in the period of transition after Elizabeth's long reign and secondly in the medieval and neo-Stoic tradition of criticism of kings, courts and courtiers. Marston's complex representation of the Jacobean court is signalled in his treatment of gender. In *The Fawn* misogynistic prescription is countered by the real political influence wielded by aristocratic women. The point of this essay then is to suggest the overlapping, if fragmented, meanings of court life that Marston presents.

I

James I was warmly welcomed by his new subjects in March 1603. As part of the traditional redress of grievances at the beginning of a new reign, the king received petitions calling for reformation both in church and state in 1603 and 1604. These covered a wide range of issues including several that had been raised in the last Elizabethan Parliament. The millenary petition, so called because it reputedly came from 1,000 ministers, urged further reform of the Elizabethan settlement. In response James convened the Hampton Court conference of divines, but the conference yielded little reform other than James's support for a new translation of the Bible. Before the first session of Parliament in 1604 petitions circulated calling for reform of ancient royal rights such as purveyance and wardship as well as monopolies; these reflected the priorities of privy councillors as well as subjects.[20] At the same time fears that court favour would now be

---

[18] J.W. Binns and H. Neville Davis suggest that *The Dutch Courtesan* (1606) was part of the entertainment prepared for Christian IV's visit to London in 1606. *Theatre Notebook*, 44.3 (1990), 118–23.

[19] Jackson and Neill, eds., *Selected Plays of John Marston*, p. xvi. BL, Sloane MS 826 is a poem on the duke of Buckingham attributed to John Marston:

> Great Buckingham's buried under a stone
> 'Twixt Heaven and Earth not such a one,
> Pope and Papists friend, the Spaniards factor
> The Palatines bone the Dunkirks Protector
> The Danes disaster, the French king's intruder
> Netherlands oppressor, the English deluder,
> The Friend of Pride, the Peer of Lust
> Th'avaricious actor of things unjust.

[20] Peck, *Northampton*, pp. 168–71.

shared with foreigners aroused opposition to the king's proposal for the Union of England and Scotland. Anti-Scots sentiment among the political elite found a particular target in the Scots at court to whom the king gave office and control of his Bedchamber.[21]

At this moment of transition, playwrights and ministers offered counsel to the new monarch. The line between advice and unacceptable criticism was hard to draw, and the French ambassador expressed dismay on 14 June 1604: 'what must be the state and condition of a prince, whom the preachers publicly from the pulpit assail, whom the comedians of the metropolis bring upon the stage, whose wife attends these representations in order to enjoy the laugh against her husband?'[22] Were *The Fawn* understood by authorities as an unflattering portrait of King James we might expect Marston to have been called before the Privy Council or even imprisoned. Marston was not, but John Burgess, a Buckinghamshire minister, was.[23] Burgess's sermon, delivered before the king at Greenwich on 19 June 1604, illustrates by contrast how Marston remained within the bounds of the politically acceptable.

When on 2 July Burgess appealed to James from prison, he admitted that at points he went beyond his text: 'some things I spake in my own phrase unpremediate as that of the swelling of princes hearts'. Still, he thought it his duty to present 'a general discourse unto a wise prince which . . . none could . . . apply to particularities'.[24] Burgess presented the people's complaints that the king had cut himself off from them and that he had evil counsellors yet claimed that his citations of Roman emperors such as Julius Caesar, Nero and Galba were not aimed at the king himself.[25]

If I had an irreverent thought in my heart to compare my sovereign to any of those evil examples which I alleged in my discourses let the Lord the searcher of hearts confound my soul and body before his presence. For the rest I could only plead (as Luther before the Emperor) for pardon of rudeness that I have not been acquainted with the tender ears of Princes.[26]

---

[21] Neil Cuddy, 'The Revival of the Entourage: The Bedchamber of James I, 1603–1625', in *The English Court*, ed. David Starkey (1987), pp. 173–225.

[22] Quoted in Finkelpearl, *John Marston of the Middle Temple*, pp. 221–2. Finkelpearl stresses the portrait of James but not the role of the queen that Beaumont suggests. Cambridge University Library (henceforth, CUL), Add. MS 335.

[23] Burgess was appointed by Sir Francis Goodwin to a benefice in Buckinghamshire on the recommendation of the second earl of Essex in 1600.

[24] CUL, Add. MS 335, fos. 59v–65, John Burgess's petition to King James, 2 July 1604. Burgess prepared 'general discourses as your Majesty might use of for your own good' and addressed 'the general murmuring and complaints which every man hears sooner than your majesty and your nearest servants as that you grace not your people'. He 'spoke them as Balaam's ass to his Majesty's understanding and not his own'.

[25] CUL, Add. MS 335, fo. 64. 'God plagued those that conspired against him; I take this for a general rule, God never spares those that rise against princes how evil so ever they be.' The speeches of Julius Caesar gave occasion for distaste and conspiracy for saying that 'the said senate (for that I think is meant by respublica was but a name only, this was a means of losing their hearts and his own greatness . . .)'. Burgess suggested that the king did have evil counsellors: 'Such evil instruments of which there is no doubt but you have more than two about though I know them not.'

[26] CUL, Add. MS 335, John Burgess's petition to King James, fos. 59v–65.

The main difference between Burgess's sermon and Marston's *The Fawn* was the former's condemnation of religious ceremony and his implication that the court leaned toward popery.

> It is generally complained that popery and licentiousness grow upon us and that the new ... urging of the ceremonies and subscription beyond law whereby 6 or 700 of the ablest ministers in the land are like to be put out: and the general depriving of religious persons if they be conscionable under the scorn of Puritanism ... make many men sigh and grieve and say in secret that these things may be the traces to Popery. ... This is the estate of your poor ministers like that of the Britons betwixt the sword of the Saxons and the Sea.[27]

Indeed, Burgess was himself expelled from his benefice the next year.

Burgess once again goes beyond *The Fawn* to endorse the contemporary perception that the Scots had a monopoly of the king's favour:

> There is nothing more grievous to subjects than enclosure of commons ... I say there is nothing more grievous unless it be monopolies ... but there is no enclosure of commons or monopolies so grievous as the enclosing or engrossing of a king's favour, as to make a monopoly of a king. What then? Would we have the favour of Princes so common to all that it should not abound especially to some: God forbid ... the favours of princes lying open as a common to all their good subjects in their proportions should yet be especially placed and bestowed on men of the chiefest use and desert.[28]

In explaining this section of the sermon Burgess wrote:

> As for the point of generality of princes favours and similitude of monopolies ... I likewise on my knees crave leave to protest that I spake it not ... because I knew that some had engrossed your favours; but because that also is muttered of as if your favours were not immediate or tool free. And because it hath been the ordinary mishap of the best princes to be enclosed.

Burgess's sermon sets Marston's *The Fawn* in relief; the sermon remains in manuscript, the play was published in 1606. The play takes up neither the religious issues nor the anti-Scots language of Burgess's sermon. *The Fawn* is more circumspect; it is not so much a realistic attack on the Jacobean court as a narrative about courts based on earlier texts. Still, Marston and Burgess were both concerned with the evils of flattery and the way in which it cut the king off from his natural advisers. Burgess cited the fifteenth-century writer Philip de Comines, *Memoires of the Reign of Louis XI*, who wrote: 'the prince is so far in God's disgrace that he flyeth the company of the wise and advanceth fools, oppressors, flatterers

---

[27] Burgess contended that he had focused on 'ceremonies for which this Church of God hath been in vexation about 50 years and though they be small things: yet they have caused great trouble ... and the course of religion hath been much hindered by them.' Such ceremonies were not impious but 'needless and scandalous ... Many a hundredth worthy ministers ... would surely die rather than use them ... Some others will much more willingly perform their subjection to your Majesty in bearing the penalty than suffer by their occasion so many to fall off to Brownism on the one hand and others to rise up in scorn and contempt of their lightness on the other hand.' Burgess admitted that he had forgotten to mention the good things that James had done.

[28] CUL, Add. MS 335, fos. 64v–65v.

and such as soothe him in all his sayings.'[29] As Frank Whigham points out in his own essay, 'flattering desire' is at the heart of *The Fawn*.[30] It was a language embraced by the court itself.

II

Baldisario Castiglione composed the most influential portrait of court life in Renaissance Italy and early modern Europe. *Il Cortegiano* (1528) was translated into English by Sir Thomas Hoby in 1561 and was wildly popular, going through many editions by 1640. Castiglione described how by cultivating humanistic learning, arts, music and sport, courtiers could win favour with their prince and, most important, serve as effective counsellors. Whether Castiglione presented the sunny humanistic agenda or the darker vision of Machiavelli's *The Prince* need not be taken up here.[31] What is crucial to note is that Marston set *The Fawn* in Urbino, the site of *The Courtier*, and yet his courtiers were anything but a humanist's ideal.[32]

Then what kind of peculiar court is this? Anti-Castiglione, anti-Urbino, Marston's most striking image is that of a ship of fools. Drawing on Sebastian Brant's fifteenth-century *Narrenschiffe*, first translated into English in 1509, Marston's caricatures resemble Mikhail Bakhtin's carnivalesque fools more than Foucault's real madmen driven away on ships from German towns.[33] His dukes and courtiers recall Erasmus's targets in *Praise of Folly*, the work that Bakhtin called 'one of the greatest creations of carnival laughter'.[34] Indeed, *The Fawn* provides a textbook case for Erasmus's diagnosis of kings and courtiers: 'Princes, though their state is doubtless happy in general, seem to me utterly wretched in this respect, that there's nobody who will tell them the truth, and they are constrained to take flatterers for friends.'[35] *The Fawn* is peopled by the traditional vices of pride, lechery, envy, wrath, avarice, gluttony and sloth. Marston's court is not Platonic and idealist; it is neo-Stoic and driven by self-interest.

---

[29] Philip de Comines, *Memoires of the Reign of Louis XI*, trans. Thomas Danett, anno 1596, Tudor Translations, 1st ser., vols. 17–18 (New York, 1967), p. 48.

[30] See Frank Whigham, 'Flattering Courtly Desire', below.

[31] See R. W. Henning and David Rosand, eds., *Castiglione, the Ideal and the Real in Renaissance Culture* (Yale, 1983). Marston refers to the machiavel when Nymphadoro warns that if Tiberio acts contrary to his wishes he 'shall find me an Italian' and have Fawn poison him to which the disguised Duke replies: 'What, ha' ye plots, projects, correspondences, and stratagems? Why are you not in better place?' (2. 114–16).

[32] I am grateful to Fritz Levy for discussion of the importance of Marston's setting of *The Fawn* in Urbino.

[33] See Desiderius Erasmus, *The Praise of Folly and Other Writings*, ed. Robert M. Adams (New York, 1989); Michel Foucault, *Madness and Civilization* (1967); H. C. Erik Middlefort, 'Madness and Civilization in Early Modern Europe', in *After the Reformation*, ed. Barbara C. Malament (Philadelphia, 1980), pp. 247–65. I am grateful to Ted Leinwand for discussion of Foucault and Middlefort on the Ship of Fools.

[34] Bakhtin, quoted in Erasmus, *The Praise of Folly*, ed. Adams, p. 317. 'Civil and social ceremonies and rituals took on a comic aspect as clowns and fools, constant participants in these festivals, mimicked serious rituals such as the tribute rendered to the victors at tournaments, the transfer of feudal rights, or the initiation of a knight,' p. 310.

[35] Erasmus, *The Praise of Folly*, p. 37.

Montaigne's *Essays*, written in the midst of the French Wars of Religion, and drawn on by Marston and other writers at the turn of the century, reflect the contemporary interest in neo-Stoicism, pessimism, self-interest and the sour taste for Tacitus.[36]

Couched in vocabulary drawn from the history and language of baronial revolt and neo-Stoicism, the language of favourites, deployed to attack Leicester in the 1570s, could easily be accommodated to the Jacobean Scots, to Robert Carr, earl of Somerset, and George Villiers, duke of Buckingham. In the 1590s plays about evil emperors and rapacious courtiers in first-century Rome and the courts of Edward II, Richard II and Henry IV flourished during the last throes of the Elizabethan regime. As J. H. Salmon suggests, 'what began as a literary convention took on the specious guise of moral truth.'[37] Together, Marston's combination of late humanism and Tacitean pessimism allowed the construction of a narrative into which it was easy to fit the Jacobean court.

If Marston's court was not Castiglione's Urbino, neither does it resemble Norbert Elias's analysis of the early modern court. Elias, who treats court society as important a formation as the state, describes how, through the manipulation of elaborate ritual, etiquette and patronage, Louis XIV uprooted his nobility to Versailles, structured their lives around court rites and effectively neutralised power independent of the Sun King.[38]

David Starkey has emphasised how personal the English court remained in the sixteenth and seventeenth century, challenging Geoffrey Elton's thesis that sixteenth-century England witnessed a 'Tudor Revolution' that bureaucratised monarchical government. Access to the king was organised by the Royal Household, especially the Privy Chamber, and, under James, the Bedchamber.[39] 'News, news, news, news!' (2. 241) was the currency that bound together city and country and undergirded advancement at court. Seeking information about Tiberio, Nymphadoro approaches Herod because 'Thou are private with the duke; thou belongest to his close stool' (1.2.46–7).

Although Marston satirises such Household officials as Groom of the Stool, though the court of Urbino circulates around the Duke and his courtiers are dependent on ducal patronage, the ceremony and ritual that ordered early modern court life is strikingly missing. Moreover, unlike Shakespeare's history plays of the 1590s, or Webster's Italian plays, such as *The White Devil*, c. 1612, and *The Duchess of Malfi*, c. 1614, Marston's

---

[36] See J. H. Salmon, 'Seneca and Tacitus in Jacobean England', in *The Mental World of the Jacobean Court*, ed. Peck, pp. 169–88. On Marston's stoicism see A. Caputi, *John Marston, Satirist* (Ithaca, 1961). In his essay on the incommodities of greatness, Montaigne wrote, 'Since we cannot attain unto it, let us revenge ourselves with railing against it.' Florio's *Montaigne* (1603), p. 552.

[37] Salmon, 'Seneca and Tacitus', pp. 178–9.

[38] Norbert Elias, *The Court Society*, trans. Edmund Jephcott (Oxford, 1983).

[39] See Neil Cuddy, 'The Revival of the Entourage: the Bedchamber of James I, 1603–1625', in *The English Court*, ed. Starkey (1987), pp. 173–225.

court of Urbino displays no independent noble power and privilege that must be honoured lest it challenge the power of the Prince.

Marston provides a telling fragment of court life that addresses James's own aspirations. If *The Fawn* satirises King James's claims to wisdom and to a singular knowledge of the *arcana imperii*, the play also celebrates the ideals of *Basilikon Doron*, the book on kingship that James wrote for his eldest son, Prince Henry. First published in 1599, the book was rushed into print in 1603 in thousands of copies by London and Edinburgh printers.[40] *Basilikon Doron* was translated and published the same year in France and translated into Italian by John Florio.[41] There James had argued that it was not enough for a good king to govern by good laws and protect his subjects by force of arms; 'if he join not therewith his virtuous life in his own person, and in the person of his Court and company; by good example alluring his subjects to the love of virtue, and hatred of vice'.[42]

III

As the play opens, Hercules, Duke of Ferrara, approaches the court of Urbino. Accompanied by his brother Renaldo, to whom he entrusts the rule of Ferrara in his absence (a motif akin to Shakespeare's in *Measure for Measure*), Hercules responds to Renaldo's question as to why he will 'break forth those stricter limits of regardful state . . . and now to unknown dangers you'll give up yourself, Ferrara's Duke, and in yourself the state, and us?' (1.1.9–14). Hercules explains that he is not abandoning his rule but disguising himself to encourage his son Tiberio to woo Dulcimel, daughter of Duke Gonzago. As Hercules seeks to secure the succession to his throne, the Duke's disguise as Fawn allows the audience and himself to see how Urbino is governed.

The play is set within the conventions of a hierarchically structured society in which law prescribes behaviour according to status. Yet Hercules as Fawn (a man without master and without history) demonstrates his ability to rise simply by flattery, the emollient that dissolves credulity.

> O mighty flattery,
> Thou easiest, commonest, and most grateful venom
> That poisons courts and all societies,

---

[40] *Basilikon Doron* in *The Political Works of James I*, ed. C. H. McIlwain (New York, 1965), p. 9. Peter Blayney argues that 11 of the 21 printers in London worked day and night and turned out 10,000 copies in three weeks. See Jenny Wormald, 'James VI and I, *Basilikon Doron* and the *Trew Law of Free Monarchies*: The Scottish Context and the English Translation', in *The Mental World of the Jacobean Court*, ed. Peck, p. 51. See also Finkelpearl, *John Marston of the Middle Temple*, p. 225.

[41] James Craigie, *The Basilikon Doron of James I* (Edinburgh, 1950), II, 63. Jean Hotman in his translation compared it to similar works by three Byzantine emperors. There is also a Spanish translation in manuscript.

[42] McIlwain, ed., *Basilikon Doron*, pp. 18, 29.

How grateful dost thou make me! Should one rail
And come to sear a vice, beware leg-rings
And the turned key on thee, when, if softer hand
Suppling a sore that itches (which should smart) –
Free speech gains foes, base fawnings steal the heart.
. . . Another's court shall show me where and how
Vice may be cured.

$$(2.580-98)^{43}$$

Marston attacks court patronage and the pretence of courtiers to any other value than self-interest.[44] Patron–client ties, which submerged one party's interest in another's to the advantage of both, pervaded early modern society.[45] Characterised by deference and bounty, loyalty and protection, patronage relationships were marked by gift-giving and surrounded with Senecan protestations that simultaneously sought to isolate such exchanges from commerce. In *De Beneficiis* Seneca had written that 'the estimation of so noble a thing should perish, if we make a merchandise of benefits. To be virtuous a man must tread all profit under foot . . . It is no benefit that hath reference to fortune, or hope of interest.'[46]

Such Senecan language of exchange surrounding patron–client ties was common in the late sixteenth and early seventeenth centuries. Moreover, in the early seventeenth century, Protestant Englishmen secularised religious vocabulary borrowed from Roman Catholicism: to gain the favour of the king who was said to bestow his bounty freely much as God granted salvation, William Trumbull, English agent in the Low Countries, was advised to direct himself to the 'right saint' at court;[47] the duke of Bucking-

---

[43] Compare Marston's language with that of Richard Niccols, *Sir Thomas Overburies Vision* (1616), pp. 21–2, 40–2:

> Ye servile sycophants, whose hopes depend
> On great mens wills; what is the utmost end
> At which ye aim? Why do ye like base curs
> Upon your patron fawn?
> Why like his spurs, will ye be ever ready at his heels
> With pleasing word to claw him, where he feels
> The humour itch? or why will ye so wait
> As to lie down and kiss the feet of state?
> And oft expose yourselves to wretched ends
> Losing your souls to make great men your friends?

[44] Compare Erasmus, *The Praise of Folly*, who described courtiers as 'the most . . . slavish, stupid, abject creatures conceivable, they fancy themselves the most distinguished of men . . . they content themselves with the gold, gems, purple robes and other insignia of virtue while relinquishing to others all concern for the virtues themselves . . . the rest of their talent is just barefaced flattery,' p. 68.

[45] See Peck, *Court Patronage and Corruption*, pp. 1–4, 12–29 and passim.

[46] Thomas Lodge, *The Works of Lucius Annaeus Seneca* (London, 1614), *On Benefits*, Book IV, ch. 1, p. 128.

[47] Roger Lockyer, *Buckingham: The Life and Political Career of George Villiers, First Duke of Buckingham 1592–1628* (1981), p. 113. In his sermon in 1604 Burgess too described patronage in religious language: 'All are their subjects ergo should have the sunshine of their sovereign, all are the brethren and companions in scot and lot (as we use to say) I mean in every burden of their troubles and therefore should have some portion in the common comfort of their favours: and indeed this is kingly graciousness to be gracious to all their good subjects and to do good like the sun that shines to all, like Christ that did good to all wheresoever he came.' CUL, Add. MS 335, fos. 59v–65.

ham was described by Francis Bacon as a 'good Angel', and Bishop Williams who wished the favourite's favour pleaded that he not be forced to pray at 'new altars'.[48] Yet Marston makes clear that at the court of Urbino, as at the court of James I, money was increasingly becoming part of the bond that bound patron and client.

Duke Hercules disguises himself as Fawn and claims to be Tiberio's 'yeoman of the bottles' (1.2.226), a reference to the importance of House-hold office as well as to the court's propensity for drink. Forswearing any similarity to the informers around the Emperor Tiberius described by Tacitus,[49] he and Herod take turns abusing their respective dukes: Herod says 'our Duke of Urbin is a man very happily mad, for he thinks himself right perfectly wise, and most demonstratively learned . . .' (1.2.259–61); Fawn obligingly refers to himself as 'noisome, cold, and . . . half-rotten' (1.2.269–70). Since each has now given hostages to fortune by revealing his true views of his master, Herod replies: 'Now dare we speak boldly as if Adam had not fallen, and made us all slaves. Hark ye, the duke is an arrant, doting ass. . . .' (1.2.271–3).

When Herod wonders at his poor clothing, Fawn hopes for better when the match is consummated between Urbino and Ferrara. Herod describes the material benefits that will then be his: 'Why then shalt thou, O yeoman of the bottles, become a maker of *magnificoes*. Thou shalt beg some odd suit and change thy old suit, pare thy beard, cleanse thy teeth, and eat apricocks, marry a rich widow . . .' (1.2.235–8).

Fawn now confesses that he is not yet a member of Tiberio's entourage, but 'if ye can prefer my service to him, I shall rest yours wholly' (1.2.285–6). Herod agrees and in return Fawn agrees to second the schemes of Herod and Nymphadoro, who attends the Duke's daughter Dulcimel. 'And we, and thou with us, blessed and enriched past that misery of possible contempt, and above the hopes of greatest conjectures' (1.2.306–8).

Once alone, the disguised Duke ruefully considers the lesson he has just learned, that upon their consecration princes are cut off from truth, a point similar to the one Burgess made in his sermon.

> I scarce had known myself.
> Thou grateful poison, sleek mischief, flattery,
> Thou dreamful slumber (that doth fall on kings
> As soft and soon as their first holy oil),
> Be thou forever damned. . . .
> But since our rank
> Hath ever been afflicted with these flies
> (That blow corruption on the sweetest virtues),

[48] James Spedding, ed., *The Letters and the Life of Francis Bacon* (7 vols., 1861–74), VI, 14. See Linda Levy Peck, 'The Culture of Exchange in Seventeenth-Century England', in *Court, Country and Culture: Essays in Early Modern British History in Honor of Perez Zagorin*, ed. Bonnelyn Kunze and Dwight Brautigam (Rochester, 1992).

[49] Blostein, ed., *Parasitaster or The Fawn*, pp. 94–5.

> I will revenge us all upon you all
> With the same stratagem we still are caught,
> Flattery itself . . . since vice is now termed fashion.

He vows to flatter all 'in all of their extremest viciousness, / Till in their own loved race they fall most lame, / And meet full butt the close of vice's shame' (1.2.325–50). Fawn's technique is simple: he always echoes, indeed amplifies, those he flatters.

As a result the Fawn's rise is stunning. At the end of Act 1 he was poorly clothed and unknown. At the opening of Act 2, where we see the court feasting, he has become a courtier, not the adviser much loved by humanists but, seemingly, a favourite of the Duke of Urbino. 'We would be private: only Faunas stay. (He is a wise fellow, daughter, a very wise fellow, for he is still just of my opinion).'

Courtiers, at once actors and audience, noted the rise and fall of favourites as a central feature of medieval and early modern European court life.[50] While favourites could serve the useful purpose of shielding the king from importunate suitors and replacing a nobility with claims to institutional power, Marston presents a humanist critique. Indeed he makes Herod the mouthpiece for Erasmus and Montaigne.

> HEROD: Did you ever see a fellow so spurted up in a moment? He has got
>   the right ear of the duke, the prince, princess, most of the lords, but all of
>   the ladies; why, he is become their only minion, usher and supporter.
> NYM: He hath gotten more loved reputation of virtue, of learning, of all
>   graces, in one hour, than all your snarling reformers have in –.
> HEROD: . . . what a fruitless labour . . . to inveigh against folly! Community
>   takes away the sense, and example the shame. No, praise me these fellows,
>   hang on their chariot wheel
> And mount with them whom fortune heaves, nay drives;
> A stoical sour virtue seldom thrives.
> Oppose such fortune . . .
> The hill of chance is paved with poor men's bones,
> And bulks of luckless souls, over whose eyes
> Their chariot wheels must ruthless grate, that rise.
>   (2.11–29)

Such a critique of favourites was echoed when the Overbury murder scandal prompted one contemporary in 1615 to condemn 'the customs of this age' and ambitious courtiers 'climbing only for greatness'. Yet at much the same time Sir Francis Bacon advised the duke of Buckingham that 'it is no new thing for Kings and Princes to have their privadoes, their favourites, their friends.'[51]

---

[50] See Peck, *Court Patronage and Corruption*, pp. 173–81. See also Robert P. Shepherd, 'Royal Favorites in the Political Discourse of Tudor and Stuart England' (Claremont Ph.D., 1985).

[51] *The Bloody Downfall of Adultery, Murder, Ambition* . . . (1615), A3v–4 (*STC* 18919.3); Spedding, ed., *Francis Bacon*, VI, 14.

Nymphadoro greets the Fawn: 'Thou art now a perfect courtier of just fashion, good grace; canst not relieve us?' To which Fawn replies 'Ha' ye any money?' (2.80–2). Later in the play the Fawn puts paid to the humanist belief that rhetoric can shape a worthy adviser to the king. 'Wherefore has heaven given man tongue but to speak to a man's own glory? He that cannot swell bigger than his natural skin, nor seem to be in more grace than he is, has not learned the very rudiments or ABC of courtship' (4.175–9).

As the two dukes discuss royal bounty, Marston lifts the veil of religious language surrounding the culture of courtly exchange to demonstrate hypocrisy on the one hand and blindness on the other. Gonzago praises Count Granuffo, who has proved his wisdom by his silent assent to everything the Duke says.[52] Fawn, so aptly named, replies

> Silence is an excellent modest grace, but especially before so instructing a wisdom as that of your excellency's. As for his advancement, you gave it most royally, because he deserves it least duly; since to give to virtuous desert is rather a due requital than a princely magnificence, when to undeservingness it is merely all bounty and free grace.
>
> GONZAGO: Well spoke ... this Faunus is a very worthy fellow, and an excellent courtier, and beloved of most of the princes of Christendom ...
>
> HERCULES: Sir, myself, my family, my fortunes, are all devoted, I protest, most religiously to your service. I vow my whole self only proud in being acknowledged by you but as your creature, and my only utmost ambition is by my sword or soul to testify how sincerely I am consecrated to your adoration. (3. 300–20)

IV

Focused around issues of kingship, courtiership and succession, *The Fawn* also displays the complex role of women in the construction of courts. The patriarchal society presented in *The Fawn* is constructed conventionally by the power of fathers over children and husbands over wives. In *The Trew Law of Free Monarchies* King James had argued that, as the father of his people, the king's obligation was 'the virtuous government of his children'.[53] Yet *The Fawn*'s patriarchal, indeed, misogynist, language is subverted by the triumph of his female characters over stupid husbands and silly fathers.[54]

---

[52] 'My Lord Granuffo, you may likewise stay, for I know you'll say nothing' (2. 473–5).

[53] *The Trew Law of Free Monarchies* in *The Political Works of James I*, ed. McIlwain, p. 85. On James's political writings see Jenny Wormald, 'James VI and I, *Basilikon Doron* and *The Trew Law of Free Monarchies*'; J. P. Sommerville, 'James I and the Divine Right of Kings: English Policy and Continental Theory', and Paul Christianson, 'Royal and Parliamentary Voices on the Ancient Constitution, *c.* 1604–1621', all in *The Mental World of the Jacobean Court*, ed. Peck, pp. 36–95.

[54] My reading of gender in *The Fawn* differs somewhat from that of Coppélia Kahn, 'Whores and Wives in Jacobean Drama', and Susan Baker, 'Sex and Marriage in *The Dutch Courtesan*', in Dorothea Kehler and Susan Baker, eds., *In Another Country: Feminist Perspectives on Renaissance Drama* (1991).

While the play addresses the accession of a male monarch, it displays court women who refuse to play subservient roles. More learned and wiser than their husbands and lovers, they nevertheless must manipulate them to achieve their ends. Fawn undertakes the same task by flattering the adulterous, the jealous, the impotent courtiers of Urbino.

Mirroring their vices, the Fawn assents to Nymphadoro's description of women as 'pretty, toying, idle, fantastic, imperfect creatures ... only created for show and pleasure' (3.20–4). The court is a marriage market for what Nymphadoro calls 'the trade of marriage' (3.71). While 'above all I affect the princess', Nymphadoro is actively courting nineteen ladies at court. 'Oh, I love a lady whose beauty is joined with fortune, above all; yet one of beauty without fortune, for some uses; nay one of fortune without beauty, for some ends; but never any that has neither fortune nor beauty, but for necessity' (3.73–7). The humour of the play, of course, lies in its resemblance to contemporary practice. Thus Sir John Holles, later earl of Clare, while hoping that his son would choose 'a gentlewoman of good blood, good kindred ... unacquainted with court conversation', negotiated with an alderman of London who offered a portion of £10,000 but preferred Sir Horace Vere's daughter, 'If Sir Horace Vere will give £5,000 and state a convenient portion of land, so much prefer I that alliance, my own profit shall give place thereunto.'[55] Nymphadoro's calculations can be matched in contemporary correspondence. 'Whose father dies first, or whose portion appeareth most, or whose fortune betters soonest, her with quiet liberty at my leisure will I elect' (3.130–2).

In response to such calculations, Duke Gonzago's daughter Dulcimel announces: 'There's a ship of fools going out. Shall I prefer thee, Nymphadoro? Thou may'st be master's mate; my father hath made Dondolo [the court fool] captain, else thou should'st have his place' (3.140–3). 'Well fooled', the ship includes officials from both court and country. Dondolo tells Fawn that

Oh, 'twas excellently thronged full: a justice of peace, though he had been one of the most illiterate asses in a country, could hardly ha' got a hanging cabin. Oh, we had first some long fortunate great politicians, that were so sottishly paradised as to think, when popular hate seconded princes' displeasure to them, any unmerited violence could seem to the world injustice; some purple fellows whom chance reared, and their own deficiencies of spirit hurled down; we had some courtiers that o'erbought their offices, and yet durst fall in love ...

When Fawn inquires, 'But why has the Duke thus laboured to have all the fools shipped out of his dominions?' Dondolo responds 'Marry, because he would play the fool himself alone, without any rival' (4.187–236).

---

[55] Peter Seddon, ed., *The Letters of Sir John Holles*, Thoroton Record Society (3 vols., Nottingham, 1975–83), II, 315, 333.

Indeed, Dulcimel dupes her father, the 'wise' Duke Gonzago: 'I will so stalk on the blind side of my all-knowing father's wit that, do what his wisdom can, he shall be my only mediator . . . he shall direct the prince the means, the very way to my bed' (3.258–64).

The Parliament of Cupid, centrepiece of the last act, sees the victory of Dulcimel and other court women. Fawn serves as Speaker, the ladies of the court act as jury. Their triumph (and Queen Anne's) is suggested by Donna Zoya's triumph over the needlessly jealous Don Zuccone. He now swears he will never suspect her again even 'if I chance to have a humour to be in a masque, you shall never grow jealous . . . or grudge at the expense' (5.344–7).

As Philip Finkelpearl has suggested, the Parliament of Cupid plays to the legal and political interests of its London audience. Cupid begins with a speech similar to King James's first speech to Parliament in 1604: 'Since multitude of laws are signs either of much tyranny in the prince or much rebellious disobedience in the subject, we rather think it fit to study how to have our old laws thoroughly executed, than to have new statutes cumbrously invented.'[56] Cupid's parody of Tudor statutes attacks the follies presented in the rest of the play. Thus 'love' was 'basely bought and sold, beauty corrupted', and men 'engrossed' (5.186–223).[57] Finally, a bawdy piece of legislation, modelled on statutes regulating retaining, is triumphantly adopted to regulate court sexuality.

Be it therefore enacted, by the sovereign authority and erected ensign of Don Cupid, with the assent of some of the lords, most of the ladies, and all the commons, that what person or persons . . . in the trade of honour, presume to wear at one time two ladies' favours, or at one time shall earnestly court two women in the way of marriage, or if any under the degree of a duke shall keep above twenty women of pleasure, a duke's brother fifteen, a lord ten, a knight or a pensioner or both four, a gentleman two, shall *ipso facto* be arrested by folly's mace, and instantly committed to the ship of fools, without either bail or mainprize.   (5.229–41)[58]

Arrested, Sir Amoroso Debile-Dosso notes the work of Fawn, the false courtier, 'all inward, inward, he lurked in the bosom of us' (5.288–9). Such discourse stretches from the language of Sir Thomas Wyatt's early sixteenth-century characterisation of courtiers as 'rather than to be, outwardly to seem', to the Overbury murder tracts which described courtiers as 'comely

---

[56] See Finkelpearl, *John Marston of the Middle Temple*, p. 225.

[57] Cupid's versions of Tudor statutes include: 'maintaining and relieving of his old soldier, maimed or dismembered in love' (5. 207–8); 'an act against the plurality of mistresses', a parody on the holding of multiple ecclesiastical benefices; 'young gallants' have 'engrossed the care or cures of divers mistresses . . . whereby their mistresses must of necessity be very ill and unsufficiently served and likewise many able portly gallants live unfurnished of competent entertainment, to the merit of their bodies.'

[58] Blostein, ed., *Parasitaster or The Fawn*, p. 224n suggests that plurality did not yet have this meaning and connects it instead to enclosure.

without, but within, nothing but rotten bones, and corrupt practices'.[59]

The ultimate gull is Gonzago himself who, in attempting to thwart the match of Tiberio for Dulcimel has, in fact, brought it about. As Hercules moves towards this final uncovering, Gonzago says, 'Of all creatures breathing, I do hate those things that struggle to seem wise, and yet are indeed fools' (5.398–400). Throughout the play Marston has displayed the silly Duke of Urbino who claims wisdom and learning and yet is constantly shown to be a fool. Welcoming Tiberio to his court to woo Dulcimel for his father Duke Hercules, Gonzago says to Granuffo:

> Men of discerning wit
> That have read Pliny can discourse, or so
> But give me practice; well-experienced age
> Is the true Delphos: I am no oracle
> But yet I'll prophesy . . .
> We have been a philosopher and spoke
> With much applause; but now age makes us wise,
> And draws our eyes to search the heart of things,
> And leave vain seemings . . . wise heads use but few words
> . . . Plain meaning shunneth art . . .
> We use no rhetoric.
>
> (1.2.150–88)

David Blostein and Philip Finkelpearl point to the similarities with King James's first speech to the English Parliament on 19 March 1604: 'I will plainly and freely in my manner tell you . . . That it becometh a King, in my opinion, to use no other eloquence than plainness and sincerity.'[60]

Or again: Gonzago says 'for as we be flesh and blood, alas, we are fools, but as we are princes, scholars, and have read Cicero *de Oratore*, I must confess there is another matter in't' (4.612–15). Referring to the wisdom that only rulers have, Gonzago admits 'what I will say or so, / Until I say, none but myself shall know' (2.508–9). Thus Marston disposes of James's *arcana imperii*.

In the final act the bifurcation of the wise and the silly king is overcome with the triumph of love and the promise of generation. Gonzago's amazement is soothed by Hercules resuming his 'own shape' as Duke of Ferrara saying 'see, my good lord, Ferrara's o'erjoyed prince meets them in fullest wish' (5.470–2). Indeed as the final act opened the disguised Duke Hercules had observed the exchange of vows of Tiberio and Dulcimel for which he had prayed. 'O bless the sheets / Of yonder chamber, that Ferrara's dukedom, / The race of princely issue, be not cursed, / And ended in abhorred barrenness' (5.6–9). Here Marston offered praise the Jacobean court could accept with pleasure.

---

[59] Kenneth Muir and Patricia Thompson, *The Collected Poems of Sir Thomas Wyatt* (Liverpool, 1969), p. 91; *The Bloody Downfall of Adultery, Murder, Ambition* (1615), A3v-4.

[60] Quoted in Blostein, ed., *Parasitaster or The Fawn*, p. 90n.

V

Marston worked within the public sphere in London created by the several Royal Households, the aristocratic households that circled them,[61] the Inns of Court, the law courts, the London companies, the heralds and the gentlemen attending Parliament in term time; that sphere allowed criticism of the court. Hercules's rueful speech about the lack of free speech in courts expresses views that might be Marston's own. 'Freeness, so't grow not to licentiousness, / Is grateful to just states. Most spotless kingdom, / And men – O happy – born under good stars, / Where what is honest you may freely think, / Speak what you think, and write what you do speak, / Not bound to servile soothings!' (1.2.331–6).[62]

The early years of James's reign saw a continuing tension in the work of dramatists who wrote court entertainments hoping for court favour and plays with which James and his Privy Council were unhappy. Marston's sunny *Fawn* with its witty attack on court flattery and pompous kings who thought themselves wise lacked the religious bite of other attacks such as that of Burgess. It was significantly different from the stronger attacks on evil counsellors and proto-Catholic policies that emerged in the 1620s, as for example in Middleton's *A Game at Chess* that made such an impression in 1624. The need for counsel was recognised within the court. In October 1605 Henry Howard, earl of Northampton, one of James's inner circle of privy councillors, wrote to the English ambassador in France:

At this instant we set hard about the preparation of matters for the Parliament. We are about to take away the scandals raised upon purveyors . . . which were the subject of exception the last time . . . The fair sweet royal hand that was wont to spread itself . . . hath now shut up itself so close . . . if men will forget the franchise of a Christmas at the first coming of our Master, when he neither knew the strength nor the weakness of his own estate (as you know that in England Christmases are seldom kept without misrule), I dare undertake that henceforth they shall have no more cause to complain of that kind of proclivity.[63]

Anti-Scots sentiment surfaced in the important parliamentary debates on the Union between 1604 and 1607. In 1610 Sir John Holles, a member of Prince Henry's Household, strongly attacked the Scots' monopoly of positions in the Bedchamber. In language not unlike that of John Burgess, Holles claimed the Scots were 'standing like mountains betwixt the beams of his grace and us . . . we most humbly beseech His Majesty his Bedchamber may be shared as well to those of our nation as to them . . . all favours and honour directly or indirectly pass through their hands; for not only they possess the royal presence, they be warm within, while the

[61] See Malcolm Smuts in *The Mental World of the Jacobean Court*, ed. Peck, pp. 99–112.
[62] Or again, 'Free speech gains foes, base fawnings steal the heart' (2. 588).
[63] BL, Stowe MS 168, fo. 169v, 10 October 1605.

Plate 9 James's Accession medal of 1603

best of ours starve without.'[64] King James took John Hoskins's 'Sicilian Vespers' speech in the Parliament of 1614 as an attack on the Scots, an attack that underlined his decision to dissolve 'The Addled Parliament' of 1614 and his unwillingness to call another until 1621.[65]

Did this public space contract or significantly change in the 1630s as the court of Charles I increasingly turned in on itself and demanded greater obedience to the political theories enunciated by the first Stuart king of

---

[64] Peck, *Court Patronage and Corruption*, p. 24.
[65] Conrad Russell, *The Addled Parliament of 1614: The Limits of Revision*, The Stenton Lecture, 1991 (Reading, 1992).

England?[66] And were these views more stringently enforced in Star Chamber and the ecclesiastical courts? With the failure to call Parliament in the 1630s were there fewer opportunities to voice these opinions in the capital?

Finally, to what extent did contemporary literary representations help shape later narratives of the Jacobean court? Is *The Fawn* a portrait of James I? After all the play ends with an anti-masque that is a procession of drunkenness, sloth, pride and plenty, folly, war, beggary attending Cupid to his throne. Such a procession was widely commented on during the visit of Christian IV when, as Sir John Harington wrote sulkily, 'we are going on, hereabouts, as if the devil was contriving every man should blow up himself, by wild riot, excess, and devastation of time and temperance'.[67] *The Fawn* presents not a real portrait of James I but a fiction that came to be current in his lifetime and which bloomed in the hothouse of Commonwealth propaganda. We respond to this portrait of James I, although it has been subjected to historical revision, because it retains its narrative force. Indeed, it is especially potent because it was shaped by narratives of court life that preceded the king's rule and which continued unabated from his accession to Thomas Scot's attacks on favourites and evil counsellors in the 1620s and Commonwealth propaganda about debauchery and popery.

Citing Tacitus and Seneca, the historian William Camden wrote a cautionary note in 1614 to those who criticised the Jacobean court:

> as the seasons of the year, so men's manners have their revolutions ... Our age is not only faulty, our ancestors have complained, we complain, and our posterity will complain, that manners are corrupted, that naughtiness reigneth, and all things wax worse and worse ... In one age there will be more adulterers, in an other time there will be excessive riot in banqueting. ... In another age cruelty and fury of civil war will flash out, and sometimes carousing and drunkenness will be counted a bravery. So vices do ruffle among themselves, and usurp one another.[68]

When Ben Jonson was called before the Council over *Sejanus*, he insisted that his play describing the climb of an unworthy favourite in first-century Rome had no political implications. Whatever Jonson's intent, King James himself provided an alternative reading of the relevance of first-century Rome to his reign. On his Accession medal he presented himself in Roman dress wearing the laurel wreath with the motto Emperor of all Britain. To his English subjects James thought he brought, like Augustus, peace, plenty and Union.[69] For James, that was truly a labour worthy of Hercules.

---

[66] See Kevin Sharpe, *Criticism and Compliment: The Politics of Literature in the England of Charles I* (Cambridge, 1987).

[67] Sir John Harington, *Nugae Antiquae* (3 vols., 1779), II, 130 (1606), Harington to Secretary Barlow.

[68] The passage continues 'As for us we may say always of ourselves: we are evil, there have been evil ... and evil there will be. There will always be tyrants, murderers, thieves, adulterers, extortioners, church-robbers, traitors and others of the same rablement.' William Camden, *Remaines Concerning Britaine* (1614), p. 198. Camden added this passage to this edition.

[69] BL, Department of Coins and Medals, 1603, King James's Accession Medal.

Flattering Courtly Desire

Frank Whigham

John Marston's little-read *Parasitaster, or The Fawn* (1604)[1] is an interregnum play, in its moment of literary production (while Elizabeth's death and the plague had closed the theatres during 1603–4), its City culture's socio-political moment (between Elizabethan and Jacobean), and in its own narrative line of event (played out before an apparently absent prince). In such a moment of closeted activity, in such a state of pause, this text presents a typifying or capturing photograph, a Foucauldian monument. It bears complex relations with these and other surrounding discursive settings – to extra-textual questions of the disguised-ruler genre, of hidden surveillance, of unseen ungratified courtly desires, public and private. In what follows I proceed in two movements: an appraisal of these varied determinants' conjunction, and an exploration of Marston's own peculiar focusing of their contradictions on the medicating conversion of appetite to flattery.

Special thanks, for rich and demanding comments on this essay, to the editors, especially Richard Strier, and to Ted Leinwand, Louis Montrose, Jo Anne Shea and Bill Worthen.

[1] The earliest possible date of performance is 9 April, 1604, when the theatres reopened after a plague closure; the Stationers' Register entry is dated 12 March, 1606. See John Marston, *Parasitaster, or The Fawn*, ed. David A. Blostein, The Revels Plays (Manchester and Baltimore, 1978), pp. 32–6. (I quote hereafter from this edition.)

The Fawn has received relatively little critical attention. For an introduction, the reader can consult the following (in addition to Blostein): Anthony Caputi, *John Marston, Satirist* (Ithaca, 1961); Philip J. Finkelpearl, *John Marston of the Middle Temple* (Cambridge, Mass., 1969); John Scott Colley, *John Marston's Theatrical Drama* (Salzburg, 1974); Michael Scott, *John Marston's Plays* (New York, 1978); R. W. Ingram, *John Marston* (Boston, 1978); Ejner J. Jensen, *John Marston, Dramatist: Themes and Imagery in the Plays* (Salzburg, 1979); George L. Geckle, *John Marston's Drama: Themes, Images, Sources* (London and Toronto, 1980). References to these sources hereafter appear in my text. For a general list of criticism see Kenneth Tucker, *John Marston: A Reference Guide* (Boston, 1985). For biographical information see Finkelpearl and Ingram and, for a good recent summary, *The Selected Plays of John Marston*, ed. MacDonald P. Jackson and Michael Neill (Cambridge, 1986).

Caputi offers the following summary, which may help to account not only for tonal mildness of the play, as he says, but for its lesser claim to critical attention. 'No one would claim for [*The Fawn*] a comic power so complex or so impressive as that of *The Malcontent*. The cardinal fact is that in *The Fawn* Marston has turned his skills to an action essentially simpler and more limited than that of *The Malcontent*. In important respects *The Fawn* turns on the familiar formula consisting of the satirist and the parade of satiric types. Marston has added to the formula the duke in disguise and has amplified it with skill and ingenuity such as he commanded only at the height of his powers. But the whole makes a relatively simple appeal and offers very few of *The Malcontent*'s possibilities for meaningful discovery and reversal and none of its opportunities to explore extremes of distress and reassurance' (*John Marston, Satirist*, p. 203). I hope to contest this last judgement, so far as the issue of reassurance goes.

I

Like many another court-focused Jacobean play, *The Fawn* processes the dyad of flattery and desire. After the tense waning years of the old queen and the exciting accession of the new king, at the exact cusp of the famous shift from Elizabethan scarcity to Jacobean inflation of honours,[2] these categories were especially foregrounded. Courtly desires long intensified by Elizabeth's anality now confronted a new scene. James and his pyramid of followers were not as yet worn out or hardened by begging, so effort seemed to have a new potential. The inward zones and boundaries of privilege, however, now took on the additional strangeness of Scots origin, seeming unintelligible, foreign and xenophobic by turns. Furthermore, in a political environment defined by categories of preferment rather than bureaucracy, advancement often seemed to proceed in secret. Personal relations (what now seems to us the private) counted as, or more than, public criteria of rationalist qualification, only dimly in view in this proto-bureaucratic setting.[3] Given such scarcity of both preferment and information, temperatures of all kinds rose.

The Jacobean stage addressed sectors of the hungry London political body much concerned with such fluctuations, and traded vigorously in relevant interrogations, speculations, provocations, analyses and fantasy gratifications. The manipulations of courtly desire had of course long served as food for the stage, but in these transition years such matter had especially local reference, and usually received disturbing, even grotesque and lurid, attention: Shakespeare's *Troilus and Cressida* (1602), *Measure for Measure* (1604), and *King Lear* (1605), and Tourneur or Middleton's *The Revenger's Tragedy* (1606) come easily to mind. Marston himself is notorious for just such disturbance, beginning with *Certain Satires* (1598); in these years he also produced *The Malcontent* (1604) and *The Dutch Courtesan* (1605), and shared in *Eastward Ho!* (1605), all caustic texts that foreground the driven struggle for secret gratifications and the newly changed environment of opportunity.

A further entanglement of the stage with its cultural locale derives from another kind of scarcity: the great year-long epidemic of bubonic plague contorted the stage's encounter generally with the phenomena of accession and access. The theatres had been closed since 19 March 1603, and the restraint of playing was apparently not lifted until 9 April of the following year.[4] Stage comment on the exciting new courtly scene was thus initially

---

[2] For the classic statement see Lawrence Stone, *The Crisis of the Aristocracy, 1558–1641* (Oxford, 1965), pp. 65–128.

[3] For basic data see J. E. Neale, 'The Elizabethan Political Scene', in *idem, Essays in Elizabethan History* (1959), pp. 59–84; and Wallace MacCaffrey, 'Place and Patronage in Elizabethan Politics', in *Elizabethan Government and Society*, ed. S. T. Bindoff *et al.* (1961), pp. 95–126.

[4] To be precise, plays had been restrained during the fatal illness of Elizabeth on 19 March, and then not resumed owing to plague, which was first reported in the suburbs on 3 March. For data see E. K. Chambers,

repressed by a natural as well as a political censorship (which followed hard upon it). James's ceremonial (that is, physical) accession to the throne was likewise truncated and privatised by the plague danger. He remained unknown to his new populace for much longer than would otherwise have been the case. Further, the specific retirements and evasions of this general lacuna helped stimulate a public sense (much confirmed on other grounds later) of the new king's personal disinclination for public dealing, so different from Elizabeth's florid ceremonial habits.[5]

It is at just this juncture that, when the theatres finally did open, a new dramatic form opened with them – what has come loosely to be called the 'disguised-ruler play'. *Measure for Measure* is the most famous of these (and *Troilus* and *Lear* show clear signs of the absent-ruler motif). Marston also wrote two, *The Malcontent* and *The Fawn*, and several other authors, including Middleton, essayed some version of the form.[6] Between 1603–4 and 1606 at least ten appeared, after which the genre faded from view. This clustering marks the set as particularly local, that is, particularly historically responsive, to the factors enumerated above. The confluent response the genre exhibits, its specific explained world, is produced by a social phenomenology of breathless attention to secret desires and absent rulers. In the typical case, a superior figure absents himself from court, disguising himself as a subject and producing a climate of surveillance; from this vantage he observes and comments upon others' privy desires, political, social and sexual; these desires are amplified by the opportunity-vacuum his absence creates; he encourages their indulgence, exposes the actors to public justice, and reaps and purveys various benefits, personal as well as collective.[7]

The Elizabethan Stage (Oxford, 1923), IV, 349–50 (Appendix E: Plague Records); and F. P. Wilson, *The Plague in Shakespeare's London* (Oxford, 1927). For much stimulation regarding the influence of this hiatus on the theatre, I am indebted to Eric S. Mallin, *Inscribing the Time: Shakespearean Contexts, 1600–1603*, forthcoming in 1995 from University of California Press. For a revisionist exploration of the effects of this variable on Shakespeare's career, see Leeds Barroll, *Politics, Plague, and Shakespeare's Theater: The Stuart Years* (Ithaca, 1991).

[5] Much has been done with James's reputation for secretiveness and dislike of the public in pursuit of topical readings of *Measure for Measure*. See, for instance, Ernest Schanzer, *The Problem Plays of Shakespeare* (New York, 1963); Josephine Waters Bennett, '*Measure for Measure' as Royal Entertainment* (New York, 1966); David L. Stevenson, *The Achievement of Shakespeare's 'Measure for Measure'* (Ithaca, 1968).

[6] Some earlier plays, prefiguring the full form of the genre, present rulers as briefly disguised, often for light comic purposes, and not for the whole play. Examples include *Fair Em* (c. 1590), *A Knack to Know a Knave* (1592), *George a Greene* (Greene?, 1599), Heywood's *Edward IV* (1599), *I Sir John Oldcastle* (Drayton, Munday, Wilson, and Hathway, 1600), Rowley's *When You See Me You Know Me* (1603–5), and, most famously, *Henry V* (1599). For fully developed specimens, see Middleton's *Phoenix* (1603–4), and the following varied efforts: John Day's *Law Tricks* (1604) and *The Isle of Gulls* (1606), Dekker and Webster's *Westward Ho!* (1604), Dekker's *Honest Whore II* (1604–5), the anonymous *London Prodigal* (1604), and Edward Sharpham's *The Fleire* (1606). For discussions of the genre see Victor Oscar Freeburg, *Disguise Plots in Elizabethan Drama: A Study in Stage Tradition* (New York, 1915); Muriel C. Bradbrook, 'Shakespeare and the Use of Disguise in Elizabethan Drama', *Essays in Criticism*, 2 (1952), 159–68; J. W. Levers's introduction to his Arden edition of *Measure for Measure* (1965); and Leonard Tennenhouse, *Power on Display: The Politics of Shakespeare's Genres* (1986), pp. 154–9.

[7] *The Revenger's Tragedy* offers a slant parallel with these plays, substituting a disguised flattering victim for the disguised flattering ruler; the meddlings and exposures are very similar, and Vindice and Hercules share the motives and methods of theatricalised revenge – endlessly permuted in the period.

The mutual readings and editings between the unseen prince and his curious and hungry commonweal constitute the essential practice of this genre. The seminal term for theorising such a dramatic action might be *humiliation*, with its derivative and correlative actions of hiding, puppetry, voyeurism, exposure, display and degradation. I speak of these not as moral but as structural phenomena, enacting positional relations, of will and power and knowledge and the Gaze, after the example of Sartre in *Being and Nothingness*.[8] The relational dyad is presented as invariably structured asymmetrically: the Gazing subject dominates the seen known object of the Gaze. If unseen, unknown, the Gazer is so much the more dominant. This figure obviously describes the doubly hierarchical relation between disguised ruler and unaware subject. It can also parse the shared practice (analogous by reversal) of playwright and audience, who bond in a voyeuristic relation of unseen comprehending dominance (which Sartre would call sadistic) both to the onstage scene and to its offstage referent.

Such a literary form mandates an effect especially relevant to *The Fawn*. Crucial moments tend to fold private and public together in complex ways. Private desires get expressed, nearly always extravagantly, in situations only apparently private; such expressions are embarrassingly overheard, witnessed, eavesdropped upon, by others standing in onstage for the audience. The witness is often the disguised prince whose absence liberates the desires, and whose power can transform, for good or ill, the desired fate. Such unwitting nakedness carries many valences for the audience; the caustic exposures of the satirist, comic trap-setting for pratfalls, even fearful productions of self-knowledge. Generally, the effects seem to be placed in simultaneous relation to the soliloquist's libidinised transport and the observer's unseen scorn, between social id and social superego.

This binary opposition works clearly in *The Malcontent*. There the favourite Mendoza luxuriates in his advancement by the usurping Duke Pietro:

What a delicious heaven is it for a man to be in a prince's favour! ... To have a general timorous respect observe a man, a stateful silence in his presence, solitariness in his absence, a confused hum and busy murmur of obsequious suitors training him: the cloth held up, the way proclaimed before him; petitionary vassals licking the pavement with their slavish knees ...   (1.5.20–9)[9]

Unknown to him, however, the true Duke Altofronto, disguised as Malevole the malcontent, sees and derides such self-defiling desires:

> How smooth to him that is in state of grace,
> How servile is the ruggedest courtier's face.

---

[8] See Jean-Paul Sartre, 'Concrete Relations with Others: Love, Masochism, Sadism', in *Being and Nothingness: An Essay on Phenomenological Ontology* (1943), trans. Hazel E. Barnes (New York, 1956) (III. 3), pp. 471–558.
[9] Cited from G. K. Hunter's Revels edition (1975).

What profit, nay what nature would keep down,
Are heaved to them are minions to a crown.
Envious ambition never sates his thirst,
Till, sucking all, he swells and swells, and bursts.

(1.4.75–80)

Though coded as indulgent and expulsive respectively, the regressive and repulsively liquid orality stabilises the play's nominal socio-political moral-ity: the lead character, like the audience, is shielded from any uncomfort-able feeling that, as usurped duke, the Malcontent spits on the very advancement he lacks. His restoration is a restoration of order, and the libidinal gratifications of Mendozas are thus both transcended and tacitly conserved in Malevole's final return to his dukedom.

However, Malevole's identity *in propria persona* is 'Altofronto': his 'true' name is 'Other'. As the name's curious turn suggests, the binary is unstable, and prone to collapse. The speaker is often, perhaps typically, witnessed voicing his or her own manipulative plans for smooth courtly climbing past unaware others. This means two things. First, when scorning observer scrutinises scorning observer, the supposed poles – of viewer and viewed, superego and id – coincide. Speaker and unseen auditor (and offstage audience) can feel, indeed savour, both the emotional transport and the alienated condescension. Second, the business of smooth climbing is based on the manipulative praxis of flattery. Fawning, however apparently submissive, is its own form of sadistic hidden-gaze dominance. These cognate effects, of passion coincident with condescension, and self-subjection coincident with covert dominance, reinforce one another.

This coincident affect is often read as a feature of Marston's psychology. The author of *Certain Satires* is frequently thought to be personally obsessed with castigating dirt, with the satirist's double taste for fondling the things he snarls at. I suggest that such affect is also – or perhaps instead – a feature of the dyads Marston writes of and for: the binary relations of unseen witnessing depicted onstage, and that of the auditors consuming the staged commodity.

In *The Fawn* Marston tries to bring these implicit contradictions to manifest textual consciousness, and to process, to find a use for them. This effort depletes the caustic tones typical of his earlier explorations, and brings the play into the field of folly rather than crime, as Jonson had it,[10] comedy rather than bitter satire. Marston is concerned in this play more with transformation or sublimation than with punishment, or amputation. Still, the categories of mild and sharp are alternatives, not opposites, and they correlate and interpenetrate in complex ways. His

---

[10] *Every Man in his Humour*, ed. Gabriele Bernhard Jackson (New Haven, 1969), Prologue 24.

efforts to process rather than expel concern the same materials as were earlier registered in more alkaline tones. What turns out to be different is that the contaminating permeations of positionality and desire are acknowledged.

This unfamiliar play has a relatively familiar plot. Hercules, Duke of Ferrara, visits the neighbouring kingdom of Urbino in disguise, presenting himself as the would-be courtier Fawn; he flatters various new comrades in their vices, eventually driving them to cathartic and transformative surfeits of self-indulgence, weeding the unweeded garden of Urbino's ineffectual Duke Gonzago, who is in like need of the moral medication of self-knowledge.

Marston's objectives are further elaborated in a marriage-plot. Hercules has a cold son, Tiberio, who refuses to marry. His father once proposed Dulcimel, daughter of Gonzago, but Tiberio remained unstirred. As the play begins, the father sends the son, as his agent, to woo Dulcimel on his behalf, hoping presumably to arouse the energies of mimetic desire.[11] Hercules then goes to Urbino to supervise the action in secret.[12] Duke Gonzago, however, crosses the plan. Anxious to promote this May–January match with his neighbour Duke Hercules, and narcissistically confident in an absurd Polonian wisdom, he relentlessly cautions his daughter against noticing Tiberio's youthful charms. She notices them anyway. Repulsed by the geriatric offer of Hercules, she sets out not only to land the passive Tiberio, but to make her father the tables-turned agent of the deflection. Her witty erotic rebellion is successful, and the satisfied Hercules prayerfully rejoices on watch below the window to her chamber while she and the repentant Tiberio renew his lineage within. (Given that Hercules's desire is for little Herculi, Tiberio's desired desire is to be mimetic indeed.)

Both marriage-plot and courtier-plot centre on distortions and gratifications of the libido. Each courtier Hercules encounters is defined by sexual deviance. Herod cuckolds his impotent brother Sir Amoroso Debile-Dosso, and is provided maintenance for these services by his sister-in-law Donna Garbetza. Nymphadoro courts every lady he sees, hilariously pledging his undying faith to each in precisely the same form of words. Don Zuccone, who has not slept with his wife for years, is convinced that his chaste Lady Zoya has cuckolded him, and bitterly proclaims the defaming 'fact' on every street corner. Hercules drives on each man to carry his courtly neurosis to a self-humiliating apotheosis, to board the emblematic

---

[11] For elaboration of his famous concept in specific relation to the Renaissance, see René Girard, *A Theater of Envy: William Shakespeare* (New York, 1991).

[12] He presents the following explanation to his brother: 'My son, as you can well witness with me, could I never persuade to marriage, although myself was then an ever-resolved widower, and though I proposed to him this very lady to whom he is gone in my right to negotiate. Now how his cooler blood will behave itself in this business would I have an only testimony. Other contents shall I give myself, as not to take love by attorney, or make my election out of tongues' (1.1.20–8).

Ship of Fools in the play's closing masque, and supposedly to depart a wiser man.

So far, both plots get adequately run by the praxis of comic humiliation; benighted narcissistic men are secretly manipulated into surfeit and public self-disclosure for the auditors' pleasure and the stage society's eventual 'good'. Marston moves beyond such familiar analysis by means of two successive narrative complications that will now focus my inquiry. First of all, Marston provides another, private, hidden and problematic motive to Hercules's visit to Urbino for lineal (if not public) surveillance. After leaving his brother in charge of Ferrara, Hercules delivers this soliloquy:

> And now, thou ceremonious sovereignty –
> Ye proud, severer, stateful complements,
> The secret arts of rule – I put you off;
> Nor ever shall those manacles of form
> Once more lock up the appetite of blood.
> 'Tis now an age of man – whilst we all strict
> Have lived in awe of carriage regular
> Apted unto my place, nor hath my life
> Once tasted of exorbitant affects,
> Wild longings, or the least of disranked shapes –
> But we must once be wild; 'tis ancient truth –
> O fortunate, whose madness falls in youth!
> Well, this is text, whoever keeps his place
> In servile station is all low and base.
> Shall I because some few may cry, 'Light, vain,'
> Beat down affection from desirèd rule?
> He that doth strive to please the world's a fool.
> To have that fellow cry, 'O mark him, grave,
> See how austerely he doth give example
> Of repressed heat and steady life',
> Whilst my forced life against the stream of blood
> Is tugged along, and all to keep the god
> Of fools and women, Nice Opinion,
> Whose strict preserving makes oft great men fools
> And fools of great men.
>
> (1.1.37–61)

Hercules, it seems, desires to ignite not only his son's libido but his own. His caretaker brother immediately and fearfully viewed the disguise-venture in just such terms, warning that 'Honour avoids not only just defame, / But flies all means that may ill voice his name' (1.1.15–16). Falsification of identity must have ulterior motives, people will think. However, Hercules appears to set out precisely to repudiate such repressive Nice Opinion, to divest himself of the 'servile station' (50) of princes, to let the 'stream of blood' follow its own channel for once.

This disruptive resolve is no sooner voiced, however, than it is strikingly transformed, resetting interpretive demand a second time. When Hercules

arrives in Urbino, he meets Herod and Nymphadoro, and after parading
their neuroses (or perhaps, as Kenneth Burke might prefer, their socioses),
they invite the Fawn to participate in a plot to advance him and themselves
by intercepting the match of Dulcimel with Hercules (partially on grounds
of gross generational unfitness, and also assuming that Tiberio will inevitably cuckold his father – both mildly moral goals by certain standards)
and promoting Nymphadoro (who thus rivals both father and son) to her
bed instead. General promotion for all is to follow. They exit, and Hercules
reflects on what he has heard. In a seizure of self-discovery ('I never knew
till now how old I was', 1.2.318) and self-transformation, he laments the
preference of princes for flattery over sharp speaking, and changes his
plans. He will revenge himself and all princes on such flatterers.

> I vow to waste this most prodigious heat,
> That falls into my age like scorching flames
> In depth of numbed December, in flattering all
> In all of their extremest viciousness,
> Till in their own loved race they fall most lame,
> And meet full butt the close of vice's shame.
>
> (1.2.345–50)

Much moved by the sight of hidden courtly desires, Hercules resolves to
transform his own inordinate lust into flattery, as a form of public service,
purging or gratifying himself and curing ('laming' – castrating?) the neighbour kingdom of its ills all at once.[13]

Marston presents us with a strange picture. Ferrara's Duke, sick of the
servile life of princes, goes in secret to the court of Urbino to go wild,
and decides to cathart his repressed heat as an unplaced courtier, by
specialising in flattery. Such a developing resolve is all the more curious
in the particular setting. Urbino was the birthplace and setting of Castiglione's *The Courtier*, dominant text of the Renaissance courtesy-literature
tradition. This tradition arose precisely in response to what the aristocracy
experienced as an epidemic of false courtliness and the corrupt social
mobility it enabled. This text strove to provide aristocratic Europe with
a lens for detecting courtly frauds, and grounded the revulsion ultimately
(in Book IV) in fear of the effects of courtly flattery. The wise prince, we
learn at Castiglione's Urbino, must fear above all to be misled by flattering
upstart counsellors who tell him what he wants to hear, in order to reap
private and destructive rewards of just the sort Gonzago's underlings
imagine.[14] Duke Hercules, escaping a life of repression, goes to this Urbino

---

[13] This spectacle of angry and repulsed excitement to imitation resembles Beatrice's ambivalent response to
DeFlores in Middleton and Rowley's *The Changeling*. 'I scarce leave trembling of an hour after' seeing him,
she says (2.1.91; cited from Joost Daalder's re-edited second New Mermaid edition, 1990). As her second lover
Alsemero observes of her response, 'There's scarce a thing but is both loved and loathed' (1.1.124).

[14] For a detailed analysis of the complex links between good and bad courtship in Castiglione, see Frank
Whigham, *Ambition and Privilege: The Social Tropes of Elizabethan Courtesy Theory* (Berkeley and Los Angeles, 1984),
passim.

to free his personal will, and flattery is – somehow – to be the site of his indulgence. What can Marston be up to?

The central interpretive challenge, it seems to me, is to interrogate this counter-intuitive and curiously specific translation of libido into flattery, to inquire into its logic and qualities and satisfactions – for Hercules, for Marston, and for his audience. David A. Blostein, *The Fawn*'s Revels editor, reading Marston in relation to neo-Stoicism, presents it as a piece of sound (early modern) psychological theory. As with physical cure via bleeding, purging and emetic, the healer of the soul encourages indulgence, surfeit, expulsion and a recovery of tempered proportion.[15] What troubles me about this move (and its analogues from comic and satiric theory) is its effective erasure of Hercules's own 'stream of blood'.[16] The interpretation enacts its own content. The interventionist flattering of the courtiers, like the vicarious courtship of Dulcimel, becomes all cure and no fun, all superego and no id. Hercules's painfully repressed private functions are sublimated fully into, colonised by, ducal propriety. Through 'moral allegory' (Blostein, p. 32) Hercules becomes the sheerly allegorical gardener-prince of *Richard II*, with none of the tyrannical surplus of the new Henry V, unto whose so-called 'grace' his 'passion is as subject / As is [his] wretches fettered in [his] prisons'.[17] Such readings as Blostein's would have us believe that Hercules quite happily satisfies his wild longings making licence plates, as convicts used to have to do in *film noir* penitentiaries.

I think we need to retain a sense of the oddness of the proposition of wasting lust in flattery, to ask why Hercules chooses *this* sublimation, to seek, perhaps, a more general way of understanding how flattery gratifies, satisfies, instantiates, 'wild longings'. This seems the more important in view of Marston's own oxymoronic identity as nastiest Elizabethan satirist and eventual Jacobean divine. He began his literary career by commoditising gross depictions of courtly lust in his satires, and ended it by departing the stage for the pulpit. I suggest that midway, in *The Fawn*, Marston

---

[15] See Blostein, ed., *Parasitaster or The Fawn*, Introduction, passim. Though I will dispute Blostein's account of this pattern (as limited), I agree with him that it requires one; most readers take it for granted.

[16] One might also object to its neglect of the historical context of flattery and desire at court. Blostein is interested in Philip Finkelpearl's arguments linking the closing masque generically with Inns of Court Christmas Revels forms, but when Finkelpearl raises Upton's argument that Gonzago is a comic portrait of James, Blostein scents 'parochialism'. 'It would be naive to claim for *The Fawn* that it is for all time, but it is rather more than merely of an age,' he says. '*The Fawn* is a minor gem, but a gem, in which diverse facets sparkle within a single comic design' (see Blostein, p. 32). While a one-to-one equivalence to James indeed seems unlikely (Hercules is perhaps an equally good candidate, as can be seen by the Duke-as-James readings of *Measure for Measure*), relations with the historical semiotics of Jacobean courtly flattery are diverse, and hardly parochial. For attention to some of these links see Whigham, *Ambition and Privilege*. For Finkelpearl on the Ship of Fools masque, see 'The Use of the Middle Temple's Christmas Revels in Marston's *The Fawne*', *Studies in Philology*, 44 (1967), 199–209.

[17] See *Henry V*, 1.2.241–3; cited from *The Complete Works of Shakespeare*, ed. David Bevington (4th edn, New York, 1992). Is it relevant that the uncomfortable theatrics of King Harry the night before Agincourt are the principal pre-Jacobean antecedent of the very disguised-ruler genre? Or that this anerotic king also woos Harfleur with the verbal sword of rape and French Kate with country-farmhouse manners?

tried to do what he shows Hercules doing: transforming a prodigious licentious urge fully into a social form that reconstitutes it (or enables its redescription) as a virtue.

So far as Marston's audiences go, a similar logic of sublimation and indulgence applies. Tabloid fascination with licentious goings-on at court combines repulsion with attraction, superego and id working together, 'each in their function serving other's need', as Kyd's Don Andrea, speaking from beyond the grave, says of his eternal soul and wanton flesh.[18] Unusual and racy sexuality was central in the public – and storied – lives of Elizabeth and James, especially in regard to potential exploitations by smooth courtiers such as Hatton and Raleigh, Carr and Buckingham. But the police function was conspicuous too; both princes were known for surveillance and micromanagement of their subjects' sexual lives. Elizabeth, famous for both arousing and blocking erotic desires, watched like a hawk for erotic action among her courtiers and ladies-in-waiting. 'A spell in the Tower or the Fleet prison was the almost invariable punishment awaiting offenders who were found out', as Neale has it, naming Raleigh and Throckmorton, Oxford and Anne Vavasour, Mr Vavasour and Mistress Southwell, and Mr Dudley and Mistress Cavendish as peccant.[19]

Here, as with honours, Elizabeth seemed mainly to manage by saying no; James preferred the controlling role of enabler. He delighted, of course, in standing for many forms of union, beginning with that of England and Scotland, and 'made it his business to arrange marriages, discourage competition, and encourage alliances among aristocratic families'.[20] His own desires for favourites such as Carr and Buckingham, sometimes even if frustrated, seem not to have been jealous. He took great interest in arranging their marriages, and indeed gave away the newly certified Frances Howard to Robin Carr. His relation to the results of such efforts was intense:

if either bride or groom was a royal favourite King James would cross-question them closely the next morning to extract the last salacious details of the events of the night. The Earl of Nottingham was allowed to get up and dress to inform the King that he had 'drawne blood of his cosen'. . . . When his daughter Elizabeth married the Prince

---

[18] Cited from *The Spanish Tragedy*, ed. J. R. Mulryne, New Mermaid ed. (2nd edn, New York, 1989), 1.1.3.

[19] J. E. Neale, *Queen Elizabeth: A Biography* (1934; rpt. New York, 1957), p. 340. In 1934 Neale thought this perfectly appropriate. When Raleigh and Elizabeth Throckmorton conceived a child together, he reports, 'both partners in sin were sent to the Tower. Very properly' (p. 340). 'Like their manners and morals, [the ladies-in-waiting's] marriage was a royal responsibility, and it was a breach of duty as well as a gross personal affront to their sovereign to marry without her leave. Elizabeth's interference in their love affairs, of which there are several well-known stories, was simply the exercise of this peculiar relationship, not the jealousy of a lascivious or envious old maid – though, indeed, "a mixture of a lie doth ever add pleasure"' (p. 340). We would no longer feel easy, I think, about Neale's term 'simply'; as for his wonderful concessive *sententia*, who he thinks is lying, and about what, and with what resultant pleasure, is far from clear. Sometimes, certainly, pleasure and duty coincide. A related example of invasiveness, in which Elizabeth called for an autopsy on one of her ladies, in order to search the cadaver's heart for physical interior marks of erotic activity, will be dealt with in a forthcoming study of anatomies by Michael Neill.

[20] Leonard Tennenhouse, 'Representing Power: *Measure for Measure* in its Time', in *The Forms of Power and the Power of Forms in the Renaissance*, ed. Stephen Greenblatt, *Genre*, 7 (1982), 153.

Palatine, 'the next morning the King went to visit these young turtles . . . and did strictly examine him whether he were his true son in law, and was sufficiently assured'. In 1617, when Frances Coke was at last forcibly wedded to Sir John Villiers, they had to stay in bed the next day until the King came to conduct his habitual *post-coitum* interrogation.[21]

When Sir Philip Herbert married Lady Susan in 1604, James gave the bride away, and said she carried herself so well that were he unmarried he would keep her rather than give her away; the next morning, Dudley Carleton told Sir Ralph Winwood, 'the King in his shirt and night-gown gave them a Reveille Matin before they were up, and spent a good time in or upon the bed, choose which you will believe.'[22] (The last phrase shows both that James's behaviour was felt to be odd by contemporaries, and that they repeated its engaged voyeurism.) Such habits of supervision, simultaneously lurid and dutiful, were typical both of both monarchs and of their courtly audiences, who preserved the many stories so well for their friends, and for us, in private letters and memoirs. These conditions suggest very strongly that the Jacobean audience's interpretive appropriation of *The Fawn* would again repeat the sublimation–indulgence binary, at once mastering and gratifying the licentious.

It must have been something of a relief, after the political uncertainties and personal whims of Elizabeth's last years, to watch the prince, whether James or Duke Hercules, channelling libido and providing unmistakably for political continuity.[23] Indeed, Hercules seems compulsive in the project:

---

[21] Stone, *The Crisis of the Aristocracy*, p. 652. In their striking mixture of direct and vicarious desire, erotic and parental coincidence, these highly Jacobean scenes bear a certain middling resemblance to the behaviour of Duke Hercules, in deputising Tiberio to woo Dulcimel for his father, and then following to watch unseen, first relishing fantasies regarding his own 'stream of blood'. It is interesting to compare two other similar moments. First, James's emotional farewell in 1615 to Carr just prior to the latter's fall: '"For God's sake, let me", said the king – "Shall I, shall I?" then lolled about his neck. "Then, for God's sake, give thy lady this kiss for me."' Surely this kiss was meant for the nominal messenger, though addressed to his wife – a displacement familiar from *Twelfth Night*, where Orsino's use of Cesario as erotic ambassador contains something of this element. (To the conveyor of this somewhat obscure story, Sir Anthony Weldon, this scene embodies the purest dissimulation. Even if we presume with him that James was here acting with duplicity, behaving lovingly precisely while ejecting Carr from his grace, I see strong authentic desire and grief present as well.) The second example, a possibly related doubling, is another affectionate farewell, James to Buckingham in 1624: 'And so God bless you, my sweet child and wife, and grant that ye may ever be a comfort to your dead dad and husband.' Here a forbidden love is delivered by translogically combining the closest forms of disparate, indeed incommensurate kinship categories of agnatic and affinal bonding. In all of these cases triangles collapse confusingly into, and thus enable, blocked binaries – though which side of the triangle is most substantial remains problematic. Given (1) that James gave away many of the brides in question (*in loco parentis*), and (2) the kinship language of his farewell to Buckingham, it is possible, as Jo Anne Shea suggests to me, that something like incest may be the enabling trope in such manoeuvres – combining categories, naming the unnamed. (Weldon's report of James's farewell to Carr is cited from *James I by his Contemporaries*, ed. Robert Ashton (1969), p. 123; I owe the comparison with *Twelfth Night* to Shannon Prosser. The king's letter to Buckingham is cited by Roger Lockyer in *Buckingham: The Life and Political Career of George Villiers, First Duke of Buckingham 1592–1628* (1981), p. 233.)

[22] *Memorials of Affairs of State* (1725), 2.43.

[23] To some degree this is an ordinary princely concern, to which Elizabeth was simply an exception. In *The Fawn* it secondarily characterises the foolish Gonzago, of course, in his misguided efforts to link Dulcimel to Hercules. However, Marston was not alone in addressing the pent-up energies of dynastic apportionment through the device of princely disguise and retirement. Both Day's *The Isle of Gulls* and Sharpham's *The Fleire* exhibit related concerns: royal fathers similarly retire, leaving the realm in others' hands, disguise themselves, and labour deviously at the dual project of arousing and channelling libido toward heir-production. (Much

he aims to secure the lineage *two* generations past himself. In fact, Marston totally relocates the direct expression of Hercules's libidinal energies. None is available to attach him to the appropriate Philocalia, whose fitness is explicitly remarked: 'There were a lady for Ferrara's duke: one of great blood, firm age, undoubted honour, above her sex, most modestly artful, though naturally modest; too excellent to be left unmatched, though few worthy to match with her' (3.1.166–70). Hercules thinks briefly, but leaves her dangling. Narratively, Marston appears to insert her only for Hercules conspicuously to ignore.[24] (Dynastically speaking, the Duke already has an heir, and Philocalia's 'firm age' presumably puts her past childbearing. This aside, perhaps we see in his incapacity to attend to her Marston registering an origin for Tiberio's coldness.)

Surely, however, despite such civic-mindedness, *The Fawn* retained something edgily pornographic, probably at several levels. The very institution of the theatre depended fundamentally upon, and renewed, pornographic energies, according to many of the hostile divines Marston was eventually to join. Philip Stubbes, for instance, speaking apoplectically of the comparatively mild drama before 1583, says, 'There is no mischief which these plays maintain not.'

Do they not maintain bawdry, infinite foolery, and renew the remembrance of heathen idolatry? Do they not induce whoredom and uncleanness? Nay, are they not rather plain devourers of maidenly virginity and chastity? For proof whereof, but mark the

---

comment also passes on English courtly corruption, as in *The Fawn*.) Day takes his plot from Sidney's *Arcadia*: Basileus takes his daughters into retirement, 'troubled by the impetuous concourse of unruly suitors'; he then issues a challenge to 'all the youthful bloods of Africa': 'whosoever (borne of princely stem) / . . . [can] by his wit and active policy / Woo, win, entice, or any way defeat / Me of my charge, my daughters of their hearts, / Shall with their loves wear my imperial crown. . . .' All this comes to pass. In *The Fleire* Piso has deposed Duke Antifront, father of Felicia and Florida; they flee to England, becoming whores to support themselves. Antifront follows, is preferred as their gatekeeper Fleire, and comments variously on the odd ways of the English. *Inter alia*, he labours to wed his daughters to husbands who would restore their honour. The younger Piso, come to England, falls for the elder daughter, and when his usurping father dies and a messenger greets him as inheritor, he makes to return to Italy, where he would summon home the wronged Antifront, marry his daughter 'in satisfaction of his wrongs', and restore him to his estate 'whilst a lived' (presumably a reservation of succession for himself). Dynastic marriage between legitimate and usurped rulers' heirs is offered as repayment, penance, whatever. At this point Antifront reveals himself: 'I tax you to your word' (5.1.294–5, 299), and apportions several other women to men as well. Cited from *Materials for the Study of the Old English Drama*, ser. 1, v. 37 (1912; rpt. Vaduz, 1963 – v. 17).

All three plays are marked by ambiguous generational conflict over sexuality: daughters are hot with unruly libido, wifeless or otherwise unsatisfied fathers simultaneously wish for and try to block its investment, and bizarre courtly disguise (scrambling rank, gender, occupation) enables much mockery and satisfaction of desire – aged and youthful, appropriate and misguided, direct and voyeuristic alike. In each case dynastic ends are finally achieved, but the means can hardly be seen as direct or selfless. These seem as much fables of sexual indulgence as sexual control.

Bradbrook notes a related pattern, a subset of the disguise-genre in which a protector disguises himself to aid a loved one, citing Kent and Edgar in *King Lear*, Flowerdale Sr in *The London Prodigal* (1605), and Friscobaldo in *The Honest Whore* (1604); the last two are fathers providing for their children in ways related to Hercules's efforts. See 'Shakespeare and the Use of Disguise', 163.

[24] A less interesting (more 'psychological') possibility is that Philocalia would be too threatening to Hercules's autonomy; he wants to go wild, but prefers manipulating his inferiors in secret. A potent wife would get too close, know him too well. We can hear the tragic version of this preference for manipulative isolate sadism in Kyd's Lorenzo's 'I'll trust myself, myself shall be my friend.'

flocking and running to theatres and curtains, daily and hourly, night and day, time and tide, to see plays and interludes; where such wanton gestures, such bawdy speeches, such laughing and fleering, such kissing and bussing, such clipping and culling, such winking and glancing of wanton eyes, and the like, is used, as is wonderful to behold. Then, these goodly pageants being done, every mate sorts to his mate, every one brings another homeward of their way very friendly, and in their secret conclaves (covertly) they play the *Sodomites*, or worse. And these be the fruits of plays or interludes for the most part.[25]

The sheer fact of Hercules's disguise disturbs his moralist brother, much as the institutional fact of the disguising and transvestite theatre did its enemies. Transvestism, both of rank and gender, seemed very close to perversion, if indeed any distance remained at all. And the spectre of voyeurism beckons the auditor, both in terms of identification and of witness, engagement and detachment. As the Shakespeare of *Measure for Measure* well knew, we enjoy watching voyeurs, both to identify and to condemn.

The particulars are complex, though. The staging of *The Fawn* by the Children of the Queen's Revels results in a specifically and especially libidinal piece of cultural practice, but one traversed by several conflicting energies. Representing one tradition, Anthony Caputi argues that the children's companies, owing to what he sees as the necessarily burlesque quality of their acting, encouraged a highly distanced audience response, to adult passions made absurd.

Marston has provided strikingly clear opportunities for the buffo antics so characteristic of the children's satiric style. The absurdity inherent in Amoroso's background in debauchery, in Herod's boasts of sexual capacity, and in Nymphadoro's prodigious ambition along these lines hardly needs comment. And the four old men in the play fairly cry out for burlesque treatment in the hands of child actors. ... (p. 211)[26]

Though this may well be an appropriate view of the children's companies, which specialised in such guying, the effect of child acting *per se* is more complex. If the presentation of *The Fawn* by the Queen's Children distances and satirises its passions and humiliations along one axis, along another it may well have embodied and aroused them. Recent scholarship has richly explored the homoerotic potential of the boy actor onstage with adults.[27] And surely, given the literal and topical referentiality of dramatic

---

[25] Cited from *The Anatomie of Abuses* (1583) by Chambers, *The Elizabethan Stage*, IV, 223–4 (Appendix C: Documents of Criticism).

[26] See also Michael Shapiro, *Children of the Revels: The Boy Companies of Shakespeare's Time and their Plays* (New York, 1977), pp. 106–7.

[27] For a sample of relevant recent work on boy actors and the homoerotic in adult-company performance, see the following important studies: Lisa Jardine, '"As boys and women are for the most part cattle of this colour": Female Roles and Elizabethan Eroticism', in *Still Harping on Daughters: Women and Drama in the Age of Shakespeare* (1983; rpt. New York, 1989), pp. 9–36; Jonathan Dollimore, 'Subjectivity, Sexuality and Transgression: The Jacobean Connection', *Renaissance Drama*, n.s., 17 (1986), 53–81; Stephen Orgel, 'Nobody's Perfect: Or Why Did the English Stage Take Boys for Women?', *South Atlantic Quarterly*, 88 (1989), 7–29; Peter Stallybrass, 'Transvestism and the "body beneath": Speculating on the Boy Actor', in *Erotic Politics: Desire on the Renaissance*

sexuality in both child-actor and adult theatre, plenty of hetero-erotic energy circulated as well.[28]

However possibly anerotic, the Children of the Queen's Revels were, as E. K. Chambers noted long ago, thoroughly racy along another axis, as the principal offenders in regard to political satire. During just these years they gave offence and were vigorously chastised in regard to Daniel's *Philotas* (1604), Chapman, Jonson and Marston's *Eastward Ho!* (1605), Day's *Isle of Gulls* (1606), and twice in 1608, with Chapman's *Byron* and another, lost play on Scottish mines, possibly by Marston.[29] Authors were called before the Privy Council, imprisoned, threatened with mutilation. Such repression surely marks the presence of great public temptation.

No matter what generic alienation or repressive management of whatever libidinal centres supervened, the sheer thematised presence of sexual motifs must have aroused complex erotic expectations before processing them. Even if dangers and unsavoury habits are finally averted or closed off, such impacted tropes as royal voyeuristic sexual manipulation, incest, seduction of and by princely heirs, cuckolding brothers or fathers, and the wilful cuckold, would have done their work along the way. We must conclude that by virtue of several contextualising institutions – the controversial early modern transvestite theatre, the children's companies and their invertingly burlesque acting styles, the reputation for dangerous topical reference that the Children of the Queen's Revels in particular enjoyed, the avant-garde taste of the Inns of Court auditors and of Marston as their satirist-playwright, the homoerotic and voyeuristic fractions of the Jacobean court in general and its former-neighbour Scottish/English king in particular, and the widespread generic interest of English audiences in unusual sexuality on both courtly and worldly stages – *The Fawn* would have been experienced by its first auditors as a specifically eroticised text summoning up both engaged libidinal arousal and disenchanted libidinal analysis.

Stage, ed. Susan Zimmerman (New York, 1992), pp. 64–83; and Theodore Leinwand, 'Redeeming Beggary/ Buggery in *Michaelmas Term*', *ELH*, 61 (1994), 53–70.

[28] See, for instance, the famous episode of Burbage and Shakespeare's rivalry for the proffered favours of a citizen auditor, preserved in John Manningham's diary; see *The Diary of John Manningham of the Middle Temple, 1602–1603*, ed. Robert Parker Sorlien (Hanover, N.H., 1976), p. 75. See too the 'Character of a Player' from Earle's *Microcosmography*: 'The waiting women spectators are over-ears in love with him, and ladies send for him to act in their chambers'; see John Earle, *Microcosmography; or, A Piece of the World Discovered in Essays and Characters* (1628; rpt. 1897), p. 61. These descriptions make the early modern stage sound very much like the erotic site of a modern rock concert.
  The effects of the issue of emotional burlesque and the children's companies are ultimately unclear. It is certainly the case that the stakes of social interaction are often displayed in this drama with alienated distance and reserve (whether Marston's, ours, or that of the materials, language and conventions of children's drama). I nonetheless regard as central the fact that a variety of social interactions are both mediated by and vehicles for desire, particularly sexual desire. Such mutual substitution is a core issue or affective centre both for James's court and the play.
  [29] See Chambers, *The Elizabethan Stage*, I, 325–7; II, 50–5. there is a suggestive overlap between this set of offending children's plays and the genre of the disguised-ruler plays: seven of the ten listed earlier, all save *Measure for Measure*, *Westward Ho!* and *The London Prodigal*, were also played by children's companies. Perhaps the companies and the genre shared something of the territory of libidinal risk.

II

How, then, to address Hercules's urge to 'waste'?[30] How does Marston bring desire and flattery into analytic relation? Begin by noticing that Hercules's liberation speech is, sexually speaking, devoid of objects. We hear of 'the appetite of blood', 'exorbitant affects', 'wild longings', 'disranked shapes', 'repressed heat', 'the stream of blood'. Any audience might reasonably expect these phrases to refer to sexual lust, but in fact there are no human bodies here.[31] 'Women' appear, generically, but as (repressive? contemptible?) worshippers of Nice Opinion.[32] Instead, I suspect, we should read this speech as referring to the libidinal constraints of public princely life. Hercules has been forever compelled to govern his actions by reference to social responsibility. He experiences a private will subjugated to his public role, as prince. The desire that has been frustrated is generic, not specifically sexual, but no less libidinal for all that. His public social moral political identity has precisely not colonised his entire self; there is a surplus, which, it seems, would out.

We can discover more about this desire by noting that Hercules's flatteries are a *revenge*:

> since our rank
> Hath ever been afflicted with these flies
> (That blow corruption on the sweetest virtues),
> I will revenge us all upon you all
> With the same stratagem we still are caught,
> Flattery itself.
>
>   (1.2.336–41)

If we see the energies of repressed heat as an unproblematic reservoir of fuel for princely public service, the transformational mechanism is occluded. It is this middle term, *flattery* – derived somehow from sublimated libido, used paradoxically for moral cleansing – that resists interpretation. We need to explore this curious transitive use, of libido as flattery, and of flattery (doubly) as public service and revenge.

Revengers generally resent having been duped, unknowingly controlled, made puppets – all the more if they are themselves figures of power. Hercules seeks revenge for being controlled through manipulations of his own self-love. The revelation of having fallen by means of flattery is especially humiliating, even more so (as Othello thinks) if inferior others have witnessed it all along. Flattery uses knowledge of the Other's deep personal needs to control him. Such knowledge of a prince, set over all,

---

[30] The word will bear many readings. Blostein would perhaps prefer *cathart*; I am more interested in *instantiate* or *indulge* or *gratify*. Other associations come to mind. Shakespeare's puns in '*expense* of spirit' and '*waste* of shame' and associations of celibacy and autoeroticism with waste are particularly interesting.

[31] A possible exception is 'disranked shapes', which might just possibly refer to (erotic) bodies; Blostein takes the phrase to mean 'disorderly imaginings'. Perhaps it is also the case that Hercules is himself now occupying a 'disranked shape'. If so, is his disguise itself, like actors' antics, an indulgence of wild desire?

[32] Perhaps an index too of Gonzago's misperception of Dulcimel.

is especially criminal. It makes a prince, as it were, a private person, steals and uses his privacy, subverts his public persona by colonising his private one. What Hercules hates is this loss, both of princely power and of a relation to himself superior to that of others. He seeks to recover such relations, to self and to others, by seizing the corrupting repertoire of flatterers for his own civic and libidinal purposes (combined as civic vehicle and libidinal tenor).[33] Duke Hercules will forcibly (re)subject others to that which has subjected him: the invisible and inescapable obligation to moral propriety – in short, something rather close to Nice Opinion. His (ultimate) allegiance to propriety conserves his ducal uprightness; in the force of its enforcement lives his privately felt revenge.[34]

Hercules begins his humiliating revenge for such subjection appropriately: in disguise. He sets aside the institutional identity that was so humiliatingly insufficient to fend off the flatterers (and that, as institutional, disabled much of his sense of personal potency, made him 'servile') in order to deprive others of epistemological access. Turning these tables aims at going from being over-known to being under-known, being known better by others to being known only by oneself;[35] in short, seizing, regaining, a control one did not realise had been degradingly stolen. Narratively, the revelation of this hitherto invisible absence is what triggers the need for – or enables – the transformation of desire into flattery. Hercules has already (1.1.50) felt his orderly princely life as 'servile' to Nice Opinion, but when his revenge-declaration targets what he takes as the typifying, forcibly essentialising strokes of flatterers (flatteries that control our self-knowledge), he shifts his sense of injury from the internal moralistic stresses of *self*-denial to those of presumptuous subjection by *others*, from 'the god / Of fools and women, Nice Opinion', to the successful manipulations of absurd underlings such as Herod and Nymphadoro.[36]

---

[33] When Hercules invokes his revenge on (all) flatterers as pursued, as in a class action suit, on behalf of all (typically) injured princes, he is generalising, depersonalising – making civic – his sense of personal injury, recovering the public transindividual identity (the king's other body) subverted by such efficacious burglary of his privacy.

[34] Such impacted densities of desire, compliment, irony and malicious revenge can be matched in Marston's own personal dealings. John Manningham's *Diary* records (p. 133) the following episode, dated 21 November 1602: 'Jo. Marston the last Christmas when he danced with Alderman More's wife's daughter, a Spaniard born, fell into a strange commendation of her wit and beauty. When he had done, she thought to pay him home, and told him that she though[t] he was a poet. "'Tis true", said he, "for poets feign, and lie, and so did I when I commended your beauty, for you are exceeding foul."' Another history of such overdetermination is borne by the trajectory of assertions, rewritings, and retractions of various complimentary and critical relations to readers and subjects in the prefatory matter of Marston's string of satiric poems. Marston's Prologus to *The Fawn* itself concludes, 'In your pleased gracings all the true life blood / Of our poor author lives; you are his very graces. / Now if that any wonder why he's drawn / To such base soothings, know his play's – *The Fawn*' (Prologus, pp. 32–5). As befits the reading offered in this essay, the closing pronouns here embrace both flattered auditor and flattering author, both 'drawn to . . . soothing'.

[35] Thus the machiavel entices the trust of others with the gestural 'you know my mind'; see, for instance, Kyd's Lorenzo (*The Spanish Tragedy*, 3.2.93).

[36] Again, perhaps another inverted link to Dulcimel, whose repudiation of Nice Opinion makes her father's attempted subjection of her produce a denial of his own self-flattering 'self-knowledge', forcibly replacing it with the home truth of his limits.

Their 'servile soothings' (1.2.336), so powerful if internalised, provide him with specific targets for compensatory abjection. He will transform insincere servility to the real thing.[37]

So, how is flattery wild, appetitive? Immediately, of course, it aims to gratify the self, but it appears to require, as a modal price, self-subjugation. The flatterer bows, scrapes, grovels, we think, selling his dignity. Yet Hercules deflects part of this recipe at once, by substituting a worthy and other-directed authorisation, of moral cure. This might well serve to deflect a sense of self-trivialisation, yet as a formulation it still screens any reticent heat from view. (I think this is part of its purpose.) The issue of control suggests something more. How might flattery be an appropriately degrading vehicle for revenge here? First, of course, as Auden has taught us, the flattering revenger takes his cue from the will of the victim: in using that will to bring about a downfall, the revenger both steals it and acts effortlessly himself.[38] Second, the victim falls to an underling, whose assumed inferiority intensifies the humiliation. Third, flattering flatterers involves the competitive triumph of mining beneath their mines: they presume to play one like a pipe, but we play them instead, besting them on their chosen turf, and they don't know it. And finally, if they have stolen and enjoyed our autonomy, we share in, steal, that pleasure, in stealing it back, assuming the subordinate role for its pleasure in its own falsity, and enjoying the recursion, only available from below, from the injured position. Perhaps, too, princes might especially seek revenge upon flatterers because they encourage their victims in self-indulgence, in precisely what a proper prince is (so hatefully for Hercules) deprived of. They anger their victims both by making them aware of the sacrifices they must continually endure, and by suggesting that they are incompetent to endure them with ease. Princely resentment of subjects often seems rather petulant, given the range of comparative privilege, but the special animus that (known) flattery can stimulate seems quite explicable.

If, then, princes hate flatterers because of these control issues, the courtier-plots delineate the gratifications of the humiliating recovery of control. Herod is encouraged toward a moral pratfall to overlook the obvious – that repeated incestuous cuckoldry of his brother will result in an heir, who will displace his father as his 'father's' heir.[39] Where Herod

---

[37] Here as throughout, Gonzago seems to be the antitype of Hercules, always known without knowing, foolishly assuming his own superiority, always explaining the opacities of his genius, eternally enabling his own manipulation and exploitation – most obviously by the always silent and thus honoured lord Granuffo. Such unconscious self-evacuation is Hercules's nightmare.

[38] See W. H. Auden, 'The Joker in the Pack', in *The Dyer's Hand and Other Essays* (1948; rpt. New York, 1968), pp. 246–72; see also Sartre. For a related consideration of effortlessness, *sprezzatura*, and the establishment of an essence of self, see Whigham, *Ambition and Privilege*, pp. 93–5.

[39] Marston mentions this eventuality earlier in his career, in *The Scourge of Villanie* (1598), Satire X: 'And tell me Ned, what might that gallant be, / Who to obtain intemperate luxury, / Cuckolds his elder brother, gets an heir, / By which his hope is turned to despair?' (pp. 27–30). (Cited from *The Poems of John Marston*, ed. Arnold Davenport (Liverpool, 1961), p. 164.) Davenport suspects 'some current piece of scandal', and compares

has been confusing terms and categories, Hercules drives him to restore and conserve order and punish himself in the process. (The fact that the heir will not be Sir Amoroso's true direct production is perhaps a surplus of pleasurable libidinality inassimilable to the project of just sublimation – unless perhaps 'it serves Sir Amoroso right', as a foolish cuckold.) Nymphadoro has also been confusing categories, all ladies with each other, all as beloved, with a view to postponing his selection until their fortunes come home, by inheritance or other means. He is justly served for this mass instrumentalisation by being exposed as a pluralist investor concerned only with quantity, and is driven into the bankruptcy of being desired by none, even the poorest, Poveia. Don Zuccone is found guilty of slander against his wife, and made to submit to a re-contract worthy of Restoration Millamant in its forward-looking charter of wifely freedom and total spousal submission, as worshipper, lover, husband, male and servant.

What of the marriage-plot? It seems to address similar power-relations in similar ways, but now arrayed not only in terms of prince/subject and gender, but also in terms of parent/child and generational power-relations. Dulcimel sets herself the virtuoso task not only of bringing Tiberio slightly more into line with his illustrious Roman forbear, but of disempowering and abasing her own forbear's hubristic sense of knowing control. Marston saves for his climactic event the exposure of Duke Gonzago as the purest of the surfeited gulls set aboard the Ship of Fools. This exposure serves not so much the social hierarchy to which Hercules owes his sense of lost and regained proper superiority, but the quasi-biological priority of youthful sexual *telos* which Gonzago thinks to appropriate and disburse to Hercules, as political capital. Dulcimel's pleasure here is that of Hercules, triumphantly duping from below.

Her actions with Tiberio suggestively confirm the central status of the control issue. Marston makes very clear that what triggers Tiberio's erotic desire for Dulcimel is her witty rebellion against her father. Initially, he repels her cleverly implicit propositions: 'O, quick, deviceful, strong-brained Dulcimel, / Thou art too full of wit to be a wife' (3.1.460–1). He speaks of her as a pleasurable object only on his aged father's behalf, thinking of her as 'the pleasure of his eyes, / And of his hands, imaginary solace of his fading life' (3.1.476–7). Hercules, present as Fawn, applauds the refusal of 'a monstrous love, / That's only out of difficulty born, / And followed only for the miracle / In the obtaining' (3.1.489–92), and calls

---

John Donne's 'The Curse' (14–16): 'In early and long scarceness may he rot, / For land which had been his, if he had not / Himself incestuously an heir begot.' (Cited from John Donne, *The Elegies and the Songs and Sonnets*, ed. Helen Gardner (Oxford, 1965), p. 40.) Gardner notes (p. 164) that these lines appear only in one version of the poem (from 1633, H 40, Group I, Dob, B); all other versions replace them with these: 'Or may he for her virtue reverence / One, that hates him only for impotence, / And equal traitors be she and his sense.' The latter lines are more familiar in subject matter, more 'literary' (perhaps deriving from Ovid, *Amores* 3.7), and less interesting. Do the singularity and the widespread substitution perhaps signal some extra-literary censoring?

upon Tiberio to 'tell her father all' (3.1.493). This suggestion makes Tiberio snap.

> Uncompassionate, vild man,
> Shall I not pity, if I cannot love?
> Or rather shall I not for pity love
> So wondrous wit in so most wondrous beauty,
> That with such rarest art and cunning means
> Entreats what I (thing valueless) am not
> Worthy but to grant, my admiration?
> Are fathers to be thought on in our loves?
> (3.1.493–8)

The very deceitfulness Tiberio decried above now becomes, after the repressive and duty-binding warnings of Fawn, the 'art' and 'wit' he is falling for. At this point Fawn immediately returns to his flattering mode, encouraging (highly sensory) self-indulgence: 'Your father, I may boldly say, he's an ass / To hope that you'll forbear to swallow / What he cannot chew' (3.1.504–6).

In fact, I think, when Fawn encouraged Tiberio to respect his father's wishes (the marital negotiation assignment) he was even then encouraging Tiberio in self-indulgence – indulgence of his inappropriate, withholding urge to chastity, a self-indulgence in fixation, analogous to the courtiers' pathologies. Yet the encouragement seems to function as a rewriting, of dutifulness as servility: that is, Hercules stimulates in his son the sense of formal servility that produced his own search for libidinal authenticity in Urbino. At the same time, in pretending that love with Dulcimel would be only a fetish of difficulty, formal rather than substantial, Hercules elicits along another axis a defiant claim to authentic capacity. Tiberio replies (moving back to the wit, forward to the body), 'Fawn, what man of so cold earth / But must love such a wit in such a body?' (510–11). At just this point admiration of wit finally gets extended to erotic desire, and the transforming pressure turns out to be not mimetic desire, but parental prohibition. (Indeed, in the final analysis Tiberio outgoes his father, who never makes the full transition to an erotic object.) Perhaps there is a productive mixture of the two pressures, in which Tiberio must ventriloquise his father's desire and enact his own desire for refusal or avoidance at the same time. In any case, Hercules's prohibition triggers rebellion, and transforms Tiberio's withholding urge into the urge for self-defining self-gift, self-desire, self-projection – the gesture that is at the same time the core of the erotic (the primal exogamy, to love another) and the foundation of autonomy, as exhibiting mastery of, ownership of, a will.

How, finally, do we return such a text to the anxious Jacobean context of the accession, with its retiring accessive prince, its desires and hopes and fears? Perhaps the first thing (and in the end one of the most important) that calls attention to itself is that this play is *comic*: that is, the frightening world of Middleton's and Webster's tragedies, of madness and murder, of what we habitually call 'Jacobean', was not immediately – in 1604 – the essential subjective correlative of James's incipient court. No stranger to the dark, Marston still seems to have written relatively happy endings for his courtly fantasies. I see this labour as that of a conjurer, summoning and welcoming a new future across the long half-life of the radioactive bitterness his early works purveyed. Perhaps we should be speaking of *warmth*, not heat, when we explore Hercules's 'stream of blood'. Still, whatever Marston's intentions, his exploration of courtly flattery and desire does many additional kinds of work. We see the licensing of desire, ubiquitous hunger, moral puppetry and mockery of excess. We see both successful and coopted challenges to hierarchies of status, gender, age and kinship. We see an attempt at the ironic and artful reclamation of courtly flattery from the cesspools of the machiavel, so that a morality of indulgence and trust can displace, or at least function alongside, the plain civic speaking recommended by Castiglione and the 'advice to prin-ces' tradition – without cankering it. The 'expense of spirit', I think Marston hopes, must not be the horizon.

It seems likely that Marston sought to enact his own wild longings, for the practices and rewards of carping and flattery alike, and to purvey such enactments to his actors' auditors, as benign vehicles for *their* enactment, in the complex spirit of what Hercules calls the 'waste' of wild desires: catharsis, assuagement, sublimation, cleansing, smuggling, practice, use, enjoyment. Whatever else, Marston compels, for Hercules, for early modern auditors, and for us, the construction and interrogation of such catalogues.

5

Ben Jonson's *Bartholomew Fair*

The Theatre constructs Puritanism

Patrick Collinson

'Marry', says one actor to another in a jest-book by Thomas Dekker, 'I have so naturally played the Puritan that many took me to be one.' On at least one occasion this compliment was returned: a real Puritan mistaken for a stage-Puritan. When, in the 1620s, the young gentlewoman Mrs Joan Drake of Esher in Surrey fell into a melancholy, perhaps a case of post-natal depression, or (depending upon your point of view) became demon-possessed, a succession of physicians of the soul were brought in to address her condition. Among the first was the already venerable and generously bearded John Dod, who reduced Mrs Drake to helpless laughter, 'in her thoughts likening him unto *Ananias*, one whom at a play in the Black-Friars she saw scoffed at, for a holy brother of *Amsterdam*'. When Dod looked pitifully upon her and told her 'what a shameless thing it was, so to laugh and jest at heavenly things', she asked him what else he was to expect, since she was, after all, under the control of Satan! To the modern reader, it may appear more relevant that Mrs Drake was said to be 'of a naturally jovial constitution', only 'accidentally melancholy'. The minister who recorded this series of spiritual encounters called himself 'an eye-witnessing actor in all her tragic-comedy'.[1]

Which preceded which, and what fashioned what? the real or the fictitious Puritan? The commonsense answer may seem to be that the real article came first. There had to be real Puritans before 'Puritans' could be scoffed at on the stage. The purpose of this brief essay will be to consider the reverse possibility: art anticipating life. This argument arises from the interest of a historian of religion in the construction of religious identities partly, and in the case of Puritanism largely, by a process of

I am grateful for the helpful comments of Professor Anne Barton and for suggestions made by Mr Jeremy Maule, my colleagues at Trinity College, Cambridge.

[1] *Non-Dramatic Works of Thomas Dekker*, ed. A. B. Grosart (1885), II, 282; *Trodden Down Strength by the God of Strength, or, Mrs Drake Revived* (attributed to John Hart but in fact by Jasper Heartwell) (1647), pp. 26–7, 4. Dod lived to be over ninety and was in his seventies when these events occurred. Later he served as chaplain to Sir Erasmus Dryden (grandfather of the poet) of Canons Ashby, Northamptonshire, and in 1630 played the part of go-between in negotiating a match between Dryden's grandson John and Elizabeth Isham, daughter of Sir John Isham of Lamport, which proved to be abortive. Nevertheless, the young Dryden assured his 'sweet heart' that Dod had been their 'constant friend' (Northamptonshire Record Office, Isham Correspondence).

negative stigmatisation, but also by a measure of reciprocal self-recognition in the stigmatised.[2] In other words, 'Puritans' in Elizabethan and Jacobean England existed by virtue of being perceived to exist, most of all by their enemies, but eventually to themselves and to each other. Puritanism was more of a process and relationship than it was state or entity. It goes without saying that this interactive process has many historical parallels in other periods and cultures. One thinks of the Italian Alpine *benandanti* or 'night-battlers' described by Professor Carlo Ginzburg, who were persuaded of their malignancy against the evidence of their own benign motives.[3]

How appropriate that John Dod should have reminded Joan Drake of one of Jonson's characters! For Jonson knew about Dod and in the winter of 1618–19 told his Scottish friend, William Drummond of Hawthornden, a bar-room joke about another gentlewoman who had longed to lie with the preacher 'for the procreation of an Angel or Saint'. But it proved 'but an ordinary birth'.[4] Dod's fortune, or misfortune, following his deprivation for nonconformity, was to spend his last forty years as the pensionary of gentlemen and gentlewomen.

There is no better place to start, and perhaps to finish, an investigation of stage-Puritanism than Jonson's *Bartholomew Fair* (rather than, it should be said, the play which Mrs Drake had seen, *The Alchemist*). Few dramatists have been more reflective than Jonson, about his art, his contractual relationship with his public, about his contemporaries. He was especially reflective about the relation of art to life, the connection between the play and the world outside the theatre, temporarily entrapped within it as audience. If Shakespeare, typically, stole the line that everyone remembers, 'All the world's a stage,' Jonson wrote, no less memorably: 'Our whole life is like a *Play*.'[5]

Bartholomew Fair was either the most verisimilitudinous of Jonson's plays or was thought to be so. As Francis Teague has shown us, this may have been most true at a period in what Jonathan Miller would call the play's afterlife,[6] when audiences were still linked by memory, their own or that of their parents, to the world which *Bartholomew Fair* refracted. But in the Restoration period the refractions passed through a further prism which was audience memory of the events of the 1640s and 1650s, when the Puritans whom Jonson had pilloried in the reign of James I cut off the

---

[2] Patrick Collinson, *The Puritan Character: Polemics and Polarities in Early Seventeenth-Century English Culture: A Paper Presented at a Clark Library Seminar 25 April 1987* (Los Angeles, 1989); Alexandra Walsham, *Church Papists: Catholicism, Conformity and Confessional Polemic in Early Modern England* (Woodbridge, 1993).

[3] Carlo Ginzburg, *I Benandanti* (Turin, 1966); translated by John and Anne Tedeschi as *The Night Battles: Witchcraft and Agrarian Cults in the Sixteenth and Seventeenth Centuries* (Baltimore, 1983). I am grateful to Richard Strier for suggesting this parallel.

[4] *Ben Jonson*, ed. C. H. Herford and Percy Simpson, I (Oxford, 1925), p. 146.

[5] *Timber, or Discoveries*, in *Ben Jonson*, VIII (Oxford, 1947), p. 597.

[6] Jonathan Miller, *Subsequent Performances* (1986).

head of his son with the crown still on it. Restoration audiences, unlike modern historians of the seventeenth century, were in no doubt that Jonson's Puritans were the same people as the rebels and regicides of the Civil War. Nor were they in the least aware that 'Puritan' was a redundant term after 1660, to be replaced by 'Nonconformist' or 'Dissenter'. Thus it was that Charles II and his subjects enjoyed the discomfiture of Zeal-of-the-Land Busy, and that Samuel Pepys discovered within himself some uncomfortable reactions. It mattered very much whether the puppet play from Act 5 was included in these Restoration productions of *Bartholomew Fair*. When it was, in a performance on 2 September 1661, Pepys thought it 'strange' that the theatre should 'dare to do it' 'and the King to countenance it', 'it being so satirical against Puritanism'. Seven years later, the diarist was more specific in his ambivalence: 'The more I see it, the more I love the wit of it, only, the business of abusing the Puritans begins to grow stale, and of no use, they being the people that at last will be found the wisest.' Pepys's dramatic criticism only made sense if he believed that the play addressed reality, albeit polemically and pejoratively. He was deaf to Jonson's warning that the play should not be mistaken topically for real life; or only on the terms that 'real life' is itself a kind of theatre.[7]

Pepys could be forgiven, for Jonson was punctilious in his realistic dramatic invention. For example, unlike Mrs Drake and many modern critics, Jonson was careful not to confuse the Puritans of *Bartholomew Fair* (1614) with the exiled Separatists of Amsterdam whose representatives, Ananias and Tribulation Wholesome, make their parodic appearance in *The Alchemist* (1610). Puritans are only glancing targets in the earlier play, the feather makers of Blackfriars. It may be that in *The Alchemist* Jonson intended to blacken the reputation of such 'professors' by associating them with more extreme sectaries, as Middleton may have done in *The Family of Love*, or Nashe in his representation of the Anabaptist commonwealth of Munster in *The Unfortunate Traveller*. But Jonson knew very well that the Blackfriars godly were of a different denomination from the 'Anabaptists' of Amsterdam, who made so much of 'the motion of the spirit'.[8]

Leah Marcus remarks: 'There is much of Jonson himself in the Puritan at *Bartholomew Fair*.' 'He might have turned Puritan himself.' What an ironical point it would make about Jonson's (shall we say?) precise interest in the subject if his father, said by him to have been 'a minister', could be shown to have been none other than Robert Johnson, a vituperative Puritan preacher with Westminster connections. In the early 1570s, Johnson picked a quarrel with Gabriel Goodman, the dean of Westminster, asking him provocatively after one of Goodman's sermons: 'As for schism,

---

[7] Francis Teague, *The Curious History of Bartholomew Fair* (1985), pp. 56, 68–74.
[8] Basil Hall, 'Puritanism: the Problem of Definition', in *Studies in Church History*, II, ed. G. J. Cuming (1965), p. 293.

who is a greater schismatic than you? . . . And as for Puritans, who is a greater Puritan than you?' At his trial, Bishop Sandys of London told Robert Johnson: 'You like well of your self, and you are stubborn and arrogant,' while the Lord Chief Justice observed: 'Sir, this is your glory and your pride, that you may come to talk thus before such an assembly, and I say to thee, thou art an arrogant and presumptuous fellow, and a seditious.' Johnson died in the prison of the Gatehouse at Westminster in about April 1574.

That the posthumous birth of 'Ben Jonson of Westminster' occurred on 11 June 1572 is a word-of-mouth matter, not confirmed by any documentary evidence. Clues to be found in two versions of *The Underwood* indicate that he may have been born in 1574, a month or two after the prison death of Johnson the minister.[9] It is rather more certain that Nathan Field, Jonson's apprentice who acted in *Bartholomew Fair*, was the son (also all but posthumous) of the 'Lenin' of Elizabethan Puritanism, John Field, a forthright critic of the stage who had dared to rebuke none other than the earl of Leicester for his theatrical patronage.[10] But I shall not attempt on this occasion to introduce these anti-Puritan playwrights to Dr Sigmund Freud.

Let us rather turn to the text. 'Down with Dagon, down with Dagon', shouts 'Rabbi' Busy as he mounts his one-man demonstration against the puppet play which consummates *Bartholomew Fair*. Now Busy, as we all know, was a Banbury man, who had given over his trade of baking Banbury cakes when he learned of some of the uses to which his products were being put, at brideales, maygames and the like. We do not know how well acquainted Jonson may have been with Banbury. Nor can he have had access to the records of the Court of Star Chamber. But it is hard to believe that the author of *Bartholomew Fair* can have been altogether ignorant of certain events in that Oxfordshire town at the turn of the century, events which had their repercussions in Star Chamber and perhaps other courts for at least ten years, the town accounts recording certain 'charges about the suit of the cross' as late as 1612.[11]

---

[9] *A Parte of a Register* (Edinburgh, 1593) printed (pp. 101–18) Johnson's own account of his trial together with his prison letters to Sandys and Goodman, reporting in vague terms the circumstances and date of his death. It was the late John Crow who in the 1960s suggested to me that Robert Johnson may have been Ben Jonson's father. There were other Robert Johnsons in the ministry of the early Elizabethan Church (but no other known to have died in 1574), and *A Parte of a Register* may confuse the matter by identifying (perhaps mistakenly) the man who died in Westminster Gatehouse with a Robert Johnson of Northampton.

[10] Patrick Collinson, 'John Field and Elizabethan Puritanism', in Collinson, *Godly People: Essays on English Protestantism and Puritanism* (1983), pp. 335–70; R. F. Brinkley, *Nathan Field, the Actor-Playwright* (New Haven, 1928).

[11] The account of the Banbury stirs which follows relies in the main on PRO, Star Chamber 5 B 31/4, supplemented by Alfred Beesly, *The History of Banbury* (1841), John Potts, *The Bailiffs and Mayors of the Borough of Banbury 1554–1904* (1904), and *Letters of Father Rivers*, ed. Henry Foley, S. J., Records of the English Province of the Society of Jesus, I (1872). The affair of the maypoles is documented in PRO, SP 12/224. See also Patrick Collinson, *The Religion of Protestants: The Church in English Society 1559–1625* (Oxford, 1982), p. 145.

What was 'the suit of the cross'? These were the years when a Puritan faction headed by the family of Wheatley or Whateley (best known from the preacher William Whateley, the legendary 'roaring boy of Banbury') was tightening its grip on Banbury's politics as well as on its culture and patterns of sociability. This faction seems to have commanded considerable support in the town but little enough in the surrounding country, certain well-disposed gentlemen excepted.[12] In the 1580s the issues had been maypoles and morris dances, pastimes which Zeal-of-the-Land Busy would in due course denounce. But now, at the turn of the century, it was the turn of the crosses.

In 1603 a bill of complaint was brought into Star Chamber concerning the toppling of Banbury Cross, or rather of two large stone crosses, ancient monuments, principal ornaments of the town, and commercial amenities: the Bread Cross and the Queen's High Cross. The High Cross was demolished on 26 July 1600 by some forty persons, variously described (by the plaintiffs) as a rent-a-mob, and (by the respondents) as workmen going about their lawful business, as instructed by the local magistracy. The bill of complaint alleged that

upon the fall of the long and large spire of the same high cross, the said rioters, profaning the words of the Holy Scripture, oftentimes cried out with a loud voice, 'God be thanked, Dagon the deluder of the people is fallen down!' and divers of them roune [ran] in a most outrageous and furious manner to strike at the stones of the same, having upon them certain pictures engraven, and there were so violent that they strove amongst themselves who should give the first blow upon the same stones and pictures.

However, upon examination, it was found that only one man, Henry Shewell, had cried out about Dagon, and but once. Asked what he meant, Shewell had indicated the carved 'pictures' on the cross. A middle-aged publican described these carvings in his evidence as very small and consisting of a picture of Christ upon the cross, 'a woman with a child in her arms' (was he no longer able to recognise the Madonna?) and 'the picture of a man, bareheaded, with a book in his hand'. Shewell would be bailiff of Banbury in the following year, 1601. The *topos* of the downfall of the Philistine image of Dagon is in fact rare in the period, making the coincidence of the Banbury case and *Bartholomew Fair* all the more striking.[13]

At this point, the reader of *Bartholomew Fair* who also has access to Star Chamber file 5 B 31/4 may be forgiven for making his own confusion of art with life, wondering what part Mr Busy may have taken in these

---

[12] A petition to Lord Burghley in favour of the preacher Thomas Brasbridge, doubtless the original Puritan evangelist of Banbury, was signed in 1590 by ninety-six townsmen (BL, Lansdowne MS 64, no. 13, fos. 43v, 44r).

[13] Ernest B. Gilman, *Iconoclasm and Poetry in the English Reformation: Down Went Dagon* (1986) collects very few examples. Milton is perhaps responsible for such resonances as the biblical story has.

deeds of iconoclasm. It only slightly spoils the effect to admit that such peculiar names as 'Zeal-of-the-Land' ('O, they all have such names, Sir,' says John Littlewit) were not much used in Banbury, being almost confined to certain parishes in East Sussex and to some parts of Northamptonshire, admittedly not a thousand miles away from Banbury. It is probable that Jonson borrowed this detail from the *Remaines Concerning Britaine* (1605), written by his schoolmaster and friend, William Camden, who unlike Jonson discussed the phenomenon in no unfriendly fashion, as involving 'no evil meaning', but only 'some singular and precise conceit'. Camden lists such names as Free-Gift, The Lord is Neare, From Above, and, significantly, since the name is echoed in *The Alchemist*, Tribulation.[14]

The Star Chamber documents reveal a more profound affinity between the worlds of real-life Banbury and fictional *Bartholomew Fair* than the possibly fortuitous conjunction of deprecations against Dagon. If the political thrust of *Bartholomew Fair* concerned the self-appointed, self-deluded reforming zeal of magistracy and ministry, Overdo and Busy (though Busy was no minister), such were the magistrates and ministers of the Oxfordshire town, as we find them reflected in this case. To what extent their rigour exceeded the law, lawyers no doubt could and can determine; whether it constituted dangerous sedition was a matter of polemical perception, in the town and in the play. In the suit of the Banbury crosses, the aggrieved enemies of the godly magistracy insisted that these acts of iconoclasm, while allegedly orderly and legal within what we may call the little commonwealth of Banbury, were perpetrated without any higher warrant than that of the town's governors. Thomas Wheatley had been overheard to say that 'he thought the queen had nothing to do in that cause'. In a celebrated trial of 1633, when Henry Sherfield the recorder of Salisbury appeared in Star Chamber on a very similar charge of unauthorised iconoclasm, perpetrated by a person of local standing and substance, Attorney General Noy recalled that, towards the end of Elizabeth's reign, such acts were undertaken by many 'of their own heads'. In particular, 'at Banbury they pulled down the cross there'.

Complaints were also made in Banbury about the conduct of the bailiff, his colleagues and his officers, in interfering with drinking and small-scale gaming in the pubs of the town. Country people in town for a night out finished up in the lock-up rather than their own beds. In 1597 an elderly tailor invited his friends to dinner on a Sunday evening, but the party

---

[14] William Camden, *Remaines of a Greater Worke, Concerning Britaine* (1605), p. 33. Richard Bancroft was more censorious of this practice in his *Daungerous Positions* (1593), p. 104. Camden was rather more critical of the fashion for conferring human names on pets and other animals. He gave the meaning of Ananias, usually thought (in Jonson) to be an ironical reference to the hypocrisy of Ananias and Sapphira in Acts of the Apostles, as 'the grace of the Lord' (*Remaines*, p. 43.) Essential reading on this topic is Nicholas Tyacke, 'Popular Puritan Mentality in Late Elizabethan England', in *The English Commonwealth 1547–1640: Essays in Politics and Society Presented to Joel Hurstfield*, ed. P. Clark *et al.* (Leicester, 1979), pp. 77–92.

was broken up by the bailiff, Richard Wheatley (a mercer by trade). When someone said that he hoped that the queen would allow a group of friends to share a joint of meat, Wheatley said: 'If the queen do allow it, yet I will not allow it.' How Jonson might have envied that line! It was Overdo to the very life, or Busy scorning the authority of the Master of the Revels who had licensed the puppet play.

Moreover the Banbury trial documents carry hostile insinuations that the motives of righteous and rigorous magistracy were not all that they might seem, 'being carried away with a covetous desire of their own private gain'. Money had been spent to excess on an extravagant silver mace, which did more for the dignity of a corrupt regime than for the good of the town. The bailiff Henry Shewell broke open the stones of the cross only 'for the iron or lead that was therein', and appropriated stones for his own private use. The new market stalls set up to replace the old crosses were let at higher rents. It has to be said that in all these complaints, responses, interrogatories and answers, the word 'Puritan', which I have used with the usual and conventional freedom in discussing them, does not so much as once appear. That too is relevant to the argument of this essay.

We do not need to say that the magistrates of Banbury were hypocritically corrupt, only that they were seen by those who resented their government to be so, and so it was in Jonson's play, which is to say Jonson's own biased perception. What Jonson's motives may have been in 1614 for mounting this most powerful and memorable of all theatrical attacks on Puritanism is discussed by Leah Marcus in her essay. To me it seems that the onslaught may have been designed to divert attention away from other issues which in the 1620s were to put the shoe on the other foot, as Margot Heinemann's 'opposition drama' turned its attention to the foreign, popish enemy rather than that supposed enemy within and paper tiger, 'seditious' native 'Puritans'. Whether or not Jonson was under some kind of royal mandate to present such a diversion, as the dedication to James I suggests and Aubrey later reported, one can see that it did him some good, as he moved from devising some politically risqué masques for Prince Henry to a more exclusive and obsequious attachment to the king.[15]

Theatricality within theatricality, fictions truer than life! *Bartholomew Fair* staged a stereotype which retained some dramatic potency into the later seventeenth century. In Thomas D'Urfey's 1690 poem, 'Collin's Walk Through London and Westminster', the country bumpkin Collin is taken

---

[15] See Graham Parry, 'The Politics of the Jacobean Masque', and Margot Heinemann, 'Drama and Opinion in the 1620s: Middleton and Massinger', both in *Theatre and Government under the Early Stuarts*, ed. J. R. Mulryne and M. Shewring (Cambridge, 1993).

to the theatre to see that 'ancient comic piece', *Bartholomew Fair*. Collin mistakes the play for some kind of reality, perhaps a Puritan meeting, and he leaps up onto the stage to rescue Zeal-of-the-Land Busy from the stocks, just as Busy had marred the puppet play within the play itself. D'Urfey's poem is, of course, more fiction, which perhaps borrowed an idea from the encounter of Samuel Butler's *Hudibras* with the 'antic show' of the skimmington, or rough riding.[16]

Although Jonson perpetuated the stage-Puritan in his most memorable form, thanks to the precision of his observation and the intensity of his polemic, he was not, of course, the inventor of the stereotype. It is strange that no one has asked who was, or at what date the stage-Puritan first trod the boards. Investigation of this neglected problem suggests (as I have hinted) that it may have been the stage-Puritan who invented, or re-invented, the Puritan, and not the other way round. The stage-Puritan cannot, I think, be traced back beyond 1588–9, the year of Martin Marprelate, the Marprelate Tracts being by a process of counter-production the unwilling midwife to that Puritanism which Jonson and so many other dramatists and satirists loved to hate.[17]

How did this happen? The Marprelate Tracts were the last desperate throe of some friend or friends of the Elizabethan Puritans as they stared political defeat in the face, the secret weapon which C. S. Lewis compared to poison gas, a substance notoriously liable to blow back into the faces of those who release it. Usually the Tracts are described as having a place in the history of something called 'English literature', and while their remarkable literary quality has not been overlooked, inordinate attention has been paid to the familiar game of 'hunt the author', as if the identification of this rare genius were the only matter of interest. Contemporaries, relatively unfamiliar with the concept of 'literature', did recognise the affinity of these pamphlets to the many libellous, rhyming 'ballads' maliciously deployed in the street wars of Elizabethan and Jacobean England.[18] The prevailing temper of this activity, after and perhaps before Martin, was anti-Puritan (whether or not the P word was employed – often it was not). Yet the more unrestrained of the Puritan preachers had made use of similar tactics, using schoolboy satirists to demolish their clerical opponents. So it was that the bishop of Exeter, in whose diocese

---

[16] Teague, *The Curious History*, pp. 76–8.

[17] The Tracts also led more obviously to what proved to be a more ephemeral stigma, 'Martinist', to which I would give a shelf-life of about ten years. In 1598–9, a man in Wells, Somerset, was ordered publicly to confess his fault for having defamed sermon-goers. 'And if they were all hanged it were not a halfpenny of harm, and all that be of Martins sect.' (Somerset County Record Office, Wells Consistory Court Book, D/D/ Con 114, unfoliated. I owe this reference to Dr Michael Moody.)

[18] C. J. Sisson, *Lost Plays of Shakespeare's Age* (Cambridge, 1936); Adam Fox, 'Aspects of Oral Culture and its Development in Early Modern England' (Cambridge Ph.D., 1993). In the trial of the Martinist John Udall, the Tracts were referred to as 'the books or libels called by the name of Martin Marprelate' (BL, Harleian MS 6849, fo. 158r).

Plate 10   Hudibras Encounters the Skimmington, by William Hogarth

this had recently happened, heard of the first Martinist tract as 'a slanderous libel lately cast abroad in London', and linked it with schoolboy libelling on the edge of his diocese; while Bishop Cooper of Winchester referred to 'libels . . . printed and spread abroad'.[19] Cultural historians are beginning to emphasise the convergence rather than divergence of orality and print. Martin Marprelate put defamatory libelling by means of the 'pastime' of ballading into the relative permanence of print, while adding a good measure of comic genius.

The Marprelate Tracts were intensely theatrical, turning the bishops, with their own inherent theatricality, into actors in so many comic jigs, which were served up with what sounds like the patter or 'rap' of the popular theatre. In a way, Martin was the resurrected persona of the comedian Richard Tarlton, who had died in early September 1588, a matter of weeks before the first tract appeared; and Martin was instantly recognised as such. In *A Whip for an Ape* (April 1589), perhaps by John Lyly, the author wrote: 'Now Tarleton's dead the consort [i.e., the dramatic company] lacks a vice; / For knave and fool thou [Martin], may'st bear prick and price.'[20] How appropriate that the Induction to *Bartholomew Fair* should include the most memorable of all posthumous references to Tarlton: 'Ho! and that man had lived to have played in *Bartholomew Fair* . . .'

The nineteenth century knew what purported to be 'Tarlton's Jig of a Horseload of Fools' (dated *c.* 1579), which included an attack on the anti-theatrical writer Stephen Gosson (who drew a more memorable riposte from Sir Philip Sidney). But this was almost certainly one of John Payne Collier's forgeries.[21] I know of no other evidence that 'Puritans' were the victims of dramatic satire before the year of Marprelate. That the grenade of satire exploded in Martin's hand was only what the graver Puritans may have expected. They had deep reservations about the Martinist strategy and were themselves the victims of Martin's biting tongue. But Martin himself may well have been surprised. For the Puritan stereotype which his satire had released from Pandora's box, sanctimonious, hypocritical and devious, bore no resemblance whatsoever to Martin's own utterly iconoclastic and picaresque persona.

The man who saw how Martin could be made to serve the contrary purpose of anti-Puritan satire appears to have been the future Archbishop Richard Bancroft, who, reported Archbishop Whitgift in an unusual testimonial, was the source of the advice that the Martinists should be answered 'after their own vein'.[22] This was in spite of some episcopal second thoughts about

---

[19] This is more extensively documented in my essay 'Ecclesiastical Vitriol: Religious Satire in the 1590s and the Invention of Puritanism', in *The Reign of Elizabeth I*, ed. John Guy (Cambridge, 1995).

[20] *The Complete Works of John Lyly*, ed. R. W. Bond, III (1890), p. 419.

[21] Arthur and Janet Ing Freeman consider it almost certain that this jig, preserved in BL, Add. MS 32380 (in a modern hand, imitating a seventeenth-century hand), was a forgery, and that the forger was Collier (Correspondence, Freeman–Collinson, October 1991).

[22] *Tracts Ascribed to Richard Bancroft*, ed. Albert Peel (Cambridge, 1953), p. xviii. Without naming him, Francis Bacon implicitly rebuked Bancroft in his 'Advertisement Touching the Controversies of the Church of England'

the wisdom or propriety of allowing matters of ecclesiastical controversy to invade the common stage and the new vogue of satire. Almost before the first anti-Martinist pamphlets appeared, Martin was whipped, 'lanced and wormed' on the stage, within the generic conventions of what C. J. Sisson called the 'operetta' of the jig.[23] Martin was vengefully 'made a Maygame upon the stage'. Among various 'tricks and devices', other Martinist characters were added to the cast. They included the enthusiastically Puritan London housewife Margaret Lawson, 'the shrew of Paul's Gate', stepping out for all the world like a transvestite pantomime dame. The evidence is skimpy,[24] but just sufficient to suggest that John Lyly was the impresario of these entertainments and to hint at the presence of authority behind Lyly, probably in the shape of Bancroft. Gabriel Harvey wrote: 'He must needs be discouraged whom they decipher.' Harvey supplies a couple of titles for these jigs: *The Zelous Love-Letter, or Corinthian Epistles to the Widow*, and *The Holie Oath of the Martinistes, That, Thinking to Sweare by His Conscience, Swore by his Concupiscence*.[25] The ambivalence of Jonson himself with respect to such 'tricks' is suggested by his censoring of 'the concupiscence of jigs and dances' in the Induction to *Bartholomew Fair*.

This was when, where and why the stage-Puritan made his entry, already equipped with the elements of an essentially simple and stable repertory: outward piety (indicated by the white of the upturned eye), inner corruption, consisting of avarice, lust and sedition – in a word, hypocrisy incarnate. The type was so well established by 1601 that Shakespeare in *Twelfth Night* could try his hand on that variant of the type who was Malvolio, of whom Maria exclaims: 'Sometimes he is a kind of Puritan', but also 'the Devil a Puritan that he is'. The ambivalence of the character depended upon audience familiarity with the type of which it was a variant, rendered, in characteristic Shakespearean style, as nuanced and open-ended. (What *did* Jonson mean when he told Drummond that Shakespeare 'wanted art'?)

The elements of the stereotype are very consistent, as we find them in Middleton's *Family of Love* (1607) (regardless of what Middleton's intended target may have been, Familists or Puritans), *The Puritan or The Widow of Watling Street* (also 1607, and once improbably attributed to Shakespeare), *Two Wise Men and All the Rest Fools* (1619); not to speak of such non-

---

(1589), which deplored 'this immodest and deformed manner of writing lately entertained, whereby matters of religion are handled in the style of the stage'. Bacon attached the greater blame to 'the invention of him who (as it seemeth) pleased himself in it as in no mean policy, that these men are to be dealt withal at their own weapons . . .' 'The second blow makes the fray' (*The Letters and the Life of Francis Bacon*, 1: *Occasional Works*, ed. J. Spedding (1861), pp. 76–7). There is an affinity between the anti-Martinist writings and some vividly satirical passages in Bancroft's own anti-Puritan polemics (unique in a future archbishop): *A Survay of the Pretended Holy Discipline* and *Daungerous Positions and Proceedings* (both 1593), and the earlier fragments published in *Tracts Ascribed to Richard Bancroft*.

[23] Sisson, *Lost Plays*, p. 127.

[24] Most of it will be found in *The Works of Thomas Nashe*, ed. A. B. Grosart, 1 (1883), pp. 59, 82–3; 111 (1885), p. 175; *Works of Lyly*, 111. 418–19; and Gabriel Harvey, *Pierces Supererogation, or A New Prayse of the Old Asse*, pp. 133–5.

[25] *Ibid.*, pp. 134–5.

dramatic texts in the style of Juvenalian satire as John Marston's *The Scourge of Villanie* (1599), an element of anti-Puritanism being *de rigueur* in this genre. That elements of the stereotype were also persistent is suggested not only by the Restoration revivals of Jonson but by the long afterlife of what may have been the most popular of all Elizabethan plays, *Mucedorus* (1590). The anti-Puritan satire in that piece consisted of a single line, but it was probably a famous line. When the play was performed before three or four hundred people at Whitney in Oxfordshire in the 1650s, that line provoked the wrath of God which expressed itself in an accident which killed six members of the audience, according to a 'providential' account of the calamity penned by a local minister.[26]

It may go too far to say that the late Elizabethan stage invented that elusive category Puritanism, thing as well as name. And yet it is a remarkable fact that the word 'Puritan' hardly ever appears in the thousands of pages written against those we call Puritans in the 1590s: the polemical works of Bancroft, Cosin, Sutcliffe and, supremely, Hooker. Instead we find 'them that seek Reformation' (whom Hooker's *Laws* addresses), 'our pretended English reformers', 'our English Disciplinarians', 'our Disciplinarian men', often just 'them'. Later conformist apologists would succumb to the polemical economy of 'Puritans'. Who persuaded them but the streets and stages of late Elizabethan and Jacobean England?

And outside ecclesiastical controversy, at a time when the issues which had first given rise to the term Puritan were in political recession and arousing less and less public interest, the Marprelate affair and its theatrical as well as literary repercussions helped, especially in the metropolitan society which is the subject of this volume, to identify the subject more sharply, answering perhaps to certain anxieties within society and even in the inner lives of individuals, of whom Ben Jonson may have been a conspicuous example. There is no doubt that Jonson's Ananias helped Mrs Drake, or the demon within her, to identify John Dod as a 'holy brother', a Puritan, whose stern admonitions were a matter for laughter and derision rather than to be taken to heart. And if there was no need to learn what a Puritan was like from the torrent of such fictions, which Martin Marprelate had served to release, it is likely that the fictions helped those exposed to them to label, laugh at, hate, and even become the Puritan who had all the time been in their midst, even within themselves. This was one way in which to respond to the pressure of an

---

[26] *Tragi-Comoedia by John Rowe*, ed. A. Freeman (New York, 1973). *Mucedorus* is included in C. F. Tucker Brooke, ed., *The Shakespeare Apocrypha: Being a Collection of Fourteen Plays Which Have Been Ascribed to Shakespeare* (Oxford, 1908). See George F. Reynolds, 'Mucedorus, Most Popular Elizabethan Play?', in *Studies in the English Renaissance Drama*, ed. Josephine W. Bennett *et al.* (1961), pp. 248–68. The famous line sounds pretty innocuous to a modern ear. The clown, called Mouse (a part written for Tarlton's heir, Will Kemp?), scared by a bear, abandons the bale of hay he has been carrying, saying that he will make his father's horse turn Puritan and observe a fast.

oppressively threatening moral climate. Paradigms such as Puritanism, which were deployed to construct and manipulate a semblance of reality, soon became part of the reality on which they imposed themselves.

When Dekker's actor claimed to have played the Puritan so naturally that many took him to be one, his companion replied: 'True . . . thou played'st the Puritan so naturally, that thou could'st never play the honest man afterwards.' Jonson, reflecting that our whole life is like a play, added that we so insist on playing others that we cannot return to our own selves.

Of Mire and Authorship

Leah S. Marcus

We know much more about the early performances of Ben Jonson's *Bartholomew Fair* than we do about the average Jacobean play. It was first acted at the new Hope Theatre, 31 October 1614, then at court before King James I the very next night, on All Saints' Day, 1 November 1614. Despite this auspicious double première, however, the play was not included in Jonson's monumental 1616 *Works*; *Bartholomew Fair* had to wait until 1640 to be issued as part of his second volume of *Works*, although it had evidently been printed under the aging Jonson's supervision as early as 1631, the date given on its title page within the 1640 volume.

In its 1640 printed form, the play is hedged about with a bristling fence of explanatory materials that link it to the occasion of its first performances. The title page announces that it was 'acted in the year, 1614. By the Lady Elizabeth's Servants. And then dedicated to King James, of most blessed memory; by the author, Benjamin Jonson'. The text itself is prefaced first by a verse 'Prologue to the King's Majesty' that probably introduced the play for the 1614 performance at court, and second by a prose 'Induction on the stage' presumably performed at the Hope Theatre for the full run of the play. It is followed by the verse 'Epilogue' printed at the end of the text, addressed to James I, and presumably performed along with the Prologue at Whitehall. We have no way of knowing, of course, what changes Jonson may have made in any of these texts between the time of composition and their much later publication. He frequently altered performance materials for print and may well have polished these, though it is most unlikely that he invented them after the fact. Even by Jonsonian standards, the text of *Bartholomew Fair* is accompanied by a large number of ancillary materials: no other play published in the first or second volume of the *Works* can boast a title-page dedication, a prologue and an epilogue to the king, although the others often carry dedications and introductions of various kinds. Why, we may ask, did Jonson choose to surround *Bartholomew Fair* in particular with such an array of supplementary texts?

One possible answer might be that he felt uneasy about the play's sprawling licence. In *Bartholomew Fair* the audience, whether viewers or readers, is treated to a highly charged, high cholesterol diet of roast pig and punk (both

Plate 11 An aquatint of a fan picture published by J. F. Setchel purporting to depict Bartholomew Fair in 1721

piping hot), gingerbread, vapours, and other vanities of the fair. The play's form is much looser than many of Jonson's previous productions; its subject matter is carnivalesque in the extreme. The Prologue, Epilogue and Induction steer readers away from a mere wallowing in the fair's carnal delights by suggesting, in a typically Jonsonian gesture, that the 'licence' of Jonson's Smithfield be measured against higher standards of decorum.

But a second answer to our question might relate to the play's unusually prominent topicality. The title page and supplementary materials included along with the printed play-text alert readers to the specific historical moment of its double première in 1614. The play is deeply enmeshed in early Jacobean struggles over law, licence and royal prerogative, and the Prologue, Epilogue and Induction invite the 'judicious' reader of the printed text to a complex set of historical reconstructions: what would the play have meant to its original audience at court or at the opening of the Hope Theatre? How would its political signification be altered by the gap in time between 1614 and 1631 or 1640?

The Prologue suggests that the playwright expected *Bartholomew Fair* to have special significance for James I, who was known for his dislike of the rhetoric and seeming obstinacy of Puritan separatists. Jonson warns the king that at this London fair, his majesty can anticipate not only the expected sights and sounds, but also the expected opposition to his authority:

> the zealous noise
> Of your land's faction, scandalised at toys,
> As babies, hobbyhorses, puppet plays,
> And such like rage, whereof the petulant ways
> Yourself have known, and have been vexed with long.[1]

And indeed, the Banbury Puritan, Zeal-of-the-Land Busy, follows this prescription, railing against the vanities of the fair as the 'shop of Satan' (3.2.38, p. 92). His thunderous volley of vituperation is interrupted temporarily by orgiastic self-abandonment to the fair's forbidden pleasures of ale and roast pig, then definitively in the debate with the puppet. His Jeremiads against the 'Dagon' of puppetry recapitulate standard Puritan arguments against the stage: the puppets have no lawful calling, they are profane, and they are an abomination because 'the male among you putteth on the apparel of the female, and the female of the male' (5.5.87–8, p. 181). In his debate with Puppet Dionysius, Busy is struck dumb by the realisation that the puppet has no sex: the demonic abominations he has found in the puppet play and the fair are the product of a psychological phenomenon that we moderns would term projection, reflections of his

---

[1] Cited from Eugene M. Waith's edition, *Ben Jonson's 'Bartholomew Fair'*, in the Yale Ben Jonson (1963; 3rd printing, New Haven, 1971), p. 23. Subsequent references will be cited by page number to this edition.

own strong but suppressed hunger for the pleasures of sacramentalism, idol worship and polymorphous self-indulgence.[2]

Jonson's Epilogue to the king points toward the same line of political critique, overriding the 'licence' of the Puritan and other enemies of the fair and restoring the right to adjudicate and reform both the fair and the play to the king:

> Your Majesty hath seen the play, and you
> Can best allow it from your ear and view.
> You know the scope of writers, and what store
> Of leave is given them, if they take not more,
> And turn it into licence. You can tell
> If we have used that leave you gave us well;
> Or whether we to rage or licence break,
> Or be profane, or make profane men speak.
> This is your power to judge, great sir, and not
> The envy of a few. Which if we have got,
> We value less what their dislike can bring,
> If it so happy be, t'have pleased the King.
>
> (p. 187)

If *Bartholomew Fair* is interpreted in terms of its Prologue and Epilogue, it can easily be read as a *tour de force* in defence of royal authority. As I argued in an extended interpretation of the play written in the late 1970s and published later in *The Politics of Mirth*, the play constructs an elaborate set of equivalences between Bartholomew Fair, under the control of the City of London, and the Jacobean theatre, under the control of James I and cleverly presented as coterminous with the fair.

What Jonson has done from this court-centred interpretive standpoint is to create a symbolic space that establishes the equivalence of two forms of entertainment, a space for the airing, contestation and eventual silencing of various systems of authority that rivalled the king's. The Puritan claims to be better able to judge than the monarchy between wholesome and abominable pastimes; Justice Adam Overdo, a caricature of a London alderman or justice of the peace, similarly claims preeminent jurisdiction over the 'enormities' of the fair. Both of them caricature Puritan and judicial opponents of James I's efforts in 1614 and after to extend royal authority into the area of plays and pastimes by overriding local attempts to suppress such harmless 'mirth'. The very habits of speech of the would-be authorities over the fair echo the rhetoric of opponents of the king's policy of toleration for 'public mirth'. Busy's ranting parodies a characteristically Puritan trick of style: the quasi-Hebraic use of repetitive

---

[2] For a fuller version of this argument, the reader is referred to ch. 2 of Leah S. Marcus, *The Politics of Mirth: Jonson, Herrick, Milton, Marvell, and the Defense of Old Holiday Pastimes* (Chicago, 1986), which the present essay will both recapitulate and interrogate.

clauses with amplification, as in the Psalms in particular; Overdo's elaborately structured rhetoric echoes the contemporary Ciceronianism associated with civic and parliamentary debate.

The Puritan and the justice are symbolically silenced in the play by the scriptural doctrine of *tu quoque*: Jonson exposes them as blinded by 'beams' while presuming to cast out the 'motes' in others' eyes; their own enormities turn out to be more dangerous to community and commonwealth than those they rail against. Having displayed the moral bankruptcy of rival authorities during the play, in the Epilogue Jonson symbolically restores authority over both play and fair to the king: the Epilogue on the printed page appears precisely where James I's servant the Master of Revels would ordinarily affix his seal permitting the play to be acted. *Bartholomew Fair* in its printed form thus functions as a powerful argument to justify and extend royal power into contested legal and religious areas. Particularly toward the end of the play, there are strong echoes of the liturgy for the Feast of St Bartholomew, one of the official feast days of the Church of England. These echoes seem to lend divine authority to the royal surveillance over the fair and over the play Jonson posits as coterminous with it. One could scarcely ask for a more forceful argument in defence of royal prerogative powers.

At the time that I constructed this argument in 1978, I was quite pleased with it. And indeed, its emphasis on viewing the play from the perspective of the monarchy was characteristic of historicist criticism from the mid- to late sixties and early seventies. Since then, however, the dominant historical models invoked by literary critics have become less court-centred; like the revisionist history on which they are based, they place – or at least should place – less emphasis on contestation and more on a broad range of political and ecclesiastical allegiances between the extremes of absolutism and nonconformity. My perspective on the play has altered accordingly, not because I consider the earlier argument to be incorrect, but because it is too narrow and rigid as interpretation, and posits too narrow an audience – perhaps an audience of one in the person of James himself. Despite Jonson's many strong ties to James I, he kept up a wide and varied network of friendships and allegiances. Some of his chief patrons, such as Lucy, countess of Bedford, were Puritan sympathisers. Jonson's readers in 1640 and after were encouraged by the framing Prologue and Epilogue to read the play in terms of its caricature of the Puritan, its affirmation of royal authority over plays and pastimes. Ironically, however, by that late date royal authority was shaky indeed. Busy's anti-theatrical sentiment was coming to predominate – within two years of the publication of Jonson's second volume of *Works* the theatres would be closed. Amidst the opening skirmishes of the Civil War, Jonson's confident appeal to the judgement of the long-dead James I must have rung hollow indeed.

Nor, in the absence of Prologue and Epilogue, would Jonson's earlier audiences in the Hope Theatre in 1614 and after have received the court-centred *Bartholomew Fair* in quite its full 'authority'. We have some evidence that Jonson designed the Induction performed before this audience to stimulate some of the same drawing of equivalences already suggested above between the institution of the theatre, under the authority of the king, and the institution of the St Bartholomew pleasure fair, under the authority of the City of London. The Prompter in the Induction is the author's legal representative, offering a mock-serious contract with the audience that sets limits on their freedom to judge it. At the end of the Induction, the Prompter notes that the author has observed a 'special decorum', the Hope Theatre being 'as dirty as Smithfield, and as stinking every whit'. But he also conveys the author's admonition: '[he] prays you to believe his ware is still the same; else you will make him justly suspect that he that is so loath to look on a baby or an hobbyhorse here, would be glad to take up a commodity of them, at any laughter, or loss, in another place' (p. 34). The 'other place' referred to is, of course, Smithfield; the Induction offers its own version of the *tu quoque* by admonishing London critics of Jonson's play, and of the theatre more generally, to look to kindred vices under their own jurisdiction that they are more willing to tolerate.

What better advocate for an author's interests than the Prompter, whose actual job in the theatre was to make sure everyone got their lines according to the book? Jonson here points to the same equivalence between the theatre and the fair that we have already discussed in connection with the Prologue and Epilogue. He also suggests that the Puritan opposition to the theatre is financially based: the zealous brethren war against it because they have not found a way to profit from it. And indeed, within the play, Puritan reforming zeal often comes down to a matter of money, as in Dame Purecraft's 'zeal' for arranging sanctified marriages between indigent Brethren in the Faith and rich widows or between poor Sisters and 'wealthy bachelors', transactions from which she herself profits handsomely (5.2.50–45–68, p. 157). But the Induction's comical contract with the reader over a range of approved readings is not supplemented by any similar statement at the end of the play. How did the play signify on the public stage, without the Epilogue to bring its swirling 'licence' safely under the authority of the king? Jonson seems simultaneously to place his audience firmly under contract through his Induction and to seduce them into breaking it through what follows. One of the main messages of the Fair is that health and communal vitality depend on the breaking of contracts – the breaking of legalism itself. To a significant degree, my court-centred reading of the play posited an audience that never was: a public audience of 1614 with the same access to the Prologue and Epilogue that readers of Jonson's *Works* from 1640 to the present have had.

To subject such a delirious and disorderly piece of comedy to such a rigid system of interpretation now seems to me to carry a strong element of defensiveness about it, a defensiveness that was both mine and Jonson's. My own zeal to organise and tidy up Jonson's Fair was an attempt to cope with the disorienting and troubling experience of reading the play, not least, I now suspect, because of the play's shabby treatment of women – its easy equation between pig and punk, its cavalier portrayal of the fallen wives of John Littlewit and the Justice Adam Overdo, its use of the site of the feminine to dismantle culturally enforced distinctions between the clean and the dirty. Readings of the play have traditionally divided between vitalist admiration for its energy and moralist condemnations of its vice: my reading allowed me to have Jonson's Fair both ways and at the same time avoid the feminist interpretive issues that I found most troubling. Rather like the reformers within the play, I too wanted to purge and order the Fair, though I saw myself as operating under the higher 'licence' of the playwright's Prologue and Epilogue. And indeed, by the time my argument appeared in book form I was troubled by its overtidiness, particularly given that Jonson's own ideological affiliations and friendships were so much more diverse than a court-centred reading of the play would suggest. What I would like to do here is disarrange my previous line of interpretation by considering the Puritan in *Bartholomew Fair* in terms of issues other than James I's war against the sabbatarians.

In particular, to what extent might the play's framing devices have been defences on Jonson's own part against other modes of interpretation or against an inchoate spirit of revelry that defies interpretation? To suggest that Jonson (or any other artist, for that matter) worked partly through the erection of barriers against self-recognition is to say nothing new. What is striking in the case of Jonson is the almost exhibitionistic vehemence with which he erects his defensive barriers, and yet the ease with which they are dismantled by the reader. There is much of Jonson himself in the Puritan at *Bartholomew Fair*. Of all the major Elizabethan and Jacobean dramatists, he was easily the most vocal in his contempt for the theatre as an institution and for its shoddy artistic standards. Busy's condemnation of the puppet play is based on the biblical injunction against cross-dressing rather than Jonsonian moral and aesthetic strictures, but it nevertheless echoes the contempt for theatrical sensationalism attributed to the author of *Bartholomew Fair* by the Bookkeeper: 'If there be never a servant-monster i' the Fair, who can help it? he says; nor a nest of antics? He is loth to make nature afraid in his plays, like those that beget Tales, Tempests, and such like drolleries, to mix his head with other men's heels, let the concupiscence of jigs and dances reign as strong as it will amongst you' (Induction, 113–18). Unlike the author of *The Tempest*, Jonson is able to remain aloof from the 'drolleries' of other men's heels. The 'concupiscence of jigs' is Busy talk – the language of contemporary Puritan and civic opposition to the drama. London authorities had recently suppressed jigs at the end of plays on grounds that they incited sexual profligacy and rebellion. In *Bartholomew Fair*'s Prologue to the king Jonson adopts a strongly anti-Puritan stance, but in the Induction at the Hope Theatre he associates himself – or allows his Bookkeeper to associate him – with the language of Jacobean anti-theatricality.

If, as Peter Stallybrass and Allon White have brilliantly suggested in a discussion of the play published almost simultaneously with mine, we look at *Bartholomew Fair* from the bottom up instead of from the top down, we see a Jonson irrevocably mired in the 'low' popular anarchic vitalism he purported to despise, a Jonson whose control over his materials was tenuous rather than masterful.[3] The enormities of the fair and of the play are, after all, the playwright's enormities: he authored them every bit as much as he did the supplementary material designed to place them under restraint. The pig woman Ursula may not be precisely a 'servant-monster' in the mode of Caliban, but she is certainly as strikingly unorthodox; her sweltering booth and succulent vapours at the centre of the play are far more memorable than Prologue, Epilogue and Induction. *Bartholomew Fair*'s defensiveness against the Puritan derives ultimately from a suppressed recognition of kinship on the part of Jonson himself. It is characteristic of Jonson to write into his work a meticulous set of discriminations among things that appear similar on the surface but need to be understood as moral opposites. It is equally characteristic of him to fail to sustain the distinctions he has taken pains to establish – to collapse them uproariously into one another, or at least allow them to contaminate one another to the extent that the playwright's 'authority' over his materials is lost. Considered from the bottom up instead of from the top downward, Jonson's hedges against free interpretation are desperately futile attempts at containing his own ludic impulses along with the populist energies he purported to despise.

Over and over again throughout the poet's works, we find Jonson airing and distancing himself from his own opinions and identity through flamboyant and nearly transparent mechanisms of displacement. We know very little about Jonson's family background, except that he identified his real father, who died before his birth, as a 'minister'. That particular term was used more of nonconformists than of Church of England men – it would be rather deliciously appropriate for Jonson's portrayal of the Banbury Puritan if, as Patrick Collinson has speculated in the essay paired with this one, his father was of the same ideological stamp. An anxiety of paternal influence is easier to demonstrate in the case of Jonson's despised stepfather, the bricklayer, who got Jonson apprenticed and apparently expected him to follow in his

---

[3] Peter Stallybrass and Allon White, *The Politics and Poetics of Transgression* (Ithaca, 1986), pp. 27–79.

own footsteps. According to Thomas Fuller's seventeenth-century report, the young Jonson lived 'in Harts-horn-lane near Charing-cross' with his mother and stepfather, probably Robert Brett, a bricklayer living on that street. It should be noted that Hartshorn Lane ran alongside an open sewer – perhaps a convenient source of raw material for Brett's trade, which required a plentiful supply of dung – but Brett had improved the open ditch along his property by building a 'little garden' over it in 1586.[4] An open sewer topped with a garden – it is an evocative image in terms of Jonson's penchant as author for revealing the bubbling vice beneath apparently serene surfaces, as in the case of the would-be correctors of Bartholomew Fair. Jonson's own stance toward concealed vices was often close to that of his Puritan reformer Zeal-of-the-Land Busy. And yet, he could never eradicate the bricklayer within: the trouble with the levelling message of the *tu quoque* is that, once set in operation, it spares no one, least of all the author himself. In Jonson, authorial control is never far distant from painful, or gleeful, self-exposure.

As an illustration of this proposition, we might briefly consider Jonson's little gem of mock-heroic scatology, his final epigram 'On the Famous Voyage', which displaces the scene of Jonson's childhood onto a vast subterranean landscape of London itself. Although I have not seen the suggestion made before, the 'Famous Voyage' was in all likelihood instigated by several noteworthy efforts on the part of the City of London to control and reverse the fouling of its water supply. Edmond Howe's continuation of John Stow's *Chronicle of England* (1615) rises to a tone of almost epic panegyric in praising engineering feats on the part of civic fathers during the previous decade for the purification of the sewers and water supply of the 'glorious City of London'. Open ditches were cleaned up and bricked over, a river was diverted through an elaborate system of conduits to bring a plentiful supply of fresh water. Howe also records various civic entertainments and ceremonies at which these heroic achievements were commemorated over the years.[5] Jonson's poem deflates that strain of civic self-congratulation by taking his readers on a tour of the continuing, and indeed ineradicable, filth underlying the apparent improvements. There is an intriguing parallel between the larger civic improvements mocked in this poem and the small improvement made by his stepfather, who covered a similar ditch with a garden. There is also an intriguing parallel between the mock-heroic uncovering of vice in the 'Famous Voyage' and the stance of the Puritan toward Bartholomew Fair. Zeal-of-the-Land Busy and Jonson's 'I' in the poem share the same love for humorous bombast, the same apparent need to feed off what they

---

[4] Cited from David Riggs, *Ben Jonson: A Life* (Cambridge, 1989), pp. 9–10.
[5] Edmond Howe, *The Annales, or Generall Chronicle of England, begun first by maister Iohn Stow, and after him continued . . . vnto the ende of this present yeere 1614* (1615), pp. 937–40.

condemn. In each case, the moralist's zeal against the monstrosity in question is all too clearly revealed as unacknowledged identification: Jonson's contemporaries were all too well aware of Jonson's humble childhood in the house of the bricklayer. What would they have made of his lovingly self-confessional catalogue of City farts and effluvia in his 'Famous Voyage'? We may wonder whether Jonson's hatred of City filth, his lifelong abhorrence/fascination with matters scatological, had something to do with the fact that he grew up alongside a sewer.

The Alchemist offers another instance of flamboyant displacement. The play's setting is Blackfriars, and Jonson himself seems to have been living in Blackfriars at the time that the play was first produced. Indeed, although we have no proof, it is tempting to postulate that the play was composed for the reopening of the Blackfriars Theatre by Richard Burbage and the King's Men in 1609–10. In 1608, James I had dissolved the Children of Blackfriars on the grounds of the boys' company's profanity and irreverence towards authority. The 'house' at Blackfriars remained vacant for a time while Burbage went through legal skirmishes to get it back from its lessee. Although I have not seen these remarked, the play offers a tempting set of equivalences between Blackfriars Theatre, a 'house' left vacant and then tenanted by rogues and mountebanks, and Lovewit's usurped 'house' in Blackfriars. The parallels would have been available to audiences in 1610, whether or not the play was performed at Blackfriars.

But how are we to read Jonson's tempting set of allegorical equivalences between Lovewit's house and Burbage's? Is the previously dissolved boys' company to be identified with the Alchemist, his boy, and his gulls, or are the King's Men just as likely to be so identified? It was they, rather than the Children of Blackfriars, who had recently occupied an empty house, in parallel with the situation of the play. We can therefore read *The Alchemist* topically either as a critique of debased theatre, like that practised by the Children of Blackfriars before the company was dissolved by the king, or as an extended critique of the theatre as practised by the King's Men – a critique of the theatre in itself, with its miraculous, shabby powers of transformation, its exploitation of a series of hapless gulls. In *The Alchemist* we are confronted with yet another instance of the poet's displacement of his own ambivalences, except that in this case the Puritans Ananias and Tribulation are more victims of the Alchemist and his subtle elixir than intrusive reformers in the manner of *Bartholomew Fair*'s Zeal-of-the-Land Busy. In *The Alchemist*, Jonson seems to suggest that the theatre needs the Puritan in the same way that the Alchemist needs his dupes. And here, as in *Bartholomew Fair*, he makes a gesture toward containing the play's explosive energies by prefacing it with a cautionary prologue calling upon the auditory to recognise the play's goal of human betterment. The printed text also includes a dedicatory epistle to Lady Wroth and an epistle to the reader-understander lamenting the 'concupiscence of dances and antics' that dominate 'this age in poetry'.[6] More Busy talk, from one who lived alongside the famous Puritans of Blackfriars.

A recent historicist study of the 'liberties' of London has depicted them (rather in the manner of the City fathers themselves) as sinkholes of licence and every form of vice.[7] But the liberties were also inhabited by large numbers of Puritans. Ecclesiastical nonconformists tended to live in 'liberties' like Blackfriars because there they were free of at least some episcopal surveillance. As Jonson himself loved to point out (there are mocking references in both *Bartholomew Fair* and *The Alchemist*), many of these 'zealous brethren' made their livings off the theatre and associated vanities as feathermakers, tiring women, and the like. Perhaps one reason Jonson kept returning to the feathermakers of Blackfriars was because they were implicated in the same ideological contradictions that Jonson was himself – making a living off an institution that a part of him heartily despised.

If we take a high moral line of interpretation like that suggested by Jonson's prefatory materials to *The Alchemist*, then we can easily enough quiet such unauthorised speculation by identifying Jonson firmly with the sensible, well-meaning character of Lovewit. The master's recovery of his house from the charlatans could then suggest a parallel Jonsonian rescue of the institution of the theatre from those elements (like the Children of Blackfriars) who had been debasing it. But the very play, *The Alchemist*, that announces this 'notable reform' is itself constituted by the outrageously funny antics of the charlatans – we encounter yet another nest of interpretive boxes in which the author becomes inextricable from the carnivalesque he professes to find wanting. Here, as in *Bartholomew Fair*, the high and low are impossible to keep distinct without a violent effort of separation on the part of the interpreter – an effort that threatens to rob the play of those very elements that make it theatrically volatile and alive.

In the late 1970s when I constructed my argument about the Puritan in *Bartholomew Fair*, I was interested in mapping out the play's topical resonances – the ways in which Jonson evokes the behaviour and rhetorical style of actual anti-theatrical spokesmen of the period. Certainly Busy's diatribes against the fair and the drama echo some of the arguments of contemporary tracts and sermons, although (as is appropriate to parody) Busy's wild, inchoate doomsday imagery goes even beyond the most colourful of those. And certainly in his Prologue to James, Jonson invites the king to see the 'zealous noise' of contemporary anti-sabbatarian sentiment in the character of the Puritan. At present, however, in parallel with Patrick Collinson's essay, I am more interested in Zeal-of-the-Land Busy as construction than as reflection. Jonson's construction of the Puritan

---

[6] Cited from Ben Jonson's *The Alchemist*, ed. Alvin B. Kernan (1974; repr. New Haven, 1979), p. 20.

[7] Steven Mullaney, *The Place of the Stage: License, Play, and Power in Renaissance England* (Chicago, 1988).

may have served his own purposes of simultaneous self-denial and self-revelation, but it obviously satisfied broader, more public hungers as well. To what extent might the stage-Puritan have been an artifact of the theatre's need to distance itself from the moral ambiguity of its own institutional status and appeal? There was obviously a market for such figures – not only James I himself but a number of his subjects took pleasure in the ritualised public dismantling of the religious hypocrite. For them, Busy may have been a reassuring character because he siphoned off to a hypothesised lunatic fringe questions about moral and social contradiction that would otherwise have had to be confronted more directly – as they were in the violent sabbatarianism of the 1640s that brought about, among other things, the closing of the theatres.

Much to his exasperation, Jonson was successful on stage only in so far as he managed to displace his high-flown authorial judiciousness onto characters like Busy and Overdo. But by doing so, inevitably, he lost authorial control. If he had not been able to create anti-theatrical Puritans like Busy, and thereby prismatically to scatter and dispel his own misgivings about the theatre, he might have turned Puritan himself. Or, at the very least, he might have felt considerably less free as a dramatist to display and revel in the pungent mire of the carnivalesque.

6

Philip Massinger's *A New Way to Pay Old Debts*

Noble Scarlet vs London Blue

Keith Lindley

Running through the text of Massinger's comedy are two conflicting approaches to the maintenance of social degree and relations in a hierarchical and highly stratified society. On the one hand, there is an apparently nostalgic portrayal of a traditional view of gentility in which the latter is seen as deriving its strength from birth and ancestry, honour and reputation, and the appropriate lifestyle, ethics and behaviour. Posited against this is a contrasting view of social rank and values that sanctioned the ruthless pursuit of self-interest in which the possession of wealth, and freedom from conventional moral and religious constraints, are the decisive factors. The first set of ideas is associated with the established landed elites, and finds its principal expression in the characters of Lord Lovell and Lady Alworth, while the conflicting view is attached to the social parvenu, epitomised by Sir Giles Overreach, who craves the kudos of elevated social rank but has little time for the contingent values and rules of conduct customarily associated with it. Massinger makes his own preference clear by condemning the voracious pursuit of new wealth in his satire of Overreach while at the same time presenting Lord Lovell and Lady Alworth as attractive ideals. The avarice and worldly ambition represented by Overreach are condemned not only from a religious standpoint but also in defence of a set of community values adhered to by Massinger and other contemporary dramatists.[1] Massinger's audience might be expected to share this outlook as a period of disruptive socio-economic change encouraged them to cling to an idealised view of a traditional society under threat.

Ideally birth and ancestry lay at the heart of true gentility. Both these qualities were conveyed most forcefully in the concept of noble blood inherited by those born to superior rank and the need to preserve that blood's purity. Despite his outward appearance, the as yet unregenerate

---

[1] L. C. Knights, *Drama and Society in the Age of Jonson* (1937), pp. 279–80, 290.

Wellborn (whose very name signals the importance of breeding) can remind
Lady Alworth that his blood 'is as noble as that which fills your veins'
(1.3.87–9).[2] She herself later lectures Lord Lovell on how noblemen, conscious of their 'eminent blood' and breeding, could not have the same
single-minded devotion to the accumulation of wealth as 'common men'
(4.1.180–7). If the traditional conventions relating to breeding were to be
observed, Overreach's driving ambition to marry his daughter, Margaret,
to Lord Lovell could never be fulfilled. The latter could not contemplate
adulterating his blood by marrying beneath his rank, 'and so leave my
issue made up of several pieces, one part scarlet and the other London-blue'
(4.1.221–6), while Margaret too urges that her 'low descent', and hence
their social incompatibility, argue against marriage to the 'noble' Lovell
(3.3.197–9). The point is driven home when Lovell eventually proposes
marriage to Lady Alworth, fully confident that she is a woman of noble
lineage and his social equal (5.1.62–6).

   This preoccupation with ancestry and lineage among the elite is one of
the most conspicuous features of early modern society. Indeed, the prestige
attached to ancient lineage stimulated a strong contemporary interest in
genealogy. In this context Wellborn's transformation into a social outcast
is rendered all the more dramatic by the later knowledge that his family's
gentility could be traced back for twenty generations. Yet in reality this
contemporary obsession with ancestry was often an attempt to disguise
the facts of upward social mobility as newcomers to gentility replaced
those families which had fallen victim to biological failure of the line or
declining fortunes. Furthermore, although social endogamy was the norm
among the upper echelons of society, and marriages between peers and
commoners were highly exceptional in the early modern period as a whole,
they were a sufficient possibility in the early seventeenth century to warrant
Overreach's belief that a union between Margaret and Lord Lovell was
feasible.[3]

   Honour, and the reputation to which it gave rise, were highly prized
genteel qualities which had to be carefully preserved against the ever-
present danger of loss. The concept of honour was an integral part of the
nobility's self-estimation and something that was conceived as being one
of the main features that distinguished them from other people.[4] From his
first appearance upon the stage, Lovell makes plain the importance he
places upon 'mine own honour', that 'fair name' and 'my fame and credit'
(3.1.38–40; 4.1.85). Alworth praises his master as being 'no scruple lessened

   [2] The edition of the play used is that edited by T. W. Craik in The New Mermaids series (Ernest Benn)
in 1964. The punctuation has been slightly modernised.
   [3] 5.1.161–3; L. Stone, *The Crisis of the Aristocracy 1558–1641* (Oxford, 1965), p. 23; K. Wrightson, *English
Society 1580–1680* (1982), pp. 47, 87; J. A. Sharpe, *Early Modern England: A Social History 1550–1760* (1987), pp.
153, 173–4.
   [4] Sharpe, *Social History*, p. 170; Stone, *Crisis*, p. 42.

in the full weight of honour' (1.2.70), while Overreach feels obliged to reassure Lovell that 'Your reputation shall stand as fair / In all good men's opinions as now' (4.1.88–9) and that he would be

> so tender
> Of what concerns you in all points of honour
> That the immaculate whiteness of your fame
> Nor your unquestioned integrity
> Shall e'er be sullied with one taint or spot
> That may take from your innocence and candour.
> (4.1.93–8)

In the same vein, immediately Lady Alworth's name is introduced into the play Wellborn applauds her as 'a noble widow, / And keeps her reputation pure and clear / From the least taint of infamy' (1.1.103–5). But honour and reputation could be damaged or lost if not jealously guarded. Lovell is reminded by Lady Alworth that 'honour / By virtuous ways achieved and bravely purchased' would be rendered 'Polluted and unwholesome' by any linkage with ill-gotten wealth (4.1.193–9). In Wellborn's case, riotous living has resulted in him losing his reputation and, until he has redeemed it 'Some noble way', he cannot be fully restored to his gentility (5.1.393–5).

It is significant that the way chosen by Wellborn to restore his reputation is to seek a military commission under Lovell so that he might serve his king and country. Despite the sharply reduced opportunities for such service in the largely peaceful decades of the early seventeenth century, the customarily close association of nobility with military service remained strong and to serve one's king and country in war was regarded as an honourable activity.[5] Lovell's own 'fair name' has been earned by displays of leadership and bravery in wars (3.1.38; 3.2.76–82; 4.1.150–1). War was 'a school / Where all the principles tending to honour / Are taught if truly followed', according to the advice bequeathed by the late Alworth, senior, to his son. 'To dare boldly / In a fair cause, and for the country's safety', and to exhibit courage, obedience to superiors and fortitude, were the essential qualities required while those who gave themselves over to 'their lusts and riots' would never deserve 'the noble name of soldiers' (1.2.99–114).

Whatever the importance attached to birth and reputation, the ultimate determinant of gentility was the possession of landed wealth. Only land could confer the correct social cachet and open the way to positions of authority and political influence.[6] Before his profligacy had taken its toll,

[5] 5.1.396–9; Stone, *Crisis*, pp. 200, 266; Sharpe, *Social History*, p. 168. For contemporary opinion about military service making gentlemen see the discussion by J. P. Cooper, 'Ideas of Gentility in Early-Modern England', in *Land, Men and Beliefs: Studies in Early-Modern History*, ed. G. E. Aylmer and J. S. Morrill (1983), pp. 43–77.

[6] Stone, *Crisis*, pp. 39–41; Wrightson, *English Society*, pp. 25, 27, 30.

Wellborn had been 'a lord of acres' which provided him with an annual income of £1,200. This wealth had been sufficient to place his late father, Sir John Wellborn, at the top end of county society and to qualify him for local positions of authority and power.[7]

Wealth derived from agrarian rents and dues supported a lavish lifestyle which was displayed in superior housing, food and dress. Sir John Wellborn had kept 'a great house' while Lady Alworth's county seat was a 'well built pile' set in the midst of rich acres (1.1.36; 4.1.66–8, 70–2). The sumptuousness of the tables laid on by Lady Alworth and Overreach for their guests proclaims their wealth and standing. By the early seventeenth century, table manners too had become a genteel requirement and hence the social distance indicated by Marrall's 'slovenly' and farcically ignorant behaviour at Lady Alworth's table.[8] Sumptuary laws may no longer have been in force,[9] yet opulence of dress still served an important function as an indicator of elevated rank. Lady Alworth's first words are instructions to her servants to 'Sort those silks well' (1.2.53) and in the following scene Wellborn makes reference to the 'costly jewels' and the 'rich clothes' that she is wearing (1.3.88–9). Likewise the household servants attending upon her, and the coach in which she travels, set Lady Alworth apart as a woman of superior status (1.2.54; 3.3.31; 3.2.40–8).

When Lady Alworth admits Wellborn and Marrall to her table, and gives gold to her cook and her stepson, or when reference is made to Sir John Wellborn's liberality to the poor, adherence to a traditional set of rules governing elite behaviour is being indicated. The ideal described by Overreach, and decisively rejected by him, is to live 'a well-governed life, / And to do right to others as ourselves' (2.1.24–6). Accordingly, the rich are expected to show hospitality, generosity and charity, and generally be good neighbours. In return they could hope to maintain social harmony, and safeguard their own privileged position, by encouraging habits of social deference among their inferiors.[10] They are also required to uphold hierarchy by observing the niceties of relative social standing even when that hierarchy has been distorted by the vagaries of fortune. Thus, in the case of his page Alworth, Lovell could 'make / A fitting difference between my foot-boy / And a gentleman by want compelled to serve me', and Alworth repays Lovell's fatherly kindness and understanding by according him obedience and deep respect (3.1. 26–30). In a more extreme instance, Margaret Overreach regards her 'new woman the Lady Downefalne', the wife of a knight imprisoned for debt, as more fitting for a companion than a servant and protests

---

[7] 1.1.32–9, 42. The play is set in Nottinghamshire. According to estimates made of the wealth of gentry families in neighbouring Yorkshire, the top 10.8% had incomes in excess of £1,000 a year (Wrightson, *English Society*, p. 25).

[8] 2.2.124–32; Stone, *Crisis*, pp. 50–1.

[9] Stone, *Crisis*, pp. 28–9.

[10] *Ibid.*, p. 42; Sharpe, *Social History*, pp. 171–2; Wrightson, *English Society*, pp. 51, 57–8.

that she blushes when she commands her 'that was once attended / With persons not inferior to myself / In birth' (3.2.38–9, 49–52).

The above portrayal of traditional gentility is an idyllic one based upon exacting standards and generally presupposing a largely static society. Yet Massinger himself lived through a fifty-year period of frequently disruptive social and economic change which was of sufficient novelty and magnitude to convince some of his contemporaries that the very bonds of society were under threat. In order to survive or even profit from this change, landed elites had to be prepared to pursue their own economic self-interests in an individualistic and competitive manner and, when necessary, jettison the restrictions imposed by traditional social values. An exceptionally fluid land market, and rising agricultural prices, provided opportunities for ambitious and resourceful men to push their way to the top, while established families who failed to adapt to changing economic conditions found themselves falling in the contrary direction. The result was a period of extraordinary social mobility with families moving up and down the social and economic scale at an unprecedentedly rapid rate.[11]

Among those who could expect to benefit from the opportunities opened up by these social and economic conditions to acquire gentility were successful City merchants, like Overreach, who used their mercantile wealth to purchase landed estates and set themselves up as rural gentry. Overreach is the kind of social climber that the Jacobean theatre loved to satirise.[12] Moving away from his mercantile roots, he has entered the world of the county gentry by apparently marrying a sister of Sir John Wellborn and accumulating substantial amounts of land. His sights are now set upon forging aristocratic links by marrying his daughter to Lord Lovell.

In contrast to the upwardly mobile Overreach are those men who have fallen upon hard times, and indeed there are several reminders in the play of the precariousness of material life, a subject on which Massinger and his fellow dramatists could testify from personal knowledge. The late Lord Alworth had experienced low fortunes, as 'Want, debts, and quarrels / Lay heavy on him', and had married wealth when taking Lady Alworth for a wife (1.3.99–101, 110–12). Consequently, although his heir, young Alworth, enjoyed his stepmother's beneficence, he has been constrained by economic necessity to seek employment, albeit of an essentially honourable nature, as a nobleman's page (3.1.28). Wellborn had inherited a name and sufficient landed property from his deceased father to place him near the top of county society, but riotous living and improvidence have reduced him to the gutter. Utterly ruined financially, ragged, lousy and foul smelling, Wellborn is being subjected to the ultimate indignity of being thrown out of a common alehouse as the play opens. He has in

---

[11] Wrightson, *English Society*, pp. 59–60, 130–1, 142, 149, 223; Stone, *Crisis*, pp. 11, 36–40.
[12] B. Ford, ed., *The New Pelican Guide to English Literature*, II: *The Age of Shakespeare* (1982), pp. 37, 477–8.

turn brought ruin upon at least two of his creditors, a vintner and a tailor (1.1; 4.2.83–7, 91–5). Overreach seeks out a servant for his daughter from among the desperate wives of knights ruined by him and eventually appoints 'the Lady Downefalne', whose husband is languishing in a debtors' prison on Overreach's instructions (2.1.78–83; 3.2.42–8).

Overreach is very much the voice of the real world in which the ruthless and unprincipled prosper and inherited status and traditional codes of behaviour provide no protection in themselves against social and economic catastrophe. With his 'heaps of ill got gold, and so much land' (3.1.83–4), and the real delight he takes in his arrival at his wealth 'these dark / And crooked ways' (4.1.135–7), Overreach is the personification of 'Mammon'. This is the approach to wealth accumulation sneered at by Lady Alworth when she alludes to how common, as opposed to noble, men 'Make sordid wealth the object and sole end / Of their industrious aims' (4.1.180–3).

The single-minded pursuit of material gain leads Overreach to repudiate completely the beliefs and values associated with traditional gentility. Reputation, which was so precious to the gentleman, holds no value whatsoever for him. While acknowledging Lovell's sensitivity on this matter when the prospect of benefiting from another's unscrupulous actions was raised, and seeking to reassure him that his reputation would remain inviolate (4.1.87–98), Overreach is totally dismissive of the notoriety he himself has earned as he has trampled his way to the top. Being branded an 'Extortioner, tyrant, cormorant, or intruder / On my poor neighbour's right, or grand encloser / Of what was common, to my private use' means nothing to him and he shrugs off the insults as 'piddling complaints / Breathed out in bitterness'. Nor is he moved by the pleas of widows and the tears of orphans, or fearful of the curses heaped upon him by whole families who have been ruined by his 'sinister practices' (4.1.111–31).

Neighbourliness, friendship and kinship are similarly rejected by Overreach. Coveting the manor of his neighbour, Master Frugal, he makes elaborate plans to acquire it by nefarious means thereby enhancing his notoriety as an intruder upon his neighbour's right. Indeed, when it comes to gaining titles for his daughter there can be no doubt that Overreach, 'without touch of conscience, / Will cut his neighbour's throat' (2.1.26–48; 1.1.159–61). 'Friendship is but a word' in Overreach's estimation, and one that he has no time for (2.1.20–2), and bonds of kinship too mean nothing to him. As he confesses to Wellborn, 'worldly men' like himself, 'when we see friends and kinsmen, / Past hope sunk in their fortunes, lend no hand / To lift 'em up, but rather set our feet / Upon their heads, to press 'em to the bottom' (3.3.50–4). Wellborn, of course, has had direct experience of this, and being Overreach's nephew has undoubtedly been a curse. Being Overreach's daughter and sole heir is little better for, in theory, it entails unquestioning obedience to an autocratic father who is prepared to sacrifice her honour and virginity to achieve his selfish ends (3.2.111–14). Friends and kin are people to be exploited, threatened and manipulated so far as he is concerned while the contemporary convention among the upper echelons of society is to accord value and respect to such associations.[13]

Religion and conscience never act as constraints upon Overreach's actions or behaviour. On the contrary, expediency is his guiding principle, as when he exhorts Margaret to 'Learn anything, / And from any creature that may make thee great; / From the devil himself' (3.2.120–2). Margaret might balk at this 'devilish doctrine' and her father's willingness to 'Cast aside religion, / The hopes of heaven, or fear of hell', but she is forced to respond on his own terms by objecting that 'In worldly policy' the ready surrender of her virginity he was advocating would not succeed in making her Lovell's wife (3.2.130–9). Later, in conversation with Lovell, Overreach declares himself uninhibited by either the hatred of all mankind in this world or the 'fear of what can fall on me hereafter' (4.1.141–2). 'Dispute not my religion, nor my faith', he proclaims, 'Though I am borne thus headlong by my will, / You may make choice of what belief you please, / To me they are equal' (4.1.145–8). A shocked Lovell recoils at the 'atheistical assertions' of 'this blasphemous beast', 'this bold, bad man' and his devilish beliefs (4.1.152, 154, 160–2). In the final scene a deranged Overreach, haunted by the widows and orphans he has wronged, fantasises about being dragged before 'the judgement seat' and having his 'ulcerous soul' scourged by furies with steel whips as he is consigned to hell (5.1.362–73). This allows Lovell to moralise that 'Here is a precedent to teach wicked men / That when they leave religion and turn atheists / Their own abilities leave 'em' (5.1.379–81).

Although it is never spelt out in the play, contemporaries would have been aware of the important function served by religion in maintaining and legitimating both social hierarchy and elite privilege and authority. By turning his back on religion, therefore, Overreach is paradoxically helping to undermine the very hierarchy that he has been so eager to climb. In fact there is a decided ambivalence in his whole attitude to social degree. On the one hand, he craves the prestige of title and aristocratic links, and can barely wait to be able to refer to 'My honourable, nay, right honourable daughter' and to bounce a noble grandson on his knee (4.1.43–5, 100–3), yet, on the other hand, he has no real respect for inherited gentility and the values ideally associated with it.

Overreach represents in a stark way the dislocation and conflict that could accompany social mobility when a City merchant, schooled in the ruthless pursuit of profit, sets out to scale the heights of a traditional

---

[13] Wrightson, *English Society*, pp. 47–8.

landed society. Recognising that there has always been 'More than a feud, a strange antipathy / Between us and true gentry' (2.1.87–9), he takes a perverse pleasure in humiliating members of the latter that he has managed to ruin. Thus he intends those ladies of knights reduced to penury to become his daughter's menial servants, for it is his 'glory, though I come from the city, / To have their issue, whom I have undone, / To kneel to mine, as bond-slaves' (2.1.81–3). When one such unfortunate gentlewoman subsequently enters Margaret's service, Overreach is keen to know whether she is being 'humble' and industrious with 'her ladyship forgotten', and Margaret's compassion for her misfortune is brushed aside with the brutal instruction to 'Trample on her' followed by the threat to cast her into prison beside her penniless husband if 'she but repines / To do thee any duty, though ne'er so servile' (3.2. 40–8).

Maintaining a merchant's pride in his affluence, Overreach is convinced that there are no differences between the parvenu and inherited superior rank that the former's wealth cannot bridge. Accordingly, Margaret has no reason to feel embarrassed at the social inversion of being served by a woman who is very much her superior in birth for, as Overreach's daughter, she is 'The blest child of my industry, and wealth' (3.2.52–3). Nor should she object that there is 'too much disparity / Between his quality and mine' when marriage with Lord Lovell is being proposed, because Overreach's 'wealth / Shall weigh his titles down, and make you equals' (3.2.100–4). Although, as has been previously noted, marriages between peers and commoners were very much the exception in early modern England, there is some evidence that at the time the play was being written there was a relatively brief and unparalleled increase in the number of matches being arranged between peers and the daughters or widows of merchants. However, the dominant view was one that continued to stress the importance of social parity when it came to aristocratic marriage and unions which were effectively an exchange of money for title, as would have been the case if Margaret had married Lovell, tended to be regarded as very squalid.[14]

The same mercantile faith in the power of money informs most of Overreach's social climbing, for in his eyes people and titles are there for the purchase. Lovell is promised a luxurious life free from financial worries after he has married Margaret. He is also promised an earldom 'if gold can do it' (4.1.104–10, 144), and in fact Overreach himself may have originally purchased his own knighthood.[15] Again the buying of titles was clearly a topic of considerable contemporary interest given the fact that titles were being sold in a quite blatant manner under James I. Knighthoods were the first dignity to be sold and, as the numbers increased and

---

[14] Stone, *Crisis*, pp. 630–2.
[15] Philip Massinger, *A New Way to Pay Old Debts*, ed. T. W. Craik (1964), p. 96n.

men like Overreach were able to assume the title, the prestige of the order
sank. A new hereditary dignity, that of baronet, was created in 1611, and
within a few years was suffering the same fate as a knighthood as indis-
criminate sales devalued it. The English peerage also underwent a phenomenal increase in its numbers during the years 1615–28 when titles were
readily available for those with sufficient cash, and Overreach would have
had little problem in purchasing an earldom for Lovell.[16] The net effect
of this inflation of honours was to blur distinctions among the upper social
strata and to reduce the respect accorded to title. In contributing to this
process, therefore, Overreach is once again helping to undermine the
existing social hierarchy.

Associated with Overreach in his villainy, and lesser contributors to the
breakdown of the old order, are the subsidiary characters of Greedy, a
justice of the peace, and Marrall, a rural attorney. Justice Greedy, with
his insatiable appetite for food figuratively underscoring his venality, has
been appointed to the commission of the peace as a result of Overreach's
patronage. With his father a tailor, Greedy's origins are relatively humble,
especially in view of the fact that he is not only a JP but is of the *quorum*
too.[17] His general demeanour, and the revelation that his surname is
'Woodcock' (with its colloquial meaning of a fool), gives Greedy a buffoon-
like status (3.2.85, 91–4). Nevertheless, having discovered that 'He that
bribes his belly / Is certain to command his soul', Overreach is not to
be disappointed in his patronage of Greedy. The latter partially and
corruptly uses his position on the county bench to secure verdicts in his
patron's favour, thereby enabling Overreach to crush those who stand in
the way of his own greed for property. It suits Overreach to remain off
the commission himself, and instead manipulate Justice Greedy from
behind the scenes, and thereby avoid both the work associated with the
office and the exposure to possible prosecution (2.1.4–21).

Partial and corrupt JPs were a fact of life in the period but they were not
the rule. The vast majority of them were nominated to the commission
because of their local prominence, and hence they were usually drawn from
the upper echelons of county society.[18] The late Sir John Wellborn, with his
breeding, wealth and authority, fitted into this picture. Like Greedy, he too
was of the *quorum* but there the comparison ends, for their social origins and
demeanour in office were very different. A sense of duty incumbent upon
men of his rank probably informed Sir John's service, in contrast to the

---

[16] Stone, *Crisis*, pp. 74–82, 84, 92–3, 103–4, 111, 120–2. Between 1615 and 1628, the numbers of the English
peerage as a whole rose from 81 to 126 and earldoms from 27 to 65 (*ibid.*, p. 104).

[17] A member of the *quorum* belonged to the prestigious inner circle of JPs whose presence was essential to
constitute a bench.

[18] J. H. Gleason, *The Justices of the Peace in England 1558–1640* (Oxford, 1969), pp. 65, 96, 120; J. S. Cockburn,
A History of the English Assizes 1558–1714 (Cambridge, 1972), pp. 103–4; J. A. Sharpe, *Crime in Early Modern
England* (1984), pp. 28–9, 39.

self-seeking of a Justice Greedy, and only death may have robbed him of the ultimate distinction of being appointed *custos rotulorum* (1.32–5).[19]

Overreach's other main agent, Marrall, is also of non-genteel stock as is pointedly emphasised by his ignorant behaviour at Lady Alworth's table. Lawyers in general, and attorneys in particular, were regarded by contemporaries with a mixture of suspicion and outright hostility. Although dishonest attorneys may not have been typical, contemporary opinion tended to see them as such and to assign to them a substantial part of the blame for the dramatic increase in litigation that they were witnessing.[20] The portrayal of Marrall's dishonesty and sharp practice, therefore, and his generally unprincipled behaviour in pursuit of his own advancement, would have struck a responsive chord in a seventeenth-century audience. Marrall is Overreach's pupil 'in the art of undoing men, / For that is our profession' who speaks the truth 'but once a year' (2.3.55–6, 76). He has no compunction whatsoever about double-crossing Overreach when he judges it to be to his advantage and is more than ready to employ his nefarious skills in the service of a new master. There is none of the genuine respect and deference in Marrall's relationship to Overreach of the kind that has been witnessed between young Alworth and his master. On the contrary, Marrall responds to the abuse he receives from his master with muttered resentment and sarcasm and takes great pleasure in ultimately betraying him. However, such treachery is not to be condoned and, far from being rewarded, Marrall is rejected by Wellborn for 'he that dares be false / To a master, though unjust, will ne'er be true / To any other' (5.1.338–42). The defence of master/servant relations was too important a matter in a hierarchical society to allow any other outcome in the play but a ruined and disgraced Marrall.[21]

The play ends with traditional order and values reaffirmed. Overreach has been utterly thwarted in his social ambitions; the cheater has been cheated and the deceiver deceived. The unprincipled pursuit of gain has ended in madness and impotence while a reformed Wellborn has recovered his material possessions and is on course to regain his honour through military service. Yet the poetic strength of Overreach's character, and his dominance of the drama until the very end, could be read as a tacit recognition on Massinger's part that it was in the ruthless pursuit of self-interest that the real future lay.

---

[19] The *custos rotulorum*, or keeper of the rolls, was the foremost JP of the county who had nominal custody of the records of the sessions of the peace. Appointment to the office carried with it considerable prestige and an implicit recognition of local preeminence.

[20] Sharpe, *Crime*, p. 146; C. W. Brooks, 'Litigants and Attorneys in the King's Bench and Common Pleas, 1560–1640', in *Legal Records and the Historian*, ed. J. H. Baker (1978), pp. 43–4, 53, 55–6.

[21] Marrall's behaviour could not be justified in terms of a virtuous servant disobeying the evil commands of a wicked master as some contemporary moral and political commentators would allow. For a full discussion of this point see R. Strier, 'Faithful Servants: Shakespeare's Praise of Disobedience', in *The Historical Renaissance: New Essays on Tudor and Stuart Literature and Culture*, ed. H. Dubrow and R. Strier (Chicago, 1988), pp. 104–33.

The Outsider as Insider

Martin Butler

I

The lurking dangers in constructing a historicist reading of *A New Way to Pay Old Debts* are twofold:[1] those of smoothing out the ideological conflicts with which the play seems to be engaged, and of reading it too transparently as a window onto the 'mental world' of its time. In the past, interpretations of the play have tended to fix it rather too neatly into a schematised context of social and economic change, in which the collision between the citizen Sir Giles Overreach and the provincial community of gentlemen and aristocrats into which he intrudes is seen as directly symbolic of the historical forces working to unsettle Massinger's England.[2] In such readings the play emerges as essentially a hysterical document of class anxiety. Sir Giles's defeat by a conspiracy of provincial elites is interpreted as an action that seeks to reverse the forward momentum of history: economic opportunism is confounded by the structure of inherited loyalties, even though outside the world of the playhouse such imaginary palliatives would not be forthcoming. I shall be arguing that this sort of reading mistakes the nature of the conflicts in the play, which prove on inspection to be much less clear-cut. Massinger does not depict two rival ideologies coming into collision but (more interestingly) a fissure within the dominant aristocratic ideology itself which is precisely tied to English circumstances in the early months of Charles I.

Moreover, I shall suggest that in historicising the play it is important not to simplify the relationship between its action and the material world to which it seems to refer. The play cannot be said to provide a simple ventriloquisation of the mental assumptions of provincial society since its

---

[1] Parts of this argument are condensed and developed from my earlier essay, 'A New Way to Pay Old Debts: Massinger's Grim Comedy', in *English Comedy*, ed. M. Cordner, P. Holland and J. Kerrigan (Cambridge, 1994), pp. 119–36. All references are to *The Plays and Poems of Philip Massinger*, ed. P. Edwards and C. Gibson (5 vols., Oxford, 1976). Quotations have been modernised.

[2] Currently the best discussions of the play are by M. Neill, 'Massinger's Patriarchy: A New Way to Pay Old Debts', *Renaissance Drama*, n.s., 10 (1979), 185–213; N. S. Leonard, 'Overreach at Bay', in *Philip Massinger: A Critical Reassessment*, ed. D. Howard (Cambridge, 1985), pp. 171–92; G. K. Paster, 'Quomodo, Sir Giles, and Triangular Desire', and P. Edwards, 'Philip Massinger: Comedy and Comical History', both in *Comedy from Shakespeare to Sheridan*, ed. A. Braunmuller and J. C. Bulman (Cranbury, N.J., 1986), pp. 165–78 and 179–93; and A. Tricomi, *Anti-Court Drama in England, 1603–1642* (Charlottesville, 1989).

representations are not unmediated. Massinger was not an omniscient observer of his society, floating free of his own historical positioning, but was himself involved in the conflicts which he describes. Consequently his play does not so much reflect its times (as an image of its society it is self-evidently far from reliable) as undertake a negotiation with them. From this point of view, its historical value does not arise from its evidential status as passive reportage but from its engagement with the stresses and conflicts of its moment of production, and from the adjudication which it attempts to make between them. Paradoxically, it is the play's very unre-liability as a 'document', its status as an intervention rather than a reflection, which makes it so historically revealing. In observing what Massinger prefers to magnify or to minimise, the clarifications which he offers, the evasions which he finds necessary or the contradictions which he seems unable to discharge, we may disclose how far his image of his society was conditioned by or in tension with the ideological assumptions of his day.

II

Certainly *A New Way to Pay Old Debts* anticipates today's historiography in its depiction of a closely bonded rural community welded together by hierarchies of deference and amity. Historians of early modern provincial society have emphasised the particularist outlook of the county community, the tendency of local horizons to loom larger than national, and the centrality to provincial life of networks of kinship and an abiding ideology of neighbourliness.[3] Within this perspective, *A New Way* seems like the localist play *par excellence*. It is rare to find a comedy in which the everyday preoccupations and genteel localism of the village world are evoked so densely. In Massinger's village (unnamed, but somewhere in Nottinghamshire) the institutions, assumptions and complex speaking tones of provincial life are concretely in evidence. At the top of the rural pyramid, Lady Alworth's household, with its nicely graded sequence of domestic officials through which visitors have to pass before reaching her presence (porter, usher, cook, steward, chambermaid and gentlewoman (2.2)), dis-plays local structures in terms of the elaborate protocols of the noble great house. At the bottom, village hierarchies are glimpsed in the social aspir-ations of Tapwell who, though a mere alehouse keeper, has achieved the lowly office of scavenger and hopes to be overseer of the poor (1.1.66–7). Throughout, the play's language is heavy with references to the 'country'

---

[3] For some examples, see K. Wrightson, *English Society 1580–1680* (1982); W. Hunt, *The Puritan Moment* (Cambridge, Mass., 1983); D. Underdown, *Revel, Riot and Rebellion: Popular Politics and Culture in England, 1603–1660* (Oxford, 1985); and A. Fletcher, *Reform in the Provinces: The Government of Stuart England* (New Haven, 1986).

or the 'shire', and the whole village treasures the memory of old Sir John Wellborn, who bore 'the whole sway of the shire; kept a great house; / Relieved the poor, and so forth' (1.1.36–7) – an ideal of neighbourliness which seems likely to continue in the social practice of Lady Alworth and her husband-to-be, Lord Lovell.

Conversely, the menace which Sir Giles Overreach represents is articulated as an offence against localist norms. His legal chicanery, insane ambition and schemes for marrying his daughter to Lord Lovell threaten to undermine both the village economy and the ethos of neighbourliness. Wellborn describes him as one who, for the sake of advancing his daughter, will 'cut his neighbour's throat' (1.1.161), and in Overreach's instructions to Marrall we learn that his way of acquiring land is to beggar the possessor by breaking his fences and involving him in actions of trespass the expense of which will force him to sell (2.1.35–42). It is striking that Massinger has doubled the intrigue plot which he found in his source, Middleton's *A Trick to Catch the Old One* (in which the principal opposition is between the usurer Hoard and the gentleman Witgood), so that Overreach seems to threaten not just an individual but the whole structure of the locality. This is one intrigue comedy in which the villain's downfall testifies not solely to the wit of a single protagonist but to the ability of the entire community to outplay him.

Yet if Overreach stands convicted of sins against neighbourliness, Massinger's scenario is still very different from that in recent historiography. Provincial historians have associated the forces of change in early modern village communities with new Puritanical elites – preachers, godly magistrates, substantial householders – whose rise had a divisive impact on provincial life. By seeking to discipline their communities according to an ethos of decent behaviour, these groupings of village notables undermined older notions of communal amity and traditional loyalty. Of this there is nothing in *A New Way* (unless one counts the scene in which Wellborn and Greedy put down Tapwell's alehouse, an event that is more revenge than reformation). It is the established gentry who remain the arbiters of village behaviour, and though Overreach is acquiring local influence and land he is absolutely no Puritan. He has no interest in changing the character of his locality but simply in achieving a controlling power within it. This power he expresses as a contest between legitimate and illegitimate gentility:

> 'tis my glory, though I come from the city,
> To have their issue, whom I have undone,
> To kneel to mine, as bond-slaves . . .
> 'Tis a rich man's pride, there having ever been
> More than a feud, a strange antipathy
> Between us and true gentry.
>
> (2.1.81–9)

This implies a scenario which owes less to close observation of provincial change than it does to the familiar ideological oppositions which structure contemporary urban comedy: birth against opportunity, land against wealth, inherited status against economic individualism. In effect, Massinger subordinates his portrayal of provincial life to city comedy antagonisms which are mapped strategically onto rural Nottinghamshire.

Further, for all its surface conservatism, the play tacitly licences a model of controlled social change. Undeniably, its action affirms a fundamentally privileged ethos. Lovell's view of the sacredness of birth is typical:

> I would not so adulterate my blood
> By marrying Margaret, and so leave my issue
> Made up of several pieces, one part scarlet
> And the other London-blue. In my own tomb
> I will inter my name first.
>
> (4.1.223–7)

His words are anticipated by Margaret, who is equally fixated on the disparity between status and wealth ('tissues matched with scarlet suit but ill' (3.2.199)), and whose respect for blood renders her utterly incapable of fulfilling her father's desire that she should order the impoverished Lady Downefalne around (3.2.38–52). Notwithstanding, the society which Massinger depicts is clearly undergoing evolution. Margaret may be an inappropriate match for a lord but she does marry Alworth – who, though a page, is still a *bona fide* gentleman likely to make a decent career out of military service – and Lovell himself weds Lady Alworth, a mere gentleman's widow for whom such an alliance means real promotion. There is thus an unspoken tension between the play's ideology of birth and its covert willingness to underwrite the necessary adaptations to money taken by impecunious gentlemen and aristocrats. Change may not be welcomed but it is happening; the important thing is that it should be gradual and accommodated to the social hegemony of the existing elites.

III

These considerations make it important to define precisely the threat that Sir Giles Overreach poses, and this is less straightforward than it seems. For all his egotism and monstrous rapacity, Overreach is far from being the typical London comedy villain, an ambitious citizen carving out a place amongst those of gentle birth by sheer force of will. Remarkably, he does not actually challenge the ideology of rank which obsesses the village inhabitants, but makes just as much a fetish of it as they do. Though he admits that he comes 'from the city', to all intents and purposes he is already a gentleman amongst gentlemen: he may rework the stock usuring citizen from earlier London comedy, but as a version of the type he has been almost totally transformed. For example, he is quite unlike the miserly Hoard in *A Trick to Catch the Old One* or Massinger's own hypocritical Luke Frugal in *The City Madam* (the height of whose ambition is to dine in solitary splendour amidst his gold). Rather, before the play begins he has moved into that genteel environment which Hoard and Luke view enviously from without. He has a knighthood, a place in the country and friends. He has status equivalent to a JP (though he refuses the honour for the sake of more nefarious considerations (2.1.10–22)) and, already boasting long-standing marital ties to the Wellborns, he is now promoting himself as a likely second husband for Lady Alworth.

More crucially, Overreach affects the manners of a gentleman, feeding high, maintaining an expensive household and living ostentatiously. Were it not that Greedy and Marrall accompany him everywhere, there would be little to distinguish him from his superiors by birth. Lady Alworth's cook says he doesn't live like 'a usurer that starves himself' (2.2.106), and he is contemptuously dismissive of Marrall's illiberal recommendations of 'thrift' (3.2.12). He may call Margaret the 'blest child of my industry and wealth' (3.2.53), but he tells Lovell that the real value of his 'industry' is the spending power which it gives him. When Lovell has become his son-in-law, he will devote his financial skills to the cause of enabling him to live like a great lord:

> As for possessions and annual rents
> Equivalent to maintain you in the port
> Your noble birth and present state requires,
> I do remove that burden from your shoulders
> And take it on mine own; for though I ruin
> The country to supply your riotous waste,
> The scourge of prodigals – want – shall never find you.
> (4.1.104–10)

With so little anxiety about conspicuous consumption, Overreach is totally at odds with any civic mentality of sober, industrious thrift. Rather, he has internalised the values of the class to which he aspires and he projects an image which has more similarities to the people with whom he collides than differences from them.

It is this likeness which makes the struggle to eject him from county society so traumatic. Though he lacks that crucial shibboleth, the cachet of gentle birth, he is in other respects not an obviously interloping outsider. This is powerfully seen, for example, in his automatic readiness to reach for that badge of gentility, his sword, repeatedly challenging his enemies to prove their truth in the field (3.2.139–44; 5.1.143, 241, 299–304). Such punctiliousness for his honour confers a kind of heroism onto him: it labels him as a participant in the aristocratic arena virtually equivalent to those with whom he competes. Equally, he is no hypocrite, since he acknowledges to Wellborn's face that his behaviour has been cruel (3.3.50–4), and he needs consciously to scale down his proud mind when it is necessary to be servile to Lovell:

> Roughness awhile leave me,
> For fawning now, a stranger to my nature,
> Must make way for me.
>
> (3.2.159–61)

These are aspects of Overreach's character which make him seem an adversary to be reckoned with, someone who fully knows the people with whom he is in conflict. Indeed, his ambitions seem as transgressive as they do precisely because he believes no less than everyone else in the absolute mystique of rank. Concurring with the general belief that the distinction is fixed 'Between us and *true* gentry' (my italics), his conviction that his gentility can never be fully legitimate reinforces the immovability of the play's assumptions about hierarchy and birth.[4]

By choosing to situate Overreach's origins in the city, Massinger has made the conflicts of *A New Way* resemble the oppositions between status and thrift that are the staple of metropolitan comedy. But on inspection the challenge which Overreach embodies proves not to be to the aristocratic ideology of power at all, but to the way that that power is used. The play's ideological content revolves around an antithesis between two differing versions of the responsibilities of patriarchy. Overreach's intended victims in the play are Wellborn and Alworth, the young impoverished gentlemen whose toe-hold on status is under threat. But really the underlying contest is between Overreach and Lovell, the ideal father against whom Sir Giles stands as a monstrous counter-type, and this emerges structurally as a struggle for control of the play's action between these rival fathers.

Overreach's defeat comes about less through the wit of the intriguers than the providence of the intriguers' patrons: it is Lovell and Lady Alworth who exert the controlling interest in the action, and the young men have relationships with them which are depicted as specially intense, emotionally charged parent–child ties. Wellborn's and Alworth's plots depend on the seeming willingness of Lady Alworth and Lovell to desire the marriages which Sir Giles thinks he and his daughter are going to achieve. When Overreach loses, power goes not to the youths (who have still to prove themselves as soldiers) but to their elders, the new Lord and Lady Lovell. They finish the play as their society's moral arbiters, securely possessed of the financial clout that had once been Sir Giles's (after her marriage, Margaret Alworth immediately turns her estates over to Lovell for disposal (5.1.387–8)). This patriarchal affirmation is all the more emphatic given that it shatters the paternal ambitions that Overreach had nursed. By marrying Margaret to Lovell and himself to Lady Alworth,

---

[4] On this point, see Paster, 'Quomodo, Sir Giles and Triangular Desire', p. 173.

Overreach has sought to become father to an extended family, in which he will control the Alworth and Wellborn estates and have the next Lord Lovell as an infant dancing on his knee (4.1.101–2). His spectral patriarchy gives force to Lovell's victory at the end, since Lovell emerges as the ideal loving father whose victory thwarts a violent tyrant. Thus the play both consolidates power in the hands of the older generation and offers an ideological contest between the self-serving Overreach and the benevolent patron Lovell.

Whether acting as father or master, Overreach is an arbitrary tyrant. He is brutal towards Margaret and Marrall, both of whom are in physical fear of him and who eventually revolt against him. Margaret he prostitutes to Lovell, tutoring her in sexual ploys and rubbishing her 'mincing modesty' with a curt 'Virgin me no virgins' (3.2.109, 112). Marrall he calls a 'slave' (5.1.95) and is incomprehending when the worm finally turns: 'Mine own varlet / Rebel against me?' (5.1.213–14). But this is only part of a more general lust for power, in which the whole world will bow to his uncontrolled tyranny. His economic advantage translates into political relationships in which 'their issue, whom I have undone, / [Will] kneel to mine, as bond-slaves' (2.1.82–3). By contrast, in Lovell's hands power is made to seem not so much naked force as the exercise of paternal responsibility. Lovell criticises 'great men' who suppose

> They part from the respect due to their honours
> If they use not all such as follow 'em
> Without distinction of their births, like slaves.
> I am not so conditioned. I can make
> A fitting difference between my foot-boy
> And a gentleman by want compelled to serve me.
> ALWORTH: 'Tis thankfully acknowledged. You have been
> More like a father to me than a master.
>
> (3.1.21–30)

Overreach may be just such a master domineering over abjects, but Alworth's language legitimates Lovell as a parent careful for his children, and he is further validated by the ethical scrupulousness of his behaviour – most notably in his refusal to take sexual advantage of Margaret when her father offers her to him (something which, remarkably, he does less for her sake than because of his consciousness of obligation to his client Alworth).

Crucially, it is intimated that Lovell's private treatment of Alworth exemplifies his character in the wider public sphere. On the one hand, he is a responsible leader, a popular army man and a patriot. Not only does he command soldiers, but,

> what's rare, is one himself,
> A bold and understanding one; and to be
> A lord and a good leader in one volume

> Is granted unto few but such as rise up
> The kingdom's glory.
>
> (3.2.78–82)

Almost certainly, behind the altruistic soldier Lovell stand those contemporary noblemen, such as Southampton, Essex, Oxford, Buccleuch, Willoughby and Danby, who in the mid-1620s were enthusiastically volunteering for the new military initiatives overseas created by the collapse of James's policy of appeasement of Spain.[5] The participation of these men in the first anti-Catholic military enterprises sanctioned by the crown since the days of Elizabeth invested them with tremendous glamour, and the 'gallant-minded, popular Lord Lovell, / The minion of the people's love' (2.1.69–70) would almost inevitably have invoked their example. We are told that Lovell is heading for the Low Countries (1.2.75) and his Hispanophobia is reinforced in his reassurance to Lady Alworth that as a 'true-born Englishman' he feels it no disparagement to marry a widow, though if he were a Spaniard he might (5.1.53). The contemporary context of new military initiatives against Spain (which are also alluded to in Massinger's *The Bondman* (1623) and *The Unnatural Combat* (1624)) helps to substantiate the specifically military and patriotic values with which Lovell is associated: honour earned in the field, in the service of a 'fair cause', upholding 'the country's safety' (1.2.107).

The representation of Lovell as an ideal patron may also evoke Massinger's personal connection with the earls of Pembroke. Massinger's father was a business agent to the second earl, and in his earliest surviving poem (*c.* 1615–20) the playwright appealed to the third earl, William Herbert, for financial support.[6] The dedication of *The Bondman* to the future fourth earl, Philip Herbert, speaks of the 'duties and service' which he owes the family,[7] and *A New Way* was published with an address to Philip Herbert's son-in-law, the earl of Carnarvon. As is well known, William and Philip Herbert were powerful courtiers who stood in a complex relationship with the crown. Great office-holders and patrons with a considerable circle of clients, they were nonetheless strongly aligned with activist sentiment at court, and were looked to for leadership by those hostile to Spain and ideologically committed to international Protestantism. Moreover, their attitude towards the favourite, Buckingham, was openly antagonistic. When *A New Way* was being written (summer 1625), the third earl was in uncomfortable alliance with Buckingham, whose promotion of war with Spain had allowed a temporary rapprochement, but in 1626 (after the military disaster at Cadiz) his brother and clients would be prominent in the parliamentary attempt to impeach the duke.[8]

---

[5] The best recent treatment of this topic is by T. Cogswell, *The Blessed Revolution: English Politics and the Coming of War 1621–1624* (Cambridge, 1989).

[6] Massinger, *Plays and Poems*, IV, 386–91.

[7] *Ibid.*, I, 313.

[8] See Cogswell, *The Blessed Revolution*, pp. 154–6; C. Russell, *Parliaments and English Politics 1621–1629* (Oxford, 1979), pp. 287–90; and M. Brennan, *Literary Patronage in the English Renaissance: The Pembroke Family* (1988).

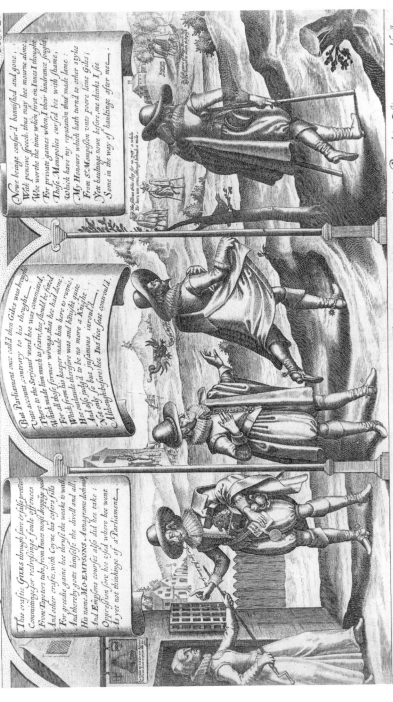

Plate 12 A satire of Sir Giles Mompesson

Of course Pembroke was not at all a soldier like Lovell, but Massinger's tie to the favourite's rival brings into focus the suggestions of barbs against Buckingham which coalesce around Overreach. Overreach, it has long been established, combines traits which link him to the hated monopolist, Sir Giles Mompesson, who had been impeached in the 1621 Parliament: particularly his name, his sharp practice at law, and his involvement in the licensing of alehouses. Mompesson was a client of Buckingham's and, as everyone knew, he was Parliament's stalking-horse for the more difficult attack on Buckingham's family, who also had fingers deep in offensive monopolies. Of course Overreach does not exactly equate with Mompesson, who was old Wiltshire gentry,[9] but the differences between them effectively strengthen the underlying allusions to Buckingham. As Margot Heinemann has argued,[10] the stress on Sir Giles's ambitions and opportunist marriages, as well as the upgrading of a comical citizen into a more threatening tyrant, associate him with anxieties which attached to a favourite who had come from nowhere and achieved almost unchallengeable power. This is not to imply that Overreach may be reduced to a topical allegory – indeed, Massinger obstructs any such application by labelling Overreach as a citizen. But the broad ideological opposition which the plot creates, between an upstart who uses his power opportunistically, and an old-style patriotically inclined nobleman whose honour has been 'By virtuous ways achieved and bravely purchased' (4.1.195), speaks to the concerns of men like Pembroke, worried in 1625 about Buckingham's hold over the new monarch and the supplantation of the older nobility by ambitious self-serving arrivistes.

IV

Given these relationships (some self-evident, some only partially disclosed) between the play and the historical circumstances within which it was written, it is easier to understand the equivocal nature of the comedy, its apparent contradictions as it seems to hesitate between celebration of the victory of Lovell and intimations that the conflicts which its action discloses cannot (or will not) readily be resolved. Ostensibly the ideology of the play is unproblematically affirmative: at the end Wellborn and the others leave for the continent and 'service / To my king and country' (5.1.397–8), which will confirm their credentials through their contribution to the royal cause. Yet as we have seen, in crucial respects the play unsettles this easy equation between king and country. For many who were unhappy

---

[9] R. C. Hoare, *The Modern History of South Wiltshire*, 1 (1822), part 2, pp. 218–19.
[10] M. Heinemann, 'Drama and Opinion in the 1620s: Middleton and Massinger', in *Theatre and Government under the Early Stuarts*, ed. J. R. Mulryne and M. Shewring (Cambridge, 1993), pp. 237–65.

with the record of Stuart kingship in the mid-1620s, hostility to Buckingham was a way by which criticism of the crown could be expressed without being taken for out-and-out subversion. On the other hand, the position of aristocratic dissenters (like Pembroke) was inherently ambivalent. For all its oppositional coding, Pembroke's antagonism towards Buckingham was not equivalent to a wish to upset the order of things any more materially: for men who criticised royal policy from within, the desire for political change coexisted uneasily with a residual social conservatism. In *A New Way*, these ambivalences translate as a series of powerful contradictions, the comedy seeming to strain after both subversion and control. It promotes respect for its aristocrats even as it raises doubts about them; it defeats one father but simultaneously reaffirms the containing values of fatherhood.

For example, however much Lovell suggests an attitude opposed to tyranny, he does not in any sense license an attack on the patriarchal system itself. On the contrary, his qualification as leader is his sophistication at discriminating between niceties of social positioning ('I can make / A fitting difference between my foot-boy / And a gentleman by want compelled to serve me' (3.1.26-8)). Though he thwarts Overreach's authoritarianism he is himself no less a patriarch, only his fatherhood is conducted in a manner acceptable to the people over whom it is exercised. The play thus avoids the imputation of being an incitement to democracy: its alternative to tyranny is not libertarianism, but willing submission to good rulers like Lovell. This is strikingly seen in the care which Massinger takes to advertise his disapproval of rebellion. Marrall, whose betrayal of his master is the basis of the play's resolution, is not rehabilitated at the end but cast out as a 'false servant' (5.1.350), disqualified forever from society. Margaret's resistance to her father is equally sensitive, and can only be condoned because she herself is otherwise entirely passive. Her tears at witnessing the madness of her father register the strains which the conclusion labours to efface. By joining the new community she has killed her parent, and in the final moments Lovell takes her affairs firmly into his own hands.

Lovell himself is discreetly idealised. Massinger does not ask any of the awkward questions about him that he poses against Overreach: we never get to know the source or extent of his income, for example, and it is emphasised that he has no social ambitions, since he refuses Overreach's offer (all too possible, given the marketing of honours to raise cash) to buy him an earldom (4.1.144). The only doubt is Alworth's considerable anxiety that when confronted with the beautiful Margaret his patron will be overwhelmed with desire and steal her from him (3.1.55–99). In the event Lovell passes the test, but there is a wobble in the play here that testifies to a more disenchanted perspective on the aristocracy than Massinger can accommodate openly. Lovell's precise behaviour towards Margaret exculpates him from blame, but this part of the action has been constructed so as to arouse anxiety about what lies behind the aristocratic parade of honour. Remarkably, the idea that great men expect to have their way was one of Overreach's presuppositions (3.2.106–7): it is as if, while idealising Lovell, space for pressing home Overreach's more sceptical view of aristocratic behaviour has been created.

If such ambiguities are obliquely raised about Lovell, with Wellborn they move to the centre, since the whole point of his role is that his honour rescues him from social suicide despite all the evidence of his personal unfitness. Wellborn is a gentleman whose indiscipline of life has caused him to forfeit his inherited status. He has wasted his patrimony in 'riots' (1.1.27), and now is at the bottom: events open with his ultimate humiliation, forcible ejection from an alehouse owned by a former servant. His recovery of his place is the play's principal action, and his career is the 'new way to pay old debts' of the title (see 4.2.28). As befits a gentleman, he is saved not by cash but by his credit. He reminds Lady Alworth of the debt of 'honour' she owes him because of his friendship with her husband (1.3.105) and, having managed to convince everyone that he is about to wed the lady, he finds as he hoped that Overreach starts to deluge him with money. He ends the play going off to earn his rehabilitation by fighting in the wars, but his revenge on the alehouse keeper Tapwell has strongly implied that even when down a gentleman has to be treated with respect.

The presentation of Wellborn so that he escapes the consequences of his actions is perhaps the play's crucial ideological manoeuvre. Certainly it is the one which is most problematic for us now, since it is difficult to know whether Wellborn is simply exculpated, or whether the play acknowledges the double standards which seem so glaring today. Of course Wellborn's rehabilitation is validated by his promises of reform, but one suspects that his wild behaviour is more easily forgiven because, whatever else, he is still a gentleman. Riot and excess are inherent in the way gentlemen live: Lady Alworth's first husband was brought low by 'Want, debts, and quarrels' (1.3.100) and young Alworth suffers from the same genteel poverty, even though his moral character is completely the reverse of Wellborn's. Moreover, the financial prodigality for which Wellborn is blamed cannot readily be distinguished from the liberality that is expected to characterise a gentleman. This is seen, for example, in his way of demonstrating his recovery of status which, inevitably, is to throw around largesse (4.2.83–110). Nonetheless, by causing us to register that the men who in this episode are loudest in the praise of Wellborn's liberality are those who were the severest censurers of his earlier excesses, Massinger foregrounds the more subversive perception that honour shines brightest when there is money around to back it up. Wellborn's admirers are not applauding some inner alienable quality of gentility, but Wellborn's recovered ability to spend with the carelessness that marks him out for a gentleman.

In this way, the question of Wellborn's own responsibility for his distresses is left nicely suspended: the outrageousness of his former life is made quite clear, but once he regains status it is permitted no longer to matter. His plot creates a stronger version of the contradiction that was only hinted at in respect of Lovell. Wellborn's qualification for gentility is the freedom with which he lives, but it was this which got him into financial difficulty in the first place. He may be blamed for his prodigality, but the play's residual admiration for the liberality of a gentleman creates a tension which cannot finally be resolved. At the end we are left with Wellborn's assurances that he will be a more sober person in future, but the play has also made it glaringly evident that in being a gentleman sobriety does not have to count for everything.

Instead, it is made to appear that Overreach is the really guilty party, and he effectively becomes the scapegoat for Wellborn's rehabilitation. In spite of what we can see of Wellborn's reckless living, the responsibility for all the world's ills is, vexingly, projected entirely onto Sir Giles. Overreach's power is provided by his daughter and his cash: as objects of aristocratic desire, they enable him to establish control in the aristocratic environment. From Overreach's point of view, it is only because the social elites are led by the drives for sex and credit that these opportunities open themselves for him. Notwithstanding, the men out of whose desires he makes his power continue to talk as though it is his ambition which has preceded and created their neediness. For example, Wellborn blames 'cormorant Overreach' (1.1.131) for the humiliations which have overtaken him, yet as Tapwell with some reason points out, whatever Overreach's sharp practice elsewhere, it is Wellborn's own riots which have put him into the citizen's debt (1.1.41–51). The same scenario will be re-enacted with emphasis in Overreach's attempted sale of Margaret to Lovell. His proposals rehearse the identical arrangement that Wellborn has had before the play begins, only this time the ideological mechanics that Wellborn suppresses are made overt.

In each case, Overreach is represented as expecting and encouraging the borrowers to waste their cash in fast living and all the usual aristocratic vices. In return for their indebtedness to him, Sir Giles assumes the guilt, being content to be blamed for avarice so that aristocrats may have their lavish spending without the imputation of dishonour. In private with Lovell he willingly shoulders the blame for whatever hard dealing is needed to support his life style:

> You run, my lord, no hazard.
> Your reputation shall stand as fair
> In all good men's opinions as now.
> Nor can my actions, though condemned for ill,

Cast any foul aspersion upon yours;
For though I do contemn report myself
As a mere sound, I still will be so tender
Of what concerns you in all points of honour
That the immaculate whiteness of your fame
Nor your unquestioned integrity
Shall e'er be sullied with one taint or spot
That may take from your innocence and candour.

(4.1.87–98)

It is thus made to appear that the moral responsibility for genteel indebtedness rests not with the debtor but with the lender, since aristocratic desire is only called into being by a preceding civic desire: the citizen's wish to lend eggs on the gentleman's wish to spend. Overreach is thereby made the scapegoat for the vices of his debtors, and though Lovell pretends to go along with these proposals, as a man of honour he professes to be deeply shocked (4.1.149–57). However, his disavowal is shadowed by what we already know about Wellborn's affairs, in which the gentleman's innocence is far less self-evident, and this uncovers the ideological work which Overreach's guilty lending is being made to perform. This polite society may eject Overreach as an external threat to its social and moral purity, but because of the way that the Lovell and Wellborn actions parallel one another it is difficult not to feel that in banishing Overreach they are exorcising a demon which they themselves have created from within.

On this analysis, Overreach can be seen as an ideological mechanism brought into being by an action which wants to critique some aspects of society's elites but which also needs to avoid calling their fundamental political hegemony into question. The play's unravelling is arranged so that even though genteel wastefulness and wilfulness are subjected to censure, ultimately the blame for their vices is projected onto the man who has profited from them. There is thus a potentially radical argument here (we see all too clearly the faults of gentlemen who get out of control), but one that resists the full consequences of its own radicalism. If this play is concerned to critique some sections of the Caroline social elites, it is equally keen to prevent that critique from being construed into an attack on their political authority as a whole.

V

It seems to me, then, that *A New Way to Pay Old Debts* stands in a fraught, two-edged relationship to its time. On the one hand, its action is designed to articulate and clarify anxieties which were widely current in the transition to the new monarch. It sets an ideal of good, patriotic, traditional paternalism against a monster of self-serving tyranny, an opposition which in ways both overt and covert was linked with the political antagonism between Pembroke and Buckingham. This in its turn is tied to a searching analysis of the relationships of power, money and status operating between the various levels of Massinger's community of social elites. On the other hand, in order to retain control of the critical thrust of this action, Massinger has to insist upon the fundamentally conservative ideology, the encompassing reverence for hierarchy and degree, by which his analysis is kept in check. Nonetheless his play's perspective is sufficiently demystified for it to disclose the element of misrecognition, the gap between what is said of the gentry and what disenchantedly they are seen to be, and these are troubling contradictions which have to be left to oscillate within the play and cannot be fully discharged at the end. They make it necessary for Overreach to implode in the last scene and for Lovell and company to be restored to their own, but since the play has already intimated the ideological mechanics in the service of which the opposition between Overreach and the rest functions, that ending feels evasive rather than fully conclusive. It does not address the way that Overreach's ambitions have been brought into being by the society which now disclaims him, nor does it acknowledge the staggering disproportion between the titanic monomania which erupts in him and the domestic tale of love and inheritance which that madness is used to resolve.

Does this mean, then, that the play fails to serve the needs of its society – that the value of its social analysis is undermined by its inability to escape involvement in the self-same contradictions which it describes? I am aware that my account of the play has a rather Greenblattian turn, and that Overreach has come out sounding like Greenblatt's account of Barabas in *The Jew of Malta*, a monster that his society creates and needs to go on creating.[11] But I do not take this to mean that the play is locked into a New Historicist cycle of subversion and containment, in which social insight is generated only for it to be relentlessly folded back into immovable economies of power. Rather, in describing the manifold and subtle relationships between this play and its world, I have been trying to imply that the tensions which it dramatises were linked historically to the potentially pre-revolutionary situation of Massinger's culture. It is not that Massinger's play wants radical change; plainly it does not, and besides, in 1625 the events of 1642 were almost literally unimaginable. Nonetheless, in the powerful way that it runs idealism up against scepticism, mystification against disenchantment, the play was working to make the tensions apparent, and by doing so it was helping to create an environment in which change might eventually become thinkable. Mass-

---

[11] S. Greenblatt, 'Marlowe, Marx, and Anti-semitism', in *Learning to Curse* (1990), pp. 40–58. I am grateful to Richard Strier for drawing this to my attention.

inger may not yet have a language to resolve his society's problems, but in giving equivalent space to the desire for stability and the pressure for change, he was helping to make these problems visible as problems. By dramatising not men's conscious mental world but the unconscious contradictions by which they lived, he was participating in that larger social process out of which a rationale for change would one day emerge.

7

The Root and Branch Petition and the Grand Remonstrance

From Petition to Remonstrance

David L. Smith

'England's Wars of Religion'; 'the last Baronial Revolt'; 'the Puritan Revolution'; 'the Great Rebellion': the myriad labels applied to the conflict which broke out in England in 1642 reflect the continuing debate over its causes and nature.[1] Most scholars would now accept that few people expected – let alone wanted – arms to be taken up. But historians are still sharply divided over the passions and motives which produced civil war. It remains difficult to establish who or what was forcing the pace of events in 1640–2, despite the abundant evidence surviving for those years. This essay will analyse and contextualise two key documents in which we can glimpse passions strong enough to destroy the 'ancient constitution', bring down the Established Church, and divide English society against itself: the Root and Branch Petition[2] and the Grand Remonstrance. These documents reflect the particular circumstances in which they were composed and they preserve, like a snapshot, one pattern of attitudes that were rapidly shifting and transient.

I

When the Long Parliament assembled on 3 November 1640 the atmosphere was one of tense expectation. Sir Henry Slingsby hoped that 'the subject'

---

[1] I am deeply grateful to David Bevington, John Morrill and Richard Strier for their very helpful comments and suggestions on earlier drafts of this essay.

[2] Throughout this essay I use the conventional title of Root and Branch Petition. However, as Richard Strier shows in his contribution to this chapter, the petition always employs the phrase 'roots and branches' in the plural, never in the singular. For the significance of this distinction, see below, pp. 226–7. I have not been able to determine the earliest instance of the label 'Root and Branch Petition'. However, the singular form of 'root and branch' can be found in contemporary sources. For example, Sir Henry Slingsby wrote in November 1640 that 'some do petition to reform [bishops], others to abolish them root and branch': *The Diary of Sir Henry Slingsby, of Scriven, Bart.*, ed. Daniel Parsons (1836), p. 66. Contemporaries also used the singular form as a shorthand for a desire to abolish episcopacy, as in Hyde's comment that Nathaniel Fiennes, Sir Henry Vane the younger, and John Hampden were 'believed to be for "root and branch"': Edward, Earl of Clarendon, *The History of the Rebellion and Civil Wars in England*, ed. W. D. Macray (6 vols., Oxford, 1888), I, 309 (Book III, § 147).

would at last secure 'a total redress of all his grievances'.[3] For many MPs, religious grievances stood at the very top of the agenda. Sir Benjamin Rudyerd urged: 'Let religion be our *Primum Quaerite*, for all things else are but *etcaeteras* to it';[4] while Sir Edward Dering insisted that 'sufferances' concerning 'the Church . . . must have the first fruits of this Parliament'.[5] The opening days of the session saw an outpouring of hostility against the recent policies of Archbishop Laud and his colleagues. Harbottle Grimston thought the Laudians intended 'to blow up the Protestant religion', while Sir John Holland lamented that 'by the usurped power and practice of some prelates . . . many great, many dangerous innovations, of doctrine, of discipline, of government have been thrust upon us'.[6] Laudian changes were almost universally denounced; but as yet not a single MP explicitly called for the abolition of episcopacy.[7]

Things were very different outside Parliament. For the godly all over England, the Long Parliament offered an unprecedented opportunity not only to destroy the Laudian ascendancy but also to reform Church government once and for all. Nowhere was this desire more intense than in the City of London.[8] Within days of the Long Parliament's opening,[9] the City ministers began to draft and circulate a petition which gained, according to contemporary estimates, between 10,000 and 20,000 signatures.[10] When one of the MPs for London, the godly merchant Alderman Isaac Penington, presented the Petition to the Commons on 11 December 1640,[11] he was accompanied by three or four hundred of the 'better' sort of citizens.[12] Some MPs were alarmed more by the Petition's provenance than by its contents. They felt that the petitioning movement smacked of 'popularity'. Lord Digby, refusing 'to flatter a multitude', later declared that he looked 'not upon this Petition as a Petition from the City of London, but from I know not what, 15,000 Londoners, all that could be got to subscribe'.[13]

---

[3] *Diary of Sir Henry Slingsby*, ed. Parsons, p. 64.

[4] *The Speeches of Sir Benjamin Rudyer in the high Court of Parliament* (1641), p. 2 (B[ritish] L[ibrary], T[homason] T[racts], E 196/2).

[5] *A Collection of Speeches made by Sir Edward Dering* (1642), p. 7 (BL, TT, E 197/1).

[6] *Mr Grimstons Speech, in the High Court of Parliament* (1642), p. 10 (BL, TT, E 198/5); *Sir Iohn Holland His Speech in Parliament* (1641), p. 2 (BL, TT, E 198/6).

[7] Cf. William M. Abbott, 'The Issue of Episcopacy in the Long Parliament, 1640–1648' (Oxford D.Phil., 1981), p. 114.

[8] *Ibid.*, p. 158.

[9] *The Letters and Journals of Robert Baillie*, ed. D. Laing (3 vols., Edinburgh, 1841–2), I, 273–4.

[10] Valerie Pearl, *London and the Outbreak of the Puritan Revolution* (Oxford, 1961), p. 214; Nicholas Tyacke, *The Fortunes of English Puritanism, 1603–1640* (1990), pp. 20–1.

[11] C[ommons] J[ournal], II, 49.

[12] *A Speech of the Honorable Nathaniel Fiennes . . . concerning Bishops and the City of London's petition* (1641), p. 2 (BL, TT, E 196/32). The French ambassador's estimate was between seven and eight hundred: P[ublic] R[ecord] O[ffice], PRO 31/3/72 (Baschet's French transcripts), fo. 642v. Sir Simonds D'Ewes put the figure at 1,500: *The Journal of Sir Simonds D'Ewes from the Beginning of the Long Parliament to the Opening of the Trial of the Earl of Strafford*, ed. Wallace Notestein (New Haven, 1923) (hereafter abbreviated as D'Ewes (N)), p. 138. According to the Scottish minister Robert Baillie, these were 'honest citizens, in their best apparel': *Letters of Baillie*, I, 280.

[13] *The Third Speech of the Lord George Digby* (1640), pp. 8–9 (BL, TT, E 196/30).

Plate 13 The Long Parliament in session, November 1640

Digby's point was that although the Petition had been signed by Londoners, it had not been officially approved by the City government.[14] Penington retorted that the Petition had 'been warranted by the hands of men of worth and known integrity', and that 'there was no course used to rake up hands'.[15] Edward Hyde later sneered that only 'a strange uningenuity [disingenuousness] and mountebankry' could have procured so many signatures.[16] Exactly how people came to sign the Petition will probably always remain murky; yet there can be little doubt that it accurately expressed the beliefs and hopes of the London godly – of congregations which included craftsmen, tradesmen and journeymen as well as ministers and aldermen.[17]

In recent years scholars have also detected a second, and secondary, influence on the Petition's formulation: that of Presbyterian Scots in London. This dimension has gradually come to light as historians have recognised that events in England need to be understood within a British context.[18] In mid-November, eleven Scottish commissioners accompanied by four chaplains arrived to negotiate a peace treaty with the king. It was their hope – though not one of their official demands – that episcopacy would be abolished in England.[19] The four ministers, of whom Robert Baillie was the most famous, quickly established close links with the London godly. Shortly after his arrival, Baillie saw a draft of the Root and Branch Petition and reported gleefully that 'all here are weary of bishops'.[20] Conrad Russell has argued that the final text shows signs of the Scots' influence;[21] and they certainly assisted in planning the Petition's presentation to the Commons.[22] However, it is important to remember that the Petition existed in draft before the Scots' arrival; and we shall see that it was typical of the many anti-episcopal petitions sent in from counties across England during 1641.

Unlike MPs' speeches in November 1640, the Petition's prime target was not Archbishop Laud and his colleagues but the actual structure of the English Church. The preamble declared that 'the government of archbishops and lord bishops, deans and archdeacons, etc.' had 'proved preju-

---

[14] Cf. Hamon L'Estrange, *The Reign of King Charles* (1656), p. 208.

[15] D'Ewes (N), p. 339.

[16] Clarendon, *History*, ed. Macray, I, 271 (Book III, §67).

[17] For a marvellous reconstruction of the mental world of one artisan who inhabited this milieu, see Paul S. Seaver, *Wallington's World: A Puritan Artisan in Seventeenth-Century London* (Stanford, 1985).

[18] The literature on this theme is burgeoning. For a cross-section, see the recent works cited in notes 19 and 22 below; and also John Morrill, *The Nature of the English Revolution* (Harlow, 1992), pp. 252–72.

[19] Conrad Russell, *The Fall of the British Monarchies, 1637–1642* (Oxford, 1991), pp. 168–70; David Stevenson, *The Scottish Revolution, 1637–1644* (Newton Abbot, 1973), pp. 214–15. This problem was first analysed in detail in Charles L. Hamilton, 'The Basis for Scottish Efforts to Create a Reformed Church in England, 1640–41', *Church History*, 30 (1961), 171–8.

[20] *Letters of Baillie*, I, 273–4.

[21] Russell, *Fall*, pp. 180–1.

[22] *Letters of Baillie*, I, 275, 280; Peter Donald, *An Uncounselled King: Charles I and the Scottish Troubles, 1637–1641* (Cambridge, 1990), p. 281.

dicial and very dangerous both to the Church and Commonwealth'.[23] Although the Laudians had highlighted the problem, especially by claiming 'their calling immediately from the Lord Jesus Christ', the government of the Church was itself intrinsically flawed. It was 'a main cause and occasion of many foul evils, pressures and grievances of a very high nature unto His Majesty's subjects in their own consciences, liberties and estates'. The Petition presented 'a schedule of particulars' supporting this claim, and demanded that 'the said government, with all its dependencies, roots and branches, may be abolished . . . and the government according to God's Word may be rightly placed amongst us'. In his contribution to this chapter, Richard Strier shows that the plural form of 'roots and branches' was highly significant, for it reflected a perception that the evil effects of episcopacy extended far beyond the confines of Church government.[24]

The 'particulars' of these 'manifold evils, pressures and grievances' comprised twenty-eight articles. The vast majority condemned the official religious policies of the 1630s.[25] They denounced 'the hindering of godly books to be printed'; 'the publishing and venting of Popish, Arminian and other dangerous books and tenets'; and 'the turning of the Communion-table altar-wise, setting images, crucifixes and conceits over them, and tapers and books upon them, and bowing or adoring to or before them'. The Petition lamented 'the growth of Popery and increase of Papists, Priests and Jesuits in sundry places, but especially about London since the Reformation'. The Laudians afforded the final proof that the Reformation of the sixteenth century had been hopelessly inadequate. It was only because England still retained 'the same way of Church government, which is in the Romish Church' that the Laudians had been able to seize the initiative. In England the Reformation had gone nothing like far enough, and further reform was necessary to end 'the great conformity and likeness both continued and increased of our Church to the Church of Rome'. Laud may have 'continued and increased' this resemblance; but its roots lay in the fact that the English Church had never been 'rightly reformed'.[26] The only answer, according to the Petition, was for England to emulate 'other reformed churches' and 'cast the prelates out also as members of the beast'.

The London Root and Branch Petition foreshadowed a wave of similar petitions from all over the country. The most moderate of these was the

---

[23] This and all subsequent quotations from the Petition are taken from the text printed in *The Constitutional Documents of the Puritan Revolution, 1625–1660*, ed. S. R. Gardiner (3rd edn, Oxford, 1906), pp. 137–44.

[24] Richard Strier, 'From Diagnosis to Operation', pp. 230–3 below.

[25] For these policies, see especially Julian Davies, *The Caroline Captivity of the Church* (Oxford, 1992); Nicholas Tyacke, *Anti-Calvinists: The Rise of English Arminianism, c. 1590–1640* (Oxford, 1987); Andrew Foster, 'Church Policies of the 1630s', in *Conflict in Early Stuart England*, ed. Richard Cust and Ann Hughes (Harlow, 1989), pp. 193–223; Peter Lake, 'The Laudian Style: Order, Uniformity and the Pursuit of the Beauty of Holiness in the 1630s', in *The Early Stuart Church, 1603–1642*, ed. Kenneth Fincham (1993), pp. 161–85.

[26] This phrase is taken from the First Admonition to the Parliament (1572), printed in *Puritan Manifestoes*, ed. W. H. Frere and C. E. Douglas (1907), pp. 8–55; quotation at p. 9.

so-called 'Ministers' Petition and Remonstrance', a digest of petitions signed by between seven and eight hundred provincial clergy, which was presented to Parliament in January 1641. This enumerated grievances against the Laudians and attacked 'corruption of matter of government in the Church', but it did not explicitly demand the abolition of episcopacy.[27] By contrast, no fewer than nineteen county petitions submitted to Parliament during 1641 called for 'the abolishing of the bishops with their hierarchical government'.[28] Whereas older accounts either devoted little space to these county petitions, or saw the London Petition as unrepresentative of the general mood, more recent research has shown that it was the tip of an iceberg.[29] Many of the county petitions closely resembled the London Petition in content and form, and Anthony Fletcher has argued that they constituted 'a national petitioning campaign' against episcopacy.[30] The petition which Sir Edward Dering presented on behalf of Kent was typical in asserting that episcopacy had been found 'by sad experience' to be 'the occasion of manifold grievances unto His Majesty's subjects, in their consciences, liberties and estates'. It concluded with a demand that 'this hierarchical power may be totally abrogated'.[31]

Such calls for root and branch reform proved deeply divisive within the House of Commons, and there were some particularly heated exchanges on 8–9 February 1641 when the House debated whether or not to refer the London Petition and the Ministers' Remonstrance to a committee. The opponents of this motion argued that the government of the Church was not intrinsically flawed, and that episcopacy should be reformed rather than abolished. They justified the office of bishop on the grounds of antiquity and 'conveniency', and portrayed it as an essential feature of 'the Church by law established'. They turned the metaphor of root and branch back on the petitioners. Viscount Falkland insisted that 'we should not root up this ancient tree as dead as it appears, till we have tried whether, by this or the like lopping of the branches, the sap which was unable to feed the whole may not serve to make what is left both grow and flourish'.[32] Lord Digby similarly urged the House not 'to root up a

---

[27] The text of this document apparently does not survive: W. A. Shaw, *A History of the English Church during the Civil Wars and under the Commonwealth, 1640–1660* (2 vols., 1900), I, 23–7; Abbott, 'Issue of Episcopacy', p. 118.

[28] D'Ewes (N), pp. 249, 283, 375; Anthony Fletcher, *The Outbreak of the English Civil War* (1981), pp. 92–6; Morrill, *Nature of the English Revolution*, pp. 77–8; Abbott, 'Issue of Episcopacy', pp. 117–18, 186–7. For petitioning to the Long Parliament in general, see James S. Hart, *Justice upon Petition* (1991), especially pp. 69–87.

[29] For the lack of attention to county petitions see, for example, S. R. Gardiner, *History of England from the Accession of James I to the Outbreak of the Civil War, 1603–1642* (10 vols., 1883–4), IX, 266. Gardiner's account of the London Petition is also astonishingly brief: *ibid.*, p. 247. The view that it was not representative of the general mood is argued in Shaw, *English Church*, I, 7–8. For more recent research, see especially Fletcher, *Outbreak*, pp. 92–6.

[30] Fletcher, *Outbreak*, p. 92.

[31] *Speeches by Dering*, pp. 20, 24. For the presentation of this petition, see D'Ewes (N), p. 249.

[32] *A Speech made to the House of Commons concerning Episcopacy, by the Lord Viscount Faulkeland* (1641), p. 15 (BL, TT, E 196/36).

good tree because there is a canker in the branches', and declared: 'Let us not destroy bishops, but make bishops such as they were in the primitive times.'[33] There was a clear anti-Laudian consensus, but the gulf was to prove unbridgeable between those who wished to reform and those who wished to abolish episcopacy.

The debates of 8–9 February 1641, however, were not confined exclusively to the question of bishops. They extended to the interrelationship between political, social and ecclesiastical hierarchies. Digby did 'not think a king can put down bishops totally with safety to monarchy'; while another future Royalist, Sir John Strangways, warned that 'if we made a parity in the Church we must at last come to a parity in the Commonwealth'.[34] The latter provoked a furious rejoinder from the hitherto obscure MP for Cambridge, Oliver Cromwell, who rejected such 'suppositions and inferences' so vigorously that he was called to the bar.[35] For Falkland, Digby, Strangways and many others, a wish to preserve episcopacy was inseparable from an attachment to the rule of law and long-established forms of government. It was precisely the inverse of this equation – that the abolition of bishops would inevitably undermine the social and political order – that Cromwell was desperately keen to deny.

These highly disputed links between the religious and secular orders bring us to an even more significant feature of this debate: its remarkable accuracy as a predictor of subsequent political allegiance. Here we see, on 8–9 February 1641, for the very first time, the convergence of a group of MPs who later formed the core of the Constitutional Royalists. Those who defended a reformed episcopacy – especially Falkland, Hyde, Strangways and Sir John Culpepper – nearly all became supporters of Charles I in 1642; while the advocates of root and branch reform – such as Cromwell, Nathaniel Fiennes, John Evelyn and Denzil Holles – all remained with Parliament during the Civil War. Whereas the constitutional issues of 1640–1 either united virtually everybody (Ship Money, the Triennial Act) or divided them along lines which bear no correlation to those of 1642 (Strafford's attainder), the debates on episcopacy forecast civil war allegiance eighteen months before a shot was fired.[36]

After prolonged debate, the Commons eventually resolved to refer the Petition to a committee, while reserving to 'itself the consideration of the main point of episcopacy when this House shall think fit'.[37] This was an important decision which, as John Morrill has observed, indicated 'that

---

[33] *Third Speech of Digby*, pp. 10, 18. For the concept of 'primitive episcopacy', see Morrill, *Nature of the English Revolution*, pp. 72, 78.

[34] *Third Speech of Digby*, p. 18; D'Ewes (N), pp. 339–40.

[35] D'Ewes (N), p. 340. Calling an MP to the bar was a disciplinary measure, 'a kind of parliamentary excommunication': Morrill, *Nature of the English Revolution*, p. 146.

[36] I justify the argument of this paragraph at greater length in my *Constitutional Royalism and the Search for Settlement, c. 1640–1649* (Cambridge, 1994).

[37] D'Ewes (N), p. 342.

the question [of episcopacy] was already accepted as an open one'.[38] It revealed a willingness to grasp nettles. But in February 1641 the nettles remained essentially religious: people were only gradually becoming aware of their political ramifications. That very same month, the smooth passage of the Triennial Act demonstrated Parliament's unity on purely constitutional issues. But by the end of the year, the Commons had polarised into two irreconcilable camps. This transformation of a dispute which was focused on Church government into a fully-fledged political confrontation will provide the context for our second document, the Grand Remonstrance of November 1641.

II

The intervening nine months between February and November 1641 decisively altered the political climate within England, and indeed Britain. They saw the completion of Parliament's attack on the institutions and 'evil counsellors' associated with Charles I's Personal Rule. Yet, despite Strafford's death and Laud's imprisonment, despite the destruction of Star Chamber and High Commission for ever, despite legal guarantees of Parliament's survival, mistrust of the king only deepened. During the spring and summer of 1641, Charles was widely suspected of complicity in the first Army Plot (a conspiracy to seize the Tower, release Strafford and dissolve Parliament), and then in the so-called 'Incident' (the attempted arrest of two of his leading Scottish opponents, Argyll and Hamilton). Charles's complicity could not be proved at the time;[39] but such episodes fuelled suspicion that he was willing to employ force and to flout the rule of law.

As 1641 progressed, however, more and more of the political elite came to feel that the greatest threat to order and stability came not from Charles I but from the radical opponents of episcopacy. All over England, the petitions against bishops coincided with spontaneous outbreaks of popular iconoclasm, with the smashing of altar-rails and other symbols of 'idolatry and superstition'. Such violence terrified the gentry. Many MPs, like Sir Edward Dering, concluded that root and branch reform was a Pandora's box which must be closed immediately before the entire social order came crashing down.[40] They therefore 'defected' to a king who had abandoned the Laudians and pledged himself to 'maintain constantly the doctrine

---

[38] Morrill, *Nature of the English Revolution*, p. 78.

[39] It has now been demonstrated beyond reasonable doubt: Conrad Russell, 'The First Army Plot of 1641', *Transactions of the Royal Historical Society*, 5th ser., 38 (1988), 85–106; Russell, *Fall*, pp. 291–4, 322–8. For the 'Incident', see Russell, *Fall*, pp. 322–8, 405, 408–9; and Donald, *An Uncounselled King*, pp. 297, 312–24, 316.

[40] Derek Hirst, 'The Defection of Sir Edward Dering, 1640–1641', *Historical Journal*, 15 (1972), 193–208.

and discipline of the Church of England'.[41] Charles became the natural rallying-point for all those who shared Edmund Waller's conviction that – despite Cromwell's vigorous denial – episcopacy formed 'a counter-scarp or outwork' protecting order and property.[42] As religious radicalism in the provinces polarised opinion, so Pym's hold on the Commons weakened.

Then, on 1 November, news reached London of a rebellion in Ireland. Fearing religious repression by the godly in England and Scotland, Irish Catholics had launched a preemptive strike against Ulster Protestants.[43] Perhaps 3,000 Protestants were massacred, a figure drastically inflated by rumour. To men like Pym, the Irish Rebellion seemed the final proof of a 'popish plot' seeking 'the subversion of religion, and destruction of [the king's] loyal subjects in both kingdoms'.[44] Determined to 'change those counsels from which such ill courses have proceeded',[45] to focus attention on Charles I's record of misgovernment, and to reunite a fragmenting House of Commons behind them, Pym and his allies introduced the 'Remonstrance of the state of the kingdom', known to history as the Grand Remonstrance.[46]

III

The Grand Remonstrance has been reinterpreted and reappropriated by successive generations of historians. It occupied a particularly hallowed place in Whig accounts of the English constitution. John Forster wrote that it contained 'the most authentic statement ever put forth of the wrongs endured by all classes of the English people during the first fifteen years of the reign of Charles the First; and, for that reason, the most complete justification upon record of the Great Rebellion'.[47] Godfrey Davies regarded

---

[41] *The Diary and Correspondence of John Evelyn*, ed. W. Bray (new edn, ed. H. B. Wheatley, 4 vols., 1906), IV, 111. Cf. *Constitutional Documents*, ed. Gardiner, p. 202.

[42] *A Speech made by Master Waller Esquire, in the Honorable House of Commons* (1641), pp. 4–5 (BL, TT, E 198/30).

[43] For the background to the Irish Rebellion, see Conrad Russell, 'The British Background to the Irish Rebellion of 1641', *Historical Research*, 61 (1988), 166–82; and Russell, *Fall*, pp. 373–99.

[44] *L[ords] J[ournal]*, IV, 431. For the very similar response of the Puritan minister Richard Baxter, see William M. Lamont, *Richard Baxter and the Millennium* (1979), especially pp. 76–88.

[45] *LJ*, IV, 431.

[46] According to John Forster, following its publication in December 1641 the Remonstrance 'thereafter . . . came to be called' the Grand Remonstrance 'to distinguish it from the many other similar State Papers of less importance, and less interest for the people, which were issued during the war': John Forster, *The Debates on the Grand Remonstrance, November and December, 1641* (1860). However, I have as yet been unable to trace a contemporary instance of the term 'Grand Remonstrance'. The earliest example that I have so far found is Laurence Echard's reference to the Commons' 'grand *Remonstrance*' (*sic*): Laurence Echard, *The History of England, from the Beginning of the Reign of King Charles the First, to the Restoration of King Charles the Second* (3 vols., 1707–18), II, 270. The fact that Echard used 'grand' with lower case and only italicised '*Remonstrance*' may suggest that the label 'Grand Remonstrance' was not widely used before he wrote. The phrase was clearly well established by 1831, when Lord Macaulay referred to 'that celebrated address to the King which is known by the name of the Grand Remonstrance': *The Works of Lord Macaulay Complete*, ed. Lady Trevelyan (8 vols., 1866), V, 572.

[47] Forster, *Debates on the Grand Remonstrance*, p. 114.

it as 'one of the most important documents in English constitutional history'; while Willson H. Coates argued that its demands advanced 'the theory of the sovereignty of Parliament'.[48] More recent scholars have located the Grand Remonstrance within a very specific political context, and have shown it to be the product of a complex gestation lasting over a year.[49]

The Grand Remonstrance originated in November 1640 with a proposal for 'an humble Remonstrance to His Majesty' for redress of grievances.[50] During the months which followed it passed through several committees and even more drafts. At one stage two remonstrances – one for religious grievances the other for secular – were envisaged.[51] By the autumn of 1641, the Remonstrance had been transformed from a private petition to Charles into a public appeal to the whole nation. It had become, as Dering later perceived,[52] an unprecedented bid to 'remonstrate downwards' to the people as well as upwards to the king. Finally, the Irish Rebellion precipitated Pym's decision to bring the Remonstrance before the Commons on 8 November 1641.[53] Over the ensuing fortnight it was further modified: an article attacking the Prayer Book was deleted;[54] and a denunciation of the Courts of Chancery, Exchequer and Wards as 'arbitrary' was changed to read 'grievous in exceeding their jurisdiction'.[55] The word 'arbitrary' still occurred three times in the final version of the Grand Remonstrance, applied to the billeting of soldiers (Article 6); the Court of the Earl Marshal (Article 42); and non-parliamentary taxation (Article 120).[56] The term 'arbitrary' was not absent from the Remonstrance,[57] but it was used exclusively in relation to matters which the Long Parliament had already redressed. The fact that the word was not applied to current grievances may well indicate that the authors of the Remonstrance were unwilling to level charges which could justify armed resistance against the king.[58] Their goal was to prevent further misuse of royal powers by persuading

---

[48] Godfrey Davies, *The Early Stuarts, 1603–1660* (Oxford, 1937), p. 118; Willson H. Coates, 'Some Observations on "The Grand Remonstrance"', *Journal of Modern History*, 4 (1932), 3.

[49] An early investigation of the drafting of the Grand Remonstrance may be found in H. L. Schoolcraft, 'The Genesis of the Grand Remonstrance', *University of Illinois Studies*, 1 (1902). I owe this reference to John Morrill. For a fuller and more recent account, see James S. Hart, 'The Political and Constitutional Origins of the Grand Remonstrance' (Portland State University M.A., 1979). I am most grateful to Professor Hart for sending me a copy of his dissertation.

[50] D'Ewes (N), p. 22; *CJ*, ii, 25, 42. The following paragraph is greatly indebted to Hart, 'Origins of the Grand Remonstrance'.

[51] *CJ*, ii, 234; Schoolcraft, 'Genesis of the Grand Remonstrance', p. 27.

[52] See below, p. 221.

[53] *The Journal of Sir Simonds D'Ewes from the first recess of the Long Parliament to the withdrawal of King Charles from London*, ed. Willson H. Coates (New Haven, 1942) (hereafter abbreviated as D'Ewes (C)), pp. 106–7; *CJ*, ii, 308.

[54] D'Ewes (C), pp. 150–1; *CJ*, ii, 317.

[55] D'Ewes (C), pp. 185–6, n. 18; *CJ*, ii, 322.

[56] *Constitutional Documents*, ed. Gardiner, pp. 209, 213, 222.

[57] Cf. Morrill, *Nature of the English Revolution*, p. 294.

[58] As John Morrill has suggested in *ibid.*, pp. 294–7.

Charles I to accept new constitutional safeguards. As long as they still believed that he might do so, they preferred to use peaceful means and consciously eschewed terminology which could imply a right to take up arms *in extremis*.[59]

The preamble to the Remonstrance blamed all England's 'evils' on 'a malignant and pernicious design of subverting the fundamental laws and principles of government, upon which the religion and justice of this kingdom are firmly established'.[60] The 'actors and promoters' of this 'design' were identified as 'Jesuited Papists', 'bishops', and 'councillors and courtiers' who 'for private ends' furthered 'the interests of some foreign princes'. Of these, 'the Jesuited counsels' were the 'most active and prevailing'. Then followed ninety-eight articles detailing the manifestations of their plot since 1625. These ranged from a pro-Catholic bias in foreign policy and the promotion of 'a conjunction between Papists and Protestants in doctrine, discipline and ceremonies', to the raising of taxes without Parliament's consent and an attempt 'to advance prerogative above law'. It is striking that none of these instances of misgovernment pre-dated the reign of Charles I. Indeed, his accession had marked a crucial turning-point, for 'in the beginning of His Majesty's reign the [Popish] party began to revive and flourish again'. The first part of the Remonstrance thus presented a comprehensive indictment of one monarch's misrule.

The next sixty-five articles described the remedies already attempted by the Long Parliament. 'The multiplied evils and corruption of fifteen years, strengthened by custom and authority', had been 'brought to judgement and reformation'. 'The arbitrary power pretended to be in His Majesty of taxing the subject, or charging their estates without consent in Parliament' was declared illegal; the 'evil counsellors' of the Personal Rule were brought to account; 'the discontinuance of Parliament' was prevented; prerogative courts such as Star Chamber and High Commission were abolished; 'the exorbitant power of bishops' was 'much abated', and steps were taken 'for maintaining godly and diligent preachers through the kingdom'. The aim throughout was to liberate the king from 'venomous councils': the drafters of the Remonstrance insisted that they desired nothing 'that should weaken the Crown either in just profit or useful power'. This qualification was critical. The Remonstrance guaranteed solely those royal powers exercised *pro bono publico* (for the public good), not those exercised *pro bono suo* (for his own benefit).[61] Behind this distinction

---

[59] As Richard Strier argues, 'From Diagnosis to Operation', pp. 237–8 below, the authors of the Remonstrance were prepared to justify *passive* disobedience. They defended those who had spoken out against earlier grievances and denied that obedience to the king was unconditional. But they were as yet unwilling to contemplate the possibility of *active* resistance. I am grateful to John Morrill and Richard Strier for advice on this point.

[60] Throughout this discussion I shall cite the final version of the Grand Remonstrance as printed in *Constitutional Documents*, ed. Gardiner, pp. 202–32.

[61] For this distinction, see Morrill, *Nature of the English Revolution*, pp. 50, 292, n. 21.

lay a conviction that Charles would only govern *pro bono publico* if Parliament ensured that he was rightfully advised.

If the first 163 articles of the Remonstrance constituted what Rudyerd termed 'the narrative historical part', the last forty-one formed 'the prophetical part'.[62] As Richard Strier argues in his companion essay, further radical changes were required 'for the perfecting of the work begun'.[63] Although the grievances attacked in the Remonstrance had arisen exclusively under Charles I, they could not be definitively redressed simply by turning the clock back to 1625. Just as the London Petition had argued that the only way to prevent a recurrence of Laudianism was to abolish episcopacy 'with all its dependencies, roots and branches', so the Remonstrance rested on a belief that the only security against further misuse of royal powers lay in fundamental constitutional reforms. This pursuit of innovation helps to explain the 'visionary' quality that Strier discerns in this last part of the Remonstrance.[64] Far-reaching measures were needed to root out 'evil counsellors' once and for all. These culminated in a request that the king 'employ such counsellors, ambassadors and other ministers in managing his business at home and abroad as the Parliament may have cause to confide in'. This was a direct assault on the king's discretionary right to choose his own advisers. Equally radical were the demands that the 'exorbitant power' of 'prelates' be reduced, that 'the monuments of idolatry' be taken away, and that a 'general synod of the most grave, pious, learned and judicious divines' be established 'to effect [religious] reformation'. Perhaps anticipating the anxieties which these words would arouse among defenders of episcopacy, the framers of the Remonstrance explicitly denied any 'desire to let loose the golden reins of discipline and government in the Church', and stated that their sole aim was 'to represent how [the king's] royal authority and trust' had 'been abused'.

Such phrases did not allay the fears of many members of the Commons, and when the final text of the Remonstrance was tabled on 22 November it caused an acrimonious debate lasting twelve hours. It crystallised attitudes towards the constitution as powerfully as the Root and Branch Petition had attitudes towards the Church. Much of the debate hinged on two issues: whether the Commons could remonstrate without consulting the Lords; and whether they should direct their advice to the people rather than the king.[65] Sir John Culpepper summed up the case against the Remonstrance thus: 'the declaration going but from this House goes but on a leg. We never desired the Lords to join. All remonstrances should

---

[62] *Memoirs of Sir Benjamin Rudyerd, Knt.*, ed. J. A. Manning (1841), p. 222.
[63] Strier, 'From Diagnosis to Operation', p. 243 below.
[64] *Ibid.*.
[65] For accounts of this debate, see Russell, *Fall*, pp. 427–9; Fletcher, *Outbreak*, pp. 149–51; Gardiner, *History*, x, 75–9.

be addressed to the king, and not to the people, because he only can redress our grievances.'[66] Culpepper was memorably supported by Dering, who 'did not dream that we should remonstrate downwards, tell stories to the people, and talk of the king as of a third person'.[67] On the other side, Pym insisted that 'the honour of the king lies in the safety of the people, and we must tell the truth. . . . The matter of the declaration is not fit for the Lords, for the matters were only agitated in this House, and again many of them are accused by it.'[68] In similar vein, Denzil Holles urged that 'all necessary truths must be told. If kings are misled by their counsellors, we may, we must, tell him of it.'[69]

Eventually the Remonstrance was passed, but only by a majority of 159 votes to 148.[70] After more wrangles, the House voted by 124 to 101 against printing the Remonstrance.[71] However, on 15 December, after further protracted debate, the Commons reversed this last decision and voted by 135 votes to 83 to authorise the printing of the Remonstrance.[72] When, on 23 December, Charles published an uncompromising answer to the Remonstrance, he professed himself 'very sensible of the disrespect' which this printing implied. He went on to defend the 'purity of doctrine' of the Church, and asserted that his choice of advisers was 'the undoubted right of the Crown of England'.[73] Charles's answer sharpened political alignments still further, for members of Parliament were now faced with a stark choice between supporting Pym's junto or rallying to the king. As Brian Wormald has argued, the Grand Remonstrance 'was of such a nature that it must create, and having created, sustain, a stronger and bitterer partisanship in the House than had existed before'.[74]

Nor was this polarisation confined to the political elite. Horror stories of Catholic atrocities against Ulster Protestants made the London godly increasingly militant.[75] In late November and throughout December the tensions within Parliament were greatly heightened by large and vociferous crowds of anti-episcopal demonstrators milling outside. A second Root and Branch Petition was drawn up and presented exactly twelve months after the first.[76] Bishops were prevented from entering the Lords, and on 27

---

[66] *Notes of proceedings in the Long Parliament . . . by Sir Ralph Verney*, ed. H. Verney (Camden Society, 1st ser., 31, 1845), p. 12.

[67] *Speeches by Dering*, p. 109.

[68] *Verney's Notes*, pp. 122–3.

[69] *Ibid.*, p. 124.

[70] D'Ewes (C), p. 186; *CJ*, II, 322.

[71] *CJ*, II, 322; Russell, *Fall*, p. 429.

[72] D'Ewes (C), p. 295; *CJ*, II, 344. The official printing of the Remonstrance is discussed in *Printing for Parliament, 1641–1700*, ed. Sheila Lambert (List and Index Society, special ser., 20, 1984), p. 4. For the title page of the first edition (Wing, E 2704; BL, TT, E 181/2), see below, plate 16.

[73] *Constitutional Documents*, ed. Gardiner, pp. 233–6. Charles's answer was drafted by Hyde: *The Life of Edward Earl of Clarendon . . . written by himself* (Oxford, 1759), pp. 44–5.

[74] Cf. B. H. G. Wormald, *Clarendon: Politics, History and Religion, 1640–1660* (Cambridge, 1951; rpt. 1989), p. 27.

[75] Pearl, *London*, pp. 221–3.

[76] D'Ewes (C), pp. 270–1.

Colonell Lunfford affaulting the Londoners at Westminfter Hall, with a great rout of ruffinly Cavaleiros

Plate *14*   The dispersal of London demonstrators by Colonel Lunsford, 27 December 1641

December several demonstrators were injured in a clash with the London Trained Bands.[77] Many believed that Pym orchestrated these demonstrations, and although this cannot be proved he certainly did nothing to stop them.[78] Furthermore, on 21 December the City of London elected a new Common Council (governing body) far more sympathetic to Pym and his junto.[79] This election indicated that Charles was gradually losing control of the capital.

Characteristically, Charles blamed everything on a small group within Parliament who 'traitorously endeavoured to subvert the fundamental laws and government of the kingdom of England' and 'to deprive the king of his regal power'.[80] Charles's fears exactly mirrored those of his leading critics expressed in the Grand Remonstrance. By the beginning of 1642, two coherent and self-sustaining conspiracy theories stood face to face, deploying remarkably similar language and levelling almost identical charges. Each accused a small minority of 'malignants' – be they 'Papists' or 'sectaries' – of trying to subvert the 'fundamental laws of England' in both church and state. Charles's version of the theory led him, on 4 January 1642, to seek the arrest of five ringleaders in the Commons and

---

[77] Russell, *Fall*, pp. 441–2.
[78] *Ibid.*, p. 433.
[79] Pearl, *London*, pp. 132–9.
[80] *Constitutional Documents*, ed. Gardiner, p. 236. For an early example of Charles's tendency to blame troubles on a small group of disaffected 'malignants', see Richard Cust, 'Charles I and a draft Declaration for the 1628 Parliament', *Historical Research*, 63 (1990), 143–61.

one in the Lords, a clearly unconstitutional use of force which turned opinion in London decisively against him.[81] Fearing for their safety, Charles and his family left the capital on 10 January. This withdrawal marked a watershed. For with the physical separation of monarch and Parliament, civil war became an immediate possibility.

---

[81] BL, Add. MS 70082 (Portland papers), unfol. (original warrant to the justices of Middlesex for the arrest of the Five Members, 4 January (1642)). For discussions of the 'attempt on the Five Members' and reactions to it, see Russell, *Fall*, pp. 447–53; and Fletcher, *Outbreak*, pp. 181–5.

From Diagnosis to Operation

Richard Strier

The essay that follows is an experiment in reading. It treats the 'Root and Branch Petition' and the 'Grand Remonstrance' as texts, with their own internal structures. I do not mean to say that I will treat these pieces as texts rather than as documents because I mean to suggest that the usefulness of these pieces as documents is increased by treating them as texts. The distinction between 'texts' and 'documents' seems to me pernicious not merely because documents are texts but also because (as I hope to show) historical documents become richer as sources of historical insight when they are treated as texts – that is, when they are read in a strong sense, subjected to 'close reading', to what Hexter calls 'macroanalysis', rather than merely being mined for hints, clues and facts or even for 'ideas'.[1] I will attempt a purely 'internal' reading of these documents. This does not mean that I will see them as not referring to the world. In fact, I will attempt to recreate, on the basis of the texts themselves, how these documents see the world. What I will not do is evaluate the truth of their pictures. I will come to these pieces with as fresh an eye (or, as Empson would say, as clean a palate) as I can – not in a state of ignorance but in a state of methodological and temporary *epochē*, 'suspension' of knowledge.[2] To do this is to run the risk of anachronism and of over- or under-weighting. On the other hand, there is the possibility of surprise, of actually finding something other than what one expected. Although I do hope to avoid both anachronism and ignorance, these are, after all, relatively easily detected, whereas finding in texts or documents what every professional already 'knows' runs the risk of making error

---

[1] On 'macroanalysis' see J. H. Hexter, 'The Rhetoric of History', in *Doing History* (Bloomington, 1971), pp. 48–50; on the effect of a 'documentary' model of knowledge on how historians tend to use their sources, see Dominick LaCapra, 'Rhetoric and History', in *History and Criticism* (Ithaca, N.Y., 1985), pp. 18, 38; for the application to intellectual history, see LaCapra, 'Rethinking Intellectual History and Reading Texts', in *Rethinking Intellectual History: Texts, Contexts, Language* (Ithaca, N.Y., 1983), pp. 32–5.

[2] For a defence of the possibility and desirability of reading with as few preconceptions as possible, see the introduction to Richard Strier, *Resistant Structures: Particularity, Radicalism, and Renaissance Texts* (Berkeley, 1995). For Empson's phrase, see 'George Herbert and Miss Tuve', *Kenyon Review*, 12 (1950), 738 (the Empson–Tuve controversy is treated in the first chapter of *Resistant Structures*). On *epochē* and ancient scepticism see David Sedley, 'The Motivation of Greek Skepticism', and Pierre Couissin, 'The Stoicism of the New Academy', in *The Skeptical Tradition*, ed. Miles Burnyeat (Berkeley, 1983), pp. 9–29, 31–63.

invisible.[3] I take heart from the assertion of H. Stuart Hughes that growth in historical knowledge can come not only through discovery of new materials but also through 'a *new reading*' of materials already available.[4]

Woeful Experience: The 'Roots and Branches' Petition

The 'humble' but also 'large' petition submitted to the Commons in December 1640 by 'many of His Majesty's subjects in and about the City of London' and elsewhere begins as if it were going to be narrowly focused.[5] Its topic will be prelatical Church-government: 'the government of archbishops, and lord bishops, and deans, and archdeacons, &c'. It then goes on to claim, however, that this 'government' has 'proved . . . very dangerous' not only to the Church but also to the Commonwealth.[6] The major rhetorical task of the document is to show how an apparently restricted matter can have had such pernicious and widespread consequences. We can get some insight into the vision and strategy of the text in noting that in speaking of 'government' – by which it seems to mean exclusively Church-government – it specifies not only Church offices but also 'their courts and ministrations in them'. A system is here hinted at, especially a judicial system. We can get further insight into the document by thinking about the kind of claim on which it is basing itself. The said 'government' and courts '*have proved* prejudicial and very dangerous'. The claim, in other words, is an empirical and consequentialist one. The argument will be conducted on empirical and historical grounds.

The second half of the opening sentence seems to contradict this. The problem with the archbishops, etc. seems to be ideological: 'they themselves having formerly held that they have their jurisdiction . . . of human authority' have recently 'claimed their calling immediately from the Lord Jesus Christ'.[7] Yet the theological claim is rejected not because it is against

---

[3] Compare Bacon's fear (and description) of the possibility of 'a kind of contract of error' in the transmission of knowledge. See Francis Bacon, *The Advancement of Learning*, ed. G. W. Kitchin (1973), p. 141 (II. xvii. 3). See also Bacon's recommendation of 'due and mature suspension' of assumptions (*Advancement*, p. 34 (I. v. 8)).

[4] H. Stuart Hughes, 'Contemporary Historiography: Progress, Paradigms, and the Regression Toward Positivism', in *Progress and Its Discontents*, ed. Gabriel A. Almond, Marvin Chodorow and Roy Harvey Pearce (Berkeley, 1982), p. 145 (emphasis in the original).

[5] The title page of the printed edition (see plate 15) describes itself as 'The First and Large Petition of the City of London and other Inhabitants thereabouts', whereas the prefatory description in the document is more modest in its self-description ('the humble Petition') and less assertive in its claim to be representing 'the City'. For the controversy over the latter claim, see David L. Smith, 'From Petition to Remonstrance', p. 212 above.

[6] I quote from the text that appears in *The Constitutional Documents of the Puritan Revolution*, ed. S. R. Gardiner (3rd edn, Oxford, 1906), pp. 137–44.

[7] I have elided the clumsy repetition of 'authority' in this clause ('jurisdiction *or authority* of human authority'), a clumsiness that reflects, I think, the difficulty of keeping 'authority' in this context on the purely 'human' level.

Scripture but because it is 'against the laws of this kingdom, and derogatory to His Majesty and his state royal'. This seems fairly abstract and technical, but the next sentence returns to empiricism ('woeful experience'), to extensiveness of effect ('a main cause and occasion of many foul evils'),[8] and to the Commonwealth rather than the 'state royal': 'grievances of a very high nature unto His Majesty's subjects'. The loci of these grievances are then specified – 'in their [the subjects'] own consciences, liberties and estates'. The petition puts first things first – 'consciences' – but makes it clear that the pernicious effects of 'the said government' are not only ('merely' would be a mistake) spiritual. 'Liberties', with its dual internal and external, subjective and objective status, mediates nicely between 'consciences' and 'estates'.

The proem – the petition proper, that is – ends with the famous plea that 'the said government, with all its dependencies, roots, and branches, may be abolished'. The 'roots and branches' idea is normally taken to refer to the radicalism of the abolition called for, of the political surgery being envisioned. This is what might be called the vertical reading of the phrase, the reading which stresses the difference between roots and branches. I would certainly not want to deny the general force and correctness of this reading, but I would suggest that we enter more fully into the mental world of this text if we read its defining phrase and image horizontally, so to speak, rather than vertically. As we have already begun to see, and as I will attempt to demonstrate at length, the central notion for the document is not depth but extensiveness – 'the said government, with all its dependencies, roots, and branches'. I would call attention to the word 'all' here (the 'dependencies' are very numerous) and especially to the plural status of 'roots'. Even this seemingly vertical term is treated 'horizontally' – in terms, that is, of multiplicity rather than origination.[9] What is surprising is that the alternative 'government according to God's Word' occupies a subordinate grammatical and rhetorical position in the petition. The content of 'government according to God's Word' is never specified – either because the authors presumed it to be well known or because they did not want to specify it – and the final vision of the proem is not of God's Word ruling in England but of the 'long and happy reign' that His Majesty will enjoy if the Petition is heeded.[10] However

---

[8] It is worth noting how careful the phrasing is here. The distinction between 'cause and occasion' seems fully meditated and intended.

[9] It is because of this – that is, for reasons of conceptual as well as textual accuracy – that I will refer to the document as the 'Roots and Branches' Petition rather than employing the more familiar singulars. The singular form never appears in the document. David L. Smith has shown (see pp. 214–15 above) that it was those who opposed the abolition of episcopacy, those who wanted the reform rather than the abolition of it, who used the image in the 'vertical' sense, emphasising the difference between the root (sound) and the branches (corrupt). As we have seen, the 'horizontal' treatment of the image tends to make the 'roots and branches' virtually identical.

[10] In the long sentence that comprises the second paragraph of the proem, there is a complex use of 'and' as a connective. It moves from a narrative function within a subjunctive structure ('that the said government

much we might think of the Roots and Branches Petition as a 'Puritan' document, the proem makes it clear that the primary strategy of the text is not going to be an appeal to God's Word but rather to 'the laws of the kingdom' and, most especially, to empiricism and to history – 'woeful experience'.

As its title page states, the 'First and Large Petition of the City of London' is also a 'Remonstrance', meaning an exposition or demonstration. The Remonstrance consists of a numbered list of paragraphs ranging (in Gardiner's edition) from three to nineteen lines, detailing 'the manifold evils, pressures, and grievances caused, practised and occasioned by the prelates and their dependents'. These triplets – 'evils, pressures, and grievances'; 'caused, practised and occasioned' – are not merely flourishes or legalistic pleonasms. The document wants to suggest the variety of ill effects and the variety of causal chains attributable to 'the prelates and their dependents'. The first of the articles, although quite brief, exemplifies a way of thinking that takes us far into the world of Roots and Branches. The two main clauses of the article are so sharply contrasting as to create what feels almost like a paradox: 'The subjecting and enthralling all ministers under them and their authority, and so by degrees exempting them from temporal power.' The prelates both enthrall and exempt the ministers. The basic premise seems to be a kind of moral mechanics: every evil produces an equal and opposite evil. In good Aristotelean fashion, the opposite of an evil is another evil. They are correlated. Wicked discipline produces equally wicked indulgence; an evil negative produces an evil positive, and vice versa. This principle is part of what gives Roots and Branches its ability to portray an evil system, a system that is perverse in all of its valences. In Article 2, doctrine is perverted through not being promulgated in its positive dimension (predestination, free grace, etc.), and in its negative dimension ('against universal grace', etc.). Godly and able men are driven from the ministry (Article 4) and consequently there is a 'great increase' of 'idle, lewd and dissolute' men in the ministry (Article 6). Evil diminishment always produces an equivalent evil increase. The downgrading of learning (Article 7) produces a 'swarming' (Article 8) of 'lascivious, idle, and unprofitable books' ('swarms' have been associated with 'the locusts of Egypt' in Article 6 – as in 'roots and branches', this is a world where proliferation and multiplicity are evil).[11] The hindering of godly books (Article 9) produces the 'venting' of Popish, Arminian, and

---

... be abolished, *and* all laws in their behalf, *and* the government according to God's Word may be rightly placed among us') to a final long clause that is ambiguous as between its present and subjunctive status ('*and* we your humble suppliants, as in duty we are bound, will daily pray . . .'), so that within the apparent assertion of good will there is a suggestion that only if the petition's demand is met will the suppliants do their benevolent praying.

[11] Whether the mention of the locusts of Egypt implies (consciously or unconsciously) that Charles is to be thought of – or is being thought of – as pharaoh is an interesting question.

THE
FIRST AND LARGE
PETITION

Of the Citie of LONDON and

other Inhabitants thereabouts:

For a Reformation in Church-government,

as also for the abolishment of Episcopacie:

WITH
A REMONSTRANCE

thereto annexed, of the many Pressures and
Grievances occasioned by the Bishops, and
the sundry inconveniences incident
to EPISCOPACIE.

The Tyrannie and Extortion practised in Ecclesiasticall Courts, together with the vnlawfulnesse of the Oath Ex Officio *: preferred to the high and honourable Court of* PARLIAMENT.

Printed *Anno Dom*. 1641.

Plate 15   The title page of the London petition, 1641

other dangerous books (Article 10). The prelates both improperly prohibit and improperly allow marriages (Article 20). Regarding holidays, they are both improperly strict (regarding saints' days – Article 21) and improperly indulgent (regarding Sundays – Article 22). They use excommunication too rigorously (Article 19) and too laxly (Article 24). The pattern is clear. All actions are conceived as having both positive and negative dimensions, and wicked actions are wicked along both axes.

The ecclesiastical content of Roots and Branches (primarily concentrated in Articles 13–18) is almost entirely negative. Likeness to 'the Romish Church' is the focus. 'Conformity with the Word' is never laid out. Where the Elizabethan Admonitions to Parliament followed the critique of the first Admonition with the platform of the second, here there is no platform, only a critique.[12] In Article 13, we watch the authors struggling to get the rhetoric of their critique in order. The government of the Church is 'the same way . . . as was in England in the time of Popery', with 'little change' except 'only the head from which it was derived'. Little change except only the head! The image is clearly not serving the argument here. The change of 'the head', as defenders of the Established Church would emphasise, seems quite significant. Later in Article 13, the petitioners get their image right. The focus is not on the transplanted head but on the remaining body – the prelates are 'members of the beast'.[13] The items of the critique are familiar and rather general: 'vestures, postures, ceremonies, and administrations'. Of these four topics, the two that are most important to this document are 'ceremonies' and, especially, as we shall see later, 'administrations'. Practices with regard to the communion table generate some heat: 'forcing people to come up thither to receive'; and especially, 'terming the altar to be the mercy-seat, or the place of God' (Article 16). This verbal practice is 'a plain device to usher in the Mass' – 'devices' are always bad in this document – and the idea of a material 'place' of God generates the most heated rhetoric in this section of what we might call 'standard admonition'. Article 17 condemns christening and consecrating churches, 'putting holiness in them; yea, reconsecrating upon pretended pollution'. This is the first 'yea' in the document (though there is a 'nay' in Article 4, on ejections of ministers). I would argue, however, that the real interest of Roots and Branches is not in this section, but rather in its presentation of the non-ecclesiastical effects of prelatical Church-government. At moments the text forgets that *Church*-government is its concern. Article 12 is on monopolies and patents (another 'swarm', though the word is not used) and all but the first of the 'dangerous tenets' listed in Article 10 are purely political ('that the subjects have no propriety in

---

[12] For the Elizabethan Admonitions to Parliament, see *Puritan Manifestoes*, ed. W. H. Frere and C. E. Douglas (1907). For commentary, see Donald J. McGinn, *The Admonition Controversy* (New Brunswick, 1949).
[13] For 'transplanted' here I am indebted to John Morrill.

their estates ... that [the king] is bound by no law'). Yet the great rhetorical and conceptual achievement of the document is to show how subtle and, as I have already suggested, how extensive the implications of bad (prelatical) Church-government in England have been.

One of the striking features of Roots and Branches is its concern with the psychological and emotional effects of the evils its describes. It takes affective states very seriously as social data. The overweening of the prelates produces 'faint-heartedness' in ministers with regard to preaching and it produces 'discouragement' in many from 'bringing up their children in learning'. 'Discouragement' is a powerful word for this text. The term recurs in the final indictment of the prelates for 'discouragement and destruction of all good subjects' (Article 28, subsection 2). It is characteristic of the thinking of this text that 'discouragement' is given a specifically sociological dimension which turns into a vision of economic disaster.[14] Many of those who became discouraged and 'departed the kingdom to Holland and other parts' were involved in the cloth trade and are now manufacturing cloth in their new locales, 'whereby wool, the great staple of the kingdom, is become of small value'. This means not only that 'trading is decayed' but also that 'many poor people want work' and 'seamen lose employment'. The economic disaster is national – 'the whole land is much impoverished' – and dishonours the kingdom and 'the government' thereof. 'Government' has now widened to include the whole administration of the kingdom, secular as well as ecclesiastical.

The intimate interweaving of the psychological, the sociological and the institutional is at the heart of Roots and Branches. Bad public policies produce bad public attitudes. The suppression of educational reform not only leads to ignorance and immorality in the approved clergymen but also thereby creates 'a loathing of the ministry' in the people (Article 7). Through the trivial and venal use of excommunication 'that sacred ordinance of God' becomes 'contemptible to all men' (Article 24). But the most powerful criticism of the prelates has to do with the effect of their attitudes, institutions, and procedures on the ordinary fabric of everyday life. We have already seen that the wicked exemption of the ministers from secular authority is presented as parallel to the wicked enthralling of them to the prelates. The text exfoliates this enthralment, and especially this exemption, in detail. The prelates interfere with the 'natural' relations among the classes. The improper 'discouragement' they create is paralleled by their improper 'encouragement of ministers to despise the temporal magistracy, the nobles, and the gentry of the land' (Article 3). The prelates' 'creatures' feel no reverence for their natural superiors and therefore 'confront whom they please' (Article 6). They put ministers upon parishes

---

[14] Derek Hirst has pointed out to me that already by 1628 (and perhaps even as early as 1610), 'the association of valour, confidence, and industry was firm'.

'without the patron's and the people's consent' (Article 26). Entering even more profoundly and wickedly into parish life, the prelates appoint ministers who encourage strife and 'live contentiously with their neighbours' (Article 3). To create contention with one's neighbours is the greatest of social sins – it is the identifying feature of English witches – and to convict the prelatical hierarchy of this sin is one of the themes of Roots and Branches.[15] The prelates thrust out of many congregations ministers who were 'diligent' and 'powerful' and who also 'lived peaceably' with their community (Article 5). Churchwardens, the keys to parish administration at the grass-roots (!) level, are pressured into causing strife: 'many churchwardens are sued, or threatened to be sued by their troublesome ministers, as perjured persons, for not presenting their parishioners' for breaches of episcopal canons (Article 22). Churchwardens are thus put in a position where they must either perjure themselves in this way or 'fall at jars continually' with their neighbours (Article 27).

The prelates' canons are interfering everywhere – with relations among neighbours, with the execution of marriages ('prohibiting of marriages without their licence . . . and licensing of marriages without banns asking'), and with work. The prohibition of working on saints' days, on pain of being fined, enforces idleness (which, of course, leads to dissoluteness – see Article 8) and places 'a very high burthen on most people, who getting their living with their daily employments, must either omit them, and be idle, or part with their money [through fines]' – whereby, Article 22 continues, 'many poor people are undone'. The great instrument through which all these interferences are managed is the system of ecclesiastical discipline. The 'sacred ordinance' with which Roots and Branches is most concerned is not the celebration of Holy Communion but the use of excommunication. The judicial function of the prelates is the key to their ultimate and most sinister aim: to replace not only God's laws but all laws with their own. The title page of the petition especially emphasises, in italic print, 'the tyranny and extortion practised in ecclesiastical courts', and it appeals to the 'high and honourable court' of Parliament (see plate 15, p. 228 above). The first of the two long Articles on excommunication (Article 19) explains how the ordinance is used to support the bishops' 'devices', though these are supported by no other law and 'appeal is denied' from the bishops' authority. The aim is total control: 'to draw all into an absolute subjection and thraldom to them and their government, spoiling both the king and the Parliament of their power'.[16] The prelates

---

[15] For the connection of witchcraft accusations in England with neighbourly strife at the village level, see Alan Macfarlane, *Witchcraft in Tudor and Stuart England: A Regional and Comparative Study* (1970), and Keith Thomas, *Religion and the Decline of Magic* (New York, 1971), chs. 16–17. This view is now quite widely held.

[16] The other long article on excommunication (Article 24) focuses on the economic rather than the political abuses of the ordinance, whereby the prelates 'have made it, as they do all other things, a hook or instrument wherewith to empty men's purses'.

and their courts take upon them the punishment of 'whoredoms and adulteries' – which they countenance for fines (Article 23) – and they take upon them many other matters which are 'determinable of right at Common Law' (Article 26). In the vision of Roots and Branches, the prelates and their courts aim to become, on a nationwide level, what Erving Goffman would call a 'total institution'.[17]

The visions of the prelates as corrupting the legal system and invading daily life coalesce in the final article, in which 'the exercising of the oath *ex officio*' and other inquisitorial proceedings are seen as 'reaching even to men's thoughts'. The 'unlawfulness of the oath *ex officio*' is explicitly mentioned on the title page of the printed edition. To reach 'even to men's thoughts' is the culmination of the aim of a 'total institution' and a violation of the fundamental juridico-metaphysical maxim that 'thought is free'.[18] Yet this article goes on to imagine an even more intimate and shocking violation. Even more horrifying than reaching into an Englishman's thoughts is invading his home – 'breaking up of men's houses and studies, taking away men's books, letters and other writings, seizing upon their estates'. No social distinctions are respected – 'fining and imprisoning of all sorts of people . . . removing them from their callings' – and even 'separating between them and their wives against both their wills'. Nothing secular is sacred. The damage extends 'to the utter infringing of the laws of the realm and the subjects' liberties', ruining both the (male) subjects

---

[17] See Erving Goffman, *Asylums: Essays on the Social Situation of Mental Patients and Other Inmates* (Chicago, 1961), Essay I: 'On the Characteristics of Total Institutions'. M. Foucault's historical analysis of 'complete and austere institutions' in *Discipline and Punish: The Birth of the Prison*, trans. A. Sheridan (1977; New York, 1979), Part 4, is very similar to Goffman's sociological–anthropological analysis. I have been unable to ascertain whether Foucault was influenced by Goffman.

[18] The phrase, 'thought is free', occurs twice in Shakespeare, most notably in *The Tempest* (at 2.2.121). It was proverbially proverbial. The first known citation of it (*c.* 1390) is as a proverb, when a character in Gower's *Confessio Amantis* states, 'I have heard said that thought is free' (see *The Oxford Dictionary of English Proverbs*, rev. F. P. Wilson (3rd edn, Oxford, 1970)). Along with some important indirect uses of the idea in Shakespeare, Tilley provides a politico-economic version of the proverb (as a proverb) in Camden, an allusion to the proverb in 1666 that suggests that it is peculiarly English, and a political explication of the proverb from a 1670 proverb collection ('Humane laws can take no cognizance of thoughts, unless they discover themselves by some overt actions'). See Morris Palmer Tilley, *A Dictionary of Proverbs in English in the Sixteenth and Seventeenth Centuries* (Ann Arbor, 1950), p. 644. In Book I of the *Commentaries*, Blackstone explains that 'a man's' (read 'a person's') 'principles, provided he keeps them to himself', and 'does not offend against the rules of public decency,' are properly 'out of the reach of human laws'; in Book IV, Blackstone explains how the laws against libel and other verbal crimes do not impinge on what he calls 'liberty of private sentiment'. See William Blackstone, *Commentaries on the Laws of England. A Facsimile of the First Edition, 1765–1769* (Chicago, 1979), I, 120; IV, 152. Queen Elizabeth repeatedly disclaimed 'inquisition of . . . opinions for their consciences in matters of faith' (see J. E. Neale, *Elizabeth I and her Parliaments* (2 vols., 1958; New York, 1966), I, 191). I am deeply grateful to my colleague, Richard H. Helmholz, of the University of Chicago Law School, for confirming my intuition that 'Thought is free' is ultimately a juridical maxim. He has called my attention to Justinian's *Digest*, 48.19.18: *Cogitationis poenam nemo patitur* ('No one is punished for thinking'). See *The Digest of Justinian*, ed. Theodore Mommsen with Paul Krueger, trans. Alan Watson (Philadelphia, 1985), IV, 850. On the controversy over the *ex officio* oath, see Mary Hume Maguire, 'Attack of the common lawyers on the oath *ex officio* as administered in the ecclesiastical courts in England', in *Essays in History and Political Theory in Honor of C. H. McIlwain* (Cambridge, Mass., 1936), ed. Carl Wittke, pp. 199–229; and Leonard W. Levy, *Origins of the Fifth Amendment* (New York, 1968). Levy's account is qualified in some detail by Charles M. Gray, 'Prohibitions and the Privilege against Self-incrimination', in *Tudor Rule and Revolution: Essays for G. R. Elton from his American Friends*, ed. DeLloyd J. Guth and John W. McKenna (Cambridge, 1982), pp. 345–367.

and – this is typical of Roots and Branches – 'their families'. The normal protection of the normal life of the subject, the Common Law, is unavailable: 'neither prohibition, *habeas corpus*, nor any other lawful remedy can be had'. It is therefore up to Parliament, under the guidance of the Lord of heaven, 'to redress these evils'. The Church, men's minds, and the whole fabric of ordinary life, the garden of the Commonwealth, must be rescued from the tentacular and pernicious kudzu, the 'roots and branches' of prelacy.

In Love with Parliaments: The 'Grand Remonstrance'

In its presentation of the evils that have affected England since the beginning of Charles's reign, the Petition and Remonstrance presented by the House of Commons to Charles on 1 December 1641 shares some of the language of the earlier Petition and Remonstrance of the Londoners to Parliament, but the 'Grand Remonstrance' is a very different document. It shares the affective language and many of the concerns of Roots and Branches – especially with violations of 'the ordinary course of justice' – but where Roots and Branches was a call for reformation of a wicked system, the Remonstrance is a cry from the heart of reformation.[19] Things have already been done; measures have been taken; the enemy is responding; further things must be done to secure the gains that have been made and to prevent imminent and long-term dangers. The Remonstrance is very much *in medias res*. It is defending itself, responding to the words and actions of The Enemy. It is a profoundly dualistic, almost Manichean document; its world is 'us' versus 'them'. In this text, the opposite of an evil is a good. And the Remonstrance is a profoundly apocalyptic document – at stake is the existence of England (and probably Scotland) as a distinct national entity.[20] The Remonstrance is obsessed with effectiveness because it sees its source, the House of Commons, as 'the only means' of combating an enemy that has not only 'endeavoured and attempted' to subvert 'the fundamental laws and principles' of English government and religion but has 'in a great measure encompassed and effected' its perfidious aim (pp. 204 and 206).[21] Parliament has taken counter-measures, but these 'will be ineffectual' unless a 'present, real and effectual course' (p. 204) be taken to suppress the continuing 'work' of the enemy (Article 61). This sense of speaking from the viewpoint of a partly accomplished but threatened and still precarious reformation – we

---

[19] Text from Gardiner, *Constitutional Documents*, ed. Gardiner, pp. 202–32, except where departures are indicated. The quotation is from Article 19.

[20] For the evil design also being against Scotland, see Articles 65–7.

[21] For the Commons as 'the only means', see Articles 70 and 180.

would say revolution – is what gives the 'Grand Remonstrance' its distinctive tone and stance.

The Petition prefixed to the Remonstrance begins with a rather fulsome delight at the king's safe return from Scotland. The House applies to the king the language of the most intimate Protestant religious experience – 'the comfort of your gracious presence'.[22] But as the sentence develops, the language of spiritual effectiveness finds a different object. The Commons desired the king's return 'to give more life and power to the dutiful and loyal counsels of your Parliament' (p. 203).[23] The Parliament, 'dutiful and loyal' as it may be, is the focus, not the king. Only Parliament can prevent 'imminent ruin and destruction'.[24] The second sentence of the Remonstrance is a very rich one, and deserves to be analysed at length. The characteristic voice of the Remonstrance emerges when it begins to characterise the problem – 'the multiplicity, sharpness, and malignity of those evils under which we have now many years suffered'. 'Multiplicity' is the centre of Roots and Branches; here the centre is 'malignity'. The word itself and its forms (not to mention synonyms) appear over two dozen times in the Remonstrance.[25] Actions are understood as expressing and manifesting inner states, and so ill-will is seen as characterising the enemy, just as the good are the 'well-affected' (see, for instance, Articles 87 and 175).

'Malignity', until our use of it to characterise tumours, had to apply to persons (or other moral agents), and the Remonstrance has no doubts about cause and agency. The long-standing and continuing evils in the kingdom 'are fomented and cherished by a corrupt and ill-affected party'. In the world of this document, 'party' is a negative word (equivalent to, but much more common than, 'faction'). A 'party' is the political manifestation of a malignant design. And a malignant design is a design for change – 'for the alteration of religion and government' (p. 203). 'Change' in the Remonstrance, as in most of the revolutionary texts of early modern Europe, is conceived as the enemy.[26] Finally, to conclude with the rich

---

[22] For the theological importance of the word and the notion of 'comfort' in the Protestant context, see Articles xi ('Of the Justification of Man') and xvii ('Of Predestination and Election') in the *Articles of Religion of the Church of England* (in *The Faith of Christendom: A Sourcebook of Creeds and Confessions*, ed. B. A. Gerrish (Cleveland, 1963). Justification by faith 'is a most wholesome Doctrine, and very full of comfort'; the doctrine of predestination is 'full of sweet, pleasant, and unspeakable comfort'.

[23] 'Life and power' are exactly the terms that those whom the Arminians, etc. 'call Puritans' (p. 207) ascribed to the words of the proper preacher. See Article 4 of Roots and Branches for diligent and 'powerful' ministers.

[24] Gardiner's text has 'eminent' rather than 'imminent' here, as does the text in *An Exact Collection of all Remonstrances . . . etc.*, printed for Edward Husbands (1643), sig. A1v. Rushworth, however, has 'imminent', which seems more appropriate in this context. See *Historical Collections . . . By John Rushworth* (8 vols., 1721), IV, 437.

[25] See, for almost random instances, pp. 203, 204, 206; Articles 69, 77, 143, and 181. For 'venomous' and 'venom', see Articles 155 and 174.

[26] Early modern revolutions are typically intended to undo (or, in this case, prevent) what is imagined as a change from a postulated earlier and proper state. For the word 'change' in the Grand Remonstrance, see pp. 206, 207, 208 and Article 65. 'That great change' referred to in Article 65 is the conversion of England to papistry.

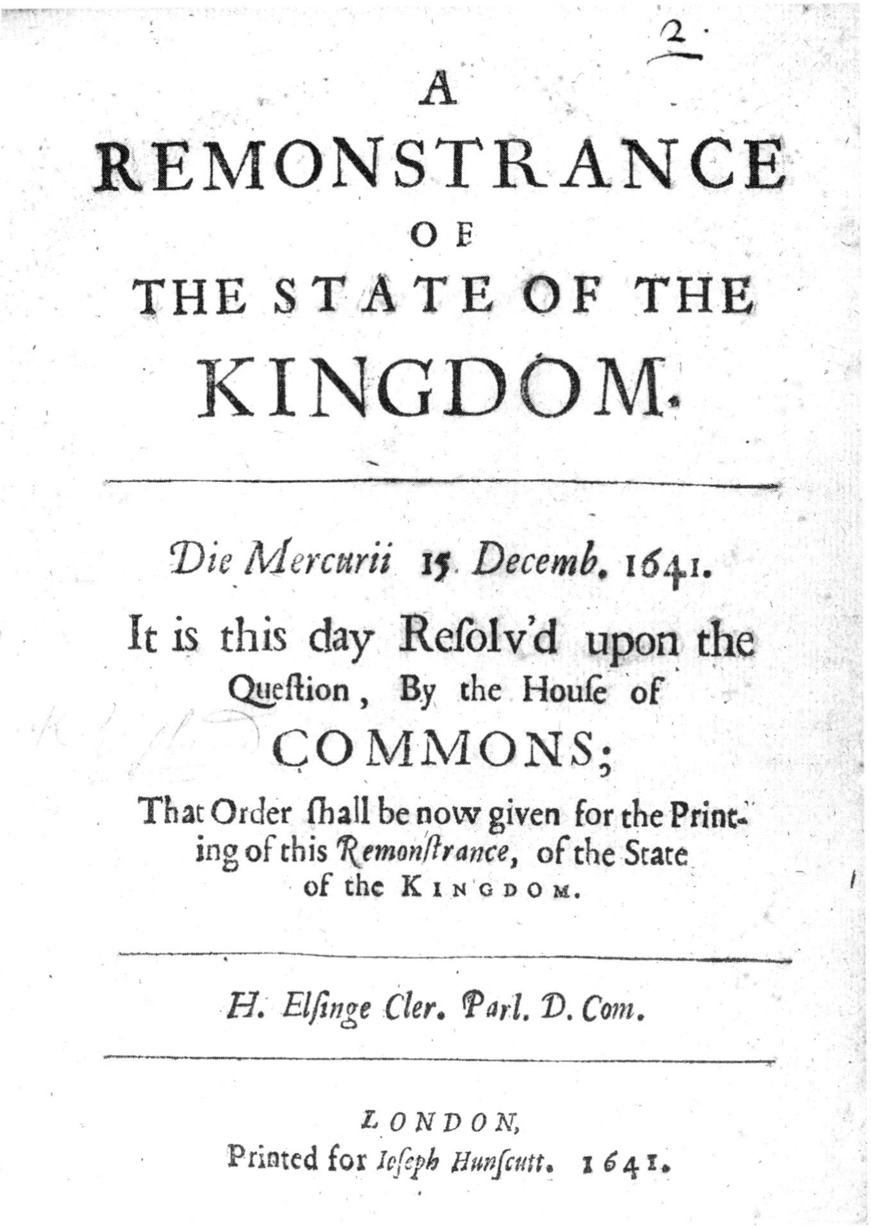

2.

A
REMONSTRANCE
O F
THE STATE OF THE
KINGDOM.

Die Mercurii 15 *Decemb.* 1641.

It is this day Refolv'd upon the Queftion, By the Houfe of

COMMONS;

That Order fhall be now given for the Printing of this *Remonftrance*, of the State of the K I N G D O M.

H. Elfinge Cler. Parl. D. Com.

L O N D O N,
Printed for *Iofeph Hunfcutt.* 1 6 4 1.

Plate 16 The title page of the Grand Remonstrance, 1641

second sentence of the Petition, it is deeply characteristic of this document that one of the main 'devices' of the malignant party is verbal – venomous words, 'scandals and imputations', directed against Parliament.

The Remonstrance is not only a more practical but also a more analytical document than Roots and Branches. The effort of Roots and Branches is primarily descriptive and evocative. The Remonstrance of the Commons speaks three times, as we know Roots and Branches never does, of 'the root' of England's troubles.[27] The analytical and political orientation of the Remonstrance can be seen in its account of one of the main strategies through which the malignant party seeks to accomplish its design:

> To cherish the Arminian part in those points wherein they agree with the Papists, to multiply and enlarge the difference between the common Protestants and those whom they call Puritans, to introduce and countenance such opinions and ceremonies as are fittest for accommodation with Popery, to increase and maintain ignorance, looseness and profaneness in the people; that of those three parties, Papists, Arminians and Libertines, they might compose a body fit to act such counsels and resolutions as were most conducible to their own ends.

This is quite carefully phrased. It does not equate Arminians with Papists and it does not entirely deny 'the difference' which has led one group of Protestants to be slandered as 'Puritans'. The mention of a 'body' might seem casual, but after listing one other malicious 'device' (slandering Parliament to the king), the document returns to the idea. It uses a kind of metaphysical conceit, drawn from the theory of matter, to explain the internal dynamics of the (supposed) three-part coalition of 'Papists, Arminians and Libertines':

> As in all compounded bodies the operations are qualified according to the predominant element, so in this mixed party, the Jesuited counsels, being most active and prevailing, may easily be discovered to have had the greatest sway in all their determinations, and if they be not prevented, are likely to devour the rest, or to turn them into their own nature. (pp. 207–8)

Moreover, later in the Remonstrance the idea of the forces of evil composing 'a body' is given a purely political twist in a vision of the pope's nuncio convoking 'the Papists of all sorts, nobility, gentry and clergy', and doing so 'after the manner of a Parliament' (Article 91). This anti-Parliament (or demonic parody, as Northrop Frye would call it) is a fearful thing: 'another state moulded within this state independent in government, contrary in interest and affection', seeking to corrupt the ignorant and to destroy those whom they could not hope to seduce (Article 92).[28] An evil body indeed.

---

[27] See Grand Remonstrance, p. 206 (where the phrase appears twice) and Article 120 (for a purely political use). Article 166 speaks of the 'long growth and deep root of those grievances'.

[28] See Northrop Frye, *Anatomy of Criticism: Four Essays* (1957; New York, 1966), p. 147.

The first section of the 'Remonstrance of the state of the kingdom' is a historical survey which emphasises offences done against Parliament.[29] Dissolutions, disregardings and subvertings are listed. The major evils, however, are violations of the privileges of Parliament: the 'close imprisonment' of various members of the House to the peril of their health and the violation of their rights to 'comfort';[30] and unjust (meaning un-Parliamentary) schemes for raising revenue. An interesting feature of the Parliamentary critique is that it cannot take place strictly on the grounds of legality. The article on taxes after 1629, during the Personal Rule, twists and turns on the issue of legality:

> After the breach of the Parliament in the fourth of His Majesty, injustice, oppression and violence broke in upon us without any restraint or moderation, and yet the first project was the great sums exacted through the whole kingdom for default of knighthood, which seemed to have some colour and shadow of a law, yet if it be rightly examined by that obsolete law which was pretended for it, it will be found to be against all the rules of justice, both in respect of the persons charged, the proportion of the fines demanded, and the absurd and unreasonable manner of their proceedings.
>
> (Article 17)

'And yet ... which seemed ... yet if it be rightly examined' – this is highly nervous and uncomfortable writing. The real ground for the critique is not legality but justice – or, even more strikingly, reason – in the abstract ('the absurd and unreasonable manner of their proceedings'). That the taxes in question were 'unreasonable' is repeated in the next two Articles. Article 17 constitutes one of those moments in which the Remonstrance is teetering on the verge of recognising its revolutionary nature.

Other such moments occur when the authors have to acknowledge that they are against, for instance, certain forms of obedience. The language of mediation and instrumentation is filled with horror in the Remonstrance, since the malignant party is adept at recruiting and manipulating 'factors', agents, 'instruments', followers and sub-parties. The most striking instance of horror at obedience is in the discussion of the selection of sheriffs under Charles (Article 50). Some sheriffs were pricked in an unusual and therefore bad way, but the House objects to others not on the basis of how they were selected but because 'such men were pricked out *as would be instruments to execute whatsoever* they [the malignant party] would have to be done' (emphasis mine). This suggests that passive disobedience – the refusal to

---

[29] It should be said again that 'Remonstrance' in these documents is primarily used in the sense of 'demonstration' rather than in the sense of complaint or accusation. Husbands's *Exact Collection* speaks of the 'Petition of the House ... which accompanies the Declaration of the State of the Kingdom' (sig. A1v).

[30] The range of this term is nicely indicated by its use in Article 12 in the phrase 'all the comforts of life' and in Article 13 to mean 'spiritual consolation' (see n. 22 above). Article 37 speaks of both the 'comfort of books' and the 'comfort and conversation' between 'men and their wives'. It should be noted that in the vocabulary of this document, the term which functions as the exact opposite of 'comfort', and has an equivalent range, is 'vexation'.

obey certain commands and therefore not 'to execute whatsoever' – is a proper thing in officials.[31] The idea that obedience and legality may not be ultimate values emerges in the second part of the historical section (Articles 1–60 of the historical section of the Remonstrance concern 1625–37; Articles 61–99 take the situation to the moment of composition). In the Short Parliament, such was the hubris of the malignant party (Article 70) that they hoped to make Parliament itself improperly obedient ('pliant to their will') and thereby 'to establish mischief by a law' (Article 72).[32] Here the possibility (happily averted) of unjust laws is explicitly acknowledged.[33] The next Article protests that the demands of the Parliaments in Scotland were condemned as 'undutiful' without the king 'hearing the reason of these demands' (Article 73). Getting a hearing for legitimate demands takes precedence over being 'dutiful'. This theme culminates in Article 99, near the end of the opening historical survey. What emerges echoes the Huguenot theory of allowed or mandated resistance by 'magistrates':[34]

> The nobility began to weary of their silence and patience, and sensible of the duty and trust which belongs to them; and thereupon some of the most ancient of them did petition His Majesty at such a time, when evil counsels were so strong, that they had occasion to expect more hazard to themselves than redress of those public evils for which they interceded.

The is a very conservative vision of a revolutionary act: it is not newcomers but 'some of the most ancient' of the nobility who feel duty-bound to speak out, at personal risk, against 'public evils', evils 'strengthened by custom and authority' (Article 106). In this context, 'duty' works against silence, obedience and patience.

The authors of this Remonstrance very much want to see themselves as defending the laws and, as I have already suggested, opposing 'innovations' (Articles 85 and 132); their aims are to 'maintain', to 'preserve', to 'restore' (Articles 58, 64, and 70). Part of the slander campaign of the malignant party was, as the Remonstrators see it, the attempt 'to work in His Majesty ill impressions and opinions of our proceedings, as if we had altogether done our own work, and not his; and had obtained from him many things

---

[31] For an exploration of the ideology of 'virtuous disobedience' in the period, and for the critique of the figure who will do 'whatsoever', see the examples and contexts adduced in Richard Strier, 'Faithful Servants: Shakespeare's Praise of Disobedience', in *The Historical Renaissance: New Essays on Tudor and Stuart Literature and Culture*, ed. Heather Dubrow and Richard Strier (Chicago, 1988), pp. 104–33.

[32] I am certain that we are intended to hear a suggestion of hubris in the syntactical and narrative structure of Article 70 – 'And such was their confidence, that ... they did now hope ...').

[33] A similar recognition occurs in the discussion of the Laudian Church canons in Article 85, where the prelates are seen as '*establishing* their own usurpations', making legal 'what they had formerly introduced without warrant of law' (emphasis mine).

[34] For this theory, see Beza's *Rights of Magistrates* in *Constitutionalism and Resistance in the Sixteenth Century*, trans. and ed. Julian H. Franklin (New York, 1969), pp. 110–13, and the *Vindiciae contra Tyrannos*, in *Constitutionalism and Resistance*, ed. Franklin, pp. 162–5.

very prejudicial to the Crown, both in respect of prerogative and profit' (Article 145). The members deeply desired 'to wipe out this slander' (Article 146). It was not, however, easy for them to do so. They could assert that they had 'ever been careful not to desire anything that should weaken the Crown either in just profit or useful power' (Article 156), but the adjectives – *just* profit, *useful* power – themselves make it clear that this asseveration begs the issue (the Commons apparently are the ones to decide what is 'just' and 'useful' for the crown). 'In respect of . . . profit', the Commons could point to the sums they raised (Articles 149–53), and argue that the abolished courts (Star Chamber and High Commission) were 'fruitful' only in oppression to 'the people' and not in profit to the king, who rarely received the fruits of these injustices (Articles 159–60). But 'in respect of prerogative', the situation was much trickier. Here the Commons convened at the end of 1640 virtually had to acknowledge its revolutionary status.

The heart of the 'Grand Remonstrance' is its second half, which begins with the calling of the present Parliament. The malignant ones seek to bring the people as well as the king 'out of love with Parliaments' (Article 162), but this document is clearly in love with Parliaments. There is something like religious awe in this Parliament's self-contemplation: 'At our first meeting, all oppositions seemed to vanish' (Article 105); 'the difficulties seemed to be insuperable, which by Divine Providence we have overcome' (Article 110). Even the economic situation is miraculous. It is hard to see what could be celebratory in contracting 'a debt to the Scots of £220,000', but 'God has so blessed the endeavours of this Parliament, that the kingdom is a great gainer by all this charge' (Article 112). A list of all the impositions and monopolies that have been suppressed (Articles 113–19) leads to a jubilant reflection on 'that which is more beneficial than all this, that the root of these evils is taken away'. The 'root of these evils' is 'the arbitrary power pretended to be in His Majesty of taxing the subject, or charging their estates without consent of Parliament'. Such behaviour is 'declared to be against law by the judgement of both Houses, and likewise by an Act of Parliament' (Article 120). The Parliament has eliminated the political root of the country's economic ills. To speak of 'the arbitrary power pretended to be in His Majesty' is not, of course, to attack the king himself – the agents of this assertion are not specified – but it is clear that it is Parliament that determines what is 'against law' and also what power is 'in His Majesty'.[35]

The whole section is an ecstasy of self-congratulation. After happily recounting its acts against 'powerful delinquents' (Article 106), the king's

---

[35] It might be worth noting that 'power pretended to be in His Majesty' does not mean that the agents in question are making believe that this power is in the king, but rather that they are asserting that it is in the king.

'evil counsellors' (Strafford, Windebank, Laud, etc. – Articles 121–4), the Parliament contemplates the laws it has passed regarding itself. These laws guarantee regular future meetings of Parliament and forbid dissolution of the present Parliament – 'which two laws', the Commons solemnly assert, 'well considered may be thought more advantageous than all the former, because they secure a full operation of the present remedy, and afford a perpetual spring of remedies for the future' (Article 126). We have already noted the Remonstrance's obsession with 'effectual' working in history and its sense that its operation is 'the only means' of combating the malignant forces that by evil means 'have had such operation' in the kingdom (p. 204). Here we see its hope for the future. The Commons wants to imagine itself in a world-historical perspective: 'The immoderate power of the Council Table, and the excessive abuse of that power is so ordered and restrained, that we may well hope that no such things as were frequently done by them, to the prejudice of the public liberty, will appear in future times but only in stories' (Article 130).[36] The 'full operation of the present remedy' (that is, the present Parliament) will – 'we may well hope' – transform history and make the recent evils seem like myths or dimly remembered facts.[37] Parliament hopes to be a 'perpetual spring of remedies'. This is clearly intended as an image of a miraculous and healing fountain flowing inexhaustibly into the future, an image that is resonant of 'living waters' and the fountain of youth. Yet I cannot help also hearing an Edenic overtone in the phrase, a reference to the perpetual (seasonal) spring and harvest of Eden or the golden age. This is reinforced by the Utopian strain that King Charles correctly detected in some of Parliament's texts ('that new Utopia of religion and government into which they endeavour to transform this kingdom').[38] This strain is clearest in the articles that mention not only the 'excellent laws and provisions' that are in preparation (Article 137), but also those that are only 'in proposition': to provide the king with a regular source for just as much revenue as he needs (and no more); to abridge 'both the delays and charges of law-suits' (always a Utopian idea); to assure a proper balance of trade; and, seemingly anti-climactically, to improve 'the herring-fishing on our coasts' (Articles 139–42).[39]

---

[36] 'Stories' in Article 130, has the primary meaning of 'histories', but also, I think, the secondary meaning of fables or myths. Derek Hirst has rightly called my attention to the element of optativeness in the language here, the element of perhaps desperate fantasy.

[37] This same sense of a possible world-historical transformation recurs in Article 167, which speaks of the advantages 'which not only the present but future ages are like to reap by the good laws and other proceedings in this Parliament'. 'Are like to reap' maintains the optative, slightly tentative tone.

[38] 'His Majesties Answer to the nineteen Propositions of both Houses of Parliament', in Husbands, *Exact Collection*, p. 315. Charles did not accuse the whole Parliament of revolutionary Utopianism, but only 'some persons, who have now too great an influence even upon both Houses'.

[39] This last item is not quite as anti-climactic as it seems. It shows an awareness of the inter-connectedness of economic and other phenomena that truly is characteristic of the tradition of More's *Utopia*. The improvement of the herring fishing 'will be of mighty use in the employment of the poor'. This is the major social good

But is not the Commons indeed doing its 'own work' and not the king's, just as its slanderers say (as in Article 145)? Although Article 130, on the abuses that have been eliminated, lists 'His Majesty's goodness' together with 'the faithful endeavours of this Parliament' among the things for which posterity will praise God, this acknowledgement does not address the constitutional question, the malicious 'slander' about 'many things very prejudicial to the Crown', especially 'in respect of prerogative'. The problem is intensified by the fact that the 'slander' seems to take hold most firmly on just the item at which the Commons is most ecstatic – the 'perpetual spring'. Article 158 finally confronts the issue:

In the bill for the continuance of the present Parliament, there seems to be some restraint of the royal power in dissolving of Parliaments, not to take it out of the Crown, but to suspend the execution of it for this time and occasion only: which was so necessary for the king's own security and the public peace, that without it we could not have undertaken any of these great charges, but must have left both armies to disorder and confusion, and the whole kingdom to blood and rapine.

This is very weak. No constitutional justification for 'the bill for the continuance of the present Parliament' is offered. The distinction between the suspension and the abolition of 'the royal power in dissolving of Parliaments' is hardly viable, since any Parliament could pass a bill for such a suspension. The only substantive appeal is to 'necessity' – to considerations of 'security' and 'public peace', which have an absolute status and 'suspend' all normal (that is, legal) considerations.

In the rest of the document, the House tries to maintain a rhetoric of working with or through the king, but this fiction is not very strongly sustained. The members can present themselves as loyal to the king – maintaining Scotland for him (through 'the vigilancy of the well-affected' – Article 175), and opposing the Irish, who have 'shaken off all bonds of obedience' (Article 177). But the fact that Parliament sees itself as the indispensable bulwark against 'destruction even of all the king's dominions' (Article 175) only serves to confirm the centrality and providential validity of its own role: 'And now what hope have we but in God, when as the only means of our subsistence and power of reformation is under Him in the Parliament?' (Article 180).

With regard to the central matter of reformation, that of Church-government, the Commons vigorously deny the scandalous charge that they 'mean to abolish all Church-government, and leave every man to his own fancy'. They fully acknowledge that the king is 'entrusted with ecclesiastical law as well as with the temporal'. Yet they make it clear that the king is to regulate the Church 'by such rules of order and discipline as

---

that it will accomplish; 'the employment of the poor' is clearly something that the House values highly. But this same 'improvement' will also provide 'a plentiful nursery of mariners', who will enable the kingdom 'in any great action'. I assume that mercantile and colonial expansion are being imagined.

are established by the Parliament' – which, they add, is the king's great council, 'in all affairs both in Church and State' (Article 182). Parliament establishes the 'rules' through which the king governs – 'in all affairs both in Church and State'. Convocation is not mentioned. Nor, in the Article that deals with the method by which 'the intended reformation' of the Church will take place, is the king. The first step will be 'a general synod of the most grave, pious, learned and judicious divines of this island; assisted with some from foreign parts, professing the same religion with us'. This synod will thoroughly consider the matter of Church-government and then 'represent the results of their consultation unto the Parliament'. These results will 'be there [in Parliament] allowed of and confirmed', and 'receive the stamp of authority, thereby to find passage and obedience throughout the kingdom' (Article 185). The 'stamp of authority' leading to 'obedience throughout the kingdom' comes from Parliament.

The Remonstrance expresses mounting exasperation with those who have slandered, traduced and maliciously misinterpreted the actions and intentions of the House, especially with regard to 'the golden reins' of Church-government and with regard to education, which 'it is our chiefest care and desire to advance' (Article 186). The exasperation culminates in a scriptural reference: 'Thus with Elijah, are we called by this malignant party the troublers of the state, and still, while we endeavour to reform their abuses, they make us the authors of those mischiefs we study to prevent' (Article 190). As with the reference to 'the locusts of Egypt' in Roots and Branches, it is difficult to estimate the intended scope of this allusion.[40] Elijah's assertion, 'I have not troubled Israel, but thou' (1 Kings 18:18), is identical in the major English translations, but were the readers of the Remonstrance – which was never intended solely (or even primarily?) for the king – to recall that the prophet's accuser was the wicked King Ahab?[41] And were the readers further intended to recall that

---

[40] On 'the locusts of Egypt', see n. 11 above.

[41] It is not clear which version of the English Bible the members would have been using. Both the Authorized Version and the Geneva Version were widely available in 1641 (and they translate the prophet's words identically in this verse). The mistake that Gardiner identifies in Rushworth, where the prophet's name appears as 'Eliab' (*Historical Collections*, IV, 450) does not help, since this is clearly a misreading of 'Eliah' (see Husbands, *Exact Collection*, p. 20), and the prophet's name appears as 'Eliiah' in all black letter print. There are both Authorized and Geneva versions that vacillate, in roman, between 'Eliiah' and 'Elijah'. On ideological grounds, one might think that the odds favour Geneva. It may be relevant to the Remonstrance that the Geneva gloss on 1 Kings 18:18 addresses the matter of slander, and urges 'true ministers' of God not only 'not to suffer the truth to be unjustly slandered', but also 'to reprove boldly the wicked slanderers *without respect of person*'. See *The Bible: That is, The Holy Scriptures* (Amsterdam?, 1640; emphasis mine). On the addressee of the Remonstrance, see the horrified reaction of Sir Edward Dering at remonstrating 'downwards' and talking 'of' rather than to the king (quoted in David L. Smith, 'From Petition to Remonstrance', p. 221 above). In the King's Answer to the Petition accompanying the Grand Remonstrance (Gardiner, *Constitutional Documents*, p. 156), the king expresses special annoyance that the Petition (and Remonstrance, which he refused to acknowledge) should already have been printed before he had a chance to respond to it. The title page of the printed edition (see plate 16) claims authority from the House of Commons for the appearance of the Remonstrance in print.

it was his wicked queen, Jezebel, who was responsible for leading Ahab astray?[42]

In any case, the Remonstrance ends with a list of items, 'for the perfecting of the work begun' (Article 191), that the king may 'be pleased to grant' (Article 192). These include a Parliamentary committee to keep track of papists and to root out conforming papists (Articles 193–4), and, most of all, virtually complete Parliamentary control over the king's selection of 'counsellors, ambassadors and other ministers' (Article 197).[43] The Commons in particular is to have complete discretion in this matter, rejecting all nominees who, though 'not legally criminal', are 'known favourer[s] of Papists', 'factors or agents' or pensioners of any foreign power, and any who have been known, *horribile dictu*, 'to speak contemptuously of either Houses of Parliament or Parliamentary proceedings' (Articles 198–203). The king is 'humbly petitioned' to grant all this – without which, the members coyly note, 'we cannot give His Majesty such supplies for the support of his own estate' as he desires (Article 197). The language of humble petition very thinly overlays the reality of threat and coercion here.

The Remonstrance ends, however, on a visionary rather than a monitory note. It returns to the language of affections, hoping that through its well-affected efforts, 'His Majesty may have cause to be in love with good counsel and good men'. By accepting the proposals of his great council – in all affairs both in Church and State – the king will finally resolve his financial woes, and 'see his own estate settled in a plentiful condition to support his honour'. More importantly, where the malignant party encouraged and produced dissensions and oppositions in the nation, the king, by following the programme, will 'see his people united' not only 'in ways of duty to him', but also in 'endeavours to the public good'. The Remonstrance ends with a vision of the king seeing 'happiness, wealth, peace and safety derived to his own kingdom, and procured to his allies by the influence of his own power and government'. This final word is lovely. There is no doubt that it primarily means 'governance', the ongoing activities of the king in his role, but in the context of the text as a whole, I cannot help thinking that it includes the suggestion of an ongoing structure as well as an ongoing action – a structure that of course centrally includes his 'great council'.[44]

---

[42] In this context it is perhaps worth recalling that one of the results of the blurring of lines between the English and the 'Romish' Church at which the Roots and Branches petition was aghast was that, because of this blurring, some Englishmen 'have restrained to pray for the conversion of our Sovereign Lady the Queen' (Roots and Branches, Article 13).

[43] On the radicalism of this proposal, see David L. Smith, p. 220 above.

[44] For helpful comments on drafts of this essay, I am deeply grateful to John Morrill, David L. Smith, Mark Kishlansky, David Underdown and, especially, Derek Hirst.

John Milton's *Eikonoklastes*

The Drama of Justice

Derek Hirst

To consider Milton's *Eikonoklastes* of 1649 under the rubric of the Theatrical City seems at first misguided. Civil war had all but cleared the stage. Some lights still flickered, it is true – compliance with the 1642 parliamentary ordinance against play-acting was less than universal, and the soldiers detailed to purify London during the Christmas and New Year season of 1648–9 found the doors of four theatres open. But the dumb show of the fall of princes performed, to the applause of bystanders, by one group of actors as they were carted off to confinement offered a fitting comment on the political fortunes of the stage.[1] As the English Revolution ran its course, would-be playgoers were translated into private consumers of the literary collections which poured from the presses.

The theatrical perspective might seem all the more unpromising when turned on Milton's long rebuttal of *Eikon Basilike*, the so-called 'king's book' of meditations on Charles I's sufferings. The nearly mechanical, point-and-counterpoint refutations in *Eikonoklastes* constitute an exercise in political demolition. The forbidding nature of that exercise,[2] and the bitter attack by this former poet and masque-writer on the superficiality of kingship, seem only to mark the final rupture of a culture in which the theatre had been intimately tied to the life of City and nation as well as court. Of course, Milton's engagement with what he denounced as the fictive and representational qualities of *Eikon Basilike* and kingship alike is unmistakable. It has invited scholars to see *Eikonoklastes* as the *locus classicus* for his emerging sense of literary corruption and its politics; and they have placed it and its themes variously, both in the cultural history of the seventeenth century and in the trajectory of Milton's career.[3] But the

---

I am grateful to Steven Zwicker and the editors for reading and commenting on an earlier draft of this essay.

[1] See C. V. Wedgwood, *The Trial of Charles I* (1964), pp. 73–4.

[2] Milton himself recognised its lack of aesthetic appeal: *The Complete Prose Works of John Milton*, ed. Don M. Wolfe *et al.* (8 vols., New Haven, 1953–82), III: 1648–1649, ed. Merritt Y. Hughes (1962) (henceforth *CPWJM* 3), pp. 433, 568.

[3] For a sample of the scholarship in these areas, see on the one hand Steven Zwicker, 'The King's head and the Politics of Literary Property: The *Eikon Basilike* and *Eikonoklastes*', in his *Lines of Authority: Politics and English Literary Culture, 1649–1689* (Cornell, 1993), pp. 37–59, and on the other Joan S. Bennett, 'God, Satan,

very visibility of Milton's denunciation of royal masquing and romancing, and theatricality too, has perhaps distracted attention from what is likely to have been his more immediate and pressing concern in 1649,[4] which had to do with situating himself and his book in relation to what was then the greatest matter of the day. This is not to say that we should turn our gaze from the theatre to politics, conventionally understood. For there are ways in which a quest for the theatrical, if redirected, can open up both the text of *Eikonoklastes* and its moment, the inception of the English republic.

At the centre of those months, dominating both press and public life, lay the king's trial and execution; and it scarcely needs the promptings of structuralists, cultural anthropologists or political scientists to remind us that there is theatre in the forensic and the punitive, all the more so when the leading character is a king.[5] On those events Milton in *Eikonoklastes* seems to withhold comment, ostentatiously standing above any petty engagement with one who, since dead, could bring Milton the victor no honour.[6] That Milton should forswear this most public drama is striking, for not only does his text show him intensely aware of the theatrical element in the life of the king, but he had built his previous work, *The Tenure of Kings and Magistrates*, around the bringing of the king to trial. Silences, like Sherlock Holmes's dog which did not bark in the night, can be significant. Listening for them, for the contemporary commonplace which a writer passes over, for the preoccupation of one which others ignore, entails of course reading widely in the textual productions of a particular moment. To read widely in the texts of 1649 is to encounter not simply the reverberations of *Eikon Basilike*, the king's book, the object of Milton's counterblast; it is also to register on every hand the repercussions of the king's trial and the controversy over the meaning of the justice enacted by that event. And it is to discover how central a protagonist Milton was in that drama.

Although the crowds could no longer wend their way to London's Bankside for bear-baiting and stage-plays, 1649 brought drama and spec-

---

and King Charles: Milton's Royal Portraits', *Publications of the Modern Language Association*, 92 (1977), 441–57; Richard Helgerson, 'Milton Reads the King's Book: Print, Performance, and the Making of a Bourgeois Idol', *Criticism*, 29 (1987), 1–25; David Loewenstein, *Milton and the Drama of History: Historical Vision, Iconoclasm, and the Literary Imagination* (Cambridge, 1990), passim.

[4] This is not to suggest that literary scholars are the only victims of truncated vision. Typical of historians' lack of interest in Milton's polemic against the kingship of Charles I are the silences in D. Underdown, *Pride's Purge* (Oxford, 1971), B. Worden, *The Rump Parliament* (Cambridge, 1974), and P. Zagorin, *History of Political Thought in the English Revolution* (1954).

[5] See especially M. Foucault, *Discipline and Punish: The Birth of the Prison* (New York, 1979); M. Walzer, *Regicide and Revolution: Speeches at the Trial of Louis XVI* (London and New York, 1974).

[6] *CPWJM 3*, pp. 337–8. Milton's silence has led one recent commentator to suggest that the king's head may indeed – as Marvell observed in his 'Horatian Ode' – have 'frighted' the republicans. Thomas I. Corns, *Uncloistered Virtue: English Political Literature 1640–1660* (Oxford, 1992), pp. 206–7; cf. Andrew Marvell, 'An Horatian Ode', ll. 69–70. For a rather different account, see below.

tacle to new heights. The victors in the English upheavals, while far less eager to eliminate their foes than were later revolutionaries,[7] did not intend to let slip their gains; insistently citing the grimmer texts of the Old Testament, they determined to avenge the fallen, and to punish the chief among their foes. Most famously, they brought their king to trial and execution. Charles was followed to the block by three prominent Royalists, while the firing squad and the rope claimed others who had been on the wrong side in the fighting of 1648 or who had sought to redirect its outcome. As the victors proudly claimed in their own adversity, when times had turned once more, they did not do this in a corner but bravely in face of the world.[8] Like those whom they succeeded, and who succeeded them at Whitehall, they recognised the importance of dramatising their power and their justice.

The drama of justice was perhaps the most visible feature of the public life of London in the first half of 1649. The king's trial held the attention not just of the preachers in their pulpits but of the City as a whole. As one newswriter put it, 'The trial of the king is the great hinge on which for this week the door of this intelligence must move.'[9] Public interest was enormous, with crowds gathering outside Westminster Hall and an extraordinary array of boats on the Thames, the occupants silently watching as the king was taken by water to Sir Robert Cotton's house, the usual landing-place for Westminster.[10] Amidst the trumpeters and horsed drummers in Palace Yard, and inside Westminster Hall as Charles refused to plead, all was spectacle. Every gesture was noted, and the ceremonial of the court received attention as careful as the arguments; particular notice was given to the refusal of courtesy on both sides – 'no congratulation or motion of hats at all' – to Charles's demeanour and bearing, and to the head which ominously broke from his cane as he angrily tapped the solicitor-general on the shoulder.[11]

It did not take much imagination – as the royalist sheet *Mercurius Pragmaticus* showed, labouring the point – to translate spectacle into theatre: 'the traitorous tragedians are upon their exit, and poor King Charles at the brink of the pit'.[12] Nor could the protagonists themselves be unaware of the audience, with masked watchers in the boxes as at any theatre; during the reading of the charge, the king 'with a quick eye and nimble gesture, turned himself oftentimes about, casting an eye not only on those that were on each side of the Court, but ever upon the spectators in the

[7] Or than their Scottish contemporaries, whose conflicts manifested a bitterness largely absent in England.
[8] See Wedgwood, *Trial of Charles I*, pp. 205–14.
[9] *The Kingdomes Weekly Intelligencer*, 16–23 Jan. 1648/9, p. 1225.
[10] See Wedgwood, *Trial of Charles I*, passim, for a fine account of both the proceedings and the press coverage.
[11] See especially *The Moderate*, 16–23 Jan. 1648/9, p. 269.
[12] *Mercurius Pragmaticus*, 23–30 Jan. 1648/9, sigs. Hhhv–Hhh2.

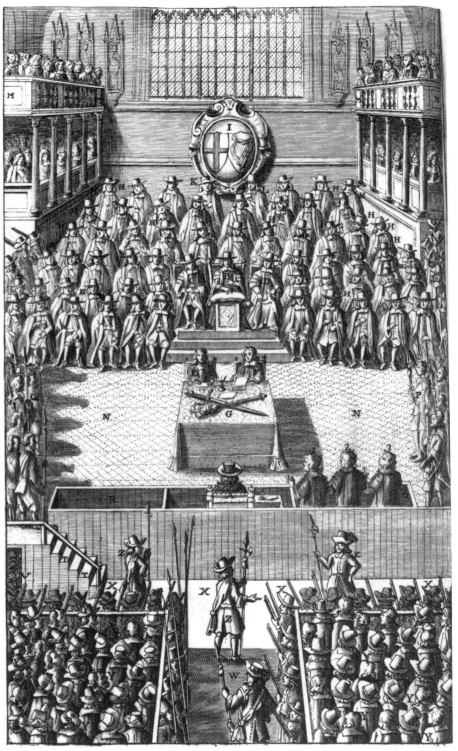

Plate 17   The High Court of Justice in session, January 1649

midst of the hall'.[13] Fully the centre of the stage now as he had been the centre of the audience in the court masques of the 1630s, Charles did not allow his sense of audience to leave him. Not for nothing did Solicitor-General Cook term the trial 'the most comprehensive, impartial and glorious piece of justice that ever was acted and executed upon the theatre of England'.[14] For his final appearance in the cold on the scaffold on 30 January, Charles dressed warmly lest any shivering be misconstrued, and pleaded in vain for a block of a more dignified height. The huge crowd testified by its silence, and then by the collective groan which a schoolboy watcher remembered to the end of his life,[15] that it had been properly moved by the spectacle.

Charles was scarcely alone in his stage sense. When his cousin the duke of Hamilton followed him to the block a few weeks later, the attendant crowds were regaled in truly baroque fashion, as the scaffold was spread with a huge sheet of scarlet silk, and a red sarcanet scarf provided to catch the severed head. The piety of the earl of Holland's protracted devotions gave entertainment of a different kind, while the journalists' muted displeasure at the speech-making, as well as the impenitence, of Lord Capel speaks of audience expectations of a proper end.[16] Those expectations crossed both national and social boundaries. Within weeks the marquis of Huntly faced the executioner in Edinburgh, urging his audience that for the royal cause they should 'stoop to a scaffold, as if it were a theatre of honour in this world', while the Leveller trooper Robert Lockyer, brought before a firing squad in St Paul's Churchyard on 29 April for mutiny, declared that he was 'willing to act his part on that dismal and bloody stage'. Lockyer's London neighbours, who gave him a ceremonial funeral designed to vie with noble exequies, understood as well as he the drama of public life.[17]

While the myriad contemporary renderings of the king's death as tragedy[18] were without question fictive, they also reflected an important reality. In 1649 politics, and in particular the politics of justice, was widely conceived of in dramatic terms. To that reality, as well as to Charles's personal history as a connoisseur of theatre, Milton surely paid tribute when at the very outset of *Eikonoklastes* he derided the theatricality of the representation of the king in the frontispiece to *Eikon Basilike*, 'set there

[13] *Perfect Weekly Account*, 17–24 Jan. 1648/9, p. 362.
[14] J. G. Muddiman, *The Trial of King Charles I* (Edinburgh, [1928]), p. 234. Cook's 'speech' forms Appendix C of this work, pp. 233–60.
[15] Nancy K. Maguire, 'The Theatrical Mask/Masque of Politics: The Case of Charles I', *Journal of British Studies*, 28 (1989), 3.
[16] See, for example, the accounts in *The Kingdoms faithfull and impartiall Scout*, 9–16 March 1648/9, *Perfect Diurnall*, 5–12 March 1648/9, *Perfect Summary of Exact Passages in Parliament*, 5–12 March 1648/9.
[17] Bulstrode Whitelocke, *Memorials* (4 vols., Oxford, 1853), III, 7, 24; *Perfect Summary*, 23–30 April 1649, p. 8; H. N. Brailsford, *The Levellers and the English Revolution* (1961), pp. 506–7.
[18] For which see Maguire, 'The Theatrical Mask/Masque of Politics', pp. 1–22.

to catch fools and silly gazers' with its effects 'begged from the old pageantry of some Twelfth-nights entertainment' or 'masking scene'. Scattered through the text, as scholars have often noted, theatrical images recur, usually in the most hostile form, as Milton condemns Charles's 'ill-acted regality' and empty 'stage-work', and the impropriety of his taste for Shakespeare at sombre moments.[19] Those scholars have with good reason connected the responses in *Eikonoklastes* with Milton's assaults on the speciousness of kingship in the later great poems. From this point until his death, Milton was preoccupied with the dangerous superficiality of monarchy. Yet, despite his contempt for the royal taste in theatrics, he did not in 1649 choose to concentrate on what was then such a dominant feature in the press. The surprise is surely not that *Eikonoklastes* has some harsh words for stage-plays and players but rather that, in all its length, it has so few. The relative prominence accorded to the dramatic in Marvell's 'Horatian Ode',[20] written slightly later, more nearly reflects the contemporary prominence of such themes.

If theatricality bulked smaller in Milton's indictment of the king and his book than did other issues, the terms of that indictment were nevertheless – and no less than the charges of stagecraft – conditioned by the crisis of the spring of 1649. Milton's noisy assertion of the manner of composition locates *Eikonoklastes* unquestionably in those months. It was 'assigned rather, than by me chosen or affected. Which was the cause both of beginning it so late, and finishing it so leisurely, in the midst of other employments and diversions.'[21] The task of answering 'the king's book' must therefore have been urged on Milton some time in the spring of 1649, 'late' that is – some months after the first appearance of *Eikon Basilike* at the end of January – but leaving sufficient time for the 'leisurely' completion and production by early October of such a long and complex text as was *Eikonoklastes*.[22] A spring inception for the work also squares with the fact that in mid-March the government was preoccupied with the task of 'satisfying the people of this nation' concerning the political and penal developments since December 1648, and most especially 'the taking of the late king's head'; that preoccupation resulted in the *Declaration of the Parliament of England* of 22 March.[23] While the general gloom and disaffection might not have warranted such an urgent response, 'the king's book' – a major rallying-point in that resurgent royalist threat which alarmed journalists and government alike[24] – made some answer impera-

---

[19] *CPWJM 3*, pp. 342–3, 355, 361, 530.

[20] In a poem of 120 lines the five lines accorded to 'that memorable scene' on which 'the royal actor' mounted 'the tragic scaffold' assume unmistakable significance.

[21] *CPWJM 3*, p. 339.

[22] The first edition came into the hands of the bookseller, George Thomason, on 6 October.

[23] *Perfect Diurnall*, 12–19 March 1648/9, p. 2377. Parliament's sense of the importance of explanations at this point was manifested in its order that its *Declaration* be printed in English, Latin, French and Dutch. Whitelocke, *Memorials*, II, 555.

[24] That threat is written all across the newspapers of these weeks.

tive. In his combative scaffold speech at the beginning of the month, Lord Capel had conjured *Eikon Basilike* when calling on his audience to rally to the young Charles II.[25] The king's book was unmistakably doing the royalists' work. So when the Rump approved 'the large declaration to give satisfaction to the people', it also referred 'the examination of the king's book' to a committee. Milton's book, with its opening condemnation of 'their intent, who published these overlate apologies and meditations of the dead king, . . . of stirring up the people', grew out of this conjuncture.[26] Indeed, the fact that the other main counterblast to the king's book should have opened with the assertion that its author too had been 'necessitated' to write suggests how much of a co-ordinated campaign was under way.[27]

The threat of renewed fighting hung over England throughout 1649. On the one hand lay dissident radicals, frustrated at the failure of political revolution to usher in social reform; but their challenge could be contained, however much the newspapers detailed Digger claims and Leveller and soldier unrest. On the other lay Charles Stuart, looking to avenge his father through Scotland and Ireland, and hopeful too of support in English centres of disaffected clericalism like London and Lancashire. Month after month, journalists related the doings of the Confederate Irish, military preparations in Scotland, the plans and movements of the young Charles, and the lamentations of pulpit orators. Early in March one reported, 'The Presbyterians and the Cavaliers do unite and join together in Scotland, that they may be better able to make another bloody war in England'; a fortnight later another warned of 'thousands of inconveniences' when malcontents 'are supported by persuasions out of the pulpit, as they have been too forward in doing in and about London'; Parliament's act for a general fast on 23 April spoke of the danger of backsliding into the abyss of renewed war; and the following month Lord General Fairfax's declaration to his soldiers as he prepared to lead them to Burford against the Levellers warned similarly of the possibility of another civil war.[28] When Milton opened *Eikonoklastes* by denouncing the efforts of those who sought 'now the third time' – a reference to the civil wars of 1642–6 and 1648 – 'to corrupt and disorder the minds of weaker men', and thus to deprive the nation of a settlement so nearly achieved and so sorely needed, he came close to paraphrasing the loyal address offered to Fairfax that March by the regiment of the regicide Richard Deane.[29] And when, throughout

[25] Not only did he ostentatiously echo the king's remorse for Strafford's death; he also ranked Charles I the most 'virtuous and sufficient prince known in the world', having, as he put it, 'had time to consider all the images of all the greatest and virtuous princes in the world'. *The Kingdoms faithfull and impartiall Scout*, 9–16 March 1648/9, pp. 44–5.

[26] *Perfect Occurrences*, 16–23 March 1648/9, p. 909; *CPWJM 3*, p. 342.

[27] *Eikon Alethine. The Pourtraiture of Truths most sacred Majesty truly suffering*, p. 1. This work came into Thomason's hands in late August 1649.

[28] *The Kingdoms faithfull Scout*, 23 Feb.–2 March 1648/9, p. 33; *The Kingdoms faithfull and impartiall Scout*, 9–16 March 1648/9, p. 49 (mispaginated); C. H. Firth and R. S. Rait, *Acts and Ordinances of the Interregnum 1642–1660* (3 vols., 1911), II, 79–81; *Perfect Occurrences*, 11–18 May 1649, pp. 1040–1.

[29] *CPWJM 3*, p. 338; *Perfect Diurnall*, 12–19 March 1648/9, p. 2375.

Eikonoklastes, Milton coupled tyranny and idolatry, kingship and superstition, as the twin evils of Charles's rule and book, he echoed Parliament's
act for a general fast, which lamented the nation's 'endeavour to relapse
into that former condition of tyranny and superstition'.[30]

The looming political instability of 1649 thus formed not only the context
but also the occasion of *Eikonoklastes*. The crisis determined many of
Milton's gestures. None of these are more celebrated than his attempt to
explode the pose of royal martyrdom adopted in the frontispiece of *Eikon
Basilike*, and the charge of idolatry he levels against the royalists in the
very title of *Eikonoklastes*. These were common themes in pro-government
argument in the early months of 1649. One radical newspaper the week
after the axe fell opened with the words, 'not death, but the cause, makes
a martyr; and who can be more unfortunate than he that is most
wicked?'[31] Another began by emphatically linking kings and idols.[32] Those
devices were soon tied to a third, the king's book, for the author of
Eikon Alethine, who preceded Milton in the controversy, opened with the
observation, 'I found an idol-worship crept in amongst you, and saw you
adoring the counterfeit portraiture of one you sometimes knew no saint.'[33]
If Milton is often castigated by historians for the lack of originality in his
political thought, the same charge might be turned against his rhetoric.
Both emerged from a crisis which preoccupied the entire political nation.

Recognition that some of Milton's arguments paralleled those used
elsewhere does not have to initiate a hunt for his borrowings. Rather, the
fact that he shared political and rhetorical ground with others suggests
the unwisdom of privileging either the biographical or the literary in any
analysis. Milton delighted in presenting himself as a voice in the wilderness,
and in the case of the divorce tracts or some of the late works such a
claim was certainly tenable. But in 1649 he occupied a recognisable
political position. Recognition of that fact suggests the plausibility of asking
of *Eikonoklastes* questions scholars normally ask of other persuasive – but not
always Miltonic – texts, questions about possible strategies and audiences.

Milton's previous controversial offering had of course been *The Tenure
of Kings and Magistrates*, a defence of the army's revolution of December
1648. While concerning himself with the general issue of the grounds of
political authority, Milton had aimed above all at the Presbyterian clergy;
not only had he carefully selected his sources from the Presbyterians'
canon, but he had closed with a long excoriation of clerical self-interest,

---

[30] Firth and Rait, *Acts and Ordinances*, II, 80.

[31] *The Moderate*, 30 Jan.–6 Feb. 1648/9, p. 285. The riposte was surely occasioned by the Christic claims
made by the royalists even in advance of *Eikon Basilike*; see, for example, *Mercurius Pragmaticus*, 23–30 Jan.
1648/9, sig. Hhhh2.

[32] *Perfect Occurrences*, 2–9 Feb. 1648/9, p. 821; cf. the letter in another paper the previous week which had
applauded the judicial proceedings 'against their head, or rather idol': *The Moderate*, 23–30 Jan. 1648/9, p. 283.

[33] *Eikon Alethine*, preface; see also *CPWJM 3*, p. 149. As others have noticed, there are a number of similarities
in wording and argument between this work and Milton's.

hypocrisy and tyranny. For, in the eyes of so many of the new regime's supporters, it was the Presbyterian clergy, with their shibboleth of the Solemn League and Covenant of 1643, who had destroyed the parliamentarian coalition in late 1648; and it was certainly the protests of the London clergy which had in January 1649 mounted the most alarming challenge to the trial of the king, and which in the spring continued to unnerve the Rump.[34] Blair Worden has demonstrated in detail the political impact in the Rump Parliament of fears of a Presbyterian backlash.[35] Such fears are written across the newspapers of these months, and they condition the *Eikon Alethine* too, a tract whose opening words – 'Having with much amazement seen many before well affected persons lately at a stand, if not in a trembling and retrograde motion' – testify graphically to the misgivings generated by revolution even amongst the godly.[36] It would have been surprising had Milton entirely forgotten the audience he had intended for *The Tenure*. And indeed, *Eikonoklastes* contains some very visible gestures in that direction. Milton's own scorn for the Presbyterian clergy was probably even greater than the king's, so that group could only have found cold comfort in Milton's reminders of the contempt for Presbyterianism revealed in the king's book.[37] Yet Milton also inserts a number of gratuitous, and much less harsh, nods in the direction of the Scots,[38] nods which suggest a very real concern to drive a wedge into the anti-Rump alliance which threatened to overwhelm all that had been fought for. In the spring and summer of 1649 it evidently seemed most feasible, or more likely most urgent,[39] to detach the Scottish Covenanters from that alliance: Charles 'would persuade the Scots that their chief interest consists in their fidelity to the Crown. But true policy will teach them to find a safer interest in the common friendship of England than in the ruins of one ejected family.'[40]

---

[34] *A Serious Representation of the Judgements of Ministers within the Province of London* (1648/9); *An Apologeticall Declaration of the Conscientious Presbyterians of London* (1648/9). The former excited a large number of replies, while the latter was widely dispersed in the country, and was reported to have been associated with a clerical campaign for forcible resistance. *The Kingdomes faithfull Scout*, 26 Jan.–2 Feb. 1648/9, pp. 1–2, 8. Parliament issued an order on 28 March against clerical meddling in politics, and in the following weeks was preparing punitive action: see especially *Perfect Diurnall*, 26 Mar.–2 April 1649, p. 2395, and 9–16 Apr. 1649, p. 2434.

[35] Worden, *The Rump Parliament*.

[36] *Eikon Alethine*, preface; this continues urgently, 'religion lies at the stake, as well as liberty.... The Presbyter and the Independent in this cause are like Hypocrates' twins, they must live and die together; yea, let our Levellers call to mind how the Curiatii, standing close together, were too strong for the three adverse combatants.'

[37] See especially the peroration with which Milton closes his chapter on Parliament's forcing of Presbyterian chaplains onto the king: 'O ye ministers, ye pluralists, whose lips preserve not knowledge, but the way ever open to your bellies, read here what work he makes among your wares, your galley pots, your balms and cordials in print, and not only your sweet sippets in widows' houses, but the huge gobbets wherewith he charges you to have devoured houses and all.... Cry him up for a saint in your pulpits, while he cries you down for atheists into Hell.' *CPWJM 3*, p. 553.

[38] See, for example, *CPWJM 3*, pp. 360, 366, 385, 445–6, 478, 546–7, 580–1.

[39] See D. Hirst, 'The English Republic and the Meaning of Britain', *Journal of Modern History*, 66 (1994), 451–86, for consideration of English attitudes to Scotland, and particularly of apprehensions of renewed war in 1649.

[40] *CPWJM 3*, p. 493.

A Miltonic appeal to Presbyterians was, by the late 1640s, bound to be an odd affair. But the divergence between the addresses to the London clergy and the addresses to the Scots is scarcely the most remarkable of the discordances in Milton's text. More striking is the discrepancy – and the political implications of the discrepancy – between Milton's chapters contesting the king's political narrative and those confronting the king's ecclesiastical claims. In the former, Milton appears as historian, political analyst, advocate, and in such guise could readily have found common ground with Presbyterians who had, after all, been part of the parliamentarian coalition which had in the war years rejected the king's claims. But when he came to challenge the king's chapters on the Covenant, on the liturgy, on Church-government, he entered what was clearly to him religious controversy; rather than alleging the historical record, he turned to scriptural warrant. And with Christian freedom his goal, the enemy now was the Presbyterians as much as the king.

There is a further, and much more important, political singularity in Milton's rhetorical stance. The author of *Eikon Alethine* had the Presbyterians as much in his sights as did Milton; yet he handled the problem of responsibility for the king's book in a very different manner. As convinced as was Milton that *Eikon Basilike* was not the king's ghostly testimony but in fact ghost-written by a cleric, the earlier controversialist used that assumption to free the king personally from the worst of his invective, reserving that for clerical forgers and royalist schemers. While perfectly happy to denounce these himself, Milton loses few opportunities to deride Charles directly as well.

Scholars have sometimes commented on the civility with which Milton the controversialist handles the king;[41] and it is true that if the comparison is made with the targets of Milton's other polemical exercises, Charles Stuart is let off lightly. But if the comparison is with other writings about the dead king in 1649 – which treated his person with considerable respect – there is no mistaking Milton's unusual vehemence. Denounced as a tyrant, typed as that 'man of blood' and the little horn of the beast Charles certainly was. While still alive, and a threat, he was indeed also derided. The week before the opening of the proceedings in Westminster Hall, one radical newspaper could report, 'The great court-fly of the nation is this week flown from Windsor to London, in order to his trial.' Once dead, the human as opposed to the political Charles Stuart was left relatively unbefouled. A fairly typical distinction was that of Solicitor-General Cook in the immediate aftermath of the execution: 'Concerning myself, I bear no more malice to the man's person than I do to my dear father. But I hate that cursed principle of tyranny that has so long lodged

---

[41] See especially Corns, *Uncloistered Virtue*, pp. 204–8.

and harboured within him . . .'[42] The reasons for such scrupulousness seem clear enough – with power gained and the king dead, the regicides and their allies had to reunite the country, or at least a viable part of it. To that end they had to present themselves as driven by principle rather than passion and personality – all the more so given the remarkable appeal of Charles's conduct in his last days, and the refraction of that conduct through the *Eikon Basilike*. Even radical newsmongers seem to have sensed the dangers in kicking the king's corpse.[43]

Measured against such a backdrop, the sheer contempt Milton shows for a king who plagiarised his prayers from a work of profane fiction, who 'thought no better of the living God than of a buzzard idol', to be worshipped only with 'polluted orts and refuse', is breathtaking. Time and again Milton spurns his enemy. He insistently casts Charles as thief and plagiarist; he mocks his marriage; he questions the extent of his vocabulary; he brutally spells out the application of Naboth's curse; he likens the king in the House of Commons in 1642 to 'some vulture in the mountains'; he repeatedly derides the spiritual bankruptcy of a man apparently unable to pray for himself.[44] It is easy to see why Milton came so close to the scaffold's steps in 1660. It is less easy to see the political reasons for the course he took in 1649. When Presbyterians were turning votaries in the growing cult of Charles the saint and martyr, what was to be gained from scorning rather than simply confronting this cult?

The answer lies in the complexity of the context as well as of Milton's objectives. Although peculiarities in his argument are sometimes too readily attributed to the dynamics of biography and the drive of his remarkable ego, Milton's enduring concerns cannot be eliminated from any topical analysis. As he showed repeatedly – and perhaps most revealingly in the extravagant portraits of the worthies of the English republic that conclude the *Second Defence* of 1654 – virtue was central to Milton's conception of political health. The converse was of course equally true: where there was political disintegration there must be sin. The political disintegration of 1648, after the high hopes of the earlier years of the war, gave rise in Milton to a fierce conviction of the presence of sin, in the English nation as a whole as it lusted after its idol-king and, above all, in that king himself. But that is scarcely the whole story. The protestations of royal

---

[42] *The Moderate*, 16–23 Jan. 1648/9, p. 261; Muddiman, *Trial of Charles I*, p. 256.

[43] This is not to deny that some Fifth Monarchy men were soon to exult in the death of the king; but the overwhelming majority of radicals spoke only in more general terms, of the fall of the old powers in the English polity.

[44] *CPWJM* 3, pp. 364, 528, 547, 393, 439, 366, 548–53. The allegations of plagiarism, theft and spiritual bankruptcy are too numerous to particularise further; see also Zwicker, 'The King's Head and the Politics of Literary Property'. It should be noted that the charge of spiritual incapacity was not infrequently levelled against formalist Anglicans – see, for example, the report of Bishop Juxon's silence after he was barred from using the Common Prayer Book at Charles's funeral: 'the doctor . . . could say nothing without book'. *Perfect Occurrences*, 9–16 Feb. 1648/9, p. 838.

piety that close every chapter of *Eikon Basilike*, and the martyr-cult they fostered, surely excited in a personality as combative as Milton's a determination to negate, to destroy, to annihilate. There are, however, strategic reasons too for the dissections of Charles's motives and the insistence on his personal delinquency. In *Eikonoklastes* Milton had on the one hand the important but relatively straightforward purpose of recounting the history of the years from 1640 to 1648 so dazzlingly glossed by the king's book. But in a work commissioned in the spring of 1649 Milton had also to encompass the task that Parliament had set itself in its 'large declaration' of March – justifying in the most delicate of circumstances the events of recent months. Milton could not have been unaware of the considerations which moved other partisans of the regime to speak only to the cause and not of the king; and as he showed in his opening gestures, he was also scarcely immune to calculations of honour. But whatever his reasoning, while he chose not to turn his readers' gaze directly to the regicide, the deepening crisis did determine Milton to confront Charles's aura as well as his history by laying bare his motives.

Despite the few words he expended in 1649 on either trial or execution, Milton became in fact an eager participant in that drama. In the introduction to *Eikonoklastes*, Milton sets the stage for a forensic encounter when he insists

> he who at the bar stood excepting against the form and manner of his judicature, and complained that he was not heard, neither he nor his friends shall have that cause now to find fault; being met and debated with in this open and monumental court of his own erecting; and not only heard uttering his whole mind at large, but answered.[45]

By refusing to acknowledge the high court of justice, Charles had deprived himself of the opportunity to present a climactic defence of his rule and his role. The enforced silence certainly frustrated him, as his ineffectual protests in Westminster Hall showed; that it frustrated others may be inferred from the prompt publication of his alleged lament at the breach of the Newport negotiations by the army revolution of December 1648, of his protest (which 'I intended to speak in Westminster Hall, on Monday 22 January, but against reason was hindered') against the jurisdiction of the high court, as well as publication of the charge that the Commonwealth's solicitor-general, John Cook, was to have delivered if the trial had run its full course.[46] But the commissioning of *Eikonoklastes* suggests that it was not simply vanity, and exasperation at a lost opportunity for professional glory which drew Cook into print. As Milton recognised, *Eikon Basilike* had become the rebuttal that Charles had been unable to present in a

---

[45] *CPWJM 3*, p. 341.
[46] *His Majesty's Declaration concerning the Treaty*, acquired by Thomason on 1 Feb. 1648/9; for Charles's protest and for Cook's intended speech, acquired by Thomason on 9 February, see Muddiman, *Trial of Charles I*, pp. 231–2, 233–60.

court he did not recognise, a court he now sought posthumously to evade by appealing to another tribunal: 'making new appeal to truth and the world', he had made his book his 'best advocate and interpreter'.[47] *Eikonoklastes* is the counter-argument, before that same 'open and monumental court'. But there is a further encounter, for *Eikon Basilike* has itself become part of the case against the king, and Milton seeks time and again to condemn Charles with the evidence of his own newly published words. Confronting the king's reflections on the Irish Revolt, Milton observes, 'of his good affection to the rebels this chapter itself is not without witness'. Indeed, the king's book has become his '*Doomsday Book*; not like that of William the Norman his predecessor, but the record and memorial of his condemnation; and discovers whatever hath befallen him to have been hastened on from divine justice by the rash and inconsiderate appeal of his own lips'.[48] The eagerness with which Milton impugns Charles's motives, pursuing the charges of plagiarism and blasphemy, determinedly underscoring Charles's impenitence, shows that for Milton, as for Cook and doubtless for many more, the trial had not ended in January.

Those scholars who have highlighted the unmistakable literary gestures in *Eikonoklastes*, and Milton's engagement with poetic fiction in *Eikon Basilike*, to establish the significance of this text for Milton's career[49] have overlooked what is surely its most frequent note. 'Justice' and its variants – 'judge', 'judgement' – recur as a virtual litany throughout,[50] as Milton pleads in this second trial. Observing that the king had been so involved in the attempt on the five members in 1642 'as to do the office of a searcher [which] argued in him no great aversation from shedding blood', Milton continues in the highest of lawyerly tones,[51] 'we insist rather upon what was actual than what was probable'. Confronting the king's opening assertion of affection for parliaments, he sarcastically observes, 'in the judgement of wise men, by laying the foundation of his defence on the avouchment of that which is so manifestly untrue, he hath given a worse foil to his own cause than when his whole forces were at any time overthrown.'[52] But it is in the momentous matter of the origins of the Irish Revolt that the forensic nature of Milton's approach becomes clearest.

---

[47] *CPWJM 3*, p. 340.

[48] *CPWJM 3*, pp. 478, 382.

[49] See the works listed in n. 3 above for citations to the abundant recent scholarship.

[50] This though Milton repeatedly condemned the author of *Eikon Basilike* for repetition, for the 'dream and tautology' of the king's insistence on his rectitude and on 'conscience, honour and reason': 'Of these repetitions I find no end': see, for example, *CPWJM 3*, pp. 456, 466, 469.

[51] This is not of course to suggest that Milton sees himself as a practiser of the English common law. As always Milton demonstrated a studied ambivalence towards the law. At one juncture he refers to others 'the more lawyerly mooting of this point, which is neither my element, nor my proper work here'; at another he notes that the position at which the king aims is 'so unlike the law of England, which lawyers say is the quintessence of reason and mature wisdom', that it must be a usurpation. 'Thus much to the law of it, by a better evidence than rolls and records, reason.' *CPWJM 3*, pp. 403, 409.

[52] *CPWJM 3*, pp. 440, 355.

Pointing to the evidence that Charles had given his commission to the rebels, Milton declaims loftily, 'against all which testimonies, likelihoods, evidences, and apparent actions of his own, being so abundant, his bare denial, though with imprecation, can no way countervail; and least of all in his own cause'. The king's own account Milton finds poor pleading – 'He falls next to flashes, and a multitude of words, in all which is contained no more than what might be the plea of any guiltiest offender.' Indeed, 'if the whole Irishry of Rebels had fee'd some advocate to speak partially and sophistically in their defence, he could have hardly dazzled better.'[53]

Milton's strenuous disclaimers in the introduction point only too clearly to his literary competition with the king's book; and he was, as we have seen, engaged in a struggle to undo its political effects. Yet he also saw himself standing at the bar – at the bar not only of the conscience of good men in 1649 but also of history. 'Allegations, not reasons are the main contents of [the king's] book; and need no more than other contrary allegations to lay the question before all men in an even balance.'[54] Milton's conviction, declared from the outset, that posterity would quite literally be passing verdict, is nowhere more explicit than in the judicial setting he gives his comments on the episode at Hull in 1642, when Sir John Hotham – whom Parliament later executed with his son for treachery – had barred the gates against the king. Charles's reflections on Hotham's conduct invite Milton's castigation of the unjust judge who repeatedly 'returns back to give sentence' on Hotham,

with a repeated condemnation, though dead long since. It was ill that somebody stood not near to whisper him that a reiterating judge is worse than a tormentor. . . . What knew he of after times, who, while he sits judging and censuring without end the fate of that unhappy father and his son at Tower Hill, knew not that the like fate attended him . . . and as little knew whether after times reserve not a greater infamy to the story of his own life and reign.[55]

And whereas *Eikon Basilike* closes emotively with Charles's meditations on death, Milton's responding chapter offers a long paean to justice, 'the strength, the kingdom, the power and majesty of all ages', set even above truth: 'Truth resigns all her outward strength to justice; justice therefore must needs be strongest, both in her own and in the strength of truth.'[56] 'Justice', justice upon 'the chief actors in the last war', had of course been the watchword of the army and its allies in Parliament through the autumn and winter of 1648–9;[57] and, after the sitting of the high court of justice,

[53] *Ibid.*, pp. 477, 478.

[54] *Ibid.*, p. 346.

[55] *Ibid.*, pp. 431–2.

[56] *Ibid.*, pp. 583–6, esp. 585.

[57] See, for example, *Perfect Diurnall*, 29 Jan.–5 Feb. 1648/9, p. 2318, or the opening of the editorial in *Perfect Occurrences*, 9–16 Feb. 1648/9, p. 833, 'That execution of law is just . . .'

justice became a matter for the most urgent contestation with the royalists.[58] Milton's closing insistence on the cosmic reach of justice only underscores the immediacy of his present concerns.

Historians who approach a text which others fold into a 'literary' canon often do so with the intention of contextualising in a fairly conventional fashion, of showing how contemporary issues and events shadowed its themes and arguments. But if instead they were to regard such texts as truly controversial – that is, embedded in, forming part of, the sediment of engagement and debate in a political culture not yet drawn into the post-Romantic separation of 'culture' from 'politics' – they might arrive at more complicated, and thus more accurate, readings. Truly to contextualise is to attend not simply to the text and its echoes of and in other writings, but also to the resonances of its tone and pitch; it is to attend as well to what is not textual, to the absences whose significance only a wide reading can determine. Such an approach may shift the focus from Milton's engagement with literary and dramatic fiction, which has preoccupied scholars, to his engagement with that drama in the courtroom which so preoccupied contemporaries. It will surely provide a more sensitive register for Milton's language of justice and kingship, the two themes central to *Eikonoklastes*. It may also add yet another dimension – that of pleader at the bar of history – to Milton's complex self-presentations.

---

[58] Thus, the younger Charles Stuart's proclamation from Amsterdam denounced the 'unjust trial' and execution of Charles I 'without law and justice', and warned, 'let them expect and prepare themselves to hear of the alarms of justice . . . my cause is balanced with justice': *Kingdoms faithfull and impartiall Scout*, 2–9 March 1648/9; compare the opening clarion of *Perfect Occurrences*, 9–16 Feb. 1648/9, p. 833, 'That execution of law is just . . .'

The Dissemination of the King

Marshall Grossman

> He who writes himself martyr by his own inscription is like an
> ill painter who, by writing on the shapeless picture which he
> hath drawn, is fain to tell passengers what shape it is, which
> else no man could imagine.[1]

The beheading of Charles Stuart on 30 January, 1649 was in theory and
in practice a punctual act. Marking a full stop to the reign, it attempted
also to excise the support given by the king's body to his role in the
symbolic economy of the monarchy. The necessity of such support may
be gauged by the anxiety that accompanies moments of monarchical
succession and the tradition according to which, in normal circumstances,
the heir is immediately elevated to the mystery of state on the death of
the incumbent king: 'the king is dead, long live the king'. In January
1649, the accession of Charles II was foreclosed by armed force, and the
judicial proceedings to which the king had been subjected underlined the
fact that it was the throne itself and not strictly the identity of its occupant
that had been put in question. The collapse in practical fact of the symbolic
system according to which the king embodies the state might be expected
to enable the rapid emergence of a new republican discourse which would
abruptly terminate and displace the prolonged struggle over whether kingship was, as the divine right royalists would have it, essential and thus
an attribute peculiar to the king's person, or, as reformers like Samuel
Rutherford argued, constitutional and thus a position established in and
posterior to law.[2] But beyond even this strategic goal stood another, more

---

[1] *The Complete Prose Works of John Milton*, gen. ed. Don M. Wolfe (8 vols., New Haven, 1953–82), III,
575. Subsequent references to Milton's prose are to this edition and will be given parenthetically with the
abbreviation CP.

[2] The divine right position is succinctly stated in James I's 'SPEECH TO BOTH HOUSES OF PARLIAMENT DELIVERED
IN THE GREAT CHAMBER AT WHITE-HALL, The Last Day of March 1607': 'For you all know that *Rex est lex
loquens*; And you have oft heard me say, that the King's will and intention, being the speaking law, ought to
be *Luce clarius* . . .,' in *The Political Works of James I*, reprinted from the edition of 1616, with an intro. by
Charles Howard McIlwain, Harvard Political Classics, vol. 1 (Cambridge, Mass., 1918), p. 291. James's word
order is strategically reversed in Samuel Rutherford's title, *Lex, Rex: The Law and the Prince. A Dispute for the
just Prerogative of King and People. Containing the* Reasons *and* Courses *of the most necessary Defensive Wars of the
Kingdom of Scotland, and of their Expedition for the aid and help of their dear Brethren of England* (1644). The constitutional
origins of monarchy are reiterated throughout Rutherford's tract; for example: 'Princedom, empire, kingdom,
or jurisdiction hath its rise from a positive and secondary law of nations, and not from the law of pure nature'
(p. 3); Monarchy 'is not by divine right, but *de jure genium*, by the law of nations' (p. 6); and 'The king by
nature is not king . . . he must be king by a politic constitution and law, and so the law in that consideration
is above the king, because it is from a civil law, that there is a king, rather any other kind of governor' (p.
231). On James I's 'projection of the self into language and of language into print' as speaking law, see
Richard Helgerson, 'Milton Reads the King's Book: Print, Performance, and the Making of a Bourgeois Idol',
Criticism, 29 (1987), 5–8; the quoted phrase appears on p. 5.

far-reaching outcome. Charles's refusal to recognise the court attests to his understanding that its assertion of the authority of the magistrate over the hereditary prince would not only challenge his person but also empty the sceptre of its meaning and open the larger question of whether even the law could logically establish a king; beyond the question of Charles Stuart's behaviour stood the question of whether any king could rule within the law, of whether republicanism was the inevitable conclusion of legislative supremacy.[3]

By irreversibly removing from the political stage the king's 'body natural', physical custody of which had for several years been a significant element in contemporary politics, the regicide offered what might be termed a pro-verbial argument to deprive its opponents of the very vocabulary of monarchy and to force contemporary discourse in the direction of a conceptual as opposed to an embodied understanding of the state. Such an understanding would view the king's power as, like that of the magistrate, the power to implement existing law, and would thus break decisively with the vestiges of an older notion which understood the law to emanate from the creative power of the king, who, as God's regent, embodied the state.[4] Thus with the act of regicide a set of words (*proverbium*), the discourse of republicanism, is thrust decisively onto the stage of London's political theatre.[5]

With the second Charles Stuart effectively off the scene, the regicide *performed* the reduction of kingship to concept by acting it out in the theatre of the real, rendering it a *fait accompli*.[6] However, the removal of the king's body was necessarily accompanied by a certain rhetoric; the struggle to control the disposition of that rhetoric demonstrates that the removal of the king as the embodiment of law and nation was an event of more difficulty and duration than might have been expected. After the seemingly decisive stroke that separated the royal head and body, a series of textual

---

[3] For a useful discussion of the disruption of the symbolic system implied by putting the monarch on trial, see Slavoj Žižek, *For they know not what they do: Enjoyment as a Political Factor* (1991), pp. 80–4.

[4] See for example Rutherford, p. 60: 'The power of all the Parliament was never given to the king, by God, the Parliament are as essentially judges as the king, and therefore the king's deed may as well be revoked, because he acteth nothing as a king; but united with his greater or lesser council, no more then the eye can see, being separated from the body.' Rutherford goes on to isolate and discredit as metaphoric the alternative etiologies that view kingly power as essentially creative, challenging in turn its derivation from that of the father over the child (pp. 11–12), that of a husband over his wife (p. 125) and that of the head over the body (p. 128).

[5] The theatrical details of the trial are described in Derek Hirst, 'The Drama of Justice', above.

[6] Royalist hopes attached to the intermittent activities of Charles II in Scotland were dashed on 3 September 1651 when Cromwell caught up with Charles's Scots at Worcester. It is an indication of the weakness of these hopes, even in the period between the execution and the battle of Worcester, that the regicide pamphlets on both sides show a notable lack of interest in the second Charles Stuart, preferring instead to continue the struggle over his father's body in the form of a struggle to inscribe the royal image: either martyr or tyrant. The way in which the absent king dominates the stage, foreclosing even the imaginary accession of his son, is further evidence of the seriousness of the regicide as a disruption of the symbolic economy. The image of the revenant king suspends the monarchy between two deaths, that of his body and that of his symbolic presence, and this impedes the movement of the son to the symbolic position of the father.

and iconic restagings of the king's death immediately supplied and prolonged Charles's presence, displacing the contested custody of the living king into a textual struggle over the staging of the regicide; this polemical conflict was, substantially, one last battle to control the body of the king. Whatever its immediate effects on the levers of government, the regicide failed in its attempt to supplant discourse by transcendent action. With or without the living body of the king, the habit of embodying power in the royal presence turned out to have always been a discursive problem, requiring ultimately a textual resolution. As Hirst suggests, the *Eikon Basilike* became the defence of royalty that Charles could not offer at the trial without becoming first a *de facto* subject.

Contemporary accounts confirm that the king's presence on the scaffold was dignified, in the view of his supporters, royal.[7] On the day of the execution a printed inscription of this royal image had already been prepared: *Eikon Basilike: The Portraiture of His Sacred Majesty in His Solitudes and Sufferings*.[8]

Because of the tremendous success of the *Eikon Basilike* in supplying as it were the absent body of the king, and because of the prestige Milton would later acquire as a canonical poet, it is tempting to imagine the textual staging of the king's death as an encounter between Milton and Charles, *Eikon Basilike* and *Eikonoklastes*. An only slightly broader view of the 'staging' and 'counter-staging' of the death of the king brings into focus two very different, yet inextricably entwined, aspects of the production of *Eikonoklastes*, one broadly historical, the other properly literary.

The first of these is the urgent polemical struggle over the regicide, beginning with the sale of the *Eikon Basilike* immediately following the execution. To characterise this context I will refer briefly to four pamphlets, which, along with the king's book, make up what we might term the '*Eikon*' series: the anonymous *Eikon Alethine*, an early republican response to the king's book; the *Eikon e pistes*, a royalist rejoinder to the *Eikon Alethine*; Milton's 'authorised' response; and the *Eikon Aklastos*, Joseph Jane's unsigned attack on *Eikonoklastes*. This polemical exchange, extending from January 1649 to 1651, is one theatre in which the textually preserved aspect of the struggle, either to keep or repudiate the king's body is played

---

[7] For a useful account of contemporary reactions to the staging of the execution, see Nancy Klein Maguire, 'The Theatrical Mask/Masque of Politics: The Case of Charles I', *Journal of British Studies*, 28 (1989), 1–22. Patricia Fumerton offers a fascinatingly detailed account of the theatricality of Charles's last acts in *Cultural Aesthetics: Renaissance Literature and the Practice of Social Ornament* (Chicago and London, 1991), pp. 1–28.

[8] Except where otherwise noted, I quote the modern edition, *Eikon Basilike: The Portraiture of His Sacred Majesty in His Solitudes and Sufferings*, ed. Philip A. Knachel, published for The Folger Shakespeare Library (Ithaca, 1966). References will be given parenthetically with the abbreviation EB. Details of the book's astonishing sales and consequently large number of editions are collected in Francis F. Madan, *A New Bibliography of the Eikon Basilike*, Oxford Bibliographical Society Publications, n.s., 3 (1949). See also Robert Wilcher, 'What was the King's Book for?: The Evolution of *Eikon Basilike*', *Yearbook of English Studies*, 21 (1991), 219–28.

out, and presumably, it is the immediate context in which Milton would have situated his efforts.[9]

The broad purpose of this chronology of regicide polemics is to bring into view a literary historical event that encloses the political events in which Milton's regicide tract was produced; to seek in the interplay of these pamphlets and the pressure of the events over which they contend the historical trace of a far-reaching encounter with the functional and ideological limits of representation as it had been accepted in the Aristotelian understanding of the Renaissance, and something of the etiology of the appearance – theoretically in *Eikonoklastes* and practically in *Paradise Lost* – of an anti-mimetic displacement of representation into *articulation*. This displacement involves a shift away from the understanding of language as a set of relations between words and things and towards an understanding of language as a set of relations among words.[10] Thus I want to suggest some of the rhetorical ways in which, under an immediate and urgent pressure to break the royal image, Milton, engaging a much broader and more profound drift away from representation, undermines not just the royal image but the connection between words and iconic representation to which he alludes in the remarks used for my epigraph. My larger interest, then, is to begin to view *Eikonoklastes* – in exemplary fashion – as at once a literary historical event broadly participating in and articulating a growing seventeenth-century scepticism towards the assumption that language *represents* – that words *stand for* – things and also a highly determined biographical event in Milton's development towards the moment when he would culminate his self-consciously crafted career with the publication of a play, 'never intended for the stage', at the climax of which his protagonist brings the theatre down on himself and his audience.[11]

Admittedly this is a larger claim about the literary and intellectual history of the seventeenth century than can be adequately supported in a

---

[9] Because Thomason did not collect the *Eikon Aklastos* and no datable information other than the year 1651 appears on the British Library and Folger copies, I am unable to state a more precise terminal date for the series. It should also be noted that my group of representative pamphlets does not exhaust the field of regicide tracts. My selection is governed by the fact that this group represents a compact portion of the field in which each succeeding pamphlet is significantly conscious of its predecessors and on the not at all trivial appearance of the word *Eikon* in the title of each tract, signalling that the debate engaged turns on the issue of an image.

[10] My discussion of the distinction between representation and articulation is indebted to Samuel Weber, *Return to Freud: Jacques Lacan's Dislocation of Psychoanalysis*, trans. Michael Levine (Cambridge, 1991), pp. 27–37 and passim. As will be shown by the discussion of *Paradise Lost* below, the phenomenon to which I refer is both broader and more specific than the transumptive allusiveness ascribed to Milton by Harold Bloom in *A Map of Misreading* (Oxford, 1975), pp. 126–43: broader because it puts in question the possibility of writing otherwise, and more specific because it positively obstructs the visual imagination.

[11] On Milton's early sense of himself as having a career see Leah Marcus, 'Milton as Historical Subject', *Milton Quarterly*, 25 (Oct., 1991), 120–7. Mary Ann Radzinowicz argues the case for seeing *Samson Agonistes* as the culmination of a long progress in *Toward Samson Agonistes: The Growth of Milton's Mind* (Princeton, 1978). On the iconoclastic import of the destruction of Dagon's temple, see Ernest Gilman, *Iconoclasm and Poetry in the English Reformation: Down Went Dagon* (Chicago, 1986), pp. 149–77.

brief essay on the regicide pamphlets. I advance it here as a speculation, intended to provoke and stimulate rather than to persuade. Whether or not it achieves that end will depend on its adequacy as a reading of the regicide pamphlets and, in turn, the support that reading may offer for the argument about *Paradise Lost* with which I will close.

I take it as given that all historical events are overdetermined. The present speculation is an attempt to move slowly forward in what proves to be a difficult problem of literary history; that is, to understand how contingent determinants like the constraints of the regicide controversy may have collaborated with or contributed to larger historical determinants (changes in land and labour valuation, for example) to bring about a literary historical event. In such a construction of literary history, 'Milton's purposes', which Hirst quite properly wishes not to see superciliously 'folded into a literary canon', emerge as key moments in the constitution of an event whose occurrence and consequences are both literary and historical.

The '*Eikon*' pamphlets may be divided into two groups according to some superficial but highly significant features. The earlier set, the *Eikon Basilike*, the *Eikon Alethine* and the *Eikon e pistes* all begin with an engraved frontispiece facing the title page.[12] The title pages feature the title in Greek centred at the top of the page, followed by an elaborate, explanatory English subtitle. Moreover the frontispiece of each of the first three texts refers sceptically to the frontispiece in the volume against which it is directed. Thus in a manner reminiscent of Hamlet's *Mousetrap*, each of these texts is preceded by a 'dumb show', that compresses its action into a mime intended to represent the inner truth of an action already familiar to its spectators.

As we might expect of a work called *Eikonoklastes*, Milton's volume omits the pictorial frontispiece. More interestingly, it also forgoes the translation of its own title, while repeating the translation of the king's: *Eikonoklastes, in Answer to a Book Entitled Eikon Basilike, The Portraiture of His Sacred Majesty in His Solitudes and Sufferings*. The volume is signed with Milton's initials ('The Author I. M.') and, in obvious contrast to the others, bears the legend 'Published by Authority', above the printer's name. The *Eikon Aklastos* resumes the scheme of Greek head and explanatory English sub-head but lacks an engraving. Its perspicacious (if tedious) rebuttal follows Milton's text in its move away from a struggle over the king's body and

---

[12] All published in London in 1649. The *Eikon Basilike*, by virtue of its unprecedented sales, exists in a wide variety of forms. The earliest issue, published by Royston, and bearing the old-style date 1648, did not include the engraving by William Marshall, which, in a variety of versions, became standard on later editions and to which Milton refers in *Eikonoklastes*. The physical descriptions of the front matter to *Eikon Basilike* included in this essay are based on the third issue of the first edition, printed by William Duggard in March 1649 and, for the first time, including the Expostulations and Prayers of the King and the *Apopthegmata* (no. 22 in Madan's listing), which I examined (along with other editions) in the Folger Library. For detailed descriptions of the various issues of the *Eikon Basilike*, see Madan.

towards an argument in which kingship is conceptually determined and structurally undermined.[13]

Thus three of the five volumes proceed from image to Greek head, to explanation, to text: a fourfold self-inscription. Milton's text alone proceeds from title to text, forgoing this preliminary self-articulation in favour of an unmediated movement to the king's title; it announces itself as the 'image breaker' and then names the portrait of the king as the image to be broken. The significance of this difference may be clarified by unpacking the articulations of title, icon and text in the other pamphlets in the series.

Since it set something of a conventional standard for the polemics that followed, the physical presentation of the *Eikon Basilike* is worthy of note. As the volume's subtitle unfolds the 'Royal Portrait' of the title's vaguely iconic Greek letters into English (plate 18), the text unfolds in a chronological series of meditations and reflections supposedly inscribed by the king on his several years' progress to the scaffold – the royal martyr iconographically established in the frontispiece.[14]

It is this doubly staged inscription of the royal image to which Milton refers when he complains of 'he who would write himself martyr by his own inscription'.[15] It is Milton's job (assigned by his employer, the Council of State), in *Eikonoklastes*, to come between the 'shapeless picture' of the iconographically generic frontispiece and the words with which the king is 'fain to tell passengers what shape it is'; that is, Milton seeks to interrupt the apposition of the reflections, prayers and meditations with which the 'king's book' purports to write the king's name on the pictured martyr. By disrupting the unity first of image and text and then of text and source, Milton attempts to come between the action that reached its climax on the scaffold and the martyrdom inscribed on it by the king's book. Where the royalist pamphlets present English subtitles as a gloss on Greek titles, and text as the unfolding

---

[13] Jane understands what is at stake in surrendering the icon when he says of the *Eikonoklastes*: 'This author doth not only dig up the bones of the dead king, but seeks to bring destruction on all kings and bury them in the ruins of their Authority' (p. 6).

[14] The debates about the authorship of EB are summarised in Knachel's introduction (EB, pp. xxxi–xxxii) and detailed in Madan and Wilcher. The scholarly consensus is that the book was produced by Dr John Gauden, based on manuscript material composed by the king over a period of time and supplied to Gauden in November or December 1647. The presence of a clerical ghost-writer was immediately detected by the author of the first republican response, the *Eikon Alethine* (1649), but no individual is identified until the Restoration, when Gauden comes forward (quietly) to claim his reward from Charles II. As will be discussed below, the questionable authorship of 'the King's Book' is, in the controversies of 1649–51, more a function of polemical strategy than available knowledge. Drawing on an unpublished paper by J. P. Kenyon, 'Charles I and the *Eikon Basilike*', Kevin Sharpe returns to the view that EB represents a faithful record of Charles's words. See *The Personal Rule of Charles I* (New Haven, 1992), pp. 179, 193, 313 and 705. (I am indebted to David Smith for this reference.) I have consulted Professor Kenyon and to his mind the question is still open, though on balance he inclines to the view that roughly the first two-thirds of the EB (up to 1646) *was* written by the king (letter of 22 August 1993). I would like to express my gratitude to Professor Kenyon for his help on this issue.

[15] See also CP, 3, 530: 'But the king and his party having lost in this quarrel their heaven upon earth, begin to make great reckoning of Eternal Life, and at an easy rate *in forma Pauperis* Canonize one another into heaven; he them in his book, they him in the portraiture before his book: but as was said before, stage-work will not do it . . .'

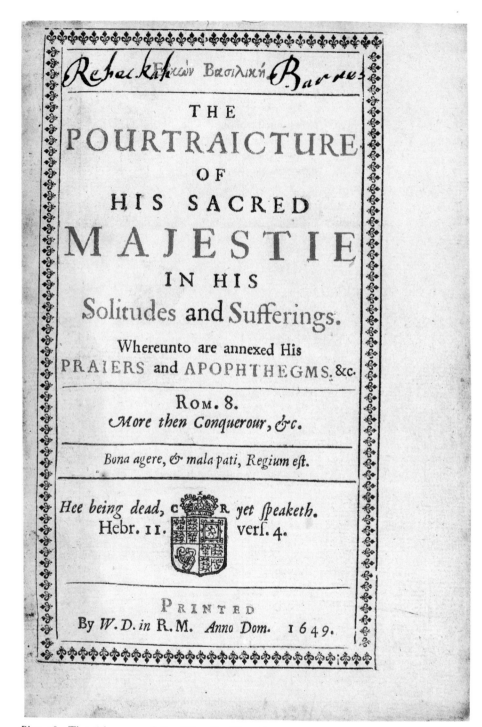

Plate 18   The title page of the *Eikon Basilike*, 1649

of the image that prefaces it, Milton locates the image to be broken in the text itself; in a profound reversal of the epideictic and mimetic tradition, he treats the icon as posterior to and a function of the word.[16]

Milton, like the author of *Eikon Alethine* before him, rebuts the 'king's' words with the king's acts, but, by working as he does to disrupt the internal unity of 'the king's book', he also transfers the scene on which the staging of the execution is contested from that of representation to that of articulation. Writing martyr by one's own inscription is not, for him, merely a matter of misrepresentation, but of improper joining, of placing together what ought to remain disjunct: he accuses Charles and his apologists of bad grammar that (as we shall see) is a kind of incest. For it is the successful inscription of martyrdom not on the king but on his image that allows his picture to prolong substantially the presence of his body, and thus to defeat Parliament's putatively unanswerable reduction of king to concept in act.

Milton's disgruntled remark about the poor painter who supplements his shapeless picture with a hermeneutically coercive text invokes and seeks to unsettle the relationship of repetition between Charles's icon in the frontispiece and expostulations such as the following from what purports to be the king's text:

But, O, let the blood of me, though their king, yet a sinner, be washed with the blood of my innocent peacemaking Redeemer; for in that Thy justice will find not only a temporary expiation but an eternal plenary satisfaction, both for my sins and the sins of my people, whom I beseech Thee still own for Thine; and when Thy wrath is appeased by my death, O remember thy mercies toward them and forgive them, O my Father, for they know not what they do. (EB, 46)

We need hardly pause to note a game as transparent as the one played in a passage like this. The execution of the king becomes an iteration of Christ's passion, through which the forgiveness called for in Christ's words from the cross, along with the redeeming power of the blood of the lamb, is transferred to the king, whose appropriation of Christ's words implies his repetition of Christ's sacrifice (as his refusal to answer the charges at his trial had appropriated Christ's silence before Pilate). It is not a question of the king repeating Christ's sacrificial act but of his rearticulating Christ's words to represent himself as Christ.

In breaking the link between image and inscription, Milton aspires to clear

---

[16] In the *Eikon Aklastos*, Jane works precisely to restore the primacy of the image as a representation of the real: 'It is not the picture but the cruelty exercised upon him, that made him a martyr, and these miscreants are enraged to see their own actions in picture, which they shamed not to commit in the face of the world' (p. 31). Here we see the traditional ideology of mimetic representation, much as it was delivered by Hamlet, 'to hold as 'twere the mirror up to nature: to show virtue her feature, scorn her own image' (3.2.22–3). Thus, for Jane, Milton and his party stand before the icon 'like guilty creatures sitting at a play' (*Hamlet*, 2.2.588): 'The traitors are loath to see the emblems of their own inhuman cruelty, and how instead of harmless pageantry they erected the theatre, of their barbarous villany at Whitehall' (p. 32). (*Hamlet* is quoted from *The Riverside Shakespeare*, ed. G. Blakemore Evans *et al.* (Boston, 1974).)

from the reader's mind the image of the royal martyr, 'which else no man
could imagine', in favour of a restored and contextualised voice, recognisable
as the king's but incapable of supporting a royal image; in fact, internally
contradictory over time and incapable of supporting any image whatsoever.

Milton's handling of the question of authorship is indicative of this
larger approach. As is implied by his title, the author of the *Eikon Alethine*,
who is principally invested in denying the king's authorship of the *Eikon
Basilike*, presents his work as uncovering a true image which has been
concealed behind a false one. The action of unveiling the truth is shown
in the frontispiece, in which a curtain, presumably bearing the image of
the royal martyr, is drawn back to reveal the clerical ghost-writer in his
doctor's cap (plate 19). The revelation of another writer behind the curtain
indicates that the text and therefore the image portrayed in it are not
that of the king. The *Eikon e pistes*, which offers its author's personal
testimony that the manuscript of the *Eikon Basilike* was in the king's hand,
engages the frontispiece to the *Eikon Alethine* with yet another unveiling
(plate 20): a hand draws back a curtain to reveal two images of King
Charles, one a seated figure wearing the crown, the other a figure standing
to the right and conferring a cap and bells on the person who stands
between the two images of Charles. This central figure, representing the
author of the *Eikon Alethine*, receives his ignominious headgear for his
inability (as the appended text explains) to understand that Charles could
be both learned and king and thus entitled both to the doctor's hat and
the crown. In marked contrast, Milton chooses both to acknowledge the
presence of a second writer and to persist in treating the *Eikon Basilike* as
the king's book: 'But as to the author of these soliloquies, whether it were
[undoubtedly] the late king as is vulgarly believed, or any secret coadjutor
. . . it can add nothing, nor shall take from the weight, if any be, or reason
which he brings' (CP, 3, 346). Milton's strategy in not challenging the
authorship is to refuse in this instance the notion of an authored text altogether and to portray both text and king as pastiche. Where the author of the
Eikon Alethine finds another writer who usurps the king's name, Milton prefers
to name the king after his book, and to pronounce the text tyrant for its
uncompensated appropriation of other men's words. In so far as books 'contain a potency of life in them to be as active as that soul was whose progeny
they are' (*Areopagitica*, CP, 2, 492), the misappropriation of another's words
is, as Milton says in reference to Charles's use of Pamela's prayer, 'a trespass
also more then usual against human right, which commands that every
author should have the property of his own work reserved to him after death
as well as living' (CP, 3, 364–5). Thus the king's purported resort to plagiarism and a ghost-writer again distinguishes his effort to 'write himself Martyr'
from the repetition-in-act of the *imitatio Christi*.[17]

---

[17] See also *Areopagitica*, CP, 2, 493: 'A good book is the precious life-blood of a master spirit, imbalmed and
treasured up on purpose to a life beyond life.'

Spectatum admissi risum teneatis .

The Curtain's drawne; All may perceiue the plot,
And Him who truely the blacke Babe begot :
Whose sable mantle makes me bold to say
A Phaeton Sol's charriot rulde that day .
Presumptuous Preist to skip into the throne ,
And make his King his Bastard Issue owne .
The Authour therefore hath conceiu'd it meet ,
The Doctor should doe penuance in this sheet .

Plate 19   The frontispiece of the *Eikon Alethine*, 1649

Authorship is a complex issue for Milton, one which occupies him throughout his career, and his treatment of it in *Eikonoklastes* may not be entirely coherent. While he mystifies and exalts the 'property' of words so as to denounce Charles's plagiarism, he also implies that a text ought to express universal reason and not the subjective position of the person from whose hand it is said to have issued. Reason, of which law ought to be a representative, is originally inscribed in a divinely ordered universe

The Curtain's drawne, all may perceive the plot :
And easly see, what yow my freind have got .
Presumptuous coxcomb th'art, that thus would'st faine ,
Murder the issue of the Kings owne braine .
If in the essence and the name of King ,
Their is Divinity: know then, yow bring.
That which conduceth to the Kings owne praise ,
As much as Crown's of Gold or wreath's of bayes.
Though as a King in's actions he did shine ,
Yet in his writings he may be Divine.
     Do not then say one skips into his throne ;
     The Docter and the King may both be one .

Plate 20   The frontispiece of the *Eikon e pistes*, 1649

and not the province of an embodied creative power.[18] To take up the issue of whether or not the text is the king's would be to accept the notion that the text represents its author and thus to accord to the king's word the prestige of the royal body. Instead, Milton presents the king's text as internally incoherent, or, as he elegantly put it when objecting to the word '*Damagogues*' as 'above [the king's] known style and orthography', 'conscious of some other author' (CP, 3, 393). It is probable that, under the pressure of his polemic (what Hirst terms his 'purposes'), Milton strategically deploys incompatible notions of authorship to discredit Charles on the one hand for failing to express himself and on the other hand for failing to efface himself before a universal and disembodied reason. However, be it contingent or intended, there is something more at stake in Milton's confused and confusing conflation of personal authorship and the disembodied voice of reason.[19]

According to Milton, the arguments of the *Eikon Basilike* are fallacious; they follow not from the facts, along the path of reason, to an inevitable conclusion, but from the will of the speaker, according to his personal needs. Yet neither are the prayers and ejaculations representative of that will. They are instead a pastiche ungrounded in the experience of the speaker they purport to represent. Both these lines of thought lead not simply to the separation of words and image but to the dispersal of the image as such. The image of the martyr is not the origin of the words, which represent him, but their posterior and deluding effect.

By placing the king's supposed repetition of Christ's sacrifice in a series of iterations that exceeds and undermines the narrative confines of the king's book, Milton works to unveil, beneath the image of the royal martyr, who, washed in the blood of the lamb, may speak redemption, not another image but rather the duplicitous words of a tyrant whose death at the hands of his outraged subjects was both just and inevitable:

Andronicus Comnenus, the Byzantine Emperor, though a most cruel tyrant, is reported by Nicetas to have been a constant reader of Saint Paul's Epistles, and by continual study had so incorporated the phrase and style of that transcendent apostle into all his familiar letters that the imitation seemed to vie with the original. Yet this availed not to deceive the people of that empire, who notwithstanding his saint's vizard, tore him to pieces for his tyranny.

(CP, 3, 361)

Milton's method in *Eikonoklastes* attempts a verbal version of the way

---

[18] For discussion of Milton's conflicted views on authorship beyond those expressed in *Eikonoklastes*, see my 'The Fruits of one's Labor in Miltonic Practice and Marxian Theory', *ELH, A Journal of English Literary History*, 59 (1992), 77–105 and '*Authors to Themselves': Milton and the Revelation of History* (Cambridge, 1987).

[19] It is perhaps useful to note that Milton's distrust of a personal style in *Eikonoklastes* may be restricted to 'discursive' as opposed to poetic (that is, inspired) writing and that this distinction may account for his sneering that 'the whole book [EB] might perhaps be intended a piece of poetry' (CP, 3, 406). Eight years earlier, he had made such a division with reference to his own polemical and poetic work in the Preface to the Second Part of *The Reason of Church Government*, CP, 1, 808.

taken by the righteous Byzantines. He dismembers the king's text by inserting hostile commentary into a string of always fragmentary quotations from the *Eikon Basilike*, disrupting the king's style by disbursing the king's text and reinscribing it as a series of falsehoods, distortions and thefts.[20]

To separate the king's text from the king's image, Milton first separates the king from the text, rendering the action of the royal martyr as the work of a royal actor whose words offend speech in the same way that the liturgy of the Prayer Book offends prayer:

[He] who prays must consult first with his heart; which in likelihood may stir up his affections; in these, having both words and matter ready-made to his lips, which is enough to make up the outward act of prayer, his affections grow lazy,' and come not up easily at the call of words not their own.
                                                          (CP, 3, 506–7)

Although the king ought to speak reason, which belongs to all, he ought also to speak authentically; that is to say, he ought to speak his felt desires in a way that testifies to the unmediated unity of his prayers and his affections.

How does the *Eikon Basilike* stage the king's prayers? What precisely is on the curtain that Milton prefers to pull down rather than draw back? Charles appears at least three times in the engraving that introduces *The Portrait of the King*, and three times again in 'The Explanation of the Emblem', which appears in doubled columns of Latin and English beneath it (plate 21). He is represented mimetically, in the kneeling figure in the centre foreground of the engraving, eyes fixed on the heavenly crown, foot spurning the worldly crown and hand grasping the crown of thorns that mediates his passage from the one to the other; this figure, which is embodied by the speaking 'I' of the explanation below, supplies the presence of Charles 'in his solitudes and sufferings' prior to his execution.

Behind the figure, in the outdoor scene on the left, are two iconographic symbols of the king: the palm, 'clogged with weights of miseries' whose nature is to rise through its oppression ('*Crescit Sub Pondere Virtus*') and 'th'unmoved rock [that] outbraves / The boistrous winds and raging waves' of the revolution ('Immota Triumphans').

The outdoor scene to the left of the wall I take to represent Charles's immediate past and the stormy present of an England wracked by civil tumult. The right hand, indoor scene, represents the calm centre of the king who withdraws from this temporal disorder into the rightly ordered world of his prayers and meditations.[21] In this respect the icon previews

---

[20] On Milton's manipulations of the king's 'style', see my 'Servile/Sterile/Style: Milton and the Question of Woman', in *Milton and the Idea of Woman*, ed. Julia Walker (Urbana, 1988), pp. 148–68.

[21] In his comments on an earlier version of this essay, David Smith observes that this depiction seems 'strangely appropriate (possibly unconsciously so) given that Charles I was always more at home ruling the interior world of the Court than his kingdom at large'.

The Explanation of the EMBLEME.

Ponderibus *genus omne mali, probrisq; gravatus,*
Vtcunq; ferenda, ferens, Palma ut Depressa, *resurgo.*

Ac, *relut uncarum* Fluctus Ventisq; *furerem*
Irati Populi Rupes immota *repello.*
Clarior è tenebris, *cælestis stella, corusco.*
Victor et æternum—felici pace triumpho.

> Auro Fulgentem *rutilo, gemmisq; micantem,*
At curis Gravidam *spernenda* calco Coronam.

Spinosam, at ferri facilem, *sno* Spes mea, *Christi*
Auxilio, *Nobis non est* tractare *molestum.*

Æternam, *fixis fidei, semperq;*—beatam
In Cælos oculis Specto, *Nobisq; paratam.*

Quod Vanum *est, sperno; quod Christi* Gratia *fovet*
Amplecti studium est: Virtutis Gloria *merces.*

Though clogg'd with weights of *miseries*
Palm-like Depress'd, I higher rise.

And as th'unmoved Rock out-brave's
The boistrous Windes and rageing waves:
So triumph I. And shine more bright
In sad Affliction's Darksom night.

That Splendid, but yet toilsom Crown
Regardlessly I trample down.

With joie I take this Crown of thorn.
Though sharp, yet easie to be born.

That heav'nlie Crown, already min,
I View with eies of Faith divine.

I slight vain things; and do embrace
Glorie, the just reward of Grace.

Τὸ Χρι ὄδεὶ ἠδίκησε τὸν πολιν. ὄδε τὸ Κάτωσε.

G.D.

Plate 21 The frontispiece of the *Eikon Basilike,* 1649

the form of the chapters that follow, which chronologically unfold the crucial steps in the king's progress to the scaffold, presenting in each a didactic treatment of a specific episode followed by a withdrawal into italicised prayers and meditations. The emblem and its explanation particularly anticipate the language of the account of 'the insolency of the tumults' in the body of the text, in which the civil disorders in London and Westminster are described as 'not like a storm at sea, which yet wants not its terror, but like an earthquake, shaking the very foundations of all' (EB, 14). In the ensuing, meditative section, faith provides shelter from the storm: 'But Thou that gatheredst the waters into one place and madest the dry land to appear, and after didst assuage the flood which drowned the world by the word of Thy power, rebuke those beasts of the people and deliver me from the rudeness and strivings of the multitude' (EB, 19). Thus the engraving compresses into a single composition what the text spells out in temporal sequence. The storm raged, the rock and trees endure, and the king is delivered through suffering to the certain hope of a heavenly crown (the open book before him reads *'in verbo tua spes mea'*). One element in the picture is curiously unnoted in the explanatory verse and only very circumspectly and belatedly introduced into the following text. Behind and to the left of the weighted palm stands a smaller and unweighted palm: Prince Charles, England's future, now on the margin but eventually to grow into his father's place in the centre foreground. Why does this junior tree remain unlabelled in a picture so redundantly explained? Perhaps because it is labelled in a non-verbal way. We have been examining the textual content of this picture. Consider now the peculiar form of its composition.

The king, kneeling in the centre foreground, receives two rays: one, emerging from the dark clouds on the upper left, that is from the tumults, cutting obliquely past the wall, and ending, apparently, in the king's left ear, is labelled *Clarior e tenebris*, light out of darkness, clarity from shadow; the other, an eyebeam, forming the right arm of a V, fixes the heavenly crown in the king's sight, *coeli specto*. Thematically the composition is simple enough. The king's understanding bringing clarity out of the darkness of civil war turns to the contemplation of eternal glory. The V traces out a classic Christian trajectory: he falls (from his earthly crown) to rise to a heavenly crown. Is it possible, however, also to see in this composition an unsettling recollection of a generic annunciation – with the king in the place of the Blessed Virgin, inseminated through the ear by the Holy Spirit, illuminated by Gabriel, and posed (as the king is) as the mediating fulcrum that carries the viewer from time (on the left) to eternity (on the right)? Without advancing the claim that the king's icon is consciously or unconsciously based on any particular prior image, I wish to call attention to the compositional similarities between William Marshall's engraving for the *Eikon Basilike* and a broad range of generic paintings. In particular, I would call attention to three compositional elements shared by the engraving and many Renaissance depictions of the Annunciation: 1, the left-right division into two distinct spaces; 2, the V of humiliation and exaltation, formed in the Carlo Crivelli *Annunciation* reproduced in plate 22, for

Plate 22   The Annunciation, by Carlo Crivelli, 1486

example, by the ray of the Holy Spirit descending from the left to Mary's ear and the folded tail of the peacock (possibly an iconographic symbol of resurrection) rising on her right; and 3, the central figure shown reading.[22]

I hesitate to push this observed compositional similarity very far; even if it were to be granted that the king's icon is indeed composed on the model of an annunciation, this fact need suggest little more than Marshall's reliance on a commonplace framework to support his composition. Yet, if I am right about what I see, the genre and the thematics of the engraving, if only in a posterior reconstruction, are not disjunct or unmotivated. This is because, in a determined way, the issues at stake in the '*Eikon*' polemics are motherhood, incarnation and incest. For, as we shall see, Milton finds a shared pattern in the frontispiece's figuring of the king as both Mary and Christ and Charles's attempt, in the *Eikon Basilike* to represent himself as both the child and the father of the law.

Milton draws precisely these implications:

Yet he professes to hold his kingly right by law; and if no law could be made but by the great counsel of a nation, which we now term a Parliament, then certainly it was a Parliament that first created kings, and not only made laws before a king was in being, but those laws especially whereby he holds his crown. He ought then to have so thought of a Parliament, if he count it not male, as of his mother, which, to civil being, created both him and the royalty he wore. And if it hath been anciently interpreted the presaging sign of a future tyrant, but to dream of copulation with his mother, what can it be less then actual tyranny to affirm waking, that the Parliament, which is his mother, can neither conceive or bring forth any authoritative act without his masculine coition. Nay, that his reason is as celestial and lifegiving to the Parliament, as the sun's influence is to the earth. What other notions but these, or such like, could swell up Caligula to think himself a God?   (CP, 3, 467)[23]

The claim that the king is the law speaking could not, in Milton's lifetime (if ever) have been held entirely separate from that of the word made flesh, and it is, I believe, notable that the most astonishing passages of

---

[22] For a general survey of Renaissance depictions of the Annunciation, see David N. Robb, 'The Iconography of the Annunciation in the Fourteenth and Fifteenth Centuries', *The Art Bulletin*, 18 (1936), 480–526. Carlo Crivelli's 1486 *Annunciation* (plate 22), now in the National Gallery, London, was commissioned for the Church of the Minori Osservanti in Ascoli to celebrate Ascoli's administrative autonomy under the papacy: thus the inscription 'Libertas Ecclesiastica'. For details, see Pietro Zampetti, *Carlo Crivelli* (Florence, 1986), pp. 284–6. Roland M. Frye cites some paintings of the Annunciation (including Crivelli's) as possible influences on Milton's depiction of Uriel riding to earth on a sunbeam (*Paradise Lost*, 4.555), in *Milton's Imagery and the Visual Arts: Iconographic Tradition in the Epic Poems* (Princeton, 1978), p. 175.

[23] The comparison to Caligula reiterates that made by Bradshaw at Charles's sentencing, as well as the reference to the 'emblem', of EB in *Eikon Alethine*: 'I never read of any that canonized themselves, but those that knew no body else would do it for them. Thus Caligula indeed made himself a God while alive, because he knew the Senate would hardly decree him divine honours after his death' (p. 2). For discussion of the specifically Oedipal thematics of *Eikonoklastes*, see Bruce Boehrer, 'Elementary Structures of Kingship: Milton, Regicide, and the Family', *Milton Studies*, 23 (1987), 97–117, and Grossman, 'Servile/Sterile/Style', pp. 148–68. A more general treatment of the psychoanalytic reading of the relations of iconoclasm, law and the desire for the mother may be found in Jean-Joseph Goux, *Symbolic Economies: After Marx and Freud*, trans. Jennifer Curtiss Gage (Ithaca, 1990), pp. 134–50.

invective in *Eikonoklastes* tease out the embarrassing confusions of gender implied by the virgin birth of a king who represents himself (in Milton's reading) as both the husband and the mother of the law, as pregnant with the cause of justice and potent to engender laws by prerogative.

To 'swell up Caligula to think himself a god', to become pregnant with oneself and so deliver a self without origin: such, according to Milton is the pattern of tyranny.[24] If to 'write himself martyr by his own inscription' betrays an ill painter and a shapeless subject, to play both Mary and Jesus bespeaks a deeper and more systemic ill. King Charles coming in his own body to the House of Commons to arrest five members on the basis of 'just motives and pregnant grounds' (EB, 11) thus recalls, in Milton's rewriting of his text, not Mary, Mother of God, but the persecuting Mary Tudor: 'and thus his pregnant motives are at last proved nothing but a tympany, or a Queen Mary's cushion' (CP, 3, 379).[25]

The comparison of Charles's charges against the five members to Mary Tudor's hysterical pregnancy of 1554, though perhaps the nastiest moment in a nasty text, is not at all adventitious in terms of the design of *Eikonoklastes*. It is, on the contrary, the point of confluence of Milton's invective against this particular king and his much broader and more radical questioning of monarchy as such. Catholic, intolerant, barren and subordinated by marriage to an enemy of English sovereignty, Mary Tudor provides Milton with an opportunity to imply Charles's effeminacy and to ridicule him for his inability to produce the expected sequilae to his 'pregnant motives'. At the same time, the comparison associates the king with a historical figure whose sinister and frightening character would be felt across the intra-Protestant divisions of 1649, reminding the recently monarchical Presbyterians of a common enemy. But, beyond these apparent motives for Milton's sly reference, the conflation of Charles Stuart and Mary Tudor is also an occasion to rethink the terms of a debate still centred on the competing claims to priority of dynasty and legislature: does the king speak the law or the law speak the king?

To appreciate this we should recall that Mary I did not claim the throne by right of inheritance but by parliamentary statute. In the Third Succession Act of 1544 Parliament had given Henry VIII the right to determine the succession rights of his daughters in his will, under the terms of which Mary came to the throne.[26] Thus Mary's accession is the result precisely of the sort of incestuous coition of king and Parliament

---

[24] Cf. in *Paradise Lost*, the genesis of Sin and Death through Satanic self-insemination (2.746–814) and Satan's claim to have been 'self-begot' (5.860).

[25] OED: Cushion 2:b: 'A swelling simulating pregnancy: sometimes called *Queen Mary's cushion*, after Mary Tudor.'

[26] The circumstances of Mary's accession and contemporary reactions to her as Queen Regnant are conveniently rehearsed in Constance Jordan, 'Woman's Rule in Sixteenth-Century British Political Thought', *Renaissance Quarterly*, 40 (1987), 421–51. On the Succession Act of 1544, see Mortimer Levine, *Tudor Dynastic Problems 1460–1571* (1973), pp. 71–5, 161–4; and Jordan, p. 425, n. 5.

that Milton sees in Charles's attempt to both 'hold his kingly right by law' and assert his royal prerogative. Implicitly, a parliamentary accommodation to Charles, as seemed to have been the Presbyterian intention before the decisive events of 1649, would reenact the circumstances of Mary's accession and once again illustrate the unworkability of even a statutorily established monarchy.[27]

In his portion of this chapter, Derek Hirst delineates the historian's task of recovering the exigent circumstances of a document like the *Eikonoklastes* from the literary scholar's task of placing such a work in the Miltonic canon, where, Hirst fears, its polemical intentions may be 'swallowed up'. By his own account, Milton saw the polemical and the prophetical sides of his career as disjunct: the work of the 'left hand' and that of a 'poet soaring in the high regions of his fancies' respectively (*Reason of Church Government*, CP, 1, 808). But, the obvious overdetermination of Milton's later style notwithstanding, the king's false pregnancy contributes to and is shaped by the more protracted birth of something of literary historical significance. Thus I propose to return now, after what has been a fairly lengthy detour through the polemical environment of 1649–51, to suggest a determined consistency between the exigent strategies of the polemicist and the canonical style of the poet.

I sought earlier to situate the *Eikonoklastes* within a literary historical movement of long duration by seeing in Milton's investment in breaking the king's image the confluence of an urgent political need to disembody the law and a slowly growing distrust of language as a representational medium. I want now to suggest that some of what Milton learned in the exigencies of the debate over the king's body may be traced, for example, in the induction to hell in Book 1 of *Paradise Lost*:

> Him the Almighty Power
> Hurled headlong flaming from th' ethereal sky
> With hideous ruin and combustion down
> To bottomless perdition, there to dwell
> In adamantine chains and penal fire,
> Who durst defy th' Omnipotent to arms.
> Nine times the space that measures day and night
> To mortal men, he with his horrid crew
> Lay vanquished, rolling in the fiery gulf
> Confounded though immortal. But his doom

---

[27] Milton's sentiments about the possible accommodation of Charles and Parliament, foreclosed by the execution, recall those of John Foxe on the failure of Mary's pregnancy. After reproducing a lengthy 'Extract of an Act for the Government of Queen Mary's Issue' passed by Parliament in 1555, Foxe remarks: 'Thus much out of the act and statute I thought to rehearse, to the intent the reader may understand, not so much how parliaments may sometimes be deceived (as by this child of Queen Mary may appear), as rather what cause we Englishmen have to render most earnest thanks unto almighty God, who so mercifully, against the opinion, expectation, and working of our adversaries, hath helped and delivered us in this case.' *The Acts and Monuments of John Foxe*, ed. Rev. Stephen Reed Cattley (1838), VI, 581.

Reserved him to more wrath; for now the thought
Both of lost happiness and lasting pain
Torments him; round he throws his baleful eyes
That witnessed huge affliction and dismay
Mixed with obdurate pride and steadfast hate.
At once as far as angels' ken he views
The dismal situation waste and wild,
A dungeon horrible, on all sides round
As one great furnace flamed, yet from those flames
No light, but rather darkness visible
Served only to discover sights of woe,
Regions of sorrow, doleful shades, where peace
And rest can never dwell, hope never comes
That comes to all.

$$(1, 44–67)^{28}$$

I want to remark in this celebrated passage a specifically anti-mimetic quality that manifests itself as the steady obtrusion of language between thought and its visualisation. This effect begins, almost immediately, in lines 46–7, first with the bilingual pun on the Latin *ruere* which linguistically identifies the 'ruin' of Lucifer with the fall the lines purport to describe, so that Satan is depicted as falling to his fall. This ruin-fall, which ends without ending on the burning lake at line 50, is pointedly, yet paradoxically, endless, a fall to '*bottomless* perdition' (which carries the English sense of 'ruin' back into the Latin *perditus*, translated as 'lost' or 'ruined'), 'there to *dwell*'. But where? In bottomless loss, in endless destruction? The 'place' of Satan's dwelling cannot be visually intuited; it must be mediated by a concept, in which time and space are not the phenomenal time and space of quotidian visual experience but are rather interpenetrating features of a rhetorically reflexive grammar. The bilingual puns suspend the reader between two languages and two times (classical and modern) as they enforce the infolded temporality in which we are to understand that the fall of the Titans in Hesiod and Homer's account of the expulsion of Hephaestus from Olympus, to which this passage alludes, are, in fact, reenactments of the originary scene here expressed by imitating these episodes of classical narrative. This curious representation of the original by an imitation of its imitations is soon reenacted (in Milton's time frame, preenacted) yet again, in the description of Mulciber, at lines 740–1.[29]

---

[28] Milton's poetry is quoted from *John Milton: Complete Poetry and Major Prose*, ed. Merritt Y. Hughes (New York, 1957). Spelling and punctuation have been modernised.

[29] See Hughes's notes to *Paradise Lost* I, 50 and 740 for the classical references. (I take the liberty of assimilating the Greek literary allusions and the Latin puns to the general term 'classical' in the paradigmatic opposition of classical/modern.) Curiously, Hughes picks up the allusion to Hephaestus (*Iliad* I, 588–95) in the passage on Mulciber but omits it from his note on the fall of Lucifer, perhaps to wall off Milton's God from Zeus's drunkenness in the Homeric account. In a deft bit of misreading Hughes ties the fall of Satan to that of the Titans by the fact that 'Here [I. 50] and in VI. 871, the devils fall for as many days as Hesiod (*Theogony*, 664–735) gives for the Titans' fall from heaven after their overthrow by the Olympian gods.' He is right about VI. 871 ('Nine days they fell') but not about I. 50. In Hughes's own edition there is a full stop at the end of

Spelling and punctuation have been modernised. With these repeated and temporally inverted imitations, Milton's language unfolds the superimpositions of time and space it first presents as the falling with falling of 'with ruin and combustion down'. The Augustinian concept within which the Fall is both the determination and the termination of history, its inception and its reduction to a series of iterative reenactments, is presented as a trace in the historical evolution of the English noun 'ruin' from the Latin verb *ruere*. To be fallen is to experience oneself as the concretisation in time of one's own actions, as Satan comes to experience himself as a perpetual falling, and to experience those actions as always having been appropriated from a preceding other.[30]

To use language in this obtrusively self-referential way is to move decisively from the visual thematics of traditional epideictics as they were deployed in the interplay of iconic and verbal portraits Milton resisted in the polemics of 1649–51. As the passage continues, it becomes even more clear that there is nothing to see here, that what is being envisioned is nothing. Lucifer, now Satan (no longer the proper referent of a proper name but generically, the Adversary, he 'who durst defy th' Omnipotent to arms'), is at once (or for nine days) falling and dwelling and lying vanquished. 'But his doom / Reserved him to more wrath.' Whose doom? Satan's fate or God's judgement? The most proximate antecedent is Satan, but the transfer of God's judgement (doom) to Satan's fate is not trivial; the implicit questioning of the grammatical identifications of subject and object, actor and acted upon, is very much to the thematic point of the passage. The hell we are given to 'see' in *Paradise Lost* is mediated by Satan's 'baleful eyes', which view not a place but a 'dismal situation'. This situation is illuminated by no external light, but rather, in perhaps the most celebrated Miltonism of all, by 'darkness visible'. If what Satan sees in the darkness visible is 'Regions of sorrow' where 'hope never comes / That comes to all', then he is what remains when all has been subtracted: an empty set, no one situated in no place. Milton's narration of Satan's fall and recovery cannot be concretised outside of a conceptual – as opposed to a visual – signification.

---

line 49, so that the passage goes on 'Nine times the Space that measures Day and Night / To mortal men, he with his horrid crew / Lay vanquished.' The period after line 49 is present in both the 1667 and 1674 editions and is not to my knowledge the site of any editorial controversy. In the argument to Book I, Milton writes 'Satan with his Angels lying on the burning Lake, thunder-struck and astonished, after *a certain space* revives' (my emphasis). Inconsistencies and expectations aside, the passage says not that Satan has fallen for nine days, but that he has lain nine days on the burning lake. Hughes's misreading of his own editing ought to serve not to devalue his scholarship, which is considerable, but to alert us to the way that rhetoric characteristically overtakes grammar in this passage. For further discussion of the classical contexts of the language Milton uses to describe the expulsion of the devils, see Edward Le Comte, *Milton Re-Viewed: Ten Essays* (New York and London, 1991), pp. 76–8.

[30] See also the transformation of the devils into snakes that attends Satan's verbal report of his success in the temptation of Adam and Eve, and which the devils are 'Yearly enjoined some say to undergo / This annual humbling certain numbered days. / To dash their pride, and joy for man seduced' (*Paradise Lost* 10. 504–77; the quoted lines are 575–7).

That hell is simply Satan's state of mind or that Satan is the absence of God's good creation is no news to Milton's readers, but Milton's way of 'showing' it in a language that resists visualisation points not to 'nature' but to the concept in which (and only in which) this description can take place. His self-consciously anti-mimetic use of language both to embody and to disembody Satan invites us to visualise evil in its regal body and then defeats our efforts in favour of the non-intuitive linguistic space in which – and only in which – the ambiguities, contradictions and agrammaticalities of evil conceived of as negation, as the privation of good, can unfold their disembodied sense. Thus I would argue that if Charles's attempt to write himself martyr in the *Eikon Basilike* proved, under Milton's scrutiny, to deliver only a Queen Mary's cushion, Milton's uncanny presentation of Satan as precisely nothing delivers Queen Mary's cushion as a literary historical event; for, Milton's exigent experiences in the regicide controversy may well have contributed to a canonical development in the way stories are told.

Index